Contents

Use of English

As this book has been written in England, it uses the appropriate English component names, phrases, and spelling. Some of these differ from those used in America. Normally, these cause no difficulty, but to make sure, a glossary is printed below. In ordering spare parts remember the parts list will probably use these words:

Glossary

English	American	English	American
Aerial	Antenna	Interior light	Dome lamp
Accelerator	Gas pedal	Layshaft (of gearbox)	Counter shaft
Alternator	Generator (AC)	Leading shoe (of brake)	Primary shoe
Anti-roll bar	Stabiliser or sway bar	Locks	Latches
Battery	Energizer	Motorway	Freeway, turnpike etc.
Bodywork	Sheet metal	Number plate	Licence plate
Bonnet (engine cover)	Hood	Paraffin	Kerosene
Boot lid	Trunk lid	Petrol	Gasoline
Boot (luggage compartment)	Trunk	Petrol tank	Gas tank
Bottom gear	1st gear	'Pinking'	'Pinging'
Bulkhead	Firewall	Quarter light	Quarter window
Camfollower or tappet	Valve lifter or tappet	Retread	Recap
Carburettor	Carburetor	Reverse	Back-up
Catch	Latch	Rocker cover	Valve cover
Choke/venturi	Barrel	Roof rack	Car-top carrier
Circlip	Snap ring	Saloon	Sedan
Clearance	Lash	Seized	Frozen
Crownwheel	Ring gear (of differential)	Side indicator lights	Side marker lights
Disc (brake)	Rotor/disk	Side light	Parking light
Propeller shaft	Driveshaft	Silencer	Muffler
Drop arm	Pitman arm	Spanner	Wrench
Drop head coupe	Convertible	Sill panel (beneath doors)	Rocker panel
Dynamo	Generator (DC)	Split cotter (for valve spring cap)	Lock (for valve spring retainer)
Earth (electrical)	Ground	Split pin	Cotter pin
Engineer's blue	Prussion blue	Steering arm	Spindle arm
Estate car	Station wagon	Sump	Oil pan
Exhaust manifold	Header	Tab washer	Tang; lock
Fast back (Coupe)	Hard top	Tailgate	Liftgate
Fault finding/diagnosis	Trouble shooting	Tappet	Valve lifter
Float chamber	Float bowl	Thrust bearing	Throw-out bearing
Free-play	Lash	Top gear	High
Freewheel	Coast	Trackrod (of steering)	Tie-rod (or connecting rod)
Gudgeon pin	Piston pin or wrist pin	Trailing shoe (of brake)	Secondary shoe
Gearchange	Shift	Transmission	Whole drive line
Gearbox	Transmission	Tyre	Tire
Halfshaft	Axle-shaft	Van	Panel wagon/van
Handbrake	Parking brake	Vice	Vise
Hood	Soft top	Wheel nut	Lug nut
Hot spot	Heat riser	Windscreen	Windshield
Indicator	Turn signal	Wing/mudguard	Fender
Interior light	Dome lamp		

Miscellaneous points

An "Oil seal" is fitted to components lubricated by grease!

A "Damper" is a "Shock absorber" it damps out bouncing, and absorbs shocks of bump impact. Both names are correct, and both are used haphazardly.

Note that British drum brakes are different from the Bendix type that is common in America, so different descriptive names result. The shoe end furthest from the hydraulic wheel cylinder is on a pivot; interconnection between the shoes as on Bendix brakes is most uncommon. Therefore the phrase "Primary" or "Secondary" shoe does not apply. A shoe is said to be Leading or Trailing. A "Leading" shoe is one on which a point on the drum, as it rotates forward, reaches the shoe at the end worked by the hydraulic cylinder before the anchor end. The opposite is a trailing shoe, and this one has no self servo from the wrapping effect of the rotating drum.

CT

Capri
Owners
kshop
ual

es

Motoring Writers

asman

0 L & XL 1593 cc ohc
0 GT 1593 cc ohc

0 Coupe 122 cu in (1993 cc) ohc

*tted with overhead-valve (ohv) type
s.*

96 1

ng Group 1977, 1986

ABCDE
FGH

Haynes Publishing Group
Sparkford Nr Yeovil
Somerset BA22 7JJ England

Haynes Publications, Inc
861 Lawrence Drive
Newbury Park
California 91320 USA

Acknowledgements

Thanks are due to the Ford Motor Company for the provision of technical information and the supply of certain illustrations used in this manual. Castrol Limited provided the necessary lubrication data.

The Section dealing with the suppression of radio interference in Chapter 10, was originated by Mr. I. P. Davey and was first published in *Motor* magazine.

The Champion Sparking Plug Company Limited provided spark plug photographs. The bodywork repair photographs used in this manual were provided by Lloyds Industries Limited who supply 'Turtle Wax', 'Dupli-Color Holts' and a range of other Holts products.

Lastly special thanks are due to all of those people at Sparkford who helped with the production of this manual, particularly, Brian Horsfall and Les Brazier, who carried out the mechanical work and took the photographs respectively; Stanley Randolph who planned the layout of each page and Rod Grainger the editor.

About this manual

Its aim

The aim of this manual is to provide full details of repair and maintenance procedures for the Capri written in a manner that the average car owner can understand. The author and those assisting him, learned about this range of models the only thorough way, by studying all the available information and then going ahead and doing the work, under typical domestic conditions and using a typical range of tools, backed only by their experience as keen car men over a number of years.

Unlike other books of this nature, therefore, the hands in most of the photographs are those of the author, and the instructions cover every step in detail, assuming no special knowledge on the part of the reader except how to use tools and equipment in a proper manner.

Every care has been taken to assure the accuracy of this manual but no liability can be accepted by the authors' or publisher's for any loss, damage or injury caused by any errors in, or omissions from, the information given.

Using the manual

The manual is divided into twelve Chapters, each covering a logical sub-division of the vehicle. The Chapters are each divided into numbered Sections, and the Sections into paragraphs (or sub-Sections). The paragraphs have decimal numbers following on from the Section number (eg; 5.3 is the third paragraph in Section 5.

The manual is freely illustrated, especially in those parts where there is a detailed sequence of operations to be carried out. There are two forms of illustration: figures and photographs. The figures are numbered in sequence with decimal numbers, according to their position in the Chapter (eg; Fig. 6.4 is the fourth illustration in Chapter 6). Photographs each have numbers which relate to the Section and paragraph of the text where the operation they show is described (eg; photo 6.31 relates to paragraph 31 of Section 6, in the same Chapter as the photo appears).

There is an alphabetical index at the back of this manual as well as a contents list at the front and on the first page of every Chapter.

Reference to the 'left' or 'right' of the vehicle is in the sense of a person in a seat facing forwards, towards the front of the car.

Where appropriate, fault diagnosis instructions are given at the end of Chapters. Accurate diagnosis of faults depends on a careful, and above all, systematic approach, so avoid the attitude: 'if all else fails, read the book'. It is better, and almost always quicker to say: 'This could be one of several things, so let's have a look at the *Haynes* manual before trying anything'.

Special tools

Wherever possible the use of special tools has been avoided and often ingenious methods have been worked out, in our own workshop, to overcome the lack of these tools. This information is included in the manual.

Sometimes there is no alternative to using the special tool for a particular job - where this is the case the method of using the tool and the tool description are included in the text. Obtaining these special tools can be quite a problem for the average do-it-yourselfer. It may be possible to borrow the tools against a deposit from your local Ford dealer, or perhaps even make the tool yourself. Special tools are manufactured for the Ford Motor Company by V. L. Churchill & Company Limited, P.O. Box 3, London Road, Daventry, Northants NN11 4NF, England and V. Lowener, D 5000 Koln 60 (Nieh), Henry Ford Strasse, Germany.

Redwing Sales of Lansdowne Road, Leamington Spa, Warwickshire, England sell proprietory tools for this model at a reasonable price. They can supply the cylinder head bolt tool and the tool used for camshaft drivebelt adjustment and oil pump bolt removal.

Introduction to the Capri 1600 and 2000 ohc

This manual covers the 1600 cc ohc engined Capri models sold in the U.K. between September 1972 and January 1974, also the 2000 cc ohc version marketed in North America between January 1971 and mid-1975.

During 1974, the bodystyle was changed to a hatchback design and the model was re-designated Capri II. The introduction of the 2000 cc ohc version to the U.K. was also coincident with the introduction of the new Mk II bodystyle. The Capri II is not covered by this manual but is the subject of another Haynes publication. Two factors should be noted in connection with these cars: (i) many components are made by Ford of Germany and/or Ford of Britain and their identification in a particular vehicle can only be made by visual inspection, (ii) a wide variety of custom packs and equipment variations has been offered during the period over which the car was marketed and detailed specifications have depended upon the sales policy and production requirements at the time the car left the British or German factories.

General dimensions, weights and capacities

Dimensions		1600 cc	2000 cc up to 1973	2000 cc after 1973
Wheelbase	... ...	100.8 in (256.0 cm)	100.8 in (256.0 cm)	100.8 in (256.0 cm)
Overall length	... ...	167.8 in (426.2 cm)	167.8 in (426.2 cm)	174.0 in (441.96 cm)
Overall width	... ...	64.8 in (164.6 cm)	64.8 in (164.6 cm)	64.8 in (164.6 cm)
Overall height	... ...	53.2 in (135.2 cm)	50.7 in (128.8 cm)	50.5 in (128.3 cm)
Ground clearance	... ...	5.4 in (13.7 cm)	5.0 in (12.7 cm)	5.0 in (12.7 cm)

Weights				
Kerb weight:				
Manual gearbox	... ...	1985 lb (900 kg)	2333 lb (1058 kg)	2356 lb (1069 kg)
GT	... ...	2030 lb (920 kg)	— —	— —
Automatic transmission	... ...	2052 lb (931 kg)	2355 lb (1068 kg)	2371 lb (1075 kg)

Capacities		1600 cc (Imperial and Metric)	2000 cc (US)
Fuel tank	... ...	10.5 gals (48.0 litres)	12 gals
Cooling system	... ...	10.5 pints (5.76 litres)	8.1 qts
Engine lubricant (including filter)	... ...	7.0 pints (3.75 litres)	4.0 qts
Rear axle	... ...	2 pints (1.13 litres)	2.32 pts
Manual gearbox	... ...	1.97 pints (1.11 litres)	2.8 pts
Auto. transmission:			
BW		11.25 pints (6.3 litres)	—
C4		—	14.4 pts
Steering gear	... ...	0.25 pint (0.15 litre)	0.31 pt

Capri 1600XL ohc (UK specification)

Capri 1600GT ohc (UK specification)

Capri 2000 ohc (USA specification)

Capri 2000 ohc (USA specification)

Buying spare parts and vehicle identification numbers

Buying spare parts

Spare parts are available from many sources, for example: Ford garages, other garages and accessory shops, and motor factors. Our advice regarding spare part sources is as follows:

Officially appointed Ford garages - This is the best source of parts which are peculiar to your car and are otherwise not generally available (eg; complete cylinder heads, internal gearbox components, badges, interior trim etc). It is also the only place at which you should buy parts if your car is still under warranty - non-Ford components may invalidate the warranty. To be sure of obtaining the correct parts it will always be necessary to give the storeman your car's vehicle identification number, and if possible, to take the 'old' part along for positive identification. Remember that many parts are available on a factory exchange scheme - any parts returned should always be clean! It obviously makes good sense to go straight to the specialists on your car for this type of part for they are best equipped to supply you.

Other garages and accessory shops - These are often very good places to buy materials and components needed for the maintenance of your car (eg; oil filters, spark plugs, bulbs, fan belts, oils and greases, touch-up paint, filler paste etc). They also sell general accessories, usually have convenient opening hours, charge lower prices and can often be found not far from home.

Motor factors - Good factors will stock all of the more important components which wear out relatively quickly (eg; clutch components, pistons, valves, exhaust systems, brake cylinders/pipes/hoses/seals/shoes and pads etc). Motor factors will often provide new or reconditioned components on a part exchange basis - this can save a considerable amount of money.

Vehicle identification numbers

Although many individual parts, and in some cases sub-assemblies, fit a number of different models it is dangerous to assume that just because they look the same, they are the same. Differences are not always easy to detect except by serial numbers.

When buying a replacement part from a Ford dealer, decide which category that part fits into (eg; engine, trim, paint etc). Then record the relevant number from the vehicle identification plate. Quote this number and the vehicle number to the storeman; he will then be able to provide you with the correct part for your individual vehicle.

The vehicle identification plate (illustrated) will be found inside the engine compartment on the front body panel or inner wing. North American models have an additional identification number (illustrated) stamped on a metal plate just inside the windscreen on the driver's side.

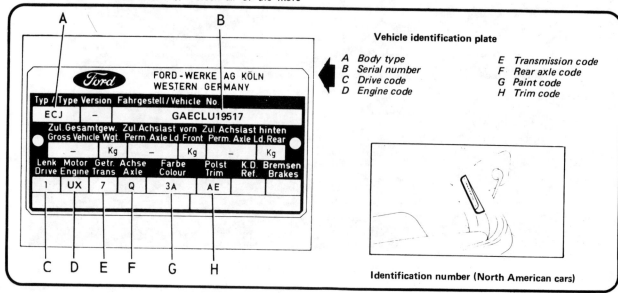

Vehicle identification plate

A Body type
B Serial number
C Drive code
D Engine code
E Transmission code
F Rear axle code
G Paint code
H Trim code

Identification number (North American cars)

Routine maintenance

Maintenance is essential for ensuring safety and desirable for the purpose of getting the best in terms of performance and economy from the car. Over the years the need for periodic lubrication - oiling, greasing and so on - has been drastically reduced if not totally eliminated. This has unfortunately tended to lead some owners to think that because no such action is required the items either no longer exist or will last for ever. This is a serious delusion. It follows therefore that the largest initial element of maintenance is visual examination. This may lead to repairs or renewals.

In the summary given here the 'essential for safety' items are shown in **bold type**. These **must** be attended to at the regular frequencies shown in order to avoid the possibility of accidents and loss of life. Other neglect results in unreliability, increased running costs, more rapid wear and more rapid depreciation of the vehicle in general.

Every 250 miles (400 km) travelled or weekly - whichever comes first

---

Steering
    Check the tyre pressures.
    Examine tyres for wear or damage.
    Is steering smooth and accurate?

Brakes
    Check reservoir fluid level.
    Is there any fall off in braking efficiency?
    Try an emergency stop. Is adjustment necessary?

Lights, wiper & horns
    Do all bulbs work at the front and rear?
    Are the headlamp beams aligned properly?
    Do the wipers and horns work?
    Check windscreen washer fluid level.

Engine
    Check the sump oil level and top up if required.
    Check the radiator coolant level and top up if required.
    Check the battery electrolyte level and top up to the level of the plates with distilled water as needed.

Every 6000 miles (9600 km)

    Renew engine oil
    Renew oil filter
    Renew fuel line filter
    Clean fuel pump filter
    Check slow-running adjustment

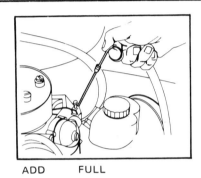

ADD   FULL

Checking engine oil

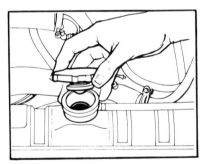

Inspecting coolant level

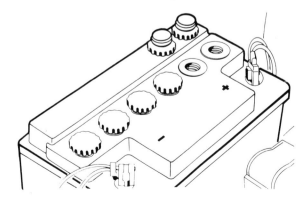

Checking battery electrolyte level

Check decel valve
Check drivebelt tension
Check and top up manual gearbox oil
Check and top up automatic transmission fluid
Check and top up rear axle lubricant.
Check brake reservoir fluid level
Check and adjust clutch free play
Check disc pad wear
Check brake shoe lining wear
Lubricate parking brake cable swivels
Inspect all brake lines and hoses for damage or deterioration
Clean and re-gap spark plugs
Clean (or renew) and adjust contact breaker points
Check and adjust valve clearances
With rocker cover removed, remove distributor rotor and crank engine on starter motor. Check that oil is discharged from the lubrication tube nozzles into the cam followers.
Lubricate door hinges, locks and controls
Check all emission control system connections and functions.

Every 12000 miles (19000 km)

Renew air cleaner element
Clean or renew PCV valve
Renew spark plugs
Check operation and clean E.G.R. valve
Check operation of temperature controlled air cleaner

deflector valve
Adjust automatic transmission brake bands (C4 type only).
Check front hub bearing adjustment

Every 18000 miles (29000 km)

Renew brake servo air filter
Check torque of rear spring 'U' bolts
Renew fuel filter
Check torque of manifold bolts.

Every 24000 miles (39000 km)

Renew crankcase emission filter within air cleaner casing
Check operation of fuel filler cap
Renew fuel evaporative charcoal canister
Check condition of cooling system hoses

Every 36000 miles (60000 km)

Clean, repack and adjust front wheel bearings
Lubricate front suspension swivel balljoints

Every two years

Drain, flush and refill the cooling system with antifreeze mixture

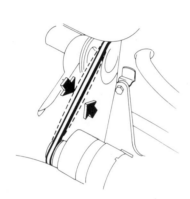

Drivebelt tension checking point

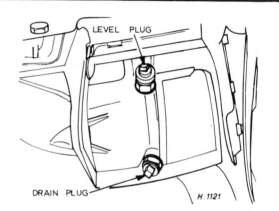

Manual gearbox filler and drain plugs

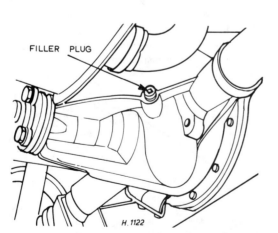

Rear axle combined filler and level plug
(on some axles this is on the rear cover plate)

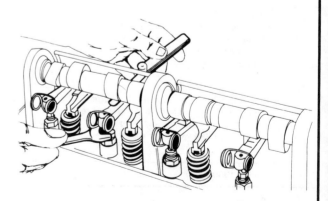

Checking valve clearances

Drain, refill and bleed the brake hydraulic system and if any sign of weeping from hydraulic component oil seals, renew all system seals and rubber components.

Periodically

The following items should be attended to as time can be spared:

Cleaning

Examination of components requires that they be cleaned. The same applies to the body of the car, inside and out, in order that deterioration due to rust or unknown damage may be detected. Certain parts of the body frame, if rusted badly, can result in the vehicle being declared unsafe and it will not pass the test for roadworthiness.

Exhaust system

An exhaust system must be leakproof, and the noise level below a certain minimum. Excessive leaks may cause carbon monoxide fumes to enter the passenger compartment. Excessive noise constitutes a public nuisance. Both these faults may cause the vehicle to be kept off the road. Repair or replace defective sections when symptoms are apparent.

Spring and autumn

Turn the air cleaner intake (not emission temperature controlled types) to the appropriate seasonal position.

Jacking points and towing

One jacking point is provided below the door sill on each side of the car. This is for use with the jack supplied with the car and should normally only be used for wheel changing. Where under-car repairs or adjustments are being carried out, never rely on the jack to support the car but always support it on axle stands or blocks placed under the bodyframe. Where a screw type or hydraulic or trolley jack is to be used, jack-up the rear of the car under the differential carrier or the front under the crossmember.

If you are towing another vehicle, attach the towrope around the rear roadspring shackle. If your car is being towed, the tow-rope should be attached to the front crossmember and the steering column unlocked. Refer to Chapter 6, part 2, for special precautions regarding towing of cars equipped with automatic transmission.

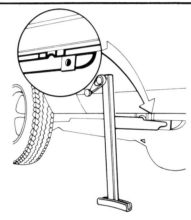

Bodysill jacking point

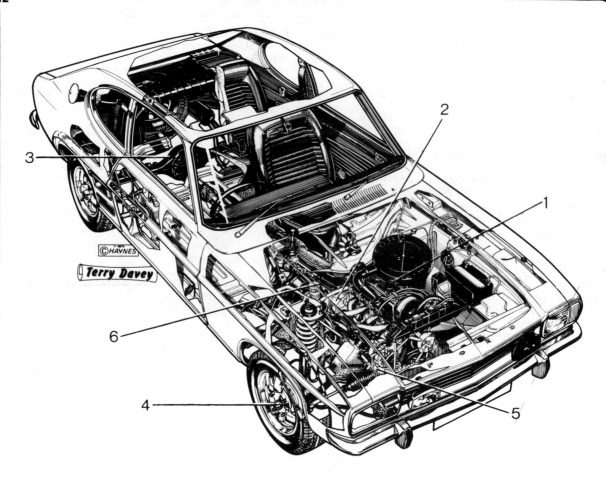

© HAYNES

Terry Davey

Lubrication chart

Component	Lubricant
1 Engine	Castrol GTX
2 Gearbox:	
Manual	Castrol Hypoy Light
Automatic	Castrol IQF Automatic Transmission Fluid
3 Rear axle	Castrol Hypoy
4 Wheel bearings	Castrol LM Grease
5 Steering gear	Castrol Hypoy
6 Braking system	Castrol Girling Universal Brake and Clutch Fluid
Handbrake linkages	Castrol LM Grease
Locks, hinges and catches	Castrol Everyman
Distributor	Castrol Everyman

Please note: *These are general recommendations only. Different operating conditions require different lubricants. Consult the handbook supplied with the car.*

Chapter 1 Engine

Contents

Specifications

Engine - general

Type	4 cylinder, in line, overhead camshaft
Valve gear operation	Cam followers via camshaft and toothed belt
Firing order	1 3 4 2
Bore:	
1600 cc	3.451 in. (87.65 mm)
2000 cc	3.575 in. (90.8 mm)
Stroke:	
1600 cc	2.6 in. (66 mm)
2000 cc	3.03 in. (76.95 mm)
Cubic capacity:	
1600 cc	1593 cc (nominal)
2000 cc	1993 cc (nominal)

Compression ratio:
1600 cc	...	...	...	...	...	...	...	9.2 : 1
2000 cc	...	...	...	...	...	...	...	8.2 : 1

	1600 cc	1600 cc GT	2000 cc
Maximum bhp (DIN) ...	72 @ 5500 rpm	88 @ 5700 rpm	98 @ 5500 rpm
Maximum torque (DIN)	86.8 lb/ft (12 kg/m) @ 2700 rpm	92 lb/ft (12.7 kg/m) @ 4000 rpm	110 lb/ft (15.4 kg/m) @ 3500 rpm

Cylinder block

	1600 cc, 1600 cc GT	2000 cc
Cast identification marks	16	20
Number of main bearings	5	5

Cylinder bore dia in. (mm) grades:
			1600 cc, 1600 cc GT	2000 cc
Standard grade				
1	... ...		3.4508–3.4512 (87.650–87.660)	3.5748–3.5752 (90.800–90.810)
2	... ...		3.4512–3.4516 (87.660–87.670)	3.5752–3.5756 (90.810–90.820)
3	... ...		3.4516–3.4520 (87.670–87.680)	3.5756–3.5760 (90.820–90.830)
4	... ...		3.4520–3.4524 (87.680–87.690)	3.5760–3.5764 (90.830–90.840)
Oversize A in. (mm)	... ...		3.4709–3.4713 (88.160–88.170)	3.5949–3.5953 (91.310–91.320)
Oversize B in. (mm)	... ...		3.4713–3.4717 (88.170–88.180)	3.5953–3.5957 (91.320–91.330)
Oversize C in. (mm)	... ...		3.4717–3.4720 (88.180–88.190)	3.5957–3.5961 (91.330–91.340)
Standard supply in service in. (mm)	... ...		3.4520–3.4524 (87.680–87.690)	3.5760–3.5764 (90.830–90.840)
Oversize 0.5 in. (mm)	... ...		3.4717–3.4720 (88.180–88.190)	3.5957–3.5961 (91.330–91.340)
Oversize 1.0 in. (mm)	... ...		3.4913–3.4917 (88.680–88.690)	3.6154–3.6157 (91.830–91.840)
Spigot bearing length in. (mm)	... ...		1.072–1.070 (27.22–27.17)	

Main bearing liners fitted: **All models**
Inner diameter:		
Standard:		
RED in. (mm)	2.2446–2.2456 (57.014–57.038)	
BLUE in. (mm)	2.2442–2.2452 (57.004–57.028)	
Crankshaft:		
Undersize:		
0.25 RED in. (mm)	2.2348–2.2357 (56.764–56.788)	
0.25 BLUE in. (mm)	2.2344–2.2354 (56.754–56.778)	
0.50 in. (mm)	2.2250–2.2263 (56.514–56.548)	
0.75 in. (mm)	2.2151–2.2164 (56.264–56.298)	
1.00 in. (mm)	2.2053–2.2066 (56.014–56.048)	
Main bearing parent bore dia:		
RED in. (mm)	2.3866–2.3870 (60.620–60.630)	
BLUE in. (mm)	2.3870–2.3874 (60.630–60.640)	

Crankshaft

Endfloat in. (mm)	0.0032–0.0110 (0.08–0.28)
Main bearing journal diameters:	
Standard:	
RED in. (mm)	2.2441–2.2437 (57.000–56.990)
BLUE in. (mm)	2.2437–2.2433 (56.990–56.980)
Undersize:	
0.25 in. (mm)	2.2338–2.2335 (56.740–56.730)
0.50 in. (mm)	2.2244–2.2240 (56.500–56.490)
0.75 in. (mm)	2.2146–2.2142 (56.250–56.240)
1.00 in. (mm)	2.2047–2.2043 (56.000–55.990)
Thrust washer thickness:	
Standard in. (mm)	0.091–0.0925 (2.3–2.35)
Undersize in. (mm)	0.098–0.100 (2.5–2.55)
Main bearing clearance in. (mm)	0.0005–0.0019 (0.014–0.048)
Crankpin journal diameter:	
Standard:	
RED in. (mm)	2.0472–2.0468 (52.000–51.990)
BLUE in. (mm)	2.0468–2.0465 (51.990–51.980)
Undersize:	
0.25 RED in. (mm)	2.0374–2.0370 (51.750–51.740)
0.25 BLUE in. (mm)	2.0370–2.0366 (51.740–51.730)
0.50 in. (mm)	2.0276–2.0272 (51.500–51.490)
0.75 in. (mm)	2.0177–2.0173 (51.250–51.240)

Camshaft

Drive ... ... Toothed belt
Thrust plate thickness:
    Type 1 in. (mm) 0.158 (4.01)
    Type 2 in. (mm) 0.157 (3.98)

Width of camshaft groove in. (mm) ... ... $0.1600 \begin{smallmatrix} +0.0028 \\ -0.0000 \end{smallmatrix} (4.064 \begin{smallmatrix} +0.070 \\ -0.000 \end{smallmatrix})$

	1600 cc, 1600 cc GT	2000 cc
Cam lift in. (mm)	0.2338 (5.938)	0.2518 (6.397)
Cam heel to toe dimensions in. (mm)	1.418–1.412 (36.01–35.87)	1.435–1.430 (36.46–36.32)
Identification colour	white	yellow

Journal diameter:
    Front in. (mm) 1.6539–1.6531 (42.01–41.99)
    Centre in. (mm) 1.7606–1.7528 (44.72–44.52)
    Rear in. (mm) 1.7720–1.7713 (45.01–44.99)
Bearing - inside diameter:
    Front in. (mm) 1.6557–1.6549 (42.055–42.035)
    Centre in. (mm) 1.7588–1.7580 (44.675–44.655)
    Rear in. (mm) 1.7381–1.7730 (45.055–45.035)
Camshaft endfloat in. (mm) 0.002–0.0035 (0.05–0.09)

Pistons

	1600 cc, 1600 cc GT	2000 cc
Piston diameter:		
Standard:		
Grade 1 in. (mm)	3.4490–3.4494 (87.605–87.615)	3.5730–3.5734 (90.755–90.765)
Grade 2 in. (mm)	3.4494–3.4498 (87.615–87.625)	3.5734–3.5738 (90.765–90.775)
Grade 3 in. (mm)	3.4498–3.4502 (87.625–87.635)	3.5738–3.5742 (90.775–90.785)
Grade 4 in. (mm)	3.4502–3.4506 (87.635–87.645)	3.5742–3.5746 (90.785–90.795)
Standard supplied in service:		
in. (mm)	3.4500–3.4510 (87.630–87.655)	3.5740–3.5750 (90.780–90.805)
Oversize supplied in service:		
0.5 in. (mm)	3.4697–3.4707 (88.130–88.155)	3.5937–3.5947 (91.280–91.305)
1.0 in. (mm)	3.4894–3.4904 (88.630–88.655)	3.6134–3.6144 (91.780–91.805)

	All models
Piston clearance in cylinder bore:	
in. (mm)	0.001–0.0024 (0.025–0.060)
Ring gap (in situ):	
Top in. (mm)	0.015–0.023 (0.38–0.58)
Centre in. (mm)	0.015–0.023 (0.38–0.58)
Bottom in. (mm)	0.0157–0.055 (0.4–1.4)
Groove gap compression	0.004 in. (0.102 mm)
Oil control	0.003 in. (0.076 mm)

Gudgeon pins

Length in. (mm) 2.83–2.87 (72–72.8)
Diameter:
    RED in. (mm) 0.94465–0.94476 (23.994–23.997)
    BLUE in. (mm) 0.94476–0.94488 (23.997–24.000)
    YELLOW in. (mm) 0.94488–0.94500 (24.000–24.003)
Clearance in piston in. (mm) 0.0002–0.00043 (0.005–0.011)
Fit in connecting rod in. (mm) 0.0007–0.00153 (0.018–0.039)

Connecting rods

Big end bore:
    RED in. (mm) 2.1653–2.1657 (55.00–55.01)
    BLUE in. (mm) 2.1657–2.1661 (55.01–55.02)
Small end bush diameter in. (mm) 0.9434–0.9439 (23.964–23.976)
Inside diameter:
    Standard:
        RED in. (mm) 2.0478–2.0487 (52.014–52.038)
        BLUE in. (mm) 2.0474–2.0483 (52.004–52.028)
    Undersize:
        0.25 RED in. (mm) 2.0379–2.0388 (51.764–51.788)
        0.25 BLUE in. (mm) 2.0376–2.0385 (51.754–51.778)
        0.50 in. (mm) 2.0281–2.0294 (51.514–51.548)
        0.75 in. (mm) 2.0183–2.0196 (51.264–51.298)
        1.00 in. (mm) 2.0084–2.0100 (51.014–51.048)
Crankpin to bearing liner clearance:
    Standard in. (mm) 0.00055–0.0018 (0.014–0.048)
    Undersize in. (mm) 0.00055–0.0023 (0.014–0.058)

Cylinder head

	1600 cc, 1600 cc GT	2000 cc
Cast identification number	6	0
Combustion chamber volume	37.5—39 cc	48.6—50.1 cc

	All models
Valve seat angle	45°
Valve guide inside diameter, inlet and exhaust:	
Standard in. (mm)	0.3174—0.3184 (8.063—8.088)
Oversize:	
0.2 in. (mm)	0.3253—0.3263 (8.263—8.288)
0.4 in. (mm)	0.3332—0.3342 (8.463—8.488)
Parent bore for camshaft bearing liners:	
Front in. (mm)	1.6557—1.6549 (42.055—42.035)
Centre in. (mm)	1.7589—1.7580 (44.675—44.655)
Rear in. (mm)	1.7738—1.7730 (45.055—45.035)

Valves

	1600 cc, 1600 cc GT	2000 cc
Valve clearance (cold):		
Inlet in. (mm)	0.008 (0.20)	0.008 (0.20)
Exhaust in. (mm)	0.010 (0.25)	0.010 (0.25)
Inlet opens	16° BTDC	18° BTDC
Inlet closes	60° ABDC	70° ABDC
Exhaust opens	58° BBDC	64° BBDC
Exhaust closes	18° ATDC	24° ATDC

Inlet valves

	1600 cc, 1600 cc GT	2000 cc
Length in. (mm)	4.449 ± 0.016 (113 ± 0.4)	4.3760 (111.15)
Valve head diameter in. (mm)	1.516 ± 0.008 (38.5 ± 0.2)	1.654 ± 0.008 (42 ± 0.2)

	All models
Valve stem diameter:	
Standard in. (mm)	0.3167—0.3159 (8.043—8.025)
Oversize:	
0.2 in. (mm)	0.3245—0.3238 (8.243—8.225)
0.4 in. (mm)	0.3324—0.3317 (8.443—8.425)
Valve stem to guide clearance in. (mm)	0.0008—0.0025 (0.020—0.063)

	1600 cc, 1600 cc GT	2000 cc
Valve lift in. (mm)	0.3730 (9.474)	0.3993 (10.142)
Valve spring free-length in. (mm)	1.73 (44)	1.73 (44)
Spring load, valve open lb (kg)	169.4 ± 6.6 (77 ± 3)	176 ± 6 (80 ± 3)
Spring load, valve closed lb (kg)	68 ± 4 (31 ± 2)	68 ± 4 (31 ± 2)
Spring length, compressed in. (mm)	0.945 (24.0)	0.945 (24.0)

Exhaust valves

	1600 cc, 1600 cc GT	2000 cc
Length in. (mm)	4.449 ± 0.19 (113 ± 0.5)	4.37 ± 0.19 (111 ± 0.5)
Valve head diameter in.	1.18 ± 0.08	1.34 ± 0.08 to 1.42 ± 0.08
(mm)	(30 ± 0.2)	(34 ± 0.2 to 36 ± 0.2)

	All models
Valve stem diameter:	
Standard in. (mm)	0.3156—0.3149 (8.017—7.999)
Oversize:	
0.2 in. (mm)	0.3235—0.3228 (8.217—8.199)
0.4 in. (mm)	0.3314—0.3307 (8.417—8.399)
Valve stem to guide clearance in. (mm)	0.0034—0.0035 (0.086—0.089)

	1600 cc, 1600 cc GT	2000 cc
Valve lift in. (mm)	0.3728 (9.47)	0.3992 (10.14)
Valve spring free-length in. (mm)	1.732 (44)	1.732 (44)
Spring load, valve open:		
lb	170 ± 6	176 ± 6
Kg	77 ± 3	80 ± 3

Lubrication

	All models
Sump capacity:	
Without filter	5.3 Imp. pints, 3.5 US qts., 3.0 litres
With filter	7 Imp. pints, 4.0 US qts., 3.75 litres
Minimum oil pressure (hot) at 2000 rpm	34 psi (standard 45—65 psi)

Torque wrench settings

	lb f ft	kg fm
Main bearing caps	70	9.7
Big-end bearing caps	32	4.4
Auxiliary shaft bolt	34	4.7
Camshaft bolt tensioner screw	34	4.7
Camshaft sprocket bolt	34	4.7
Crankshaft pulley bolt	40	5.5
Cylinder head bolts:		
Stage 1	20	2.8
Stage 2	40	5.5
Stage 3	75	10.4
Flywheel bolts	50	6.9
Rocker arm ball stud nut	34	4.7
Spark plugs	20	2.8
Water pump bolts	30	4.1
Clutch bellhousing bolts	30	4.1
Torque converter housing bolts	35	4.8
Torque converter to driveplate	40	5.5
Driveplate to crankshaft	55	7.6
Oil pump to cylinder block	20	2.8
Thermostat housing bolts	25	3.5

1 General description

The engine fitted to models covered by the manual is of four cylinder overhead camshaft design.

An exploded view identifying the main components is shown in Fig. 1.1.

The cylinder head is of the crossflow design with the inlet manifold one side and the exhaust manifold on the other. As flat topped pistons are used, the combustion chambers are contained in the cylinder head.

The combined crankcase and cylinder block is made of cast iron and houses the pistons and crankshaft. Attached to the underside of the crankcase is a pressed steel sump which acts as a reservoir for the engine oil. Full information on the lubricating system will be found in Section 24.

The cast iron cylinder head is mounted on top of the cylinder block and acts as a support for the overhead camshaft. The slightly angled valves operate directly in the cylinder head and are controlled by the camshaft via cam followers. The camshaft is operated by a toothed reinforced rubber belt from the crankshaft. To eliminate backlash and prevent slackness of the belt a spring loaded tensioner in the form of a jockey wheel is in contact with the back of the belt. It serves two further functions, to keep the belt away from the water pump and to increase the contact area of the camshaft and crankshaft sprocket.

The drive belt also drives the auxiliary shaft sprocket and it is from this shaft that the oil pump, distributor and fuel pump operate.

The inlet manifold is mounted on the left-hand side of the cylinder head and to this the carburettor is fitted. A water jacket is incorporated in the inlet manifold so that the petrol air charge may be correctly prepared before entering the combustion chambers.

The exhaust manifold is mounted on the right-hand side of the cylinder head and connects to a single downpipe and silencer system.

Aluminium alloy pistons are connected to the crankshaft by H section forged steel connecting rods and gudgeon pins. The gudgeon pin is a press fit in the little end of the connecting rod but a floating fit in the piston boss. Two compression rings and one scraper ring, all located above the gudgeon pin, are fitted.

The forged crankshaft runs in five main bearings and end float is accommodated by fitting thrust washers each side of the centre main bearings.

Before commencing any overhaul work on the engine refer to Section 8, where information is given about special tools required to remove the cylinder head, drive belt tensioner and oil pump.

2 Major operations possible with engine in place

The following major operations can be carried out to the engine with it in place in the bodyshell:

1 *Removal and replacement of cylinder head*
2 *Removal and replacement of camshaft drive belt*
3 *Removal and replacement of engine front mountings*
4 *Removal and replacement of camshaft (after first removing cylinder head and cam followers)*

3 Major operations requiring engine removal

The following major operations can be carried out with the engine out of the bodyframe on the bench or floor:

1 *Removal and replacement of auxiliary shaft*
2 *Removal and replacement of oil pump*
3 *Removal and replacement of pistons and connecting rods*
4 *Removal and replacement of crankshaft and main bearings*
5 *Removal and replacement of flywheel*
6 *Removal and replacement of crankshaft rear oil seal*
7 *Removal and replacement of camshaft (see Section 2, item 4)*

4 Methods of engine removal

The engine may be lifted out together with the gearbox or separated from the gearbox and lifted out by itself. If the gearbox is left attached the disadvantage is that the engine has to be tilted to a very steep angle to get it out. Unless both the engine and gearbox are being repaired or overhauled together there is no other reason for removing them as one complete unit.

5 Engine removal (less gearbox)

1 The do-it-yourself owner should be able to remove the engine fairly easily in about 4 hours. It is essential to have a good hoist and two axle stands if an inspection pit or ramp is not available.
2 The sequence of operations listed in this section is not critical as the position of the person undertaking the work, or the tool in his hand, will determine to a certain extent the order in which the work is tackled. Obviously the engine cannot be removed until everything is disconnected from it and the following sequence will ensure that nothing is forgotten.
3 Open the bonnet.
4 Place a container of suitable size under the radiator and one

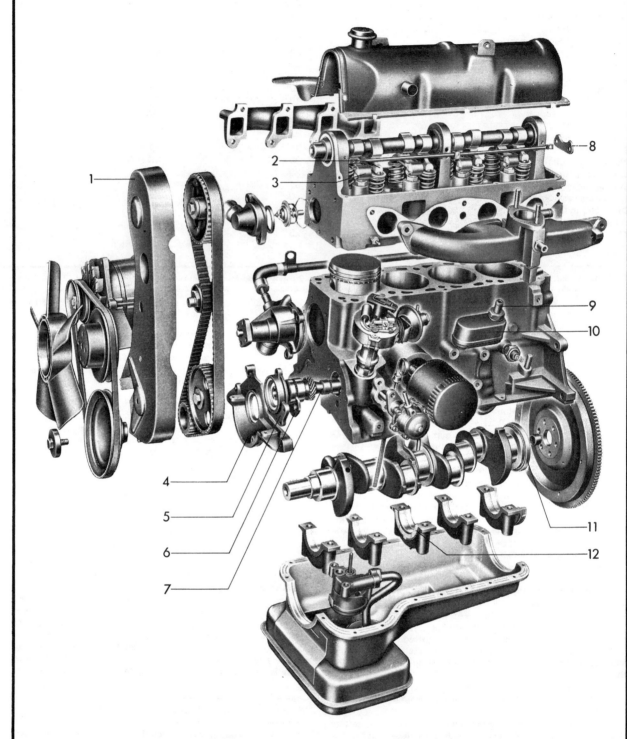

Fig. 1.1. Engine (1600 cc single venturi carburettor) - major components

1 *Guard, toothed belt drive*	7 *Auxiliary shaft*
2 *Cam follower*	8 *Thrust plate, camshaft*
3 *Cam follower spring*	9 *Ventilation valve*
4 *Timing cover, crankshaft*	10 *Oil separator*
5 *Timing cover auxiliary shaft*	11 *Oil seal, crankshaft*
6 *Thrust plate, auxiliary shaft*	12 *Central main bearing*

under the engine and drain the cooling system as described in Chapter 2. Do not drain the water in the garage or the place where the engine is to be removed if receptacles are not at hand to catch the water.

5 Place a container of at least 8 pints (9.608 US pints/4.55 litres) under the engine sump and remove the oil drain plug. Allow the oil to drain out and then refit the plug.

6 Place old blankets over the wing and across the cowl to prevent damage to the paintwork.

7 It is easier if two assistants are available so that the bonnet can be supported whilst the hinges are being released.

8 Using a pencil mark the outline of the hinges on the bonnet.

9 Undo and remove the four nuts and washers and bolts that secure the hinges to the bonnet.

10 Release the bonnet stay and carefully lift the bonnet over the front of the engine compartment.

11 Refer to Chapter 3 and remove the air cleaner and carburettor adaptor.

12 Disconnect the battery, release the battery clamp and lift away from its tray.

13 Refer to Chapter 2 and remove the radiator and shroud from the engine compartment.

14 Where air conditioning is installed, remove the compressor from its mounting bracket and push it to one side of the engine compartment. On no account disconnect any part of the system as lethal refrigerant gas will be released. The evacuation and recharging of the refrigeration circuit of the air conditioning system are jobs for your Ford dealer or refrigeration engineer.

15 Disconnect all emission control connections according to the system employed (see Chapter 3).

16 *Automatic choke:* Slacken the clips and disconnect the heater hose from the water pump and carburettor automatic choke.

17 Release the clip and detach the multi-pin plug from the rear of the alternator. Also disconnect the servo vacuum hose from the inlet manifold.

18 *Manual choke:* Disconnect choke inner and outer cables at the carburettor.

19 Disconnect the accelerator cable from the bellcrank assembly, and the bellcrank to carburettor shaft swivel.

20 Undo and remove the two cap screws that secure the throttle shaft bellcrank to the inlet manifold. Move the bellcrank assembly to one side. Where automatic transmission is fitted, disconnect the 'kickdown' cable.

21 Slacken the clip and detach the flexible fuel line from the fuel tank pipe. Plug the end of the fuel tank pipe to prevent loss of petrol and dirt ingress.

22 Make a note of the electrical connections at the ignition coil and disconnect the primary lead and HT cable from the coil.

23 Locate the oil pressure switch and water temperature gauge sender unit and disconnect the terminal connectors. Tuck the leads out of the way.

24 Make sure the handbrake is applied. Chock the rear wheels and jack up the front of the car. Support on firmly based stands and remove the roadwheels.

25 Refer to Chapter 10 and remove the starter motor.

26 Soak the exhaust downpipe to manifold securing nuts with penetrating oil and remove the nuts. Tap the clamp plate free from the studs.

27 Remove the rear engine cover plate and bracket assembly from the clutch housing. Detach the bracket assembly from the cylinder block and swing it back out of the way.

28 *Manual gearbox:* Undo and remove the clutch housing lower securing bolts and washers.

29 *Automatic transmission:* Disconnect the converter from the flexplate by turning the crankshaft until a bolt is visible and then remove it. Repeat until all bolts have been removed. Next undo and remove the converter housing to cylinder block securing bolts.

30 Undo and remove the nut securing each engine mounting insulator to the underbody bracket. Remove the plain washers.

31 If engine lifting facilities are limited the car should now be lowered. If the wheels were removed they should now be

refitted.

32 Using a garage hydraulic jack support the weight of the gearbox/automatic transmission unit.

33 Support the weight of the engine using suitable chains or rope positioned on the existing lifting brackets.

34 Check that all electrical cables and controls have been disconnected and tucked well out of the way.

35 Undo and remove the remaining clutch housing (manual gearbox) or torque converter housing (automatic transmission) securing bolts and washers.

36 Carefully raise the engine to free the mountings and pull slightly forward. It will now be necessary to tilt the engine at a fairly steep angle so that the sump clears the front grille panels. Continue to raise the engine until the sump is just above the front panel.

37 The engine should now be drawn forward or the car pushed rearward until the engine is clear of the car. Lower the unit to the floor.

38 Thoroughly clean the exterior of the engine with paraffin or a water soluble solvent type cleaner.

6 Engine removal (with manual gearbox attached)

1 Proceed exactly as described in Section 5 up to, and including paragraph 24, then 26 to 28 inclusive and finally 30 and 31.

2 Unscrew the gearbox drain plug and allow the oil to drain away for five minutes. Replace the drain plug.

3 *2000 cc models.* Working under the car detach the three remote control selector rods from the gearbox. See Chapter 6.

4 *1600 cc models.* Refer to Chapter 6 and remove the gearchange lever from inside the car.

5 Support the weight of the gearbox using a small jack located adjacent to the drain plug.

6 Undo and remove the centre bolt which locates the gearbox extension housing into the support member. Then making sure the gearbox support jack is firmly in position, undo and remove the four bolts and washers that secure the crossmember to the underside of the body. Lift away the crossmember.

7 With the crossmember removed it is now an easy task to disconnect the speedometer cable from the gearbox by removing the circlip and withdrawing the cable.

8 Detach the reverse light cable at its snap connector.

9 Wrap rope slings around the engine and take up the slack.

10 Check that all cables and controls have been detached and safely tucked out of the way.

11 With the jack under the gearbox still in position start lifting and at the same time, once the front mountings have been cleared, move the engine forward until the propeller shaft is released. Support it until clear, and then lower and rest it on a suitable block so as not to strain the centre bearing.

12 Due to the fact that the gearbox is attached, the engine will have to be lifted out at a much steeper angle than for removing the engine on its own. As the weight is more towards the rear, it will be fairly easy to achieve the necessary angle.

13 Continue to raise the engine and move it forwards at the necessary angle. At this stage the forward edge of the bellhousing is likely to catch against the front crossmember and the tail of the gearbox will need raising until the whole unit is forward and clear of it.

14 Finally the whole unit will rise clear and if the maximum height of the lifting tackle has been reached, it will be necessary to swing the unit so that the tail can be lifted clear whilst the hoist is moved away or the car lowered from its axle stands and pushed from under the unit. (It will be necessary to tie up the propeller shaft front end).

15 The whole unit should be lowered to the ground (or bench) as soon as possible and the gearbox may then be separated from the engine.

7 Engine removal (with automatic transmission attached)

It is recommended that the engine should not be removed

whilst still attached to the automatic transmission, because of the weight involved. If it is necessary to remove both units refer to Chapter 6 and remove the transmission unit first. Then remove the engine, as described in Section 5 but disregarding information on detachment from the transmission unit.

8 Engine - dismantling general

1 It is best to mount the engine on a dismantling stand, but if this is not available, stand the engine on a strong bench at a comfortable working height. Failing this, it can be stripped down on the floor.
2 During the dismantling process, the greatest care should be taken to keep the exposed parts free from dirt. As an aid to achieving this thoroughly clean down the outside of the engine, first removing all traces of oil and congealed dirt.
3 A good grease solvent will make the job much easier, for, after the solvent has been applied and allowed to stand for a time, a vigorous jet of water will wash off the solvent and grease with it. If the dirt is thick and deeply embedded, work the solvent into it with a strong stiff brush.
4 Finally wipe down the exterior of the engine with a rag and only then, when it is quite clean, should the dismantling process begin. As the engine is stripped, clean each part in a bath of paraffin.
5 Never immerse parts with oilways (eg; crankshaft) in paraffin. To clean these parts, wipe down carefully with a petrol dampened rag. Oilways can be cleaned out with a piece of wire. If an air line is available, all parts can be blown dry and the oilways blown through as an added precaution.
6 Re-use of old gaskets is false economy. To avoid the possibility of trouble after the engine has been reassembled **always** use new gaskets throughout.
7 Do not throw away the old gaskets, for sometimes it happens that an immediate replacement cannot be found and the old gasket is then very useful as a template. Hang up the gaskets as they are removed.
8 To strip the engine, it is best to work from the top down. The sump provides a firm base on which the engine can be supported in an upright position. When the stage is reached where the crankshaft must be removed, the engine can be turned on its side and all other work carried out with it in this position.
9 Wherever possible, replace nuts, bolts and washers (nuts and bolts finger tight) from wherever they were removed. This helps to avoid loss and muddle. If they cannot be replaced then hang them out in a fashion that is clear from whence they came.
10 Before dismantling begins it is important that three special tools are obtained otherwise certain work cannot be carried out. This includes removal of the cylinder head. The special tools are shown in the photo.

9 Ancillary components - removal

Before basic engine dismantling begins, it is necessary to strip it of ancillary components.

    a) *Fuel system components (Chapter 3)*
       Carburettor and manifold assembly
       Exhaust manifold
       Fuel pump
       Fuel line
    b) *Ignition system components (Chapter 4)*
       Spark plugs
       Distributor
    c) *Electrical system components (Chapter 10)*
       Alternator
       Starter motor
    d) *Cooling system components (Chapter 2)*
       Fan and hub
       Water pump
       Thermostat housing and thermostat
       Water temperature indicator sender unit

    e) *Engine*
       Oil filter
       Oil pressure sender unit
       Oil level dipstick
       Oil filler cap and top cover
       Engine mountings
       Crankcase ventilation valve and oil separator
       Emission control components (Decel valve, spark delay valve, air pump, EGR valve etc: see Chapter 3)
    f) *Clutch (Chapter 5)*
       Clutch pressure plate assembly
       Clutch friction plate assembly

All nuts and bolts associated with the foregoing. Some of these items have to be removed for individual servicing or renewal periodically and details can be found in the appropriate Chapter.

10 Cylinder head removal - engine in car

1 Open the bonnet and using a soft pencil mark the outline of both the hinges at the bonnet to act as a datum for refitting.
2 With the help of a second person to take the weight of the bonnet, undo and remove the hinge to bonnet securing bolts with plain and spring washers. There are two bolts to each hinge.
3 Lift away the bonnet and put in a safe place where it will not be scratched.
4 Refer to Chapter 10, and remove the battery.
5 Refer to Chapter 3, and remove the air cleaner assembly from the top of the carburettor.
6 Mark the HT leads so that they may be refitted in their original positions and detach them from the spark plugs.
7 Release the HT lead rubber moulding from the clip on the top of the cover.
8 Spring back the clips securing the distributor cap to the distributor body. Lift off the distributor cap.
9 Detach the HT lead from the centre of the ignition coil. Remove the distributor cap from the engine compartment.
10 Refer to Chapter 2 and drain the cooling system.
11 Refer to Chapter 3 and remove the carburettor.
12 The combined insulation spacer and gasket may now be lifted from the studs. Note that it is marked 'TOP FRONT' and it must be refitted the correct way round.
13 Slacken the clip securing the hose to the inlet manifold branch pipe adaptor and pull off the hose.
14 Slacken the clip securing the hose to the adaptor at the centre of the manifold and pull off the hose.
15 Undo and remove the self lock nuts and bolts securing the inlet manifold to the side of the cylinder head. Note that one of the manifold securing bolts also retains the air cleaner support bracket.
16 Lift away the inlet manifold and recover the manifold gasket.
17 Undo and remove the two nuts that secure the exhaust downpipe and clamp plate to the exhaust manifold.
18 Slide the clamp plate down the exhaust pipe.
19 Detach the thermal transmitter electric cable from the inlet manifold side of the cylinder head (photo).
20 Slacken the radiator top hose clips and completely remove the hose (photo).
21 Undo and remove the bolts, spring and plain washers that secure the top cover to the cylinder head (photos).
22 Lift away the top cover (photo).
23 Undo and remove the two self lock nuts that secure the heat deflector plate to the top of the exhaust manifold. Lift away the deflector plate (photo).
24 Undo and remove the bolts, spring and plain washers that secure the toothed drive belt guard (photo).
25 Lift away the guard (photo).
26 Release the tension from the drive belt by slackening the spring loaded roller mounting plate securing bolt (photo).

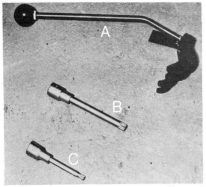

8.10 Three special tools for dismantling A - valve spring compressor, B - cylinder head bolt wrench, C - oil pump bolt wrench

10.19 Thermal transmitter electric cable detachment

10.20 Slackening radiator top hose clip

10.21A Removing a top cover bolt

10.21B Removing a top cover flange bolt

10.22 Removing top cover

10.23 Removing heat deflector plate

10.24 Removing belt guard bolt

10.25 Removing belt guard

10.26 Releasing belt tensioner mounting plate securing bolt

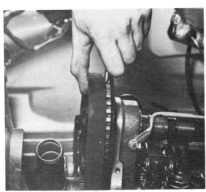

10.27 Removing belt from camshaft sprocket

10.28 Slackening cylinder head securing bolts

27 Lift the toothed drive belt from the camshaft sprocket (photo).

28 Using Ford service tool 21 - 002 together with a socket wrench (photo), slacken the cylinder head securing bolts in a diagonal and progressive manner until all are free from tension. Remove the ten bolts noting that because of the special shape of the bolt head no washers are used. Unfortunately there is no other tool suitable to slot into the bolt head so do not attempt to improvise which will only cause damage to the bolt. A proprietary version of this tool is available from Redwing Sales (See Section 8.10 and page 2).

29 The cylinder head may now be removed by lifting upward (photo). If the head is stuck, try to rock it to break the seal. Under no circumstances try to prise it apart from the cylinder block with a screwdriver or cold chisel, as damage may be done to the faces of the cylinder head and block. If the head will not readily free, turn the engine over by the flywheel using the starter motor, as the compression in the cylinders will often break the cylinder head joint. If this fails to work, strike the head sharply with a plastic headed or wooden hammer, or with a metal hammer with an interposed piece of wood to cushion the blow. Under no circumstances hit the head directly with a metal hammer as this may cause the casting to fracture. Several sharp taps with the hammer, at the same time pulling upward, should free the head. Lift the head off and place to one side (photo).

11 Cylinder head removal - engine on bench

The procedure for removing the cylinder head with the engine on the bench is similar to that for removal when the engine is in the car, with the exception of disconnecting the controls and services. Refer to Section 10 and follow the sequence given in paragraphs 21 to 29, inclusive.

12 Auxiliary shaft - removal

1 Using a metal bar lock the auxiliary shaft sprocket and with an open ended spanner undo and remove the bolt and washer securing the sprocket to the shaft (photo).
2 Undo and remove the three bolts and spring washers that secure the auxiliary shaft timing cover to the cylinder block (photo).
3 Lift away the timing cover (photo).
4 Undo and remove the two cross head screws securing the auxiliary shaft thrust plate to the cylinder block (photo).
5 Lift away the thrust plate (photo).
6 The auxiliary shaft may now be drawn forward and then lifted away (photo).

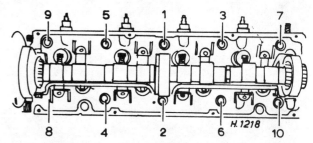

Fig. 1.2. Cylinder head bolt tightening or releasing diagram (Secs. 10 and 59)

13 Flywheel (or driveplate - auto. trans.) - backplate and sump - removal

1 With the clutch removed as described in Chapter 5, lock the flywheel using a screwdriver in mesh with the starter ring gear and undo the six bolts securing the flywheel to the crankshaft in a diagonal and progressive manner (photo). Lift away the bolts.
2 Mark the relative position of the flywheel and crankshaft and then lift away the flywheel (photo).
3 Undo the remaining engine backplate securing bolts and ease the backplate from the two dowels. Lift away the backplate (photo).
4 Undo and remove the bolts that secure the sump to the underside of the crankcase (photo).
5 Lift away the sump and its gasket (photo).

14 Oil pump and strainer - removal

1 Undo and remove the bolt and spring washer securing the oil pump pick up pipe support bracket to the crankcase.
2 Using Ford special tool 21 - 020, undo the two special bolts that secure the oil pump to the underside of the crankcase. Unfortunately there is no other tool suitable to slot into the bolt head so do not attempt to improvise which will only cause damage to the bolt (photo).
3 Lift away the oil pump and strainer assembly (photo).
4 Carefully lift away the oil pump drive making a special note of which way round it is fitted (photo).

15 Crankshaft pulley, sprocket and timing cover - removal

1 Lock the crankshaft using a block of soft wood placed

10.29A Cylinder head removal

10.29B Engine with cylinder head removed

12.1 Removing auxiliary shaft securing bolt

12.2 Removing auxiliary shaft timing cover securing bolts

12.3 Removing auxiliary shaft timing cover

12.4 Removing thrust plate securing bolt

12.5 Lifting away thrust plate

12.6 Withdrawing auxiliary shaft

13.1 Removing flywheel bolts

13.2 Lifting away flywheel

13.3 Backplate removal

13.4 Removing sump securing bolts

13.5 Lifting away sump

14.2 Removing oil pump bolts

14.3 Lifting away oil pump and pick-up pipe

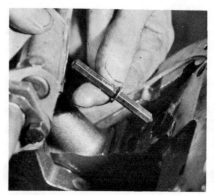
14.4 Removing oil pump driveshaft

15.3 Removal of sprocket from crankshaft

15.5 Removing timing cover and gasket

16.1 Piston identification marks stamped on crown

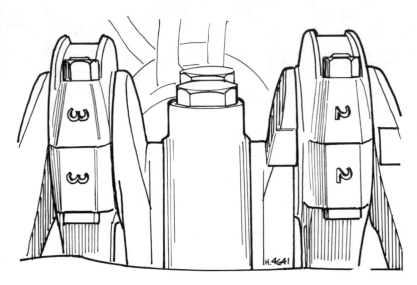
Fig. 1.3. Big-end bearing cap and connecting rod identification marks (Sec. 16)

16.3 Removing a big-end cap

17.1 Main bearing cap identification marks

17.3 Lifting away No. 2 main bearing cap

17.4 Removing rear main bearing cap

between a crankshaft web and the crankcase then using a socket and suitable extension, undo the bolt that secures the crankshaft pulley. Recover the large diameter plain washer.

2 Using a large screwdriver ease the pulley from the crankshaft. Recover the large diameter plain washer.

3 Again using the screwdriver ease the sprocket from the crankshaft (photo).

4 Undo and remove the bolts and spring washers securing the timing cover to the front of the crankcase.

5 Lift away the timing cover and the gasket (photo).

16 Pistons, connecting rods and big-end bearings - removal

1 Note that the pistons have an arrow marked on the crown showing the forward facing side (photo). Inspect the big-end bearing caps and connecting rods to make sure identification marks are visible. This is to ensure that the correct end caps are fitted to the correct connecting rods and the connecting rods placed in their respective bores (Fig. 1.3).

2 Undo the big-end nuts and place to one side in the order in which they were removed.

3 Remove the big-end caps, taking care to keep them in the right order and the correct way round. Also ensure that the shell bearings are kept with their correct connecting rods unless the rods are to be renewed (photo).

4 If the big-end caps are difficult to remove, they may be gently tapped with a soft faced hammer.

5 To remove the shell bearings press the bearing opposite the groove in both the connecting rod and its cap, and the bearing will slide out easily.

6 Withdraw the pistons and connecting rods upward and ensure that they are kept in the correct order for replacement in the same bore as they were originally fitted.

17 Crankshaft and main bearing - removal

With the engine removed from the car and separated from the gearbox, remove the drive belt, crankshaft pulley and sprocket, flywheel and backplate, oil pump, big-end bearings and pistons.

1 Make sure that identification marks are visible on the main bearing end caps, so that they may be refitted in their original positions and also the correct way round (photo).

2 Undo by one turn at a time the bolts which hold the five bearing caps.

3 Lift away each main bearing cap and the bottom half of each bearing shell, taking care to keep the bearing shell in the right caps (photo).

4 When removing the rear main bearing end cap note that this also retains the crankshaft rear oil seal (photo).

5 When removing the centre main bearing, note the bottom semi-circular halves of the thrust washers, one half lying on either side of the main bearing. Lay them with the centre main bearing along the correct side.

6 As the centre and rear bearing caps are accurately located by dowels it may be necessary to gently tap the end caps to release them.

7 Slightly rotate the crankshaft to free the upper halves of the bearing shells and thrust washers which can be extracted and placed over the correct bearing cap.

8 Carefully lift away the crankshaft rear oil seal (photo).

9 Remove the crankshaft by lifting it away from the crankcase (photo).

18 Camshaft drivebelt - removal

It is possible to remove the drivebelt with the engine in situ but experience has shown that this type of belt is very reliable and unlikely to break or stretch considerably. However, during a major engine overhaul it is recommended that a new belt is fitted.

1 Refer to Chapter 2 and drain the cooling system. Slacken the top hose securing clips and remove the top hose.

2 Slacken the alternator mounting bolts and push the unit towards the engine. Lift away the fan belt.

3 Undo and remove the bolts that secure the drivebelt guard to the front of the engine. Lift away the guard.

4 Slacken the belt tensioner mounting plate securing bolt and release the tension on the belt.

5 Place the car in gear (manual gearbox only), and apply the brakes firmly. Undo and remove the bolt and plain washer that secure the crankshaft pulley to the nose of the crankshaft. On automatic cars, remove the starter and jam the driveplate ring gear.

6 Using a screwdriver carefully ease off the pulley (photo).

7 Recover the plain large diameter washer.

8 The drivebelt may now be lifted away (photo).

19 Valves - removal

1 To enable the valves to be removed a special valve spring compressor is required. This has a part number of 21 - 005. However, it is just possible to use a universal valve spring compressor provided extreme caution is taken.

2 Make a special note of how the cam follower springs are fitted and, using a screwdriver, remove these from the cam followers (photo).

3 Back off fully the cam follower adjustment and remove the cam followers. Keep these in their respective order so that they can be refitted in their original positions.

4 Using the valve spring compressor, compress the valve springs and lift out the collets (photo).

5 Remove the spring cap and spring and using a screwdriver prise the oil retainer caps out of their seats. Remove the valves and keep in their respective order, unless they are so badly worn that they are to be renewed. If they are going to be used again, place them in a sheet of card having eight numbered holes

17.8 Lifting away crankshaft rear oil seal

17.9 Cylinder block and crankcase with crankshaft removed

18.6 Lifting away crankshaft pulley

18.8 Drivebelt removal

19.2 Removing a cam follower spring

19.4 Compressing a valve spring

20.1 Removing camshaft oil pipe

20.2 Camshaft oil pipe drillings

20.3 Using a metal bar to lock camshaft sprocket

20.4 Removing camshaft sprocket

20.5 Removing camshaft thrust plate securing bolts

20.6 Removing camshaft thrust plate

20.7 Tapping camshaft through bearings towards rear

20.8 Removing camshaft

20.9 Removing camshaft oil seal

corresponding with the relative positions of the valves when fitted. Also keep the valve springs caps etc., in the correct order.

6   If necessary unscrew the ball head bolts.

20 Camshaft - removal

The camshaft can only be removed after the cylinder head has been withdrawn from the block or the engine has been lifted from the car. The camshaft has to be removed to the rear due to the larger bearings being at the rear end. First remove the cam followers as described in Section 19.

1   Undo and remove the bolts, spring washers and bracket that secure the camshaft lubrication pipe. Lift away the pipe (photo).

2   Carefully inspect the fine oil drillings in the pipe to make sure that none are blocked (photo).

3   Using a metal bar, lock the camshaft drive sprocket then undo and remove the sprocket securing bolt and washer (photo).

4   Using a soft faced hammer or screwdriver ease the sprocket from the camshaft (photo).

5   Undo and remove the two bolts and spring washers that secure the camshaft thrust plate to the rear bearing support (photo).

6   Lift away the thrust plate noting which way round it is fitted

(photo).

7   The camshaft may now be removed by using a soft faced hammer and tapping rearward. Take care not to cut the fingers when the camshaft is being handled as the sides of the lobes can be sharp (photo).

8   Lift the camshaft through the bearing inserts as the lobes can damage the soft metal surfaces (photo).

9   If the oil seal has hardened or become damaged, it may be removed by prising out with a screwdriver (photo).

21 Thermostat housing and camshaft belt tensioner - removal

1   Removal of these parts will usually only be necessary if the cylinder head is to be completely dismantled.

2   Undo and remove the two bolts and spring washers that secure the thermostat housing to the front face of the cylinder head.

3   Lift away the thermostat housing and recover its gasket (photo).

4   Undo and remove the bolt and spring washer securing the belt tensioner to the cylinder head. It will be necessary to override the tension using a screwdriver as a lever (photos).

5   Using Ford special tool number 21 - 012, (the tool for

21.3 Removing thermostat housing

21.4A Removing belt tensioner mounting plate bolt

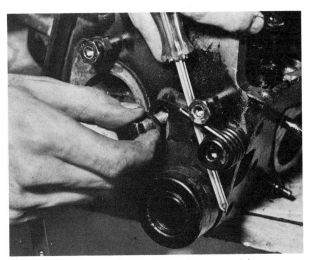
21.4B Easing off the spring tensioner with a screwdriver

21.5 Using special tool to remove mounting plate and spring securing bolt

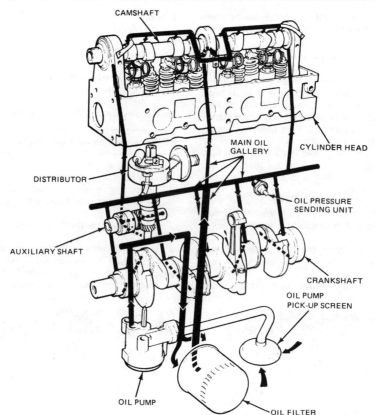

Fig. 1.4. Engine lubrication system (Sec. 24)

removal of the oil pump securing bolts) unscrew the tensioner mounting plate and spring securing bolt and lift away the tensioner assembly (photo).

22 Gudgeon pin - removal

A press fit gudgeon pin is used and it is important that no damage is caused during removal and refitting. Because of this, should it be necessary to fit new pistons, take the parts along to the local dealer who will have the special equipment to do this job.

23 Piston rings - removal

1 To remove the piston rings, slide them carefully over the top of the piston, taking care not to scratch the aluminium alloy; never slide them off the bottom of the piston skirt. It is very easy to break the cast iron piston rings if they are pulled off roughly, so this operation should be done with extreme care. It is helpful to make use of an old 0.020 inch (0.5 mm) feeler gauge.
2 Lift one end of the piston ring to be removed out of its groove and insert under it the end of the feeler gauge.
3 Slide the feeler gauge slowly round the piston and, as the ring comes out of its groove, apply slight upward pressure so that it rests on the land above. It can then be eased off the piston with the feeler gauge stopping it from slipping into an empty groove if it is any but the top piston ring that is being removed.

24 Lubrication and crankcase ventilation systems - description

The pressed steel oil sump is attached to the underside of the crankcase and acts as a reservoir for the engine oil. The oil pump draws oil through a strainer located under the oil surface, passes

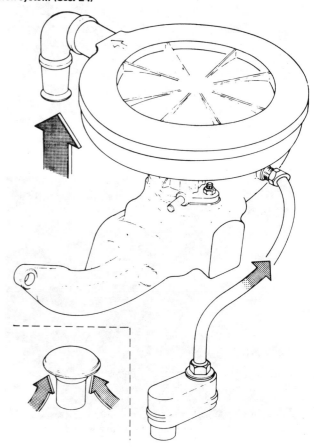

Fig. 1.5. Crankcase ventilation system (1600 cc engine) (Sec. 24)

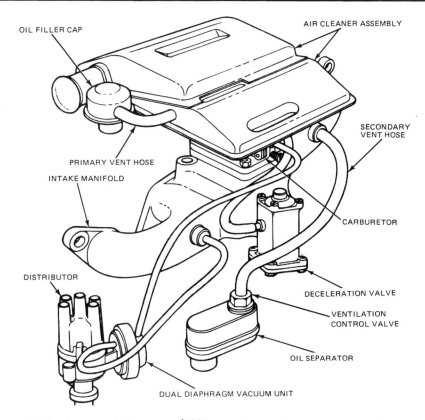

OIL FILLER CAP

AIR CLEANER ASSEMBLY

SECONDARY
VENT HOSE

PRIMARY VENT HOSE

INTAKE MANIFOLD

CARBURETOR

DISTRIBUTOR

DECELERATION VALVE

VENTILATION
CONTROL VALVE

OIL SEPARATOR

DUAL DIAPHRAGM VACUUM UNIT

Fig. 1.6. Crankcase ventilation system (2000 cc engine with full emission control (Sec. 24)

it along a short passage and into the full flow oil filter. The freshly filtered oil flows from the centre of the filter element and enters the main gallery. Five small drillings connect the main gallery to the five main bearings. The big-end bearings are supplied with oil by the front and rear main bearings via skew oil bores.

When the crankshaft is rotating, oil is thrown from the hole in each big-end bearing and splashes the thrust side of the piston. Lubrication for the auxiliary shaft is directly from the main gallery.

The distributor shaft is supplied with oil passing along a drilling inside the auxiliary shaft.

A further three drillings connect the main oil gallery to the overhead camshaft. The centre camshaft bearing has a semi-circular groove from which oil is passed along a pipe running parallel with the camshaft. The pipe is drilled opposite to each cam and cam follower so providing lubrication to the cams and cam followers. Oil then passes back to the sump via large drillings in the cylinder head and cylinder block.

A semi-enclosed engine ventilation system is used to control crankcase vapour. It is controlled by the amount of air drawn in by the engine when running and the throughput of the regulator valve.

The fresh air drawn in passes through the oil filter pipe and enters the engine top cover. It then passes through the crankcase and vent valve in the oil separator which is located on the left-hand side of the engine, from where it is drawn by the running engine so that its combustion takes place together with the petrol/air mixture prepared by the carburettor. The vent valve controls the air throughput relative to the given engine load.

25 Oil pump - dismantling, inspection and reassembly

1   If oil pump wear is suspected it is possible to obtain a repair kit. Check for wear first as described later in this section and if confirmed obtain an overhaul kit or a new pump. The two rotors

are a matched pair and form a single replacement unit. Where the rotor assembly is to be re-used the outer rotor, prior to dismantling, must be marked on its front face in order to ensure correct reassembly.

2   Undo and remove the two bolts and spring washers that secure the intake cowl to the oil pump body. Lift away the cowl and its gasket (Fig. 1.7).

3   Note the relative position of the oil pump cover and body and then undo and remove the three bolts and spring washers. Lift away the cover.

4   Carefully remove the rotors from the housing.

5   Using a centre punch tap a hole in the centre of the pressure relief valve sealing plug, (make a note to obtain a new one).

6   Screw in a self tapping screw and using an open ended spanner withdraw the sealing plug (Fig. 1.8).

7   Thoroughly clean all parts in petrol or paraffin and wipe dry using a non-fluffy rag. The necessary clearances may now be checked using a machined straight edge (a good steel rule) and a

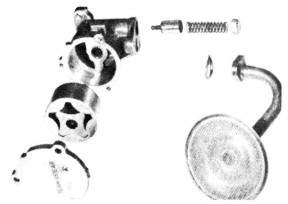

Fig. 1.7. Components of oil pump (Sec. 25)

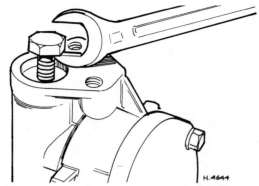

Fig. 1.8. Removing oil pump sealing plug (Sec. 25)

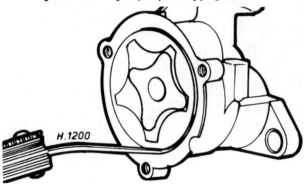

Fig. 1.9. Checking oil pump rotor clearance (Sec. 25)

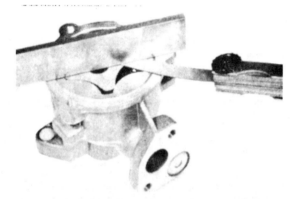

Fig. 1.10. Checking oil pump endfloat (Sec. 25)

set of feeler gauges. The critical clearances are between the lobes of the centre rotor and convex faces of the outer rotor, between the rotor and the pump body and between both rotors and the end cover plate.

8   The rotor lobe clearances may be checked using feeler gauges and should be within the limits 0.002 - 0.008 inch (0.05 - 0.20 mm).

9   The clearance between the outer rotor and pump body should be within the limits 0.006 - 0.012 inch (0.15 - 0.30 mm).

10 The endfloat clearance may be measured by placing a steel straight edge across the end of the pump and measuring the gap between the rotors and the straight edge. The gap in either rotor should be within the limits 0.0012 - 0.004 inch (0.03 - 0.10 mm) (Fig. 1.10).

11 If the only excessive clearances are endfloat, it is possible to reduce them by removing the rotors and lapping the face of the body on a flat bed until the necessary clearances are obtained. It must be emphasised, however, that the face of the body must remain perfectly flat and square to the axis of the rotor spindle otherwise the clearances will not be equal and the end cover will not be a pressure tight fit to the body. It is worth trying, of course, if the pump is in need of renewal anyway but unless

done properly it could seriously jeopardise the rest of the overhaul. Any variations in the other two clearances should be overcome with a new unit.

12 With all parts scrupulously clean first refit the relief valve and spring and lightly lubricate with engine oil.

13 Using a suitable diameter drift drive in a new sealing plug, flat side outwards until it is flush with the intake cowl bearing face.

14 Well lubricate both rotors with engine oil and insert into the body. Fit the oil pump cover and secure with the three bolts in a diagonal and progressive manner. Do not overtighten.

15 Fit the intermediate shaft into the rotor driveshaft and make sure that the rotor turns freely.

16 Fit the cowl to the pump body, using a new gasket and secure with the two bolts.

26 Oil filter - removal and refitting

The oil filter is a complete throw away cartridge screwed into the left-hand side of the cylinder block. Simply unscrew the old unit, clean the seating on the block and lubricate with engine oil.

Screw the new one into position taking care not to cross the thread. Continue until the sealing ring just touches the block face then tighten one half turn. Always run the engine and check for signs of leaks after installation.

27 Engine components - examination for wear - general

When the engine has been stripped down and all parts properly cleaned decisions have to be made as to what needs renewal and the following sections tell the examiner what to look for. In any border line case it is always best to decide in favour of a new part. Even if a part may still be serviceable its life will have been reduced by wear and the degree of trouble needed to replace it in the future must be taken into consideration. However, these things are relative and it depends on whether a quick 'survival' job is being done or whether the car as a whole is being regarded as having many thousands of miles of useful and economical life remaining.

28 Crankshaft - examination and renovation

1   Look at the main bearing journals and the crankpins and if there are any scratches or score marks then the shaft will need regrinding. Such conditions will nearly always be accompanied by similar deterioration in the matching bearing shells.

2   Each bearing journal should also be round and can be checked with a micrometer or caliper gauge around the periphery at several points. If there is more than 0.001 inch (0.0154 mm) of ovality regrinding is necessary.

3   A main Ford agent or motor engineering specialist will be able to decide to what extent regrinding is necessary and also supply the special undersize shell bearing to match whatever may need grinding off.

4   Before taking the crankshaft for regrinding check also the cylinder bores and pistons as it may be advantageous to have the whole engine reconditioned at the same time.

5   During any major engine repair, prise out the clutch pilot bearing from the rear end of the crankshaft; this may require the use of a hook-ended tool to get behind the bearing. Fit the replacement bearing with the seal outwards (where applicable) so that it is just below the surface of the crankshaft flange.

29 Crankshaft, main and big-end bearings - examination and renovation

1   With careful servicing and regular oil and filter changes bearings will last for a very long time but they can still fail for unforeseen reasons. With big-end bearings the indication of failure is a regular rhythmic loud knocking from the crankcase. The frequency depends on engine speed and is particularly noticeable when the engine is under load. This symptom is accompanied by a fall in oil pressure although this is not normally noticeable

unless an oil pressure gauge is fitted. Main bearing failure is usually indicated by serious vibration, particularly at higher engine revolutions, accompanied by a more significant drop in oil pressure and a 'rumbling' noise.

2 In the section on big-end bearing removal it was mentioned that this could be done with the engine still in the car. If the failure is sudden and the engine has a low mileage since new or overhaul this is possibly worth doing. Bearing shells in good condition have bearing surfaces with a smooth, even matt silver/grey colour all over. Worn bearings will show patches of a different colour when the bearing metal has worn away and exposed the underlay. Damaged bearings will be pitted or scored. It is always well worthwhile fitting new shells as their cost is relatively low. If the crankshaft is in good condition it is merely a question of obtaining another set of standard size. A reground crankshaft will need bearing shells as a matter of course.

30 Cylinder bores - examination and renovation

1 A new cylinder is perfectly round and the walls parallel throughout its length. The action of the piston tends to wear the walls at right angles to the gudgeon pin due to side thrust. This wear takes place principally on that section of the cylinder swept by the piston rings.

2 It is possible to get an indication of bore wear by removing the cylinder head with the engine still in the car. With the piston down in the bore first signs of wear can be seen and felt just below the top of the bore where the top piston ring reaches and there will be a noticeable lip. If there is no lip it is fairly reasonable to expect that bore wear is not severe and any lack of compression or excessive oil consumption is due to worn or broken piston rings (see Section 31).

3 If it is possible to obtain a bore measuring micrometer, measure the bore in the thrust plane below the lip and again at the bottom of the cylinder in the same plane. If the difference is more than 0.003 inch (0.0762 mm) then a rebore is necessary. Similarly, a difference of 0.003 inch (0.0762 mm) or more across the bore diameter is a sign of ovality calling for rebore.

4 Any bore which is significantly scratched or scored will need reboring. This symptom usually indicates that the piston or rings are damaged also in the cylinder. In the event of only one cylinder being in need of reboring it will still be necessary for all four to be bored and fitted with new oversize pistons and rings. Your Ford agent or local motor engineering specialist will be able to rebore and obtain the necessary matched pistons. If the crankshaft is undergoing regrinding also, it is a good idea to let the same firm renovate and reassemble the crankshaft and pistons to the block. A reputable firm normally gives a guarantee for such work. In cases where engines have been rebored already to their maximum new cylinder liners are available which may be fitted. In such cases the same reboring processes have to be followed and the service of a specialist engineering firm are required.

31 Pistons and piston rings - examination and renovation

1 Worn pistons and rings can usually be diagnosed when the symptoms of excessive oil consumption and lower compression occur and are sometimes, though not always, associated with worn cylinder bores. Compression testers that fit into the spark plug holes are available and these can indicate where low compression is occuring. Wear usually accelerates the longer it is left so when the symptoms occur, early action can possibly save the expense of a rebore.

2 Another symptom of piston wear is piston slap - a knocking noise from the crankcase not to be confused with big-end bearing failure. It can be heard clearly at low engine speed when there is no load (idling for example) and is much less audible when the engine speed increases. Piston wear usually occurs in the skirt or lower end of the piston and is indicated by vertical streaks in the worn area which is always on the thrust side. It can also be seen where the skirt thickness is different.

3 Piston ring wear can be checked by first removing the rings from the pistons as described in Section 23. Then place the rings in the cylinder bores from the top, pushing them down about 1½ inches with the crown of a piston (from which the rings have been removed), so that they rest square in the cylinder. Then measure the gap at the ends of the ring with a feeler gauge. If it exceeds 0.023 inch (0.58 mm) for the two top compression rings, or 0.055 inch (1.4 mm) for the lower oil control ring then they need renewal (Fig. 1.11).

4 The grooves in which the rings locate in the piston can also become enlarged in use. The clearance between ring and piston in the groove, should not exceed 0.004 inch (0.102 mm) for the top two compression rings and 0.003 inch (0.076 mm) for the lower oil control ring (Fig. 1.12).

5 However, it is rare that a piston is only worn in the ring grooves and the need to replace them for this fault alone is hardly ever encountered. Whenever pistons are renewed the weight of the four piston/connecting rod assemblies should be kept within the limit variations of 8 gms to maintain engine balance.

32 Connecting rods and gudgeon pins - examination and renovation

1 Gudgeon pins are a shrink fit into the connecting rods. Neither of these would normally need replacement unless the pistons were being changed, in which case the new pistons would automatically be supplied with new gudgeon pins.

2 Connecting rods are not subject to wear but in extreme circumstances such as engine seizure they could be distorted. Such conditions may be visually apparent but where doubt exists they should be changed. The bearing caps should also be examined for indications of filing down which may have been attempted in the mistaken idea that bearing slackness could be

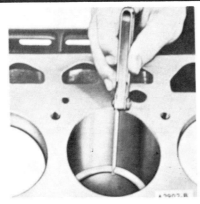
Fig. 1.11. Checking piston ring end gap (Sec. 31)

Fig. 1.12. Checking piston ring groove clearance (Sec. 31)

remedied in this way. If there are such signs then the connecting rods should be renewed.

33 Camshaft and camshaft bearings - examination and renovation

1   The camshaft bearing bushes should be examined for signs of scoring and pitting. If they need renewal they will have to be dealt with professionally as, although it may be relatively easy to remove the old bushes, the correct fitting of new ones requires special tools. If they are not fitted evenly and square from the very start they can be distorted thus causing localised wear in a very short time. See your Ford dealer or local engineering specialist for this work.

2   The camshaft itself may show signs of wear on the bearing journals or cam lobes. The main decision to take is what degree of wear justifies renewal, which is costly. Any signs of scoring or damage to the bearing journals cannot be removed by regrinding. Renewal of the whole camshaft is the only solution.

3   The cam lobes themselves may show signs of ridging or pitting on the high points. If ridging is light then it may be possible to smooth it out with fine emery. The cam lobes however, are surface hardened and once this is penetrated wear will be very rapid thereafter.

Excessive cam follower wear - note

If excessive cam follower wear is evident (and possibly excessive cam lobe wear), this may be due to a malfunction of the valve drive lubrication tube. If this has occurred, renew the tube and the cam follower. If more than one cam follower is excessively worn, renew the camshaft, all the cam followers and the lubrication tube; this also applies where excessive cam lobe wear is found.

4   During any operation which requires removal of the valve rocker cover, ensure that oil is being discharged from the lubrication tube nozzles by cranking the engine on the starter motor. During routine maintenance operations this can be done after checking the valve clearances.

34 Cam followers (tappets) - examination and renovation

1   The faces of the cam followers bearing on the camshaft should show no signs of pitting, scoring or other forms of wear. They should not be a loose sloppy fit on the ballheaded bolt.

2   Inspect the face which bears onto the valve stem and if pitted the cam follower must be renewed.

Note: Where excessive cam lobe wear is evident, refer to the note in the following Section.

35 Valves and valve seats - examination and renovation

1   With the valves removed from the cylinder heads examine the heads for signs of cracking, burning away and pitting of the edge where it seats in the port. The seats of the valves in the cylinder head should also be examined for the same signs. Usually it is the valve that deteriorates first but if a bad valve is not rectified the seat will suffer and this is more difficult to repair.

2   Provided there are no obvious signs of serious pitting the valve should be ground with its seat. This may be done by placing a smear of carborundum paste on the edge of the valve and, using a suction type valve holder, grinding the valve in situ. This is done with a semi-rotary action, rotating the handle of the valve holder between the hands and lifting it occasionally to re-distribute the traces of paste. Use a coarse paste to start with. As soon as a matt grey unbroken line appears on both the valve and seat the valve is 'ground in'. All traces of carbon should also be cleaned from the head and neck of the valve stem. A wire brush mounted in a power drill is a quick and effective way of doing this.

3   A new valve should be ground into the seat in the same way as the old valve.

4   Another form of valve wear can occur on the stem where it runs in the guide in the cylinder head. This can be detected by

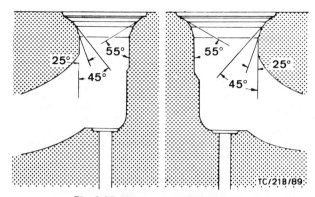

Fig. 1.13. Valve seat angles (Sec. 35)

trying to rock the valve from side to side. If there is any movement at all it is an indication that the valve stem or guide is worn. Check the stem first with a micrometer at points along and around its length and if they are not within the specified size new valves will probably solve the problem. If the guides are worn, however, they will need reboring for oversize valves or for fitting guide inserts. The valve seats will also need recutting to ensure they are concentric with the stems. This work should be given to your Ford dealer or local engineering works.

5   When valve seats are badly burnt or pitted, requiring replacement, inserts may be fitted - or renewed if already fitted once before - and once again this is a specialist task to be carried out by a suitable engineering firm.

6   When all valve grinding is completed it is essential that every trace of grinding paste is removed from the valves and ports in the cylinder head. This should be done by thoroughly washing in petrol or paraffin and blowing out with a jet of air. If particles of carborundum should work their way into the engine they would cause havoc with bearings or cylinder walls.

36 Timing sprockets and belt - examination and renovation

1   Any wear which takes place in the timing mechanism will be on the teeth of the drivebelt or due to stretch of the fabric. Whenever the engine is to be stripped for major overhaul a new belt should be fitted.

2   It is very unusual for the timing gears (sprockets) to wear at the teeth. If the securing bolt/nuts have been loose it is possible for the keyway or hub bore to wear. Check these two points and if damage or wear is evident a new gear must be obtained.

37 Auxiliary shaft - examination and renovation

1   The auxiliary shaft drives the oil pump and distributor through meshed gears and short driveshafts.

2   The fuel pump is also driven from an eccentric on the auxiliary shaft through the medium of a short rod.

3   Examine the gear teeth on the auxiliary shaft, if they are worn or chipped, renew the shaft.

4   Examine the shaft bearing surfaces and if grooves or scores are apparent, renew the shaft.

38 Flywheel ring gear - examination and renovation

1   If the ring gear is badly worn or has missing teeth it should be renewed. The old ring can be removed from the flywheel by cutting a notch between two teeth with a hacksaw and then splitting it with a cold chisel.

2   To fit a new ring gear requires heating the ring to 400°F (204°C). This can be done by polishing four equally spaced sections of the gear, laying it on a suitable heat resistant surface

(such as fire bricks) and heating it evenly with a blow lamp or torch until the polished areas turn a light yellow tinge. Do not overheat or the hard wearing properties will be lost. The gear has a chamfered inner edge which should go against the shoulder when put on the flywheel. When hot enough place the gear in position quickly, tapping it home, and letting it cool naturally without quenching in any way.

39 Driveplate (auto. trans.) ring gear - examination and renovation

1 If the starter ring gear is worn on the driveplate (automatic transmission) it is recommended that the driveplate be renewed complete.

40 Cylinder head and piston crowns - decarbonisation

1 When the cylinder head is removed, either in the course of an overhaul or for inspection of bores or valve condition when the engine is in the car, it is normal to remove all carbon deposits from the piston crowns and heads.
2 This is best done with a cup shaped wire brush and an electric drill. This is fairly straightforward when the engine is dismantled and the pistons removed. Sometimes hard spots of carbon are not completely removed except by a scraper. When cleaning the pistons with a scraper, take care not to damage the surface of the piston in any way.
3 When the engine is in the car certain precautions must be taken when decarbonising the piston crowns in order to prevent dislodged pieces of carbon falling into the interior of the engine which could cause damage to cylinder bores, pistons and rings - or if allowed into the water passages - damage to the water pump. Turn the engine so that the piston being worked on is at the top of its stroke and then mask off the adjacent cylinder bores and all surrounding water jacket orifices with paper and adhesive tape. Press grease into the gap all round the piston to keep carbon particles out and then scrape all carbon away by hand carefully. Do not use a power drill and wire brush when the engine is in the car as it will virtually be impossible to keep all the carbon dust clear of the engine. When completed, carefully clear out the grease around the rim of the piston with a matchstick or something similar - bringing any carbon particles with it. Repeat the process on the other piston crown. It is not recommended that a ring of carbon is left round the edge of the piston on the theory that it will aid oil consumption. This was valid in the earlier days of long stroke low revving engines but modern engines, fuels and lubricants cause less carbon deposits anyway and any left behind tends merely to cause hot spots.

41 Valve guides - examination and renovation

Examine the valve guides internally for wear. If the valves are

a very loose fit in the guides and there is the slightest suspicion of lateral rocking using a new valve, then the guides will have to be reamed and oversize valves, fitted. This is a job best left to the local dealer.

42 Sump - examination and renovation

Wash out the sump in petrol and wipe dry. Inspect the exterior for signs of damage or excessive rust. Should such a condition be evident a new sump must be purchased. To ensure an oil tight joint scrape away all traces of the old gasket from the cylinder block mating face.

43 Engine reassembly - general

All components of the engine must be clean - oil, sludge and old gaskets removed. The working area should be clear and clean. In addition to the normal range of good quality socket spanners and general tools which are essential, the following must be available before reassembling begins:

1 Complete set of new gaskets
2 Supply of clean rags
3 Clean oil can full of clean engine oil
4 All new spare parts as necessary

44 Crankshaft - installation

1 Wipe the bearing shell location in the crankcase with a soft non-fluffy rag.
2 Wipe the crankshaft journals with a soft non-fluffy rag.
3 If the old main bearing shells are to be replaced (not to do so is a false economy unless they are virtually new) fit the five upper halves of the main bearing shells to their location in the crankcase (photo).
4 Identify each main bearing cap and place in order. The number is cast onto the cap and with intermediate caps an arrow is also marked so that the cap is fitted the correct way round (photo).
5 Wipe the cap bearing shell location with a soft non-fluffy rag.
6 Fit the bearing half shell onto each main bearing cap (photo).
7 Fit the bearing half shell into each location in the crankcase.
8 Apply a little grease to each side of the centre main bearings so as to retain the thrust washers (photo).
9 Fit the upper halves of the thrust washers into their grooves, either side of the main bearing. The slots must face outwards (photo).
10 Lubricate the crankshaft journal and the upper and lower main bearing shells with engine oil (photo).
11 Carefully lower the crankshaft into the crankcase (photo).
12 Lubricate the crankshaft main bearing journals again and then fit No. 1 bearing cap (photo). Fit the two securing bolts but

44.3 Inserting bearing shells into crankcase

44.4 Main bearing cap identification marks

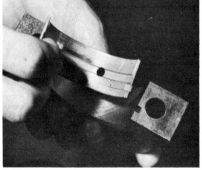
44.6 Fitting bearing shell to main bearing cap

44.8 Applying grease to either side of centre main bearing

44.9 Fitting thrust washers to centre main bearing

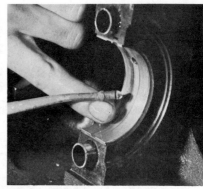
44.10 Lubricating bearing shells

44.11 Fitting crankshaft to crankcase

44.12 Refitting No. 1 main bearing cap

44.13 Applying jointing compound to rear main bearing cap joint

44.14 Refitting main bearing cap

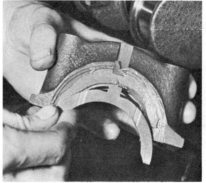
44.15 Fitting thrust washers to centre main bearing cap

44.16 Main bearing caps in position

44.17 Tightening main bearing cap securing bolts

44.18 Using feeler gauge to check end-float of crankshaft

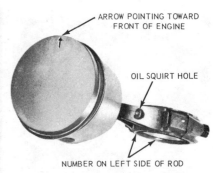

ARROW POINTING TOWARD FRONT OF ENGINE

OIL SQUIRT HOLE

NUMBER ON LEFT SIDE OF ROD

Fig. 1.14. Correct alignment of piston and connecting rod (Sec. 45)

do not tighten yet.

13 Apply a little jointing compound to the crankshaft rear main bearing cap location (photo).

14 Next fit No. 5 cap (photo). Fit the two securing bolts but as before do not tighten yet.

15 Apply a little grease to each side of the centre main bearing cap so as to retain the thrust washers. Fit the thrust washers with the tag located in the groove and the slots facing outward (photo).

16 Fit the centre main bearing cap and the two securing bolts. Then refit the intermediate main bearing caps. Make sure that the arrows always point towards the front of the engine (photo).

17 Lightly tighten all main cap securing bolts and then fully tighten in a progressive manner to the specified torque (photo).

18 Using a screwdriver ease the crankshaft fully forward and with feeler gauges check the clearance between the crankshaft journal side and the thrust washers. The clearance must not exceed 0.0032 - 0.0110 inch (0.08 - 0.28 mm). Undersize thrust washers are available (photo).

19 Test the crankshaft for rotation. Should it be stiff to turn or possess high spots, a most careful inspection must be made with a micrometer, preferably by a qualified mechanic, to get to the root of the trouble. It is very seldom that any trouble of this nature is experienced when fitting the crankshaft.

45 Pistons and connecting rods - reassembly

1 These operations will have been carried out by your dealer (see Section 22) but it is wise to check that the alignment of the piston to the rod has been correctly carried out as shown in Fig. 1.14.

46 Piston rings - installation

1 Check that the piston ring grooves and oilways are thoroughly clean and unblocked. Piston rings must always be fitted over the head of the piston and never from the bottom.

2 The easiest method to use when fitting rings is to position two or three feeler blades vertically at the top of the piston and place the rings one at a time, starting with the bottom oil control ring, over the feeler gauges.

3 The feeler gauge, complete with ring can then be slid down the piston over the other piston ring grooves until the correct groove is reached. The piston ring is then slid gently off the feeler gauge into the groove.

4 An alternative method is to fit the rings by holding them slightly open with the thumbs and both of the index fingers. This method requires a steady hand and great care as it is easy to twist or open the ring too much and break it.

47 Pistons - installation

The piston, complete with connecting rods, can be fitted to the cylinder bores in the following sequence:-

1 With a wad of clean rag wipe the cylinder bores clean.

2 The pistons, complete with connecting rods, are fitted to their bores from the top of the block.

3 Position the piston ring gaps in accordance with the diagram (photo) (Fig. 1.15).

4 Well lubricate the piston and rings with engine oil (photo).

5 Fit a universal piston ring compressor and prepare to insert the first piston into the bore. Make sure it is the correct piston/connecting rod assembly for that particular bore, that the connecting rod is the correct way round and that the front of the piston is towards the front of the bore, ie towards the front of the engine.

6 Again lubricate the piston skirt and insert into the bore up to the bottom of the piston ring compressor (photo).

7 Gently but firmly tap the piston through the piston ring compressor and into the cylinder bore with a wooden or plastic hammer (Fig. 1.16).

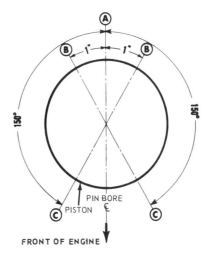

Fig. 1.15. Piston ring gap positioning diagram (Sec. 47)

A   Oil control ring spacer gap
B   Oil control ring rail gaps
C   Compression ring gaps

47.3 Positioning ring gaps

47.4 Lubricating pistons prior to refitting

47.6 Piston ring compressor correctly positioned

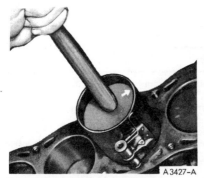
Fig. 1.16. Installing a piston/
connecting rod assembly (Sec. 47)

48.6 Refitting big-end cap securing nuts

48.7 Tightening big-end cap securing nuts

49.2 Inserting oil pump driveshaft

49.3 Tightening oil pump securing bolts

50.1 Refitting rectangular shaped seals

50.2 Fitting seal into rear main bearing
cap

50.3 Refitting crankshaft rear oil seal

50.4 Tapping oil seal into position

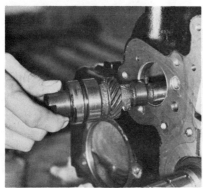
51.1 Refitting auxiliary shaft

51.2 Locating thrust plate

51.3 Tightening thrust plate securing
screws

48 Connecting rod to crankshaft - reassembly

1 The connecting rod clean, wipe half of the big-end bearing cap and the underside of the shell bearing, and fit the shell bearing in position with its locating tongue engaged with the corresponding cut out in the rod.
2 If the old bearings are nearly new and are being refitted then ensure that they are replaced in their correct locations on the correct rods.
3 Generously lubricate the crankpin journals with engine oil and turn the crankshaft so that the crankpin is in the lowest position for the connecting rods to be drawn onto it.
4 Wipe the connecting rod bearing cap and back of the shell bearing clean, and fit the shell bearing in position ensuring that the locating tongue at the back of the bearing engages with the locating groove in the connecting rod cap.
5 Generously lubricate the shell bearing and offer up the connecting rod bearing cap to the connecting rod.
6 Refit the connecting rod nuts (photo).
7 Tighten the bolts with a torque wrench to the specified figure (photo).
8 When all the connecting rods have been fitted, rotate the crankshaft to check that everything is free, and that there are no high spots causing binding. The bottom half of the engine is now nearly built up.

49 Oil pump - refitting

1 Wipe the mating faces of the oil pump and underside of the cylinder block.
2 Insert the hexagonal driveshaft into the end of the oil pump (photo).
3 Offer up the oil pump and refit the two special bolts. Using Ford special tool 21 - 020 and a torque wrench, tighten the two bolts to the specified torque (photo).
4 Refit the spring washer and the bolt securing the oil pump pick up pipe support bracket to the crankcase.

50 Crankshaft rear oil seal - refitting

1 Apply some jointing compound to the slot on each side of the rear main bearing cap and insert a rectangular shaped seal (photo).
2 Apply some jointing compound to the slot in the rear main bearing cap and carefully insert the shaped seal (photo).
3 Lightly smear some grease on the crankshaft rear oil seal and carefully ease it over the end of the crankshaft. The spring must be inwards (photo).
4 Using a soft metal drift carefully tap the seal into position (photo).

51 Auxiliary shaft and crankshaft timing covers - refitting

1 Carefully insert the auxiliary shaft into the front face of the cylinder block (photo).
2 Position the thrust plate into its groove in the auxiliary shaft (countersunk faces of the holes facing outward) and refit the two crosshead screws (photo).
3 Tighten the two screws using a Phillips screwdriver and an open-ended spanner (photo).
4 Smear some grease on the cylinder block face of a new gasket and carefully fit into position (photo).
5 Apply some jointing compound to the slot in the underside of the crankshaft timing cover. Insert the shaped seal.
6 Offer up the timing cover and secure with the bolts and spring washers (photo).
7 Smear some grease onto the seal located in the auxiliary shaft timing cover and carefully ease the cover over the end of the auxiliary shaft.
8 Secure the auxiliary shaft timing cover with the four bolts and spring washers (photo).

52 Sump - installation

1 Wipe the mating faces of the underside of the crankcase and the sump.
2 Smear some grease on the underside of the crankcase.

51.4 Positioning new gasket on cylinder block front face

51.6A Refitting crankshaft timing cover

51.6B Tightening crankshaft timing cover securing bolts

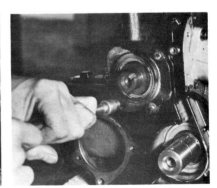

51.8 Tightening auxiliary shaft timing cover securing bolts

3 Fit the sump gasket making sure that the bolt holes line up (Fig. 1.17).
4 Offer the sump up to the gasket taking care not to dislodge the gasket and secure in position with the bolts (photo).
5 Tighten the sump bolts in a progressive manner, in the order shown in Fig. 1.18. Do not overtighten or the joint gasket will be over-compressed.

53 Crankshaft and auxiliary shaft sprockets - refitting

1 Fit the keys to the crankshaft and auxiliary shaft keyways (photo).
2 Fit the sprocket to the front of the crankshaft (photo).
3 Tap the sprocket fully home.
4 Slide the large diameter washer onto the front of the crankshaft (photo).
5 Fit the crankshaft pulley (photo).
6 Fit the washer and crankshaft retaining bolt (photo).
7 Lock the crankshaft pulley with a tommy bar and fully tighten the bolt (photo).
8 Fit the auxiliary shaft sprocket and washer and fully tighten the bolt (photo).

54 Water pump - refitting

1 Make sure that all traces of the old gasket are removed and then smear some grease on the gasket face of the cylinder block.
2 Fit a new gasket to the cylinder block.
3 Offer up the water pump and secure in position with the four bolts and spring washers (photo).

55 Flywheel and clutch (or driveplate - auto. trans.) - refitting

1 Remove all traces of the shaped seal from the backplate and apply a little adhesive to it. Fit a new seal to the backplate (photo).
2 Wipe the mating faces of the backplate and cylinder block and carefully fit the backplate to the two dowels (photo).
3 Wipe the mating faces of the flywheel and crankshaft and offer up the flywheel to the crankshaft aligning the previously made marks unless new parts have been fitted.
4 Fit the six crankshaft securing bolts and lightly tighten.
5 Lock the flywheel using a screwdriver engaged in the starter ring gear and tighten the securing bolts in a diagonal and progressive manner to the specified torque wrench setting (photo).
6 Refit the clutch disc and pressure plate assembly to the flywheel making sure the disc is the right way round (flatter side to flywheel). Centralise the clutch (as described in Chapter 5) before finally tightening the pressure plate cover bolts to the specified torque wrench setting.
7 Refitting the driveplate (auto. transmission) is simply a matter of bolting it to the crankshaft rear flange.

56 Valves - refitting

1 With the valves suitably ground in (see Section 35) and kept in their correct order start with No. 1 cylinder and insert the valve into its guide (photo).
2 Lubricate the valve stem with engine oil and slide on a new oil seal. The spring must be uppermost as shown in this photo.
3 Fit the valve spring and cap (photo).
4 Using a universal valve spring compressor, compress the valve spring until the split collets can be slid into position (photo). Note these collets have serrations which engage in slots in the valve stem. Release the valve spring compressor.
5 Repeat this procedure until all eight valves and valve springs are fitted.

Fig. 1.17. Correct fitment of sump gasket at front and rear main bearing caps (Sec. 52)

52.4 New gaskets fitted to greased underside of crankcase ready for sump

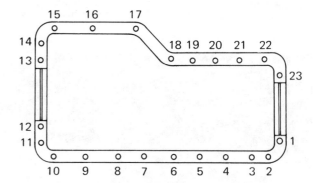

Fig. 1.18. Sump bolt tightening sequence (Sec. 52)

53.1 Refitting Woodruff key to crankshaft

53.2 Sliding on crankshaft sprocket

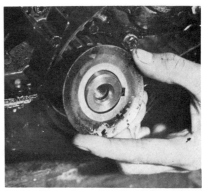
53.4 Refitting large diameter plain washer (dished side visible from front)

53.5 Refitting crankshaft pulley

53.6 Crankshaft pulley securing bolt and large washer

53.7 Tightening pulley securing bolt

53.8 Fitting sprocket to auxiliary shaft

54.3 Water pump offered up to mating face fitted with new gasket

55.1 Fitting new gasket to backplate

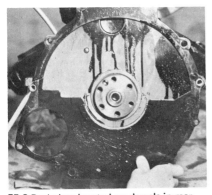
55.2 Backplate located on dowels in rear of engine block

55.5 Fully tightening securing bolts

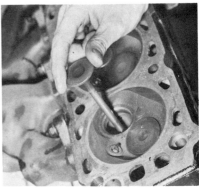
56.1 Inserting valve into valve guide

56.2 Sliding seal down valve stem

56.3 Replacing valve spring cap

56.4 Refitting valve collets

57.1 Camshaft oil seal correctly fitted

57.3 Threading camshaft through bearings

57.4 Lubricating camshaft bearings

57.6 Locating camshaft thrust plate

57.7 Tightening camshaft thrust plate retaining bolts

57.8 Fitting Woodruff key to camshaft

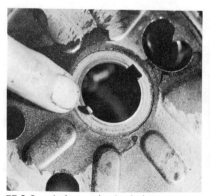
57.9 Camshaft sprocket backplate tag

57.10 Camshaft sprocket backplate refitted

57.11 Refitting sprocket

57 Camshaft - installation

1   If the oil seal was removed (Section 20) a new one should be fitted taking care that it is fitted the correct way round. Gently tap it into position so that it does not tilt (photo).
2   Apply some grease to the lip of the oil seal. Wipe the three bearing surfaces with a clean non-fluffy rag.
3   Lift the camshaft through the rear bearing taking care not to damage the bearing surfaces with the sharp edges of the cam lobes. Also take care not to cut the fingers (photo).
4   When the journals are ready to be inserted into the bearings lubricate the bearings with engine oil (photo).
5   Push the camshaft through the bearings until the locating groove in the rear of the camshaft is just rearward of the bearing carrier.
6   Slide the thrust plate into engagement with the camshaft taking care to fit it the correct way round as previously noted (photo).
7   Secure the thrust plate with the two bolts and spring washers (photo).
8   Check that the keyway in the end of the camshaft is clean and the key is free from burrs. Fit the key into the keyway (photo).
9   Locate the tag on the camshaft sprocket backplate and this must locate in the second groove in the camshaft sprocket (photo).
10 Fit the camshaft sprocket backplate, tag facing outwards (photo).
11 Fit the camshaft sprocket to the end of the camshaft so that the raised webs face the front and with a soft faced hammer make sure it is fully home (photo).
12 Refit the thick plain washer and securing bolt (photo).

58 Cam followers (tappets) - refitting

1   Undo the ball headed bolt locknut and screw down the bolt fully. This will facilitate refitting the cam followers (photo).
2   Rotate the camshaft until the cam lobe is away from the top of the cylinder head. Pass the cam follower under the back of the cam until the cup is over the ball headed bolt (photo).
3   Engage the cup with the ball headed bolt (photo).
4   Refit the cam follower spring by engaging the ends of the spring with the anchor on the ball headed bolt (photo).
5   Using the fingers pull the spring up and then over the top of the cam follower (photo).
6   Repeat the above sequence for the remaining seven cam followers.
7   Check that the jet holes in the camshaft lubrication pipe are free and offer up to the camshaft bearing pedestals (photo).
8   Refit the pipe, spring washer and securing bolts.

59 Cylinder head - installation

1   Wipe the mating faces of the cylinder head and cylinder block.
2   Carefully place a new gasket on the cylinder block and check to ensure that it is the correct way up and the right way round (photo).
3   Gently lower the cylinder head being as accurate as possible first time so that the gasket is not dislodged (photo).
4   Refit the cylinder head bolts taking care not to damage the gasket if it has moved (photo).
5   Using the Ford special tool 21 - 002 tighten all the bolts (photo), progressively in stages, to the torque settings specified in Specifications Section (Fig. 1.2).

57.12 Fitting camshaft sprocket securing bolt and plain washer

58.1 Slackening ball headed bolt locknut

58.2 Passing cam follower under camshaft

58.3 Cap locating over ball headed bolt

58.4 Cam follower spring engaged with the anchor

58.5A Cam follower spring being lifted over cam follower

58.5B Cam follower spring correctly fitted

58.7 Replacing lubrication pipe

59.2 Positioning cylinder head gasket on top of cylinder block

59.3 Lowering cylinder head onto gasket

59.4 Replacing cylinder head bolts

59.5 Special tool engaged in cylinder head bolt

60.1 Refitting drivebelt tensioner

60.3 Using screwdriver to relieve tension of spring

61.3 Lining up camshaft timing marks

61.4 Engaging camshaft belt with crankshaft sprocket

61.7A Replacing drivebelt guard

61.7B Locating guard between washer and pedestal

60 Camshaft belt tensioner and thermostat housing - refitting

1 Thread the shaped bolt through the spring and tensioner plate and screw the bolt into the cylinder head (photo).
2 Tighten the bolt securely using Ford special tool 21 - 020.
3 Using a screwdriver to overcome the tension of the spring, position the plate so that its securing bolt can be screwed into the cylinder head (photo).
4 Clean the mating faces of the cylinder head and thermostat housing and fit a new gasket.
5 Offer up the thermostat housing and secure in position with the two bolts and spring washers.
6 Tighten the bolts to the specified torque wrench settings.

61 Camshaft belt refitting and camshaft timing

1 Using a socket wrench applied to the crankshaft pulley bolt, turn the crankshaft until No. 1 piston is at TDC. This position can be established by removing No. 1 spark plug and placing the finger over the hole to feel the compression being generated. As soon as this pressure is felt, continue turning the crankshaft until the 'O' mark on the crankshaft pulley is opposite the pointer.
2 If the crankshaft pulley is not yet fitted, then the procedure is similar but the keyway in the crankshaft sprocket must be vertical to provide the TDC (top-dead-centre) position. In this case, the crankshaft can still be turned without the pulley, provided the pulley bolt is temporarily screwed in.
3 Rotate the camshaft until the pointer is in alignment with the dot mark on the front bearing pedestal. To achieve this always rotate the camshaft in the direction shown in Fig. 1.20.
4 Engage the drive belt with the crankshaft sprocket and auxiliary shaft sprocket. Pass the back of the belt over the tensioner jockey wheel and then slide it into mesh with the camshaft sprocket (photo).
5 Slacken the tensioner plate securing bolt and allow the tensioner to settle by rotating the crankshaft twice. Retighten the tensioner plate securing bolt.
6 Line up the timing marks and check that these are correct indicating the belt has been correctly refitted.
7 Refit the drive belt guard, easing the guard into engagement with the bolt and large plain washer located under the water pump (photos).
8 Refit the guard securing bolts and fully tighten.

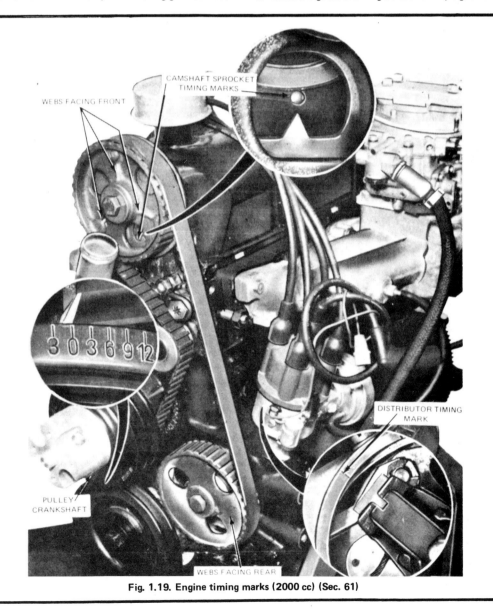

Fig. 1.19. Engine timing marks (2000 cc) (Sec. 61)

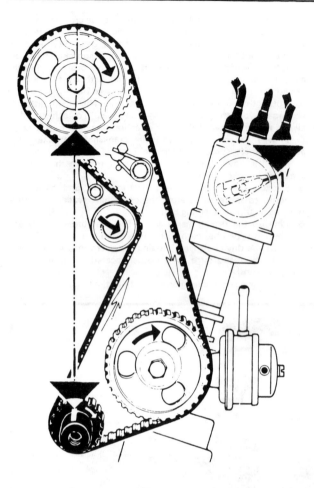

Fig. 1.20. Timing marks (crankshaft pulley removed) on 1600 cc engine (Sec. 61)

62 Valve clearances - checking and adjusting

1   With the engine top cover removed, turn the crankshaft until the two cams of one cylinder point upward to form a 'V'. This will ensure that the cam follower will be at the back of the cam.

2   Using feeler gauges as shown in this photo check the clearance which should be as shown in Specifications (Fig. 1.21).

3   If adjustment is necessary, using open-ended spanners, slacken the ball headed bolt securing locknut (photo).

4   Screw the ball headed bolt up or down as necessary until the required clearance is obtained (photo). Retighten the locknut.

5   Repeat the operations on the other valves.

6   An alternative method of adjusting the valves is to work to the following table:

Valves depressed	Valves to adjust
1 ex. 4 in.	6 in. 7 ex.
6 in. 7 ex.	1 ex. 4 in.
2 in. 5 ex.	3 ex. 8 in.
3 ex. 8 in.	2 in. 5 ex.

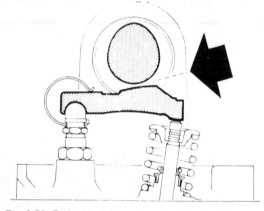

Fig. 1.21. Feeler blade insertion point for checking valve clearance (Sec. 62)

62.2 Checking cam follower clearance   **62.3 Slackening ball headed bolt locknut**   **62.4 Adjusting ball headed bolt**

7   Refit the engine top cover (Fig. 1.22). The valve clearances must be checked and adjusted when the engine has been run to normal operating temperature.

63 Ancillary components - refitting

1   The exhaust manifold is best replaced before putting the engine back into the car as it provides a very useful hold if the engine has to be manhandled at all. Select the new gasket and fit the correct way round.

2   Replace the manifold and tighten the bolts evenly.

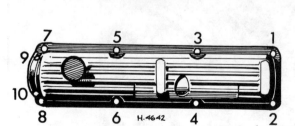

Fig. 1.22. Top cover bolt tightening sequence diagram (Sec. 62)

3   Install the ancillary components after reference to Section 9 and to the relevant Chapters.

64 Engine installation (less gearbox)

1   The engine must be positioned suitably so that the sling used to remove it can be refitted easily and the lifting tackle hooked on. Position the engine the right way round in front of the car and then raise it so that it may be brought into position over the car and the car rolled into position underneath it.
2   The gearbox should be jacked up to its approximately normal position.
3   Lower the engine steadily into the engine compartment, keeping all ancillary wires, pipes and cables well clear of the side. It is best to have a second person guiding the engine while it is being lowered.
4   The tricky part is finally mating the engine to the gearbox, which involves locating the gearbox input shaft into the clutch housing and flywheel. Provided that the clutch friction plate has been centred correctly as described in Chapter 5, there should be little difficulty. Grease the splines of the gearbox input shaft first. It may be necessary to rock the engine from side to side in order to get the engine fully home. Under no circumstances let any strain be imparted on the gearbox input shaft. This could occur if the shaft was not fully located and the engine was raised or lowered more than the amount required for very slight adjustment of position.
5   As soon as the engine is fully up to the gearbox bellhousing replace the bolts holding the two together.
6   Now finally lower the engine onto the mounting brackets and secure in position.
7   Replace all electrical connections, the fuel lines and carburettor linkages, cooling system hoses and radiator in the reverse order to that described in Section 5.
8   Reconnect the clutch cable as described in Chapter 5, replace the exhaust pipe and reconnect to the manifold. Replace the plate covering the lower half of the bellhousing and remove the supporting jack.
9   Fill the engine with fresh oil and replace the coolant.

65 Engine installation (less automatic transmission)

1   Having left the automatic transmission in the car (as recommended because of the weight) the engine must now be installed and reconnected to the transmission.
2   This is similar to installation where a manual gearbox is used but the following points must be noted.
3   Make sure that the torque converter is pushed fully to the rear so that the oil pump drive tangs are fully engaged.
4   Align the driveplate to torque converter mating marks made before removal.
5   Reconnect the speed selector linkage and 'kick-down' cable and check and adjust them, as described in Chapter 6.
6   When the transmission reaches normal operating temperature check the fluid level and top-up to make up for that lost when the torque converter was disturbed.

66 Engine installation (with manual gearbox attached)

1   The gearbox should be refitted to the engine, taking the same precautions as described in the preceding Section for the gearbox input shaft.
2   The general principles of lifting the engine/gearbox assembly

are the same as for the engine above, but the gearbox will tilt everything to a much steeper angle. Replacement will certainly require the assistance of a second person.
3   Lift the gearbox end of the unit into the engine compartment (unless you are fortunate enough to have a hoist with a very high lift) and then lower and guide the unit down. One of the first things to be done is to reconnect the propeller shaft into the gearbox extension casing so someone should be ready to lift and guide the propeller shaft into position as soon as the gearbox is near enough. This cannot be done after the unit has been lowered beyond a certain position.
4   If a trolley jack is available this is the time to place it under the gearbox so that as the engine is lowered further the rear end can be supported and raised as necessary - at the same time being able to roll back as required. Without such a jack, support the rear in such a way that it can slide if possible. In any case the gearbox will have to be jacked and held up in position when the unit nears its final position.
5   Locate the front mounting brackets and secure in position.
6   Refit the speedometer drive cable with the gearbox drive sprocket and refit the circlip and bolt. This should be done before the gearbox supporting crossmember is in place.
7   Jack-up the rear of the gearbox and position the crossmember to the bodyframe. Then replace and tighten down the securing bolts.
8   Reconnect the gearshift control according to type (see Chapter 6).
9   Reconnect the clutch cable and adjust as described in Chapter 5 and reconnect the reverse light wire. The final connections should then be made and in addition to the engine lubricant and coolant the gearbox should also be refilled with fresh oil.

67 Engine - initial start-up after overhaul or major repair

1   Make sure that the battery is fully charged and connected. Ensure that all lubricants, coolant and fuel are replenished.
2   If the fuel system has been dismantled it will require several revolutions of the engine on the starter motor to pump the petrol up to the carburettor.
3   As soon as the engine fires and runs, keep it going at a fast tickover only (no faster) and bring it up to normal working temperature.
4   As the engine warms up there will be odd smells and some smoke from parts getting hot and burning off oil deposits. The signs to look for are leaks of water or oil which will be obvious. Check the exhaust pipe and manifold connections as these do not always find their exact gas tight position until the warmth and vibration have acted on them and it is almost certain that they will need tightening further. This should be done, of course, with the engine stopped.
5   When normal running temperature has been reached, adjust the engine idle speed as described in Chapter 3.
6   Stop the engine and wait for a few minutes to see if any lubricant or coolant is dripping when the engine is stationary.
7   After the engine has run for 20 minutes remove the engine top cover and recheck the tightness of the cylinder head bolts.
8   Check the tightness of the sump bolts. In both cases use a torque wrench.
9   Road test the car to check that the timing is correct and that the engine is giving the necessary smoothness and power. Do not race the engine - if new bearings and/or pistons have been fitted it should be treated as a new engine and run in at a reduced speed for the first 1000 miles (2000 km).

For fault diagnosis see page 46.

68 Fault diagnosis - engine

Symptoms	Reason/s
Engine fails to turn over when starter button operated	Discharged or defective battery
	Dirty or loose battery leads
	Defective starter solenoid or switch
	Engine earth strap disconnected
	Jammed starter motor drive pinion
	Defective starter motor
Engine turns over but will not start	Ignition damp or wet
	Ignition leads to spark plugs loose
	Shorted or disconnected low tension leads
	Dirty, incorrectly set or pitted contact breaker points
	Faulty condenser
	Defective ignition switch
	Ignition LT leads connected wrong way round
	Faulty coil
	Contact breaker point spring earthed or broken
	No petrol in petrol tank
	Vapour lock in fuel line (in hot conditions or at high altitude)
	Blocked float chamber needle valve
	Fuel pump filter blocked
	Choked or blocked carburettor jets
	Faulty fuel pump
	Too much choke allowing to rich a mixture to wet plugs
	Float damaged or leaking or needle not seating
	Float lever incorrectly adjusted
Engine stalls and will not start	Ignition failure - sudden
	Ignition failure - misfiring precludes total stoppage
	Ignition failure - in severe rain or after traversing water splash
	No petrol in petrol tank
	Petrol tank breather choked
	Sudden obstruction in carburettor
	Water in fuel system
Engine misfires or idles unevenly	Ignition leads loose
	Battery leads loose on terminals
	Battery earth strap loose on body attachment point
	Engine earth leads loose
	Low tension leads to SW and CB terminals on coil loose
	Low tension lead from CB terminal side to distributor loose
	Dirty, or incorrectly gapped spark plugs
	Dirty, incorrectly set or pitted contact breaker points
	Tracking across distributor cap
	Ignition too retarded
	Faulty coil
	Mixture too weak
	Air leak in carburettor
	Air leak at inlet manifold to cylinder head, or inlet manifold to carburettor
	Incorrect valve clearances
	Burnt out exhaust valves
	Sticking or leaking valves
	Wear or broken valve springs
	Worn valve guides or stems
	Worn pistons and piston rings
Lack of power and poor compression	Burnt out exhaust valves
	Sticking or leaking valves
	Worn valve guides and stems
	Weak or broken valve springs
	Blown cylinder head gasket (accompanied by increase in noise)
	Worn pistons and piston rings
	Worn or scored cylinder bores
	Ignition timing wrongly set. Too advanced or retarded
	Contact breaker points incorrectly gapped
	Incorrect valve clearances
	Incorrectly set spark plugs
	Carburettor too rich or too weak

Symptoms	Reason/s
	Dirty contact breaker points
	Fuel filters blocked causing top end fuel starvation
	Distributor automatic balance weights or vacuum advance and retard mechanisms not functioning correctly
	Faulty fuel pump giving top end fuel starvation
Excessive oil consumption	Badly worn, perished or missing valve stem oil seals
	Excessively worn valve stems and valve guides
	Worn piston rings
	Worn pistons and cylinder bores
	Excessive piston ring gap allowing blow-by
	Piston oil return holes choked
Oil being lost due to leaks	Leaking oil filter gasket
	Leaking cover gasket
	Leaking timing
	Leaking sump gasket
	Loose sump plug
Unusual noises from engine	Incorrect valve clearances
	Worn big-end bearing (regular heavy knocking)
	Worn main bearings (rumbling and vibration)
	Out of balance crankshaft (knocking , rumbling and vibration)

Chapter 2 Cooling system

Contents

Specifications

System type ... ...   Pressurised system, assisted by pump and fan

Thermostat:

Type	Wax
Location	Top water outlet tube
Starts to open	185° to 192°F (85° to 89°C)
Fully open	210° to 216°F (99° to 102°C)

Radiator:

Type	Corrugated fin
Pressure cap opens	13 lb/in^2 (0.91 kg/cm^2)

Water pump:

Type	Centrifugal

Fan:

Number of blades	6
Tension	50 lb (22.68 kg)
Free-play of drivebelt	0.5 inch (12.7 mm)

Cooling system capacity:

1600 cc models with heater	10.5 Imp. pints (5.76 litres)
2000 cc models with heater	16 US pints (7.5 litres)

Torque wrench settings	lb f ft	kg f m
Fan blades	10	1.4
Water pump bolts	15	2.1
Thermostat housing bolts	20	2.8
Alternator mounting and adjustment bolts	25	3.5

1 General description

The engine cooling water is circulated by a thermo-syphon and water pump assisted system, and the whole system is pressurised. This is both to prevent the loss of water down the overflow pipe with the radiator cap in position and to prevent premature boiling in adverse conditions. The radiator cap is pressurised to 13 lb/sq in (0.91 kg/cm^2). This has the effect of considerably increasing the boiling point of the coolant. If the water temperature goes above the increased boiling point the extra pressure in the system forces the internal part of the cap off its seat, thus exposing the overflow pipe down which the steam from the boiling water escapes thereby relieving the pressure. It is, therefore, important to check that the radiator

cap is in good condition and that the spring behind the sealing washer has not weakened. The cooling system comprises the radiator, top and bottom water hoses, heater hose, the impeller water pump (mounted on the front of the engine, it carries the fan blades, and is driven by the fan belt), the thermostat and the two drain taps. The inlet manifold is water heated, also the automatic choke.

The system functions in the following fashion. Cold water in the bottom of the radiator circulates up the lower radiator hose to the water pump where it is pushed round the water passages in the cylinder block, helping to keep the cylinder bores and pistons cool.

The water then travels up into the cylinder head and circulates round the combustion spaces and valve seats absorbing more heat, and then, when the engine is at its correct operating

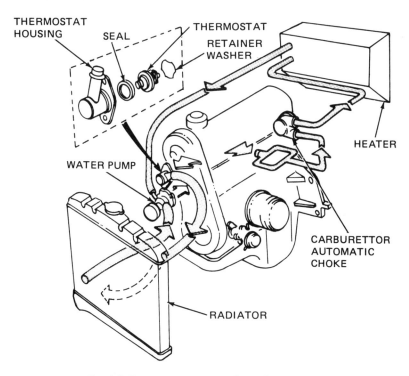

THERMOSTAT HOUSING
SEAL
THERMOSTAT RETAINER WASHER
HEATER
WATER PUMP
CARBURETTOR AUTOMATIC CHOKE
RADIATOR

Fig. 2.1. Engine cooling system (Sec. 1)

temperature, travels out of the cylinder head, past the open thermostat into the upper radiator hose and so into the radiator header tank.

The water travels down the radiator where it is rapidly cooled by the in-rush of cold air through the radiator core which is created by both the fan and the motion of the car. The water, now much cooler, reaches the bottom of the radiator when the cycle is repeated.

When the engine is cold the thermostat (which is a valve which opens and closes according to the temperature of the water) maintains the circulation of the same water in the engine.

Only when the correct minimum operating temperature has been reached, as shown in the Specification, does the thermostat begin to open, allowing water to return to the radiator.

2 Cooling system - draining

1 If the engine is cold, remove the filler cap from the radiator by turning the cap anti-clockwise. If the engine is hot, then turn the filler cap very slightly until pressure in the system has had time to be released. Use a rag over the cap to protect your hand from escaping steam. If with the engine very hot the cap is released suddenly, the drop in pressure can result in the water boiling. With the pressure released the cap can be removed.
2 If antifreeze is used in the cooling system, drain it into a bowl having a capacity of at least 13 Imp. pints (15.6 US pints, 7.4 litres) for re-use.
3 Open the drain plug located on the rear of the radiator lower tank next to the bottom hose. Also remove the engine drain plug which is located at the rear left-hand side of the cylinder block (photo).
4 When the water has finished running, probe the drain plug orifices with a short piece of wire to dislodge any particles of rust or sediment which may be causing a blockage.
5 It is important to note that the heater cannot be drained completely during the cold weather so an antifreeze solution must be used. Always use an antifreeze with an ethylene glycol or glycerine base.

2.3 Cylinder block drain plug removal

3 Cooling system - flushing

1 In time the cooling system will gradually lose its efficiency as the radiator becomes choked with rust, scale deposits from the water, and other sediment. To clean the system out, remove the radiator filler cap and drain plug and leave water running in the filler cap neck for ten to fifteen minutes.
2 In very bad cases the radiator should be reverse flushed. This can be done with the radiator in position. The cylinder block plug is removed and a hose with a suitable tapered adaptor placed in the drain plug hole. Water under pressure is then forced through the radiator and out of the heater tank filler cap neck.
3 It is recommended that some polythene sheeting is placed over the engine to stop water finding its way into the electrical

system.

4   The hose should now be removed and placed in the radiator cap filler neck, and the radiator washed out in the usual manner.

4   Cooling system - filling

1   Refit the cylinder block and radiator drain plugs.
2   Fill the system slowly to ensure that no air lock develops. If a heater is fitted, check that the valve in the heater is open (control at HOT), otherwise an air lock may form in the heater. The best type of water to use in the cooling system is rain water; use this whenever possible.
3   Do not fill the system higher than within 0.5 inch (12.7 mm) of the filler neck. Overfilling will merely result in wastage, which is especially to be avoided when antifreeze is in use.
4   It is usually found that air locks develop in the heater radiator so the system should be vented during refilling by detaching the heater supply hose from the elbow connection on the water outlet housing.
5   Pour coolant into the radiator filler neck whilst the end of the heater supply hose is held at the elbow connection height. When a constant stream of water flows from the supply hose quickly refit the hose. If venting is not carried out it is possible for the engine to overheat. Should the engine overheat for no apparent reason then the system should be vented before seeking other causes.
6   Only use antifreeze mixture with a glycerine or ethylene glycol base.
7   Replace the filler cap and turn it firmly clockwise to lock it in position.

5   Radiator - removal, inspection and cleaning

1   Drain the cooling system, as described in Section 2 of this Chapter.
2   Slacken the two clips which hold the top and bottom radiator hoses on the radiator and carefully pull off the two hoses.
3   Disconnect the automatic transmission oil cooler pipes from the botom section of the radiator if automatic transmission is fitted. Plug the unions and hoses to stop water or dirt ingress.
4   Undo and remove the four bolts that secure the radiator shroud to the radiator side panels and move the shroud over the fan blades. This is only applicable when a shroud is fitted.
5   Undo and remove the four bolts that secure the radiator to the front panel. The radiator may now be lifted upwards and away from the engine compartment. The fragile matrix must not be touched by the fan blades as it easily punctures.
6   Lift the radiator shroud from over the fan blades and remove from the engine compartment.
7   With the radiator away from the car any leaks can be soldered or repaired with a suitable material. Clean out the inside of the radiator by flushing as described earlier in this Chapter. When the radiator is out of the car it is advantageous to turn it upside down and reverse flush. Clean the exterior of the radiator by carefully using a compressed air jet or a strong jet of water to clear away any road dirt, flies etc.
8   Inspect the radiator hoses for cracks, internal or external perishing and damage resulting from overtightening of the securing clips. Also inspect the overflow pipe. Renew the hose if suspect. Examine the radiator hose clips and renew them if they are rusted or distorted.
9   The drain plug and washer should be renewed if leaking or with worn threads, but first ensure the leak is not caused by a faulty fibre washer.

6   Radiator - installation

1   Refitting the radiator and shroud (if fitted) is the reverse sequence to removal (see Section 5).

2   If new hoses are to be fitted they can be a little difficult to fit on the radiator so lubricate them with a little soap.
3   Refill the cooling system, as described in Section 4.

7   Thermostat - removal, testing and refitting

1   Partially drain the cooling system (usually 4 Imp. pints, 4.8 US pints, 2.27 litres is enough) as described in Section 2.
2   Slacken the top radiator hose to the thermostat housing and remove the hose.
3   Undo and remove the two bolts and spring washers that secure the thermostat housing to the cylinder head.
4   Carefully lift the thermostat housing away from the cylinder head. Recover the joint washer adhering to either the housing or cylinder head.
5   Using a screwdriver ease the clip securing the thermostat to the housing (Fig. 2.2). Note which way round the thermostat is fitted in the housing and also that the bridge is 90º to the outlet.
6   The thermostat may now be withdrawn from the housing. Recover the seal from inside the housing (photo).
7   Test the thermostat for correct functioning by suspending it on a string in a saucepan of cold water together with a thermometer. Heat the water and note the temperature at which the thermostat begins to open. This should be 85 - 89ºC (185 - 192ºF). It is advantageous in winter to fit a thermostat that does not open too early. Continue heating the water until the thermostat is fully open. Then let it cool down naturally.

Fig. 2.2. Extracting thermostat clip (Sec. 7)

7.6 Removing thermostat sealing ring

8　If the thermostat does not fully open in boiling water, or does not close down as the water cools, then it must be discarded and a new one fitted. Should the thermostat be stuck open when cold this will usually be apparent when removing it from the housing.

9　Refitting the thermostat is the reverse sequence to removal. Always ensure that the thermostat housing and cylinder head mating faces are clean and flat. If the thermostat housing is badly corroded fit a new housing. Always use a new gasket. Tighten the two securing bolts to the specified torque wrench setting.

10　If a new winter thermostat is fitted, provided the summer one is still functioning correctly, it can be placed on one side and refitted in the spring. Thermostats should last for two or three years before renewal becomes desirable.

8　Water pump - removal and installation

1　Drain the cooling system, as described in Section 2.

2　Refer to Section 5 and remove the radiator (and shroud if fitted).

3　Slacken the alternator mounting bolts and push the alternator towards the cylinder block. Lift away the fan belt (Fig. 2.3).

4　Undo and remove the four bolts and washers that secure the fan assembly to the water pump spindle hub. Lift away the fan and pulley (Fig. 2.4).

5　Slacken the clip that secures the heater hose to the water pump. Pull the hose from its union on the water pump.

6　Undo and remove the four bolts and spring washers that secure the water pump and recover the gasket

7　Refitting the water pump is the reverse sequence to removal. The following additional points should however be noted:

　　a) *Make sure the mating faces of the cylinder block and water pump are clean. Always use a new gasket.*

　　b) *Tighten the water pump securing bolts to the correct torque.*

　　c) *Tighten the water pump fan and pulley bolts to the specified torque wrench setting.*

9　Water pump - dismantling and overhaul

1　Before undertaking the dismantling of a water pump to effect a repair, check that all parts are available. It may be quicker and more economic to replace the complete unit.

2　Refer to Fig. 2.7 and using a universal three leg puller and suitable thrust block draw the hub from the shaft.

3　Carefully pull out the bearing retaining clip from the slot in the water pump housing. On some water pumps this clip is not fitted.

4　Using a soft faced hammer drive the shaft and bearing assembly out towards the rear of the pump body.

5　The impeller vane is removed from the spindle by using a universal three leg puller and suitable thrust block.

6　Remove the seal and the slinger by splitting the latter with the aid of a sharp cold chisel.

7　Carefully inspect the condition of the shaft and bearing assembly and if it shows signs of wear or corrosion, new parts should be obtained. If it was found that coolant was leaking from the pump, a new seal should be obtained. If it was evident that the pulley hub or impeller were a loose fit they must be renewed. The repair kit available comprises a new shaft and bearing assembly, a slinger seal, bush, clip and gasket.

8　To reassemble the water pump first fit the shaft and bearing assembly to the housing, larger end of the shaft to the front of the housing, and press the assembly into the housing until the front of the bearing is flush with the pump housing.

9　Refit the bearing locating clip.

10　Next press the pump pulley onto the front end of the shaft until the end of the shaft is flush with the end of the hub.

11　Press the new slinger flanged end first onto the shaft until the non-flanged end is approximately 0.5 inch (13 mm) from the shaft end. To act as a rough guide the flanged end on the slinger

Fig. 2.3. Alternator mounting bolts (Sec. 8)

Fig. 2.4. Removing fan and pulley (Sec. 8)

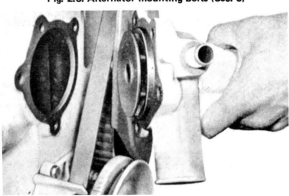
Fig. 2.5. Removing water pump (Sec. 8)

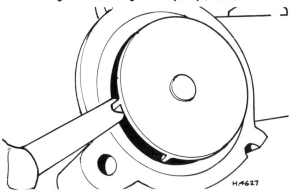
Fig. 2.6. Checking water pump impeller clearance (Sec. 9)

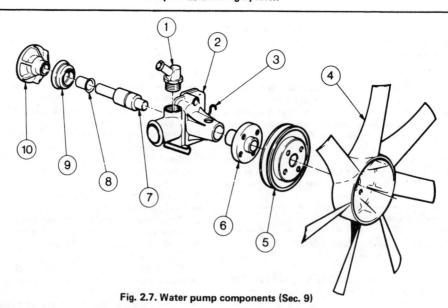

Fig. 2.7. Water pump components (Sec. 9)

1 Heater connection	4 Cooling fan	7 Shaft and bearing	9 Seal assembly
2 Pump body	5 Fan pulley	assembly	10 Impeller
3 Bearing retainer	6 Pulley hub	8 Slinger	

will be just in line with the impeller side of the window in the water pump body.

12 Place the new seal over the shaft and into the counterbore in the water pump housing and then press the impeller onto the shaft until a clearance of 0.03 inch (0.76 mm) is obtained between the impeller and the housing face (Fig. 2.6). Whilst this is being carried out the slinger will be pushed into its final position by the impeller.

10 Drivebelt - removal and refitting

If the fanbelt is worn or has stretched unduly, it should be renewed. Often the reason for replacement is that the belt has broken in service. It is recommended that a spare belt be always carried in the car.

1 Loosen the alternator mounting bolts and move the alternator towards the engine.

2 Slip the old belt over the crankshaft, alternator and water pump pulley wheels and lift it off over the fan blades.

3 Put a new belt onto the three pulleys and adjust it, as described in Section 11. **Note:** After fitting a new belt it will require adjustment after 250 miles (400 km).

11 Drivebelt - adjustment

1 It is important to keep the fanbelt correctly adjusted and it is considered that this should be a regular maintenance task every 6,000 miles (10,000 km). If the belt is loose it will slip, wear rapidly and cause the alternator and water pump to malfunction. If the belt is too tight the alternator and water pump bearings will wear rapidly causing premature failure of these components.

2 The fan belt tension is correct when there is 0.5 inch (12.7 mm) of lateral movement at the mid point position of the belt run between the alternator pulley and the water pump.

3 To adjust the fan belt, slacken the alternator securing bolts and move the alternator in or out until the correct tension is obtained. It is easier if the alternator bolts are only slackened a little so it requires some effort to move the alternator. In this way the tension of the belt can be arrived at more quickly than by making frequent adjustment.

4 When the correct adjustment has been obtained fully tighten the alternator mounting bolts (Fig. 2.8).

5 If air conditioning is fitted, the compressor drivebelt is adjusted by means of the idler pulley (Figs. 2.9 and 2.10).

Fig. 2.8. Drivebelt (1) and alternator adjusting strap bolt (2) (Sec. 11)

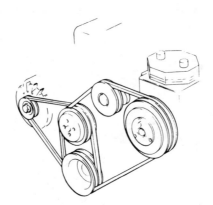

Fig. 2.9. Drivebelt arrangement with air conditioner compressor (Sec. 11)

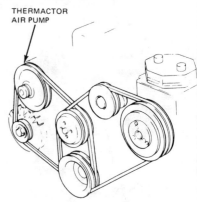

Fig. 2.10. Drivebelt arrangement with air conditioner compressor and emission control air pump (Sec. 11)

12 Temperature gauge - fault finding

1 If the temperature gauge fails to work, either the gauge, the sender unit, the wiring or the connections are at fault.
2 It is not possible to repair the gauge or the sender unit and they must be replaced by new units if at fault.
3 First check the wiring connections are sound. Check the wiring for breaks using an ohmmeter. The sender unit and gauge should be tested by substitution.

13 Temperature gauge sender unit - removal and refitting

1 Partially drain the cooling system, as described in Section 2.
2 Detach the terminal connector from the sender unit.
3 Unscrew the old sender unit with a suitably sized socket or box spanner (the unit is located in the cylinder head just below the manifold on the left-hand side) (Fig. 2.11).
4 Apply a little conductive water resistant sealer to the threads of the new sender unit and screw into position. Take care not to overtighten.
5 Refit the terminal connector and top-up the cooling system, as described in Section 4.

14 Antifreeze and corrosion inhibiting mixtures

1 It is recommended that the system is filled with an antifreeze mixture where climatic conditions warrant its use. The cooling system should be drained, flushed and refilled every alternate autumn. The use of antifreeze solutions for periods of longer than two years is likely to cause damage and encourage the formation of rust and scale due to the corrosion inhibitors gradually losing their efficiency. If the use of antifreeze mixture is not necessary because of favourable climatic conditions, never use ordinary water but always fill the system with a corrosion inhibiting mixture of recommended brand to protect the engine against rust and corrosion.
2 Before adding antifreeze to the system, check all hose

Fig. 2.11. Location of water temperature sender unit (Sec. 13)

connections and check the tightness of the cylinder head bolts as such solutions are searching. The cooling system should be drained and refilled with clean water as previously explained, before adding antifreeze.
3 The quantity of antifreeze which should be used for various levels of protection is given in the table below, expressed as a percentage of the system capacity.

Antifreeze volume	Protection to	Safe pump circulation
25%	$-26^{o}C$ $(-15^{o}F)$	$-12^{o}C$ $(10^{o}F)$
30%	$-33^{o}C$ $(-28^{o}F)$	$-16^{o}C$ $(-3^{o}F)$
35%	$-39^{o}C$ $(-38^{o}F)$	$-20^{o}C$ $(-4^{o}F)$

4 Where the cooling system contains an antifreeze or corrosion inhibiting solution any topping-up should be done with a solution made up in similar proportions to the original in order to avoid dilution.

Fault diagnosis - cooling system

Symptom	Reason
Overheating	Low coolant level
	Faulty radiator pressure cap
	Thermostat stuck shut
	Drivebelt slipping or incorrectly tensioned
	Clogged radiator matrix
	Incorrect engine timing
	Corroded system
Cool running	Incorrect type thermostat
Slow warm up	Thermostat stuck open
Coolant loss	Faulty radiator pressure cap
	Split hose
	Leaking water pump to block joint
	Leaking core plug
	Blown cylinder head gasket

Chapter 3 Carburation; fuel, exhaust and emission control systems

Contents

Specifications

Fuel tank

Location ... ... Rear mounted
Capacity ... ... 10.5 Imp. gals, 12 US gals, 48 litres

Fuel pump

Type ... ... Mechanically operated by pushrod from engine auxiliary shaft
Delivery pressure ... ... 3.75 to 5.0 lb/in^2 (0.26 to 0.35 kg/cm^2)

Carburettor - application

1600 cc engine ... ... Ford single venturi downdraught
1600 cc GT ... ... Weber, dual barrel
2000 cc:
   (Up to 1974) ... ... Ford Motorcraft 5200 2V dual barrel carburettor
   (1974 onwards) ... ... Ford Motorcraft 5200 2V dual barrel carburettor with
supplementary quick warm-up electric choke

Carburettor specifications	1600 cc engine	1600 cc GT engine	2000 cc engine
Throttle bore diameter:			
Primary	1.42 in (36.0 mm)	1.26 in (32.0 mm)	1.26 in (32.0 mm)
Secondary	—	1.42 in (36.0 mm)	1.42 in (36.0 mm)
Venturi diameter:			
Primary	1.10 in (28.0 mm)	1.02 in (26.0 mm)	1.02 in (26.0 mm)
Secondary	—	1.06 in (27.0 mm)	1.06 in (27.0 mm)
Main jets:			
Primary	137	135	125
Secondary	—	150	160
Air correction jet:			
Primary	140	170	160
Secondary	—	140	140

	1600 cc engine	1600 cc GT engine	2000 cc engine
Idling jet:			
Primary	80	50	50
Secondary	—	45	50
Idle air bleed:			
1st	110	170	170
2nd	100	70	70
Accelerator pump jet	55	50	50
Enrichment pipe jet	—	F50	F50
Power jet	90	100	100
Float needle valve	2.0 mm	2.0 mm	2.0 mm
Float level (raised)	1.1 in (28.0 mm)	1.4 in (35.5 mm)	1.4 in (35.5 mm)
Float level (hanging)	1.4 in (35.0 mm)	2.0 in (51.0 mm)	2.0 in (51.0 mm)
Choke plate pull down	0.10 in (2.54 mm)	0.12 to 0.24 in (3.0 to 6.0 mm)	0.12 to 0.24 in (3.0 to 6.0 mm)
De-choke dimension	0.17 to 0.21 in (4.32 to 5.33 mm)	0.138 to 0.158 in (3.5 to 4.0 mm)	0.138 to 0.158 in (3.5 to 4.0 mm)
Accelerator pump stroke	0.12 in (3.0 mm)	—	—
Idling speed:			
Manual gearbox	725 to 775 rom	725 to 775 rpm	725 to 775 rpm
Auto. trans. (in 'N')	600 to 650 rpm	725 to 775 rpm	725 to 775 rpm
Fast idle speed	1900 to 2100 rpm	2900 to 3100 rpm	2900 to 3100 rpm

Torque wrench settings	lb f ft	kg f m
Fuel pump to cylinder block	20	2.8
Carburettor flange nuts	18	2.5
Air pump bracket to engine	25	3.5
Air pump to bracket	18	2.5
Exhaust downpipe flange nuts	25	3.5
Manifold nuts	20	2.8

1 General description

1 The fuel system comprises a rear mounted fuel tank, a fuel pump, mechanically operated from an eccentric on the engine auxiliary shaft, a carburettor and all the necessary fuel lines, filters and a fuel gauge.

2 Cars operating in North America (2000 cc engine) are equipped with one or more emission control systems, depending on operating territory and date of production. These systems are described later in this Chapter.

2 Air cleaner (1600 cc) - element renewal

1 Remove the lid securing screws and the lid from the air cleaner (Fig. 3.1).

2 Extract the element and wipe out the interior of the air cleaner casing.

3 If a mileage of 12000 miles (19000 km) has been covered since the element was last renewed, discard it and fit a new one.

4 If the renewal mileage has not been reached, tap the element sharply on the bench to remove any adhering dust and refit it but positioning it so that a fresh surface is presented to the air intake spout.

5 Refit the lid and screws.

6 In spring and autumn remember to move the air intake to the appropriate seasonal position.

3 Air cleaner (1600 cc GT) - element renewal

1 The operations are similar to those described in the preceding Section except that the air cleaner lid is secured by spring clips.

Fig. 3.1. 1600 cc type air cleaner element (1) and lid (2) (Sec. 2)

4 Air cleaner (2000 cc) - description and element renewal

1 This type of air cleaner incorporates a temperature operated valve and duct mechanism. This arrangement regulates the intake of air from the engine compartment and the heater box adjacent to the exhaust manifold so that the carburettor is always supplied with air at a temperature of between 90° and 100°F (32° to 38°C) and this assists in the reduction of noxious exhaust gases (Fig. 3.2 and 3.3).

2 Every 12,000 miles (19,000 km) unscrew and remove the nuts which secure the housing cover to the air cleaner adaptor.

3 Lift off the housing and extract the filter element (Fig. 3.4).

4 If the element is dirty and discoloured, renew it after wiping out the air cleaner body.

5 Assembly is a reversal of dismantling and removal.

6 On some air cleaners, the crankcase ventilation (PCV) hose has its own independent filter within the air cleaner housing.

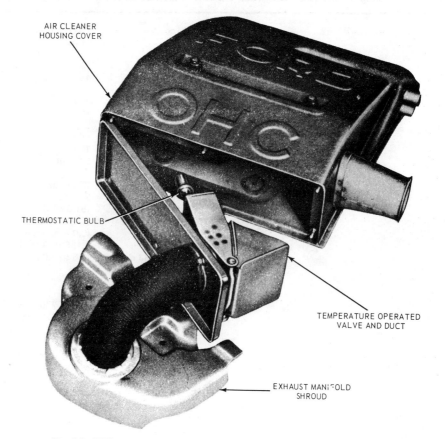

Fig. 3.2. 2000 cc type temperature controlled air cleaner duct (Sec. 4)

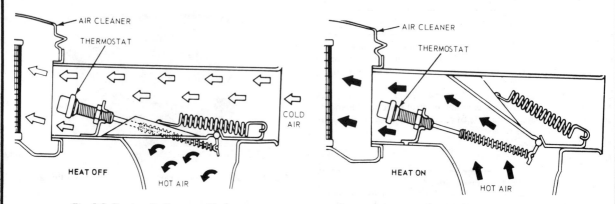

Fig. 3.3. Duct and valve assembly (temperature controlled air cleaner) - principle of operation (Sec. 4)

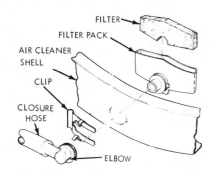

Fig. 3.4. PCV hose filter within air cleaner body (Sec. 4)

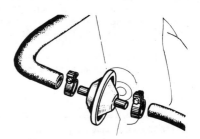

Fig. 3.5. Fuel line filter (Sec. 5)

5   In-line fuel filter - renewal

1   Every 6,000 miles (9,600 km) the air cleaner should be removed and the fuel hoses disconnected from the (now accessible) fuel line filter (Fig. 3.5).
2   Install the new filter, the correct way round and clamp the new hose clips supplied, securely.
3   Test for leaks with the engine running and then refit the air cleaner.

6   Fuel pump - description

The mechanical fuel pump is mounted on the left-hand side of the engine and is driven by an auxiliary shaft. It is not recommended that this type of pump be dismantled for repair other than cleaning the filter and sediment cap. Should a fault appear in the pump it may be tested and if confirmed it must be discarded and a new one obtained. One of two designs may be fitted, this depends on the availability at the production time of the car (Fig. 3.6).

7   Fuel pump - removal and refitting

1   Remove the inlet and outlet pipes at the pump and plug the ends to stop petrol loss or dirt finding its way into the fuel system.
2   Undo and remove two bolts and spring washers that secure the pump to the cylinder block.
3   Lift away the fuel pump and gasket and recover the pushrod, (Fig. 3.7)
4   Refitting the fuel pump is the reverse sequence to removal but there are several additional points that should be noted:
   a) Do not forget to refit the pushrod.
   b) Tighten the pump securing bolts to the specified torque.
   c) Before reconnecting the pipe from the fuel tank to the pump inlet, move the end to a position lower than the fuel tank so that fuel can syphon out. Quickly connect the pipe to the pump inlet.
   d) Disconnect the pipe at the carburettor and turn the engine over until petrol issues from the open end. Quickly connect the pipe to the carburettor union. This last operation will help to prime the pump.

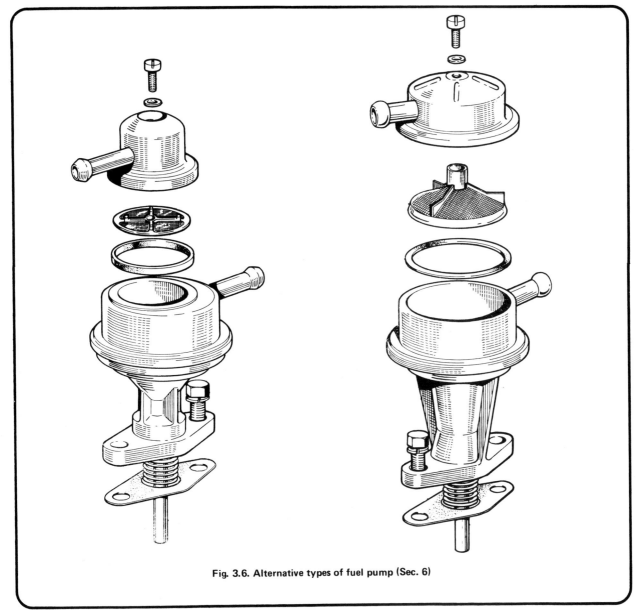

Fig. 3.6. Alternative types of fuel pump (Sec. 6)

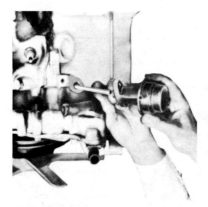

Fig. 3.7. Removing fuel pump and operating rod (Sec. 7)

9.2 Lifting away fuel pump sediment cap, filter and seal

9.3 Removal of filter from fuel pump sediment cap

8 Fuel pump - testing

Assuming that the fuel lines and unions are in good condition and that there are no leaks anywhere, check the performance of the fuel pump in the following manner. Disconnect the fuel pipe at the carburettor inlet union, and the high tension lead to the coil and with a suitable container or large rag in position to catch the ejected fuel, turn the engine over. A good spurt of petrol should emerge from the end of the pipe every second revolution.

9 Fuel pump - cleaning

1   Detach the fuel pipe from the pump inlet tube.
2   Undo and remove the centre screw and 'O' ring and lift off the sediment cap, filter and seal. (photo)
3   Thoroughly clean the sediment cap, filter and pumping chamber using a paintbrush and clean petrol to remove any sediment. (photo)
4   To reassemble is the reverse sequence to dismantling. Do not overtighten the centre screw as it could distort the sediment cap.

10 Carburettors - general description

On 1600 cc cars, a single venturi down draught carburettor is used.

On 1600 cc GT Cars, a Weber dual barrel down draught carburettor is fitted.

On 2000 cc cars, a dual barrel carburettor is installed. All models have an automatic choke, water heated from the engine cooling system and late carburettors on 2000 cc engine have a supplementary electrically heated choke to assist in rapid warming up and to reduce the emission of noxious gases during the rich running of the initial warming-up period.

The single venturi carburettor, incorporates idling, main power valve and accelerator pump systems. The float chamber is externally vented. The carburettor comprises two castings, the upper and lower bodies. The upper body incorporates the float chamber cover and pivot brackets, fuel inlet components, choke plate and the main and power valve system, idling system and accelerator pump discharge nozzle (Fig. 3.8).
The lower body incorporates the float chamber, the throttle barrel and venturi, throttle valve components, adjustment screws, accelerator pump and distributor vacuum connection.

The dual barrel carburettors operate on similar principles and they incorporate a fully automatic strangler type choke to ensure easy starting whilst the engine is cold. The float chamber

Fig. 3.8. Ford single venturi carburettor (Sec. 10)

is internally vented (Fig. 3.9).
The carburettor body comprises two castings which form the upper and lower bodies. The upper incorporates the float chamber cover, float pivot brackets, fuel inlet union, gauze filter, spring loaded needle valve, twin air intakes, choke plates and the section of the power valve controlled by vacuum.
Incorporated in the lower body is the float chamber, accelerator pump, two throttle barrels and integral main ventures, throttle plates, spindles, levers, jets and the petrol power valve.
The throttle plate opening is in a preset sequence so that the primary starts to open first and is then followed by the secondary in such a manner that both plates reach full throttle position at the same time. The primary barrel, throttle plate and venturi are smaller than the secondary, whereas the auxiliary venturi size is identical in both the primary and secondary barrels.
All the carburation systems are located in the lower body and the main progression systems operate in both barrels, whilst the idling and the power valve systems operate in the primary barrel only and the full load enrichment system in the secondary barrel.
The accelerator pump discharges fuel into the primary barrel.
A connection for the vacuum required to control the distributor advance/retard vacuum unit is located on the lower body.

11 Carburettor (1600 cc and 1600 cc GT) - slow running adjustment

1   Run the engine until normal operating temperature is reached.
2   Adjust the throttle speed screw until the specified idling speed is obtained (Figs. 3.10 and 3.11).
3   Now unscrew (anticlockwise) the mixture control screw until the engine begins to run unevenly ('hunts').

Fig. 3.9. Motorcraft model 5200 carburettor (Sec. 10)

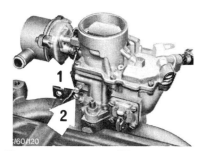

Fig. 3.10. Throttle speed screw (1) and mixture screw (2) on Ford single venturi carburettor (Sec. 11)

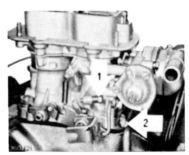

Fig. 3.11. Throttle speed screw (1) and mixture screw (2) on Weber dual barrel carburettor (Sec. 11)

4 Screw the mixture control screw in, until the engine runs evenly and then re-adjust the throttle speed screw, if necessary, to obtain the correct slow running speed.

5 This method of adjustment is basic and it is recommended that a final tuning is made using a device such as a Colortune, a vacuum gauge or an exhaust gas analyser in accordance with the manufacturer's instructions.

12 Carburettor (2000 cc) - slow running adjustment

1 To carry out these adjustments it is necessary to use specialist tuning equipment so that the result will be within the Federal requirements. Full information is given in this Section to enable the engine to be started and the car driven to the local dealer.

2 The carburettor fitted is equipped with idle fuel mixture adjustment limiters which control the maximum idle richness thereby preventing over rich idle adjustment. The plastic idle limiter cap is fitted on the head of the idle fuel mixture adjusting screw. Any adjustment to be made must therefore be within the range of the limiter and no attempt may be made to render the limiter inoperative. If it is not possible to obtain a satisfactory idle speed then the ignition and engine settings must be checked as well as the parts of the fuel system.

3 Start the engine and with the bonnet in the half raised position run the engine at a speed of 1500 rpm for a period of at least 20 minutes. This may be achieved by positioning the fast idle screw or cam follower on the kickdown step of the fast idle cam.

4 The ignition timing and distributor advance/retard system must now be checked for correct operation. This work requires specialist equipment.

5 Disconnect the carburettor - to - decel valve hose at the valve. Plug the decel valve fitting. (See Section 23).

6 *Manual gearbox.* The gear change lever must be in the neutral position.

7 *Automatic transmission,* The selector lever must be in the drive position except when an exhaust gas analyser is in use. Take care not to open the throttle wide and chock all wheels.

8 Adjust the engine curb idle speed until the engine runs evenly at a reasonable idle speed (Fig. 3.12).

9 Now turn the mixture idle adjustment screw inwards to obtain the smoothly running condition within the range of the idler limiter (Fig. 3.13).

10 Check the exhaust gas CO content using an exhaust gas analyser.

13 Carburettor - removal and installation

1 Open the bonnet and remove the air cleaner assembly as detailed earlier in this Chapter.

2 Partially drain the cooling system and collect in a suitable

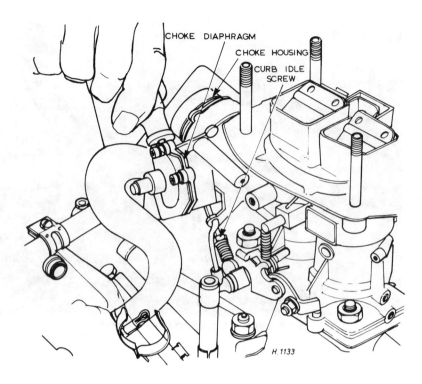

CHOKE DIAPHRAGM

CHOKE HOUSING

CURB IDLE SCREW

H. 1133

Fig. 3.12. Adjusting curb idle speed (2000 cc carburettor) (Sec. 12)

Choke housing

Idle mixture screw

Hot idle compensator

Fig. 3.13. Engine idle mixture adjustment (2000 cc carburettor) (Sec. 12)

capacity container if antifreeze is in use.

3 Slacken the clips securing the hoses to the automatic choke housing and carefully separate the hoses from the housing.

4 Slacken the fuel pipe retaining clip at the float chamber union and detach the flexible hose.

5 Detach the ventilation tube from the top of the float chamber (1600 cc only).

6 Release the distributor automatic advance pipe from the side of the carburettor.

7 Disconnect the throttle control rod from the throttle shaft.

8 Undo the nuts that secure the carburettor flange and remove the nuts and spring washer.

9 Carefully lift away the carburettor and its gasket.

10 Replacement is a straightforward reversal of the removal sequence but note the following additional points:

   a) *Remove all traces of the old carburettor gasket, clean the mating flanges and fit a new gasket in place.*

   b) *Refill the cooling system as described in Chapter 2.*

14 Carburettors - dismantling and reassembly - general

1 With time the component parts of the carburettor will wear and petrol consumption increase. The diameter of drillings and jets may alter, and air and fuel leaks may develop round spindles and other moving parts. Because of the high degree of precision involved it is best to purchase an exchange carburettor. This is one of the few instances where it is better to take the latter course rather than to rebuild the component oneself.

2 It may be neccessary to partially dismantle the carburettor to clear a blocked jet. The accelerator pump itself may need attention and gaskets may need renewal, providing care is taken there is no reason why the carburettor may not be completely reconditioned at home, but ensure a full repair kit can be obtained before you strip the carburettor down. **Never** poke out jets with wire or similar to clean them but blow them out with compressed air or air from a tyre pump.

3 When a 2000 cc engine type carburettor has been refitted or the controls adjusted it is imperative that the car be taken to the local dealer to have any adjustments made so that it complies with the Federal Regulations (US models only).

15 Single venturi type carburettor (1600 cc) - overhaul and adjustment

1 Unscrew and remove the fast idle cam retaining screw and withdraw the cam (Fig. 3.14).

2 Remove the upper body, also the automatic choke housing cover.

3 From within the automatic choke housing extract the retaining screw and remove the thermostatic lever, piston and associated parts (Fig. 3.15).

4 Withdraw the pivot pin and remove the float and needle valve (Fig. 3.16).

5 Unscrew the fuel inlet needle valve housing and extract the filter and washer.

6 Unscrew and remove the main jet.

7 Only if essential, dismantle the choke butterfly valve plate and shaft. Invert the lower body and eject the accelerator pump ball and weight.

8 Unscrew the accelerator pump cover and disconnect the cover from the operating link. Extract the flexible diaphragm and return spring (Fig. 3.17).

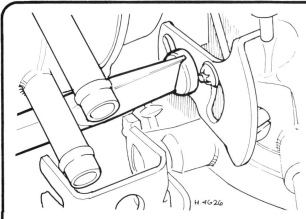

Fig. 3.14. Removing fast idle cam (single venturi carburettor) (Sec. 15)

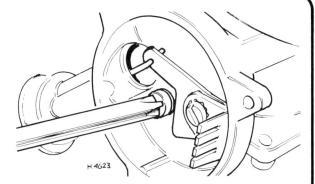

Fig. 3.15. Removing thermostatic components screw from auto. choke housing (single venturi carburettor) (Sec. 15)

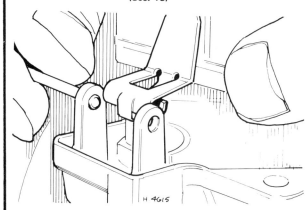

Fig. 3.16. Extracting float pivot pin (single venturi carburettor) (Sec. 15)

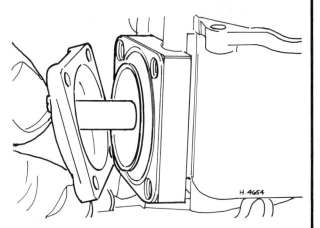

Fig. 3.17. Removing accelerator pump cover (single venturi carburettor) (Sec. 15)

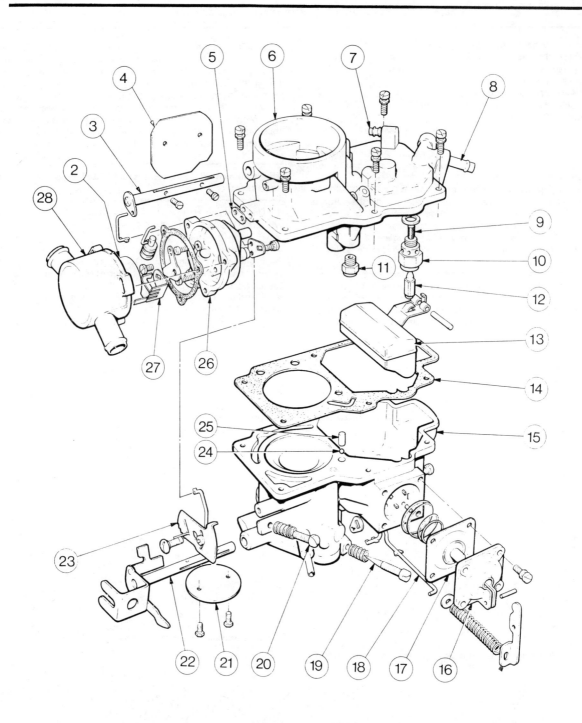

Fig. 3.18. Exploded view of Ford single venturi carburettor

2	Automatic choke bi-metal spring	8	Fuel inlet
3	Choke valve shaft	9	Filter
4	Choke valve plate	10	Fuel inlet valve housing
5	Vacuum passage gasket	11	Main jet
6	Upper body	12	Inlet needle valve
7	External vent	13	Float

14	Gasket
15	Lower body
16	Accelerator pump cover
17	Diaphragm
18	Rod
19	Mixture control screw
20	Throttle speed screw
21	Throttle valve plate

22	Throttle valve shaft
23	Fast idle cam
24	Accelerator pump ball
25	Accelerator pump weight
26	Automatic choke housing
27	Thermostatic spring lever
28	Automatic choke housing cover

9 Only if essential, dismantle the throttle butterfly valve plate and shaft.

10 Clean all components in fuel or a suitable solvent and inspect for wear or damage. When reassembling, use all the parts supplied in the repair kit.

11 If the throttle valve has been dismantled, insert the shaft and then attach the small oval-shaped plate to the shaft so that the 'O' mark on the plate is furthest from the carburettor body.

12 Locate the throttle valve plate in the slot in the shaft so that the indentations are furthest from the mixture control screw. The securing screws should be fully tightened and peened with the throttle plate in the closed position (Fig. 3.20).

13 Assemble the accelerator pump and insert the ball and weight in the lower body.

14 Insert the automatic choke thermostatic lever shaft and plate into the housing. Assemble the piston link and levers, and secure with the retaining screw (Fig. 3.21).

15 If the choke valve plate has been dismantled, reassemble it to the shaft and tighten and peen the securing screws with the valve plate in the fully closed position.

16 Locate a new gasket on the vacuum passage and then offer up the automatic choke housing to the upper body and at the same time engage the 'U' link with the thermostatic lever operating shaft plate. Secure the housing with the retaining screws.

17 Assemble the fuel inlet valve housing and filter to the upper body and insert the needle valve (Fig. 3.22).

18 Assemble the float and pivot and then check the float adjustment in the following way:

Float level adjustment

19 Hold the carburettor upper body vertically so that the weight of the float is resting on the needle valve. Measure the distance between the bottom of the float and the face of the upper body. This should be 1.1 in. (28.0 mm) otherwise bend the tab which rests against the needle valve (Fig. 3.23).

Fig. 3.19. Correct installation of throttle valve shaft and plate (single venturi carburettor) (Sec. 15)

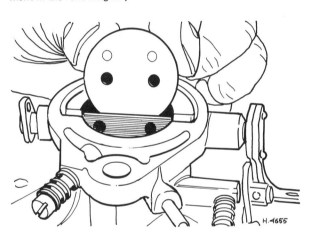

Fig. 3.20. Alignment of throttle valve plate (single venturi carburettor) (Sec. 15)

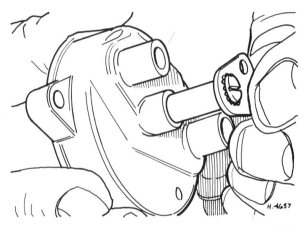

Fig. 3.21. Installing automatic choke thermostatic lever shaft (single venturi carburettor) (Sec. 15)

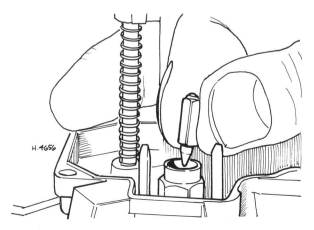

Fig. 3.22. Installing fuel inlet needle valve (single venturi carburettor) (Sec. 15)

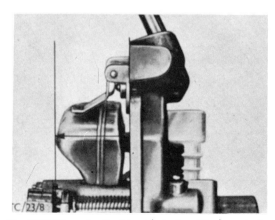

Fig. 3.23. Measuring float level (raised position) on single venturi carburettor (Sec. 15)

20 Now hold the upper body so that the float hangs free and again measure the distance between the bottom of the float and the face of the upper body. This dimension should be 1.4 in (35.0 mm) otherwise bend the stop tab on the end of the float arm (Fig. 3.24).

21 Continue reassembly by screwing in the main jet and then assemble the upper and lower carburettor bodies using a new gasket.

22 Position the automatic choke fast idle cam and link and insert the shouldered screw. Check the choke plate pull down, as described in the following way.

Choke plate pull-down adjustment

23 Depress the vacuum piston until the vacuum bleed port is exposed and then insert a piece of wire into the port and raise the piston until the wire is trapped. Holding the piston in this position, close the choke valve plate with the fingers, at the same time partially opening the throttle for the fast idle tab to clear the cam.

24 Check the gap between the edge of the choke valve plate and the carburettor body using a suitable twist drill or rod. This gap should be 0.10 in. (2.54 mm) otherwise bend the choke thermostat lever at point 'C'. With the choke plate held in the pull-down position, check the alignment of the fast idle tab and 'V' mark (see paragraph 27) (Fig. 3.25).

Accelerator pump stroke adjustment

25 Unscrew the throttle stop screw a few turns until the throttle valve plate is fully closed. Depress the diaphragm plunger fully and check the clearance between the operating lever and plunger using a rod or twist drill. This clearance should be 0.12 in. (3.0 mm) otherwise carefully bend the swan neck of the operating rod. Reset the throttle stop screw when the carburettor has been installed on the engine (Fig. 3.26).

26 Using a new gasket, refit the automatic choke cover to the housing making sure that the spring engages in the centre slot of the thermostatic lever and aligning the centre housing and cover marks. Reassembly is now complete but if new components have been fitted, carry out the following three checks and adjustments:

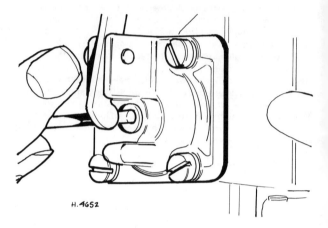

Fig. 3.26. Checking accelerator pump stroke (single venturi carburettor) (Sec. 15)

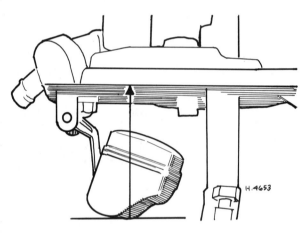

Fig. 3.24. Measuring float level (suspended position) on single venturi carburettor (Sec. 15)

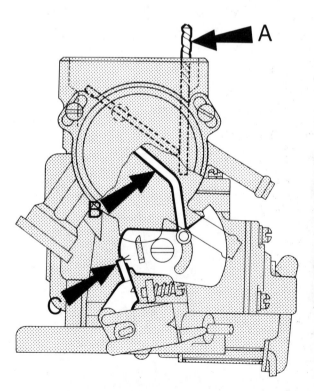

Fig. 3.27. Fast idle cam 'V' mark alignment diagram (single venturi carburettor) (Sec. 15)

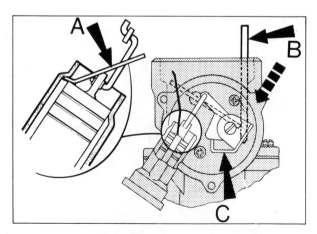

Fig. 3.25. Choke plate pull down diagram (single venturi carburettor) (Sec. 15)

A Piston retaining wire   B Gap gauge   C Thermostat lever

A Gap gauge   B Link   C Fast idle tab

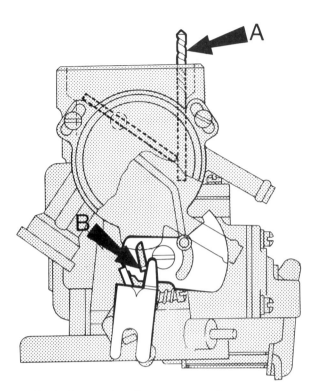

Fig. 3.28. De-choke adjustment diagram (single venturi carburettor) (Sec. 15)

A Gap gauge   B Fast idle cam projection

'V' mark alignment

27 Take a rod or twist drill 0.167 in. (4.25 mm) in diameter and insert it between the edge of the choke plate and the carburettor body as the plate is held in the closed position with the fingers.
28 Open the throttle slightly so that the fast idle cam attains its natural position. If necessary, bend the fast idle cam link to align the 'V' mark on the cam with the throttle lever fast idle tab. (Fig. 3.27).

De-choke adjustment

29 Open the throttle slightly so that the choke plate will close under the action of the bi-metal spring. Now open the throttle fully and hold it against its stop.
30 With the throttle held in this position, use a rod or twist drill to check the clearance between the bottom edge of the choke valve plate and the carburettor body. This clearance should be between 0.17 and 0.21 in. (4.32 and 5.33 mm) otherwise bend the projection on the fast idle cam (Fig. 3.28).

---

16 Dual barrel carburettor (1600 cc GT) - overhaul and adjustment

---

1 Before dismantling wash the exterior of the carburettor and wipe dry using a non-fluffy rag. Select a clean area of the workbench and lay several layers of newspaper on the top. Obtain several small containers for putting some of the small parts in, which could be easily lost. Whenever a part is to be removed look at it first so that it may be refitted in its original position. As each part is removed place it in order along one edge of the newspaper so that by using this method reassembly is made easier.
2 All parts of the carburettor are shown in Fig. 3.31.
3 Unscrew and remove the fuel filter retainer from the upper body. Recover the cylindrical filter.
4 Disconnect the choke plate operating rod at its upper end.
5 Undo and remove the screws and spring washers that retain the upper body to the lower body. Lift away the upper body and the gasket (Fig. 3.29).
6 Carefully extract the float pivot pin and lift out the float assembly followed by the needle valve.
7 Using a box spanner unscrew the needle valve carrier.
8 Remove the choke thermostatic spring cover and housing and then remove the automatic choke assembly from the carburettor body. Unscrew and remove the three screws which secure the vacuum diaphragm cover to the automatic choke housing and remove the diaphragm components (Fig. 3.30).
9 Undo and remove the four screws and spring washers that secure the accelerator pump cover to the lower body. Lift away the cover gasket, diaphragm and spring.
10 If necessary using a parallel pin punch, drive out the pivot pin from the plain end and lift away the accelerator pump lever.
11 Also if necessary remove the split pin (or clip) that retains the upper end of the choke plate operating rod to the spindle lever and detach. Remove the dust seal from the air cleaner flange.
12 Undo the two screws securing each choke plate to the shaft. Lift away the choke plates. Remove the burrs from the threaded holes and then withdraw the shaft.
13 Obtain a selection of screwdrivers with the ends in good condition and square so that the jets may be removed without damage.

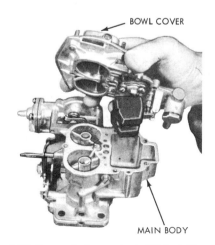

Fig. 3.29. Removal of upper body (Weber) (Sec. 16)

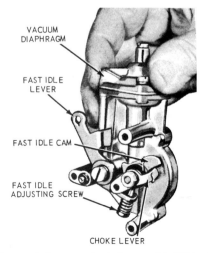

Fig. 3.30. Removal of automatic choke assembly (Weber) (Sec. 16)

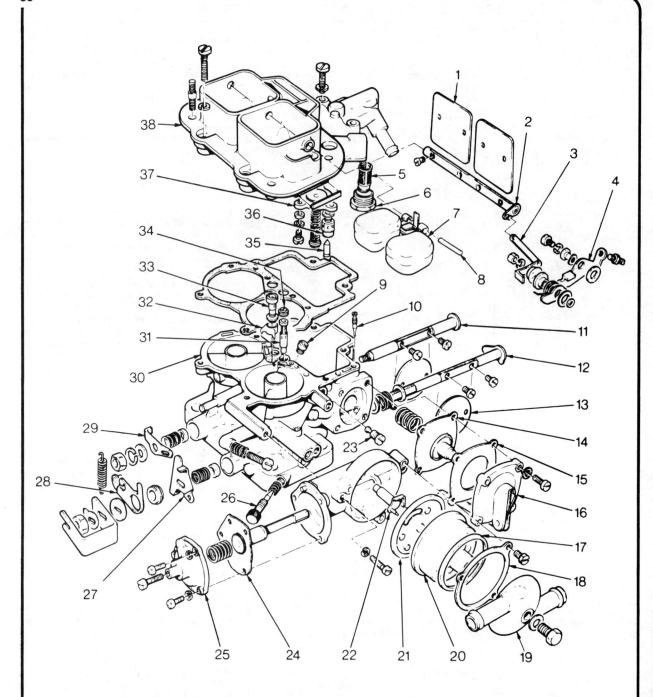

Fig. 3.31. Component parts of Weber carburettor (1600 cc GT) (Sec. 16)

1	Choke plate
2	Choke plate shaft
3	Choke plate lever assembly
4	Fast idle lever
5	Filter
6	Filter retaining screw
7	Float
8	Float pivot pin
9	Main jet (primary)
10	Accelerator blanking plug
11	Secondary throttle shaft
12	Primary throttle shaft
13	Throttle plate
14	Accelerator pump diaphragm
15	Gasket
16	Accelerator pump cover
17	Gasket
18	Retaining ring
19	Auto. choke cover
20	Thermostatic spring housing
21	Insulating gasket assembly
22	Shaft and lever assembly
23	Slow running jet and holder assembly
24	Diaphragm and shaft assembly
25	Cover
26	Mixture control screw
27	Throttle stop lever
28	Throttle control lever
29	Secondary throttle lever
30	Lower body
31	Primary diffuser tube
32	Accelerator pump discharge jet
33	Accelerator pump discharge jet ball check valve
34	Primary main air correction jet
35	Needle valve
36	Needle valve housing
37	Spring loaded diaphragm assembly
38	Upper body

14 Unscrew the primary and secondary main jets from the base of the float chamber. **Do not** remove the power valve from the centre (Fig. 3.32).

15 Unscrew and remove the accelerator pump discharge valve from the top of the carburettor body together with the discharge jet.

16 Unscrew the air correction jets from the top of the lower carburettor body. Invert the latter and slide out the emulsion tubes.

17 Unscrew the two idling jet holders, one from either side of the carburettor body and remove the idling jets.

18 Remove the volume control screw and spring from the base of the body.

19 Unhook the secondary throttle return spring from the secondary throttle control lever and then unscrew the nut located on the primary throttle shaft. Remove the throttle control lever, spacer, secondary throttle control lever, bush, waved washer, fast idler lever, washer, slow running stop lever and spring from the spindle.

20 Unscrew and remove the nut, washer and lever from the secondary throttle spindle.

21 Undo the two screws that secure each throttle plate to the shaft. Lift away the two throttle plates. Remove the burrs from the threaded holes and then withdraw the shaft.

22 Dismantling is now complete and all parts should be thoroughly washed and cleaned in petrol. Remove any sediment in the float chamber and drillings but take care not to scratch the fine drillings whilst doing so. Remove all traces of old gaskets using a sharp knife. When all parts are clean reassembly can begin.

23 To reassemble first insert the fuel filter into the upper body and screw in the retaining plug.

24 Insert the choke spindle in its bore, locate the choke plate in the shaft with the minus (−) sign uppermost. Secure the choke plates in position with two screws each. Peen over the threaded ends to lock.

25 Fit the dust seal to the air cleaner mounting flange.

26 Carefully insert the choke rod through the seal and connect it to the choke spindle lever.

27 Position the spring loaded automatic choke diaphragm assembly in the upper body and secure with three screws and spring washers.

28 Using a box spanner screw in the needle valve housing. A new fibre washer should always be fitted under the housing.

29 Fit the needle valve into the housing (make sure it is the correct way up). Offer up the float to the pivot bracket and retain in position with the pivot pin. Check the float adjustment, as described in the next sub-Section.

Float level adjustment

30 Invert the upper body and using a ruler or vernier gauge, measure the clearance between the surface of the upper body and the bottom of the float. This dimension should be 1.4 in. (35.5 mm). To adjust bend tang 'A' (Figs. 3.33 and 3.34).

31 Now hold the upper body the normal way up and again measure the distance between the surface of the upper body and the bottom of the float. This should be 2.0 in (51.0 mm). To adjust, bend tang 'B'. Make sure that both floats are level (Figs. 3.34 and 3.35).

32 The emulsion tubes, air correction jets and the primary and secondary main jets may next be refitted to their locations in the lower body.

33 Position the idling jets within their holders and then fit the assemblies together with new 'O' rings, one to each side of the lower body.

34 Locate the discharge valve, fitted with a new washer to both the top and lower face, onto the discharge valve and secure the assembly to the lower body.

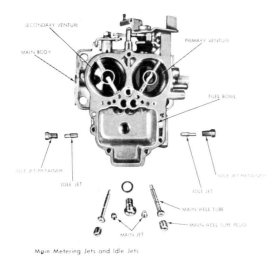

Main Metering Jets and Idle Jets

Fig. 3.32. Location of jets (Weber) (Sec. 16)

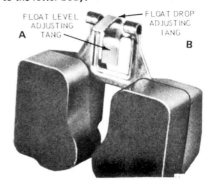

Fig. 3.34. Adjustment of float assembly (Sec. 16)

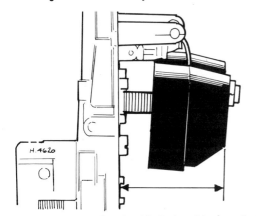

Fig. 3.33. Checking float level (raised position) on dual barrel carburettor (Sec. 16)

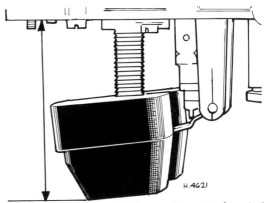

Fig. 3.35. Checking float level (suspended position) on dual barrel carburettor (Sec. 16)

35 Position a new gasket, diaphragm and spring onto the accelerator pump cover and secure the cover assembly with the four screws and spring washers.

36 Refit the volume control screw and spring to the base of the lower body.

37 Slide the throttle shafts into their appropriate bores and fit the throttle plates into the shafts so that the 78° mark is towards the base of the lower body. Secure the throttle plates with two screws each and peen over the ends to stop them working loose.

38 Fit the lever and washer onto the secondary throttle spindle and secure with the nut and spring washer.

39 Slide the following parts onto the primary throttle shaft: spring, slow running top lever, washer, fast idle lever, wave washer, bush, secondary throttle control lever, spacer.

40 Next engage the secondary throttle return spring with the throttle control lever. Locate the choke operating lever, spring and washer and retain in position with the screw.

41 Fit a new gasket onto the top face of the lower body and offer up the upper body to the lower body. Secure the two body halves with the retaining screws and spring washers.

42 Check the clearance between the secondary throttle plate and the carburettor body at its widest point with the secondary throttle closed, adjust the stop until the specified clearance is obtained of 0.0015 in (0.038 mm) (Fig. 3.36).

43 Refit the accelerator pump lever and secure with the pin. Carefully drive the pin home until the serrated end is flush with the casting.

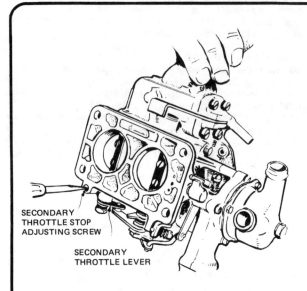

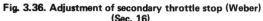

Fig. 3.36. Adjustment of secondary throttle stop (Weber) (Sec. 16)

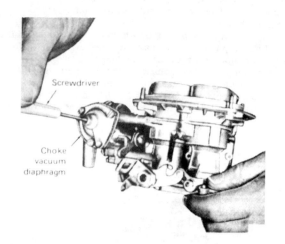

Fig. 3.38. Adjustment of automatic choke during reassembly (Weber) (Sec. 16) (The threads must be flush with inside of cover)

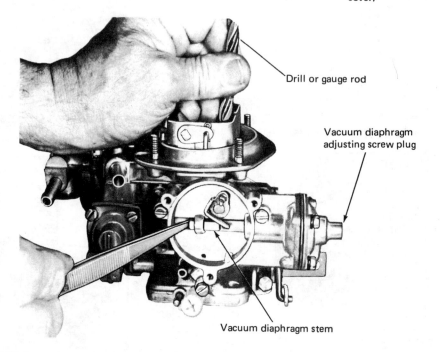

Fig. 3.37. Pushing in vacuum diaphragm stem during measurement of choke plate pull down (Sec. 16)

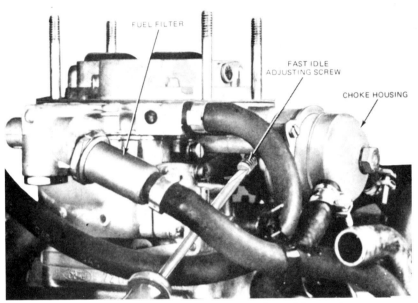

Fig. 3.39. Adjustment of fast idle speed (Weber) (Sec. 16)

44 The automatic choke is all that remains to be fitted. Position the diaphragm and shaft assembly within the inner choke housing. Locate the spring and cover on the diaphragm and retain with the screws.

45 Place the insulation gasket on the inner housing and follow this with the thermostatic spring housing. Take care to ensure that the spring loop engages with the crankpin. Check the choke plate pull-down, as described in the next sub-Section.

Choke plate pull down - adjustment

46 Set the fast idle lever on the top step of the fast idle cam.

47 Carefully depress the diaphragm stem to its stop (Fig. 3.37).

48 Now measure the clearance between the lower edge of the choke plate and the carburettor body. This should be between 0.12 and 0.24 in. (3.0 and 6.0 mm).

49 If necessary, adjust by removing the diaphragm cover plug and turning the adjusting screw as necessary.

50 Align the locating marks on the automatic choke housing and secure with locking ring and screws.

51 Reassembly is now complete, but if new components have been fitted, carry out the following checks and adjustments:

De-choke clearance - adjustment

52 Gently hold the throttle lever in the fully open position and then apply pressure to the top edge of the choke plate so eliminating any slackness in the choke linkage.

53 Measure the distance between the lower edge of the choke plate and the air intake wall. This should be between 0.138 to 0.158 in. (3.5 to 4.0 mm). If adjustment is necessary bend the tabs on the fast idle lever where it touches the fast idle cam.

Fast idle cam clearance

54 Insert an 0.156 in. (3.969 mm) diameter drill between the lower edge of the choke valve plate and the carburettor body.

55 Hold the fast idle screw on the second step of the fast idle cam and measure the clearance between the tang of the choke lever and the arm on the fast idle cam. If necessary, bend the choke lever to adjust. The following two adjustments should be carried out after the carburettor has been refitted to the engine.

Choke thermostatic spring housing - adjustment

56 Refer to Section 3, and remove the air cleaner assembly.

57 Slacken the three choke cover retaining screws. It is

permissible for the cover to be rotated slightly without partially draining the cooling system.

58 Move the choke cover 0.125 inch (3.175 mm) to weaken (anticlockwise) from the index mark. It will be observed that a small punch mark indicates the correct location.

59 Retighten the three cover retaining screws and finally refit the air cleaner.

Fast idle speed - adjustment

60 To adjust the engine fast idle first run the engine until it reaches its normal operating temperature (Fig. 3.39).

61 Adjust the position of the fast idle screw on the second step of the fast idle cam until it is against the shoulder on the first step.

62 The fast idle speed should now be set to specification by adjusting the screw in, or out.

17 Dual barrel carburettor (2000 cc engine) - overhaul and adjustment

1 The carburettors fitted to the 2000 cc engine are similar to the 1600 cc Weber type unit and differ only in detail (Figs. 3.40 and 3.41).

2 The carburettor fitted to late model cars incorporates an electric (supplementary) choke and other minor modifications.

3 Refer to Specifications Section for precise details of jet calibrations etc.

18 Emission control systems - description and application

1 All cars are fitted with a *positive crankcase ventilation (PCV) system,* as described in Section 24, Chapter 1.

2 Cars fitted with the 2000 cc power unit and destined for operation in North America may be equipped with one or more of the following systems depending on date of manufacture.

(i)   *Temperature controlled air cleaner,* as described in Section 4 of this Chapter.

(ii)   *Fuel evaporative emission control,* to contain petrol vapours which evaporate from the fuel tank and the fuel bowl of the carburettor. The vapours are stored in an activated carbon canister when the engine is not running but when the engine is

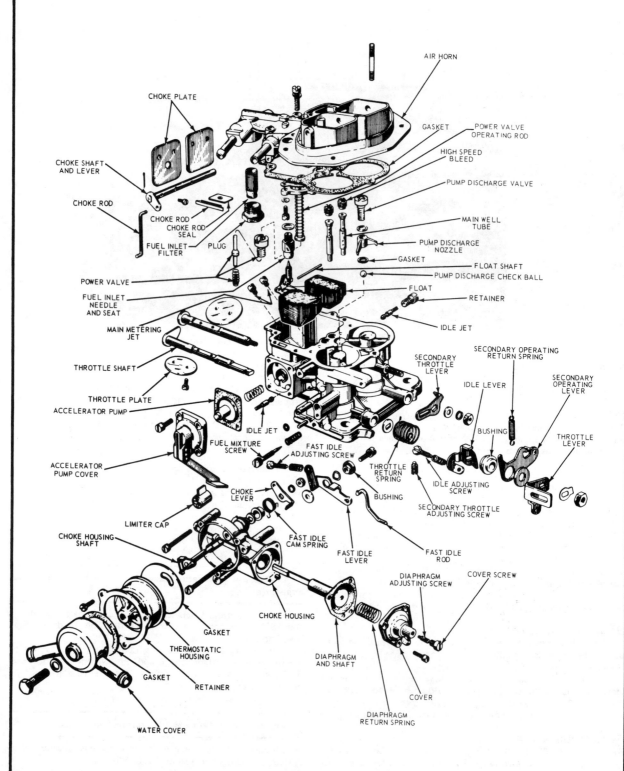

Fig. 3.40. Exploded view of Motorcraft dual barrel carburettor (2000 cc engine) up to 1974 (Sec. 17)

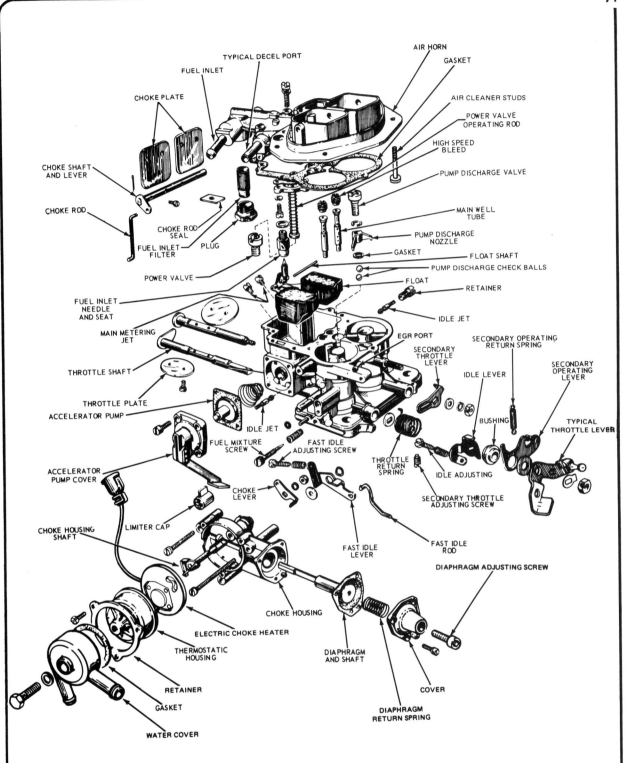

Fig. 3.41. Exploded view of Motorcraft dual barrel carburettor (2000 cc engine) 1974 onwards (Sec. 17)

started and running, they are drawn into the intake manifold and burned during the normal combustion cycle.

(iii)   Exhaust gas recirculation (E.G.R.) designed to reduce the emission of nitrogen oxides from the exhaust by reducing the combustion chamber temperature through the introduction, or recycling of small quantities of exhaust gas.

(iv)   Air injection (thermactor) system. By using an engine driven air pump, fresh air is injected into the hot exhaust gas stream as it leaves the exhaust ports. This causes a certain amount of after burning (oxidisation) to reduce the concentrations of hydro carbons and carbon monoxide in the exhaust gas. The system is only installed on cars operating in

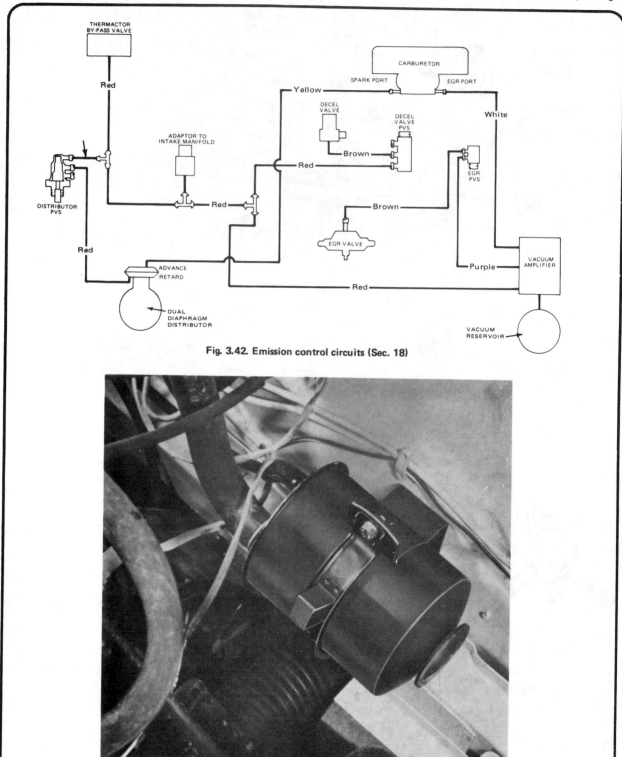

Fig. 3.42. Emission control circuits (Sec. 18)

Fig. 3.43. Fuel evaporative emission control system charcoal canister (Sec. 19)

California.

(v)   Spark delay valve (SDV). This is essentially a supplementary ignition advance/retard device to retard the ignition spark during periods of brisk acceleration when under normal ignition timing conditions, heavy concentrations of rich mixture would be emitted.

(vi)   Deceleration (decel) valves, used to provide an enriched mixture during periods of deceleration. The valves provide momentary fuel/air flow by bypassing the carburettor when the throttle valve is closed. The valve is only used on cars with manual transmission.

3   It is emphasised that in order to ensure the lowest possible emission levels, the engine condition and state of tune must be as specified before any adjustment or servicing of individual emission control systems can have full effect.

19 Fuel evaporative emission control system - maintenance

1   Periodically check the security of the connecting hoses and the operation of the fuel tank filler cap valves. The valves can be tested by removing the cap and alternately blowing and sucking the valves.

2   Every 24,000 miles (39,000 km) disconnect the hoses from the charcoal canister which is mounted within the engine compartment, dismount the canister and renew it (Fig. 3.43).

20 Exhaust gas recirculation (E.G.R.) system - maintenance

1   Periodically inspect the condition and security of the system vacuum hoses.

2   Every 12,000 miles (19,000 km), remove the E.G.R. valve for cleaning.

3   Check the small orifice in the valve body for deposits and clear it with a small twist drill but on no account enlarge the hole.

4   *With valves that can be dismantled,* separate the diaphragm section and then clean all deposits from the metal components using a wire brush or scraper. Reassemble using a new gasket.

5   In a similar manner, remove the deposits from the exhaust gas passages in the carburettor spacer and the exhaust gas passage in the intake manifold. The carburettor will have to be removed and probably the intake manifold to permit a thorough job to be made of the cleaning. Do not allow any particles or dust to enter the engine or carburettor during these operations.

6   *With valves which are sealed* and cannot be dismantled, renew them complete at the specified mileage as indicated for cleaning the valves which can be dismantled.

7   Any malfunction of the E.G.R. system can only be checked out with special equipment and provided all connections are secure it will probably be more realistic to eliminate the problem by substituting a new E.G.R. valve for the original one.

21 Air injection (thermactor) system - maintenance

1   Periodically inspect the condition and security of the system connecting hoses.

2   Check the air pump drivebelt tension and adjust if necessary to provide a total deflection of ½ in. (12.7 mm) at the mid-point of the longest run of the belt (see Chapter 2).

3   Any malfunction of the system will require the use of special testing equipment but provided the air pump is producing a good air pressure (remove hose to verify) the non-return valves can be checked in the following way: (Fig. 3.44).

4   Run the engine until normal operating temperature is reached.

5   Disconnect the air supply hose from the non-return valve. Visually inspect the position of the valve plate inside the valve body. It should be lightly seated away from the air or exhaust manifold.

6   Insert a probe into the hose nozzle of the non-return valve

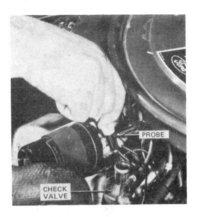

Fig. 3.44. Checking non-return valve (Thermactor system) (Sec. 21)

and depress the valve plate. Release the probe and the plate should return freely to its original position.

7   Repeat the foregoing operations if a second non-return valve is incorporated in the system.

8   Leaving the hoses disconnected, start the engine and slowly increase the engine speed to 1500 rpm at the same time watching for the escape of exhaust fumes from the non-return valves. Where this is evident or the valve is stuck closed, renew the valve complete. The valve will flutter at engine idling speeds; this is a normal condition.

9   A final test can be carried out by disconnecting the hose which runs between the bypass valve and the non-return valve. Disconnect from the bypass valve end (Fig. 3.45).

10 Start the engine and allow it to idle. Check that air is flowing from the bypass valve hose connecting port to the exhaust ports. For a period of between 5 to 8 seconds, pinch the end of the bypass valve vacuum hose to simulate the air bypass cycle. Airflow through the bypass valve should stop or diminish for a short period proving the valve to be serviceable.

11 After a very high mileage has been covered, the centrifugal filter fan of the air pump may require renewal. To do this, loosen the air pump mountings to relieve the drivebelt tension and remove the pump pulley.

12 Prise the outer disc loose and extract the filter fan with a pair of pliers. Do not attempt to remove the metal drive hub (Fig. 3.46).

13 Draw the new filter fan into position using the pulley and securing bolts.

14 A new fan may squeak initially until the outer sealing lip has worn in.

15 Re-install the drivebelt and adjust the tension.

16 Tighten the air pump mounting and adjustment bolts to the specified torque wrench settings.

22 Spark delay valve (SDV) - testing

1   Special equipment is required to test this valve and it is recommended that it is either tested by your dealer if a fault is suspected, or it is checked by substitution of a new valve.

23 Deceleration (decel) valve - checking and adjustment

1   Malfunction or incorrect adjustment of this valve can cause excessively high engine idling speed.

2   Rough idling or evidence of an excessively weak mixture may be due to a split decel valve diaphragm. To eliminate this possibility, have the engine idling and at normal operating temperature. Place a finger over the small hole in the base of the valve and if the idling quality improves or there is a marked change in

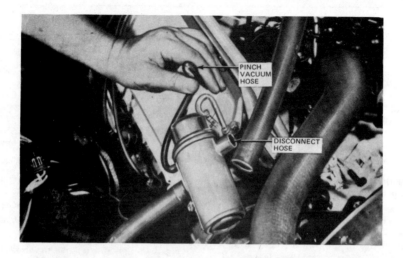

Fig. 3.45. Checking bypass valve (Thermactor system) (Sec. 21)

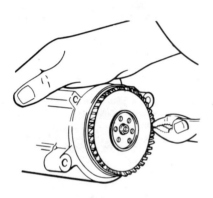

Fig. 3.46. Removing filter fan from air pump (Thermactor system) (Sec. 21)

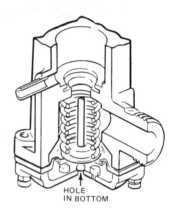

Fig. 3.47. Cutaway view of deceleration valve (Sec. 23)

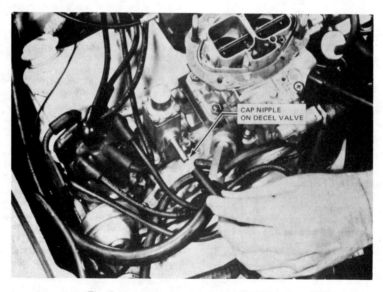

Fig. 3.48. Testing deceleration valve (Sec. 23)

engine speed then the diaphragm is split and must be renewed.

3   If the foregoing test proves satisfactory, then proceed to check the valve adjustment. A tachometer must be connected to the engine and it should be attached in accordance with the maker's instructions.

4   Disconnect the hose, which runs between the decel valve and the carburettor (from the decel valve) and then cap the valve nipple (Fig. 3.48).

5   Increase the engine speed to 3,000 rpm and hold it there for about 5 seconds. Release the throttle when the engine speed should return to idling. If this is not the case, check the accelerator linkage for freedom of movement. If this is operating correctly, remove the cap from the valve nipple and 'tee' a vacuum gauge into the hose which runs between the decel valve and the carburettor.

6   Increase the engine speed to 3,000 rpm and hold for 5 seconds. Release the throttle and check the time taken for the vacuum gauge needle to drop to zero. This should be between 2 and 5 seconds.

7   If the time taken is outside the period specified, adjust the valve by turning the screw inwards to reduce the time taken for closure or unscrew it to increase the time.

8   If altering the position of the screw has no effect, renew the valve.

9   Malfunctioning of the decel valve can be caused by incorrect initial (static) ignition timing or a rich carburettor mixture.

24 Fuel tank - removal and installation

1   The fuel tank is located in the rear luggage compartment with the filler pipe connected to the flush fitting pressure and vacuum sensitive filler cap located in the right-hand quarter panel. The filler pipe is connected to vertically mounted tank by a convoluted hose.

2   Remove the filler cap and using a length of rubber hose approximately ½ inch bore, syphon out as much petrol as possible.

3   Disconnect the battery earth terminal.

4   Slacken the clip that secures the flexible hose to the fuel tank neck.

5   Disconnect the fuel and vapour lines from the tank.

6   Undo and remove the four bolts and spring washers that secure the fuel tank and partially lower the tank.

7   Disconnect the fuel tank sender unit cable and lift away the fuel tank.

8   If necessary detach the sender unit by rotating the lock ring. Carefully withdraw the sender unit ensuring the float arm is not

bent. Recover the sealing ring. It may be necessary to tilt the unit to assist removal. Note the float arm hangs down when in the fitted position.

9   Refitting the sender unit and the fuel tank is the reverse sequence to removal. Test the operation of the sender unit by switching on the ignition. Wait 30 seconds and observe the gauge reading.

25 Fuel tank - cleaning and repair

1   With time it is likely that sediment will collect in the bottom of the fuel tank. Condensation, resulting in rust and other impurities will usually be found in the fuel tank of any car more than three or four years old.

2   When the tank is removed, it should be vigorously flushed out and turned upside down and if facilities are available, steam cleaned.

3   Never weld, solder or bring a naked light close to an empty fuel tank unless it has been steamed out for at least two hours or washed internally with boiling water and detergent several times. If using the latter method finally fill the tank with boiling water and detergent and allow to stand for at least three hours.

26 Accelerator pedal - removal and refitting

1   Release the throttle cable clip and detach the throttle cable from the lever on the accelerator pedal shaft.

2   Carefully disconnect the accelerator pedal return spring.

3   Withdraw the retaining pins from each side of the right-hand bush.

4   The accelerator pedal and shaft may now be withdrawn from the pedal mounting bracket.

5   Refitting the accelerator pedal is the reverse sequence to removal. Lubricate the bushes and cable attachment with a little grease.

6   It is now necessary to adjust the accelerator pedal position.

7   *Manual transmission:* Place a 0.015 inch (0.381 mm) feeler gauge between the return stop and the pedal arms. Adjust the return stop located under the instrument panel until the front face of the accelerator pedal pad is 4.5 inch (114.3 mm) from the front panel. Now adjust the accelerator cable to remove slackness (Fig. 3.51).

8   *Automatic transmission:* Detach the accelerator cable at the bell crank ball joint. Now adjust the accelerator pedal pad length to 4.5 inch (114.3 mm) from the top face of the pedal to the floor by turning the pedal stop adjustment bolt which is located

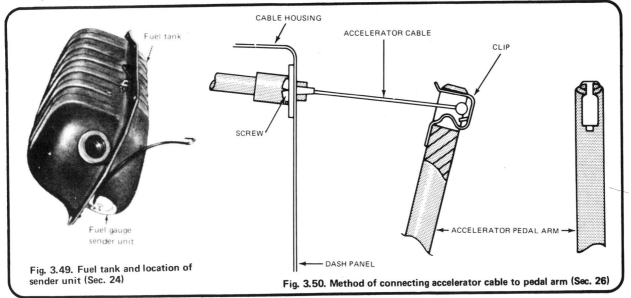

Fig. 3.49. Fuel tank and location of sender unit (Sec. 24)

Fig. 3.50. Method of connecting accelerator cable to pedal arm (Sec. 26)

under the instrument panel. If necessary reset the engine idle speed. Adjust the accelerator cable until it just slides into the bell crank ball joint and reconnect. Finally remove the air cleaner and ensure that the carburettor throttle plates open fully and return to the idle position when the pedal is released.

27 Accelerator cable - renewal

1 Open the bonnet and detach the accelerator cable from the accelerator lever ball stud.
2 Slacken the two cable adjustment nuts on the bracket and slip the cable from the bracket.
3 Detach the cable from the accelerator pedal shaft lever.
4 Remove the cable retainer at the dash panel and remove the

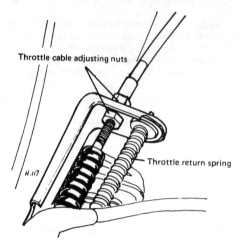

Fig. 3.51. Accelerator cable adjustment (Secs. 26 and 27)

cable.
5 Refitting the cable is the reverse sequence to removal.
6 Adjust as described in the preceding Section.

28 Exhaust system and manifolds

1 The design of the inlet and exhaust manifolds varies between the models, as illustrated. Always tighten manifold bolts and nuts to the specified torque and sequence (Figs. 3.52 to 3.57).
2 The silencers and exhaust pipe are suspended on flexible mountings and supported with rigid brackets (Figs. 3.58 and 3.59).
3 Examination of the exhaust pipe and silencers at regular intervals is worthwhile as small defects may be repairable when, if left they will almost certainly require renewal of one of the sections of the system. Also, any leaks, apart from the noise factor, may cause poisonous exhaust gases to get inside the car which can be unpleasant, to say the least, even in mild concentrations. Prolonged inhalation could cause sickness and giddiness.
4 As the sleeve connections and clamps are usually very difficult to separate it is quicker and easier in the long run to remove the complete system from the car when renewing a section. It can be expensive if another section is damaged when trying to separate a bad section from it.
5 To remove the system first remove the bolts holding the tail pipe bracket to the body. Support the rear silencer on something to prevent cracking or kinking the pipes elsewhere.
6 Disconnect the centre mounting.
7 Disconnect the manifold to downpipe connecting flange and then withdraw the complete exhaust system from below and out to the rear of the vehicle. If necessary, jack up the rear of the vehicle to provide more clearance.
8 Badly corroded clamps should be cut off and new ones purchased. Cut the bad sections from the system, clean up the socket joints and insert the new sections but do not tighten the clamps at this stage.
9 Install the complete system to the car by attaching the

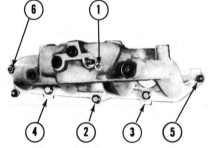

Fig. 3.52. Inlet manifold nut tightening sequence (Sec. 28)

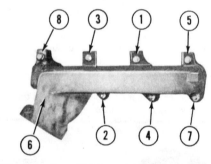

Fig. 3.53. Exhaust manifold nut tightening sequence (Sec. 28)

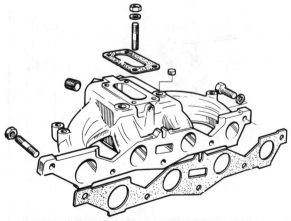

Fig. 3.54. Inlet manifold (1600 cc GT and 2000 cc) (Sec. 28)

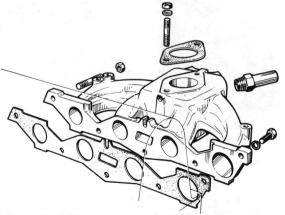

Fig. 3.55. Inlet manifold (1600 cc) (Sec. 28)

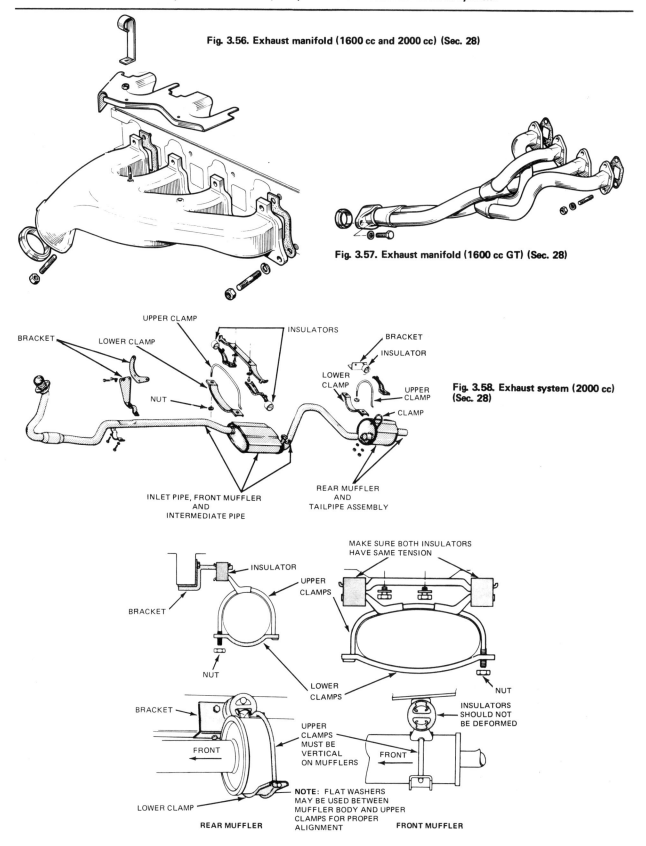

Fig. 3.56. Exhaust manifold (1600 cc and 2000 cc) (Sec. 28)

Fig. 3.57. Exhaust manifold (1600 cc GT) (Sec. 28)

Fig. 3.58. Exhaust system (2000 cc) (Sec. 28)

Fig. 3.59. Exhaust system mountings (2000 cc) (Sec. 28)

mountings. Now twist the sections of the system to obtain correct alignment and then deflect the silencers and pipes sideways to ensure that they do not foul any adjacent components. Finally tighten the clamps and mountings.

29 Fault diagnosis - fuel system

Symptom	Reason/s
Excessive fuel consumption*	Air filter choked
	General leaks from fuel system
	Float chamber fuel level too high
	Rich mixture
	Incorrect valve clearances
	Dragging brakes
	Tyres under inflated

May also be caused by faulty condenser or sticking counterweights in distributor

Symptom	Reason/s
Insufficient fuel delivery or weak mixture	Clogged fuel line filter
	Fuel inlet valve stuck
	Faulty fuel pump
	Leaking fuel pump unions
	Leaking inlet manifold gasket
	Leaking carburettor mounting flange gasket
	Incorrect mixture adjustment
	Smell of petrol after switching off engine at high ambient temperature
	Faulty float chamber vent hose. Fit modified hose.

30 Fault diagnosis - emission control system

Symptom	Reason/s
P.C.V. system	
Escaping fumes from engine	Clogged P.C.V. valve
	Split or collapsed hoses
Fuel evaporative control system	
Fuel odour or rough running engine	Choked carbon canister
	Stuck filler cap valve
	Collapsed or split hoses
Air injection system (Thermactor)	
Fume emission from exhaust pipe	Slack air pump drive belt
	Split or collapsed hoses
	Clogged air pump filter fan
	Defective air pump
	Leaking pressure relief valve
Exhaust gas recirculation system (E.G.R.)	
Rough idling	Faulty or dirty E.G.R. valve
	Disconnected or split vacuum hose
	Leaking valve gasket
Deceleration valve	
Rough idling	Split valve diaphragm

Chapter 4 Ignition system

Contents

Specifications

Distributor

Make	Bosch or Ford (Motorcraft)
Type:	
1600 cc and 1600 cc GT	Mechanical contact breaker with centrifugal and vacuum advance
2000 cc (up to 1974)	Mechanical contact breaker with centrifugal and vacuum advance
2000 cc (1974 onwards)	Mechanical contact breaker with centrifugal advance and dual diaphragm vacuum capsule
Contact breaker points gap	0.023 to 0.027 in. (0.58 to 0.69 mm)
Rotation	Clockwise, viewed from above
Drive	Gear on auxiliary shaft

	1600 cc	1600 cc GT	2000 cc*
Ignition timing (static)	6° BTDC	4° BTDC	6° BTDC
*except California (auto. trans.) which is	—	—	10° BTDC**
**Also consult individual vehicle tune-up sticker			
Dwell angle (Motorcraft distributor)		38 to 40°	
Dwell angle (Bosch distributor)		48 to 52°	

Firing order ... ...   1 - 3 - 4 - 2

Coil
Type	Oil filled used in conjunction with 1.5 ohm ballast resistor

Spark plugs
Type:	
1600 cc and 1600 cc GT	Autolite BF22
2000 cc	Motorcraft BF32
Size	18 mm
Gap	0.025 in. (0.64 mm)

Condenser
Capacity	0.21 to 0.25 m.fd

Torque wrench settings
	lb f ft	kg f m
Spark plug	26	3.6

1 General description

In order that the engine can run correctly it is necessary for an electrical spark to ignite the fuel/air mixture in the combustion chamber at exactly the right moment in relation to engine speed and load. The ignition system is based on feeding low tension voltage from the battery to the coil where it is converted to high tension voltage. The high tension voltage is powerful enough to jump the spark plug gap in the cylinders many times a second under high compression pressures, providing that the system is in good condition and that all adjustments are correct.

The ignition system is divided into two circuits, low tension and high tension.

The low tension circuit (sometimes known as the primary)

consists of the battery, lead to the control box, lead to the ignition switch, lead from the ignition switch to the low tension or primary coil windings (terminal +), and the lead from the low tension coil windings (coil terminal −) to the contact breaker points and condenser in the distributor.

The high tension circuit consists of the high tension or secondary coil windings, the heavy ignition lead from the centre of the coil to the centre of the distributor cap, the rotor arm, and the spark plug leads and spark plugs.

The system functions in the following manner. Low tension voltage is changed in the coil into high tension voltage by the opening and closing of the contact breaker points in the low tension circuit. High tension voltage is then fed via the carbon brush in the centre of the distributor cap to the rotor arm of the distributor cap, and each time it comes in line with one of the four metal segments in the cap, which are connected to the spark plug leads, the opening and closing of the contact breaker points causes the high tension voltage to build up, jump the gap from the rotor arm to the appropriate metal segment and so via the spark plug lead to the spark plug, where it finally jumps the spark plug gap before going to earth.

The ignition is advanced and retarded automatically, to ensure the spark occurs at just the right instant for the particular load at the prevailing engine speed.

The ignition advance is controlled both mechanically and by a vacuum operated system. The mechanical governor comprises two weights, which move out from the distributor shaft as the engine speed rises due to centrifugal force. As they move outward they rotate the cam relative to the distributor shaft, and so advance the spark. The weights are held in position by two light springs and it is the tension of the springs which is largely responsible for correct spark advancement.

The vacuum control consists of a diaphragm, one side of which is connected via a small bore tube to the carburettor, and the other side to the contact breaker plate. Depression in the inlet manifold and carburettor, which varies with engine speed and throttle opening, causes the diaphragm to move so moving the contact breaker plate, and advancing or retarding the spark. A fine degree of control is achieved by a spring in the vacuum assembly.

On cars with 2000 cc engines a dual diaphragm type distributor may be encountered according to the date of manufacture and the emission control systems employed. The outer diaphragm is connected to carburettor vacuum (above the throttle valve plates) to advance the ignition timing. The inner diaphragm is connected to intake manifold vacuum so that when vacuum conditions are high during engine idle or deceleration, the ignition timing will be retarded to help reduce the emission of unburned hydrocarbons.

Where a dual diaphragm distributor is fitted, one or more ported vacuum switches (PVS) are incorporated in the vacuum lines (see Section 16).

The wiring harness includes a high resistance wire in the ignition coil feed circuit and it is very important that only a 'ballast resistor' type ignition coil is used. The lead is identified by its white with grey colour tracer colour coding and has a resistance of 1.4 - 1.6 ohms. The starter solenoid has an extra terminal so that a lead from the solenoid to the coil supplies current direct to the coil when the starter motor is operated. The ballast resistor wire is therefore by-passed and battery voltage is fed to the ignition system so giving easier starting.

2 Contact breaker points - adjustment

1 To adjust the contact breaker points to the correct gap, first release the two clips securing the distributor cap to the distributor body, and lift away the cap. Clean the cap inside and out with a dry cloth. It is unlikely that the four segments will be badly burned or scored, but if they are the cap will have to be renewed.

2 Inspect the carbon brush contact located in the top of the cap to ensure that it is not broken and stands proud of the plastic surface.

3 Lift away the rotor arm and check the contact spring on the top of the rotor arm. It must be clean and have adequate tension to ensure good contact.

4 Gently prise the contact breaker points open to examine the condition of their faces. If they are rough, pitted or dirty it will be necessary to remove them for resurfacing, or for replacement points to be fitted.

5 Assuming the points are satisfactory, or that they have been cleaned or renewed, measure the gap between the points with feeler gauges but first slowly turn the crankshaft until the heel of the breaker arm is on the highest point of the cam. The gap should be between 0.023 and 0.027 in. (0.58 and 0.69 mm).

6 If the gap varies from that specified, slacken the single securing screw on Bosch type distributors or two screws on Ford type distributors, to release the contact breaker plate (photo).

7 Adjust the contact breaker gap by inserting a screwdriver in the notched hole in the contact breaker plate. Turn clockwise to increase and anti-clockwise to decrease the gap. When the gap is correct, tighten the securing screw/s and check the gap again (photo).

8 Replace the rotor arm and distributor cap. Retain in position with the two clips.

9 The use of a dwell meter is recommended for accurate points gap setting.

2.6 Slackening contact plate screw (Ford)

2.7 Resetting contact breaker points (Ford)

3 Contact breaker points - renewal

1 If the contact breaker points are burned, pitted or badly worn, they must be removed and either renewed or their faces must be ground smooth.

2 Lift off the rotor arm by pulling it straight up from the top end of the cam spindle.

3 **Bosch**

a) Detach the low tension lead terminal from the internal terminal post and then undo and remove the screw that retains the contact breaker assembly to the base plate. Lift away the two contact breaker points.

b) To refit the points first locate the fixed point and lightly tighten the retaining screw. Smear a trace of grease onto the cam to lubricate the moving point heel and then fit the moving point pivot and reset the gap as described in Section 2.

4 **Ford**

a) Slacken the self-tapping screw securing the condenser and low tension lead to the contact breaker point assembly. Slide out the forked ends of the lead terminals.

b) Undo and remove the two screws that secure the contact breaker points assembly to the distributor base plate. Lift away the points assembly.

c) To refit the points is the reverse sequence to removal. Smear a trace of grease onto the cam to lubricate the moving point heel, and then reset the gap as described in Section 2.

5 Refit the rotor arm, distributor cap and retaining clips.

4 Condenser - removal, testing and refitting

1 The purpose of the condenser (capacitor) is to ensure that when the contact breaker points open there is no sparking across them which would waste voltage and cause wear.

2 The condenser is fitted in parallel with the contact breaker points. If it develops a short circuit, it will cause ignition failure as the contact breaker points will be prevented from correctly interrupting the low tension circuit.

3 If the engine becomes very difficult to start or begins to miss after several miles of running and the breaker points show signs of excessive burning then the condition of the condenser must be suspect. One further test can be made by separating the points by hand with the ignition switched on. If this is accompanied by a bright flash, it is indicative that the condenser has failed.

4 Without special test equipment the only safe way to diagnose condenser trouble is to replace a suspected unit with a new one and note if there is any improvement.

5 To remove the condenser from the distributor take off the distributor cap and rotor arm.

6 *Bosch:* Release the condenser cable from the side of the distributor body and then undo and remove the screw that secures the condenser to the side of the distributor body. Lift away the condenser.

7 *Ford:* Slacken the self-tapping screw holding the condenser lead and low tension lead to the contact breaker points. Slide out the forked terminal on the end of the condenser low tension lead. Undo and remove the condenser retaining screw and remove the condenser from the breaker plate.

8 To refit the condenser, simply reverse the order of removal.

5 Distributor - lubrication

1 It is important that the distributor cam is lubricated with vaseline (petroleum jelly) or grease at 3,000 miles (5,000 km) or 3 monthly intervals. Also the automatic timing control weights and cam spindle are lubricated with engine oil.

2 Great care should be taken not to use too much lubricant as any excess that finds its way onto the contact breaker points could cause burning and misfiring.

3 To gain access to the cam spindle, lift away the distributor

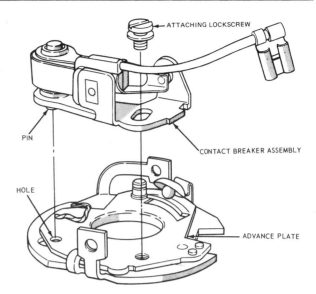

Fig. 4.1. Bosch type distributor contact breaker points and baseplate assembly (Sec. 3)

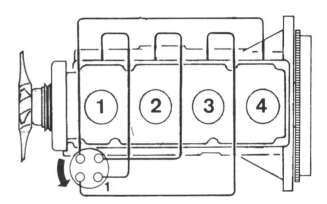

Fig. 4.2. Correct fitment of HT leads (Sec. 6)

cap and rotor arm. Apply no more than two drops of engine oil onto the felt pad. This will run down the spindle when the engine is hot and lubricate the bearings.

4 To lubricate the automatic timing control allow a few drops of oil to pass through the holes in the contact breaker base plate through which the four sided cam emerges. Apply not more than one drop of oil to the pivot post of the moving contact breaker point. Wipe away excess oil and refit the rotor arm and distributor cap.

6 Distributor - removal

1 To remove the distributor from the engine, mark the four spark plug leads so that they may be refitted to the correct plugs and pull off the four spark plug leads (Fig. 4.2).

2 Disconnect the high tension lead from the centre of the distributor cap by gripping the end cap and pulling. Also disconnect the low tension lead from the ignition coil.

3 Pull off the rubber union holding the vacuum pipe to the distributor vacuum advance housing. On dual diaphragm distributors, disconnect both vacuum pipes.

4 If it is not wished to disturb the timing turn the crankshaft until the timing marks are in line and the rotor arm is pointing to number 1 spark plug segment in the distributor cap. This will facilitate refitting the distributor providing the crankshaft is not moved whilst the distributor is away from the engine.

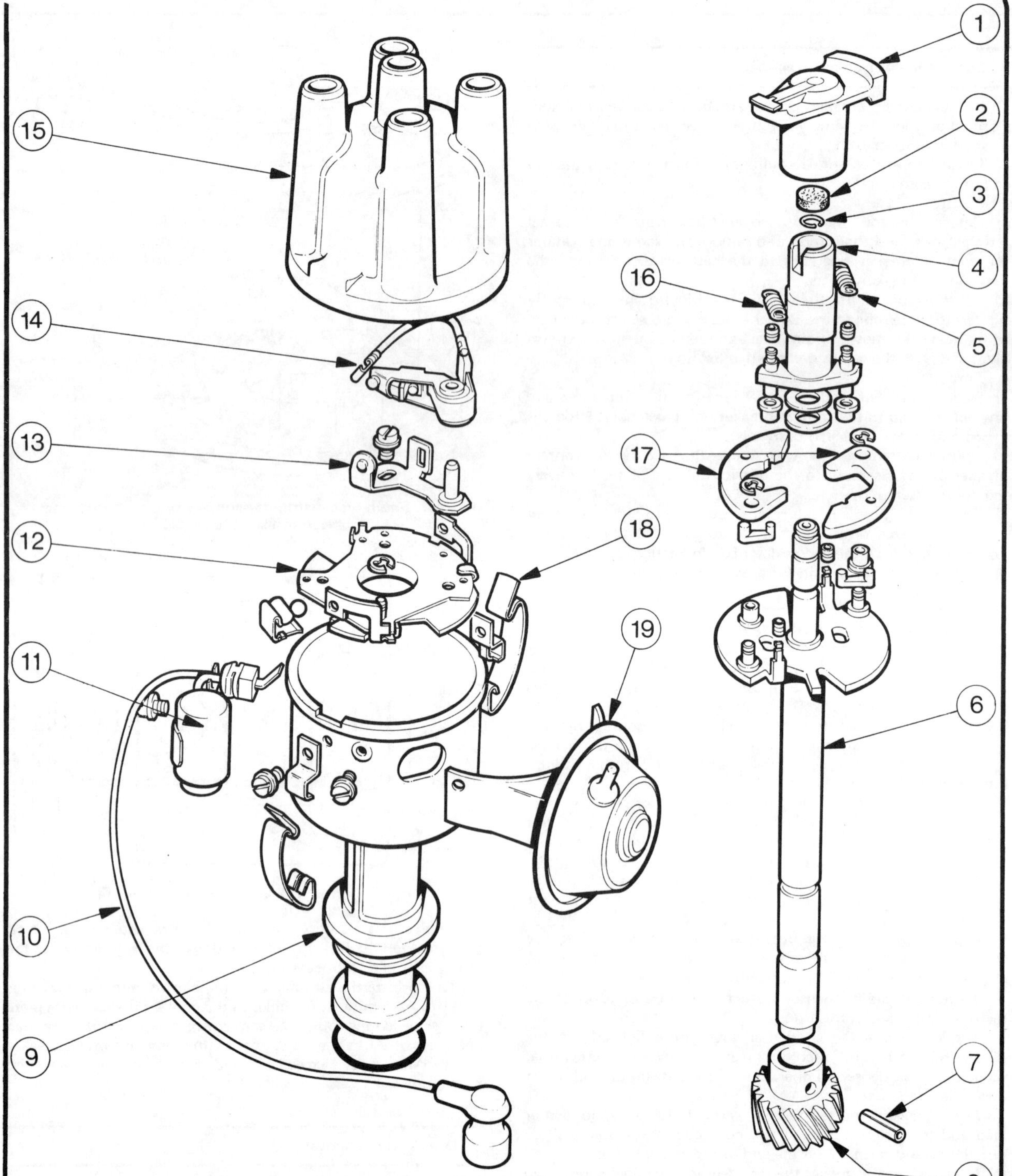

Fig. 4.3. Exploded view of Bosch distributor (Sec. 7)

1	Rotor	6	Shaft	11	Condenser	16	Counterweight spring
2	Lubricating felt	7	Roll pin	12	Baseplate	17	Counterweights
3	Circlip	8	Gear	13	Contact point (fixed)	18	Cap clip
4	Cam	9	Body	14	Contact point (movable)	19	Vacuum capsule
5	Counterweight spring	10	LT lead	15	Cap		unit

5 Remove the distributor body clamp bolt which holds the distributor clamp plate to the engine and lift out the distributor. (Fig. 4.4).

7 Distributor (Bosch) - dismantling

1 With the distributor on the bench, release the two spring clips retaining the cap and lift away the cap (Fig. 4.3).
2 Pull the rotor arm off the distributor cam spindle.
3 Remove the contact breaker points as described in Section 3.
4 Unscrew and remove the condenser securing screw and lift away the condenser and connector.
5 Next carefully remove the 'U' shaped clip from the pull rod of the vacuum unit.
6 Undo and remove the two screws securing the vacuum unit to the side of the distributor body. Lift away the vacuum unit.
7 Undo and remove the screws which fix the distributor cap spring clip retainer to the side of the distributor body. Lift away the two clips and retainers. This will also release the breaker plate assembly.
8 Lift away the contact breaker plate assembly from the inside of the distributor body.
9 Separate the breaker plate by removing the spring clip that holds the lower and upper plates together.
10 It is important that the primary and secondary springs of the automatic advance system are refitted in their original position during reassembly so the springs, weights, and upper plate must be marked accordingly.
11 Unhook the springs from the posts on the centrifugal weights.
12 Using a screwdriver release the cam from the cam spindle and recover the felt pad, lock ring, and thrust washers from the cam. Release the two springs from the cam plate and lift away the centrifugal weights and washers (Fig. 4.5).
13 Should it be necessary to remove the drive gear, using a suitable diameter parallel pin punch tap out the gear lock pin.
14 The gear may now be drawn off the shaft with a universal puller. If there are no means of holding the legs these must be bound together with wire to stop them springing apart during removal.
15 Finally withdraw the shaft from the distributor body.

8 Distributor (Ford) - dismantling

1 Remove the distributor cap and pull off the rotor arm.
2 Next prise off the small circlip from the vacuum unit pivot post.
3 Take out the two screws that hold the breaker plate to the distributor body and lift away.

4 Undo and remove the condenser retaining screw and lift away the condenser.
5 Take off the circlip, flat washer and wave washer from the base plate pivot post. Separate the two plates by bringing the holding down screw through the keyhole slot in the lower plate. Be careful not to lose the spring now left on the pivot post.
6 Pull the low tension lead and grommet from the lower plate.
7 Undo the two screws holding the vacuum unit to the body. Take off the unit.
8 To dismantle the vacuum unit, unscrew the bolt on the end of the unit and withdraw the vacuum spring, stop and shims.
9 The mechanical advance is next removed but first make a careful note of the assembly particularly which spring fits which post and the position of the advance springs. Then remove the advance springs.
10 Prise off the circlips from the governor weight pivot pins and take out the weights.
11 Dismantle the spindle by taking out the felt pad in the top of the spindle. Expand the exposed circlip and take it out.
12 Now mark which slot in the mechanical advance plate is occupied by the advance stop which stands up from the action plate, and lift the cam from the spindle.
13 It is only necessary to remove the spindle and lower plate if it is excessively worn. If this is the case, with a suitable diameter parallel pin punch tap out the gear lock pin.
14 The gear may now be drawn off the shaft using a suitable puller.
15 Finally withdraw the shaft from the distributor body.

9 Distributor - inspection and repair

1 Check the contact breaker points for wear as described in Section 2. Check the distributor cap for signs of tracking indicated by a thin black line between the segments. Renew the cap if any signs of tracking are found.
2 If the metal portion of the rotor arm is badly burned or loose, renew the arm. If only slightly burned clean the end with a fine file. Check that the contact spring has adequate pressure and the bearing surface is clean and in good condition.
3 Check that the carbon brush in the distributor cap is unbroken and stands proud of its holder.
4 Examine the centrifugal weights and pivots for wear and the advance springs for slackness. They can best be checked by comparing with new parts. If they are slack they must be renewed.
5 Check the points assembly for fit on the breaker plate, and the cam follower for wear.
6 Examine the fit of the spindle in the distributor body. If there is excessive side movement it will be necessary to either fit a new bush or obtain a new body.

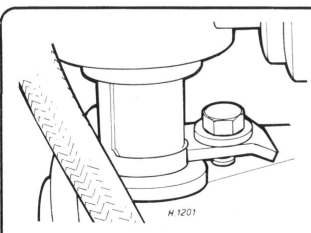

Fig. 4.4. Distributor clamp plate and securing bolt (Sec. 6)

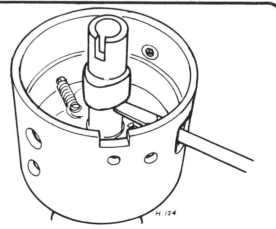

Fig. 4.5. Removal of cam from cam spindle (Bosch) (Sec. 7)

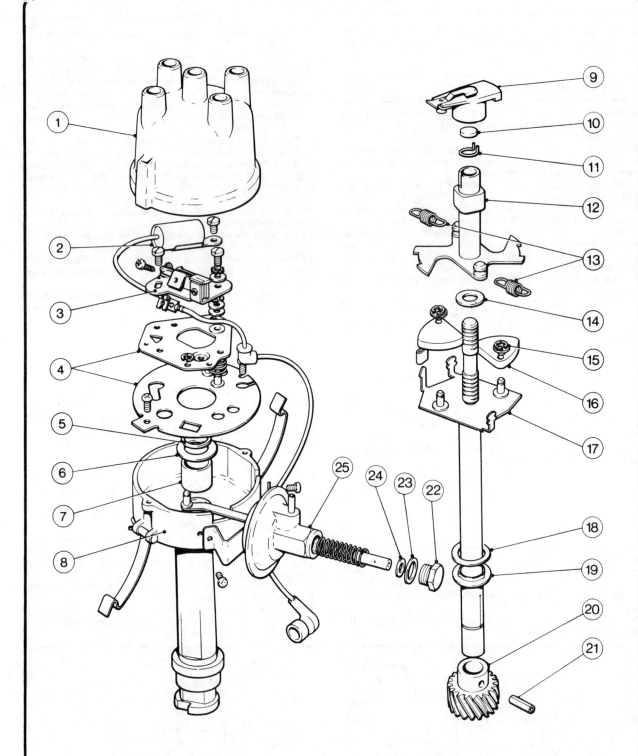

Fig. 4.6. Exploded view of Ford distributor (Sec. 8)

1	Cap	7	Bush	13	Counterweight springs	19	Washer
2	Condenser	8	Body	14	Washer	20	Gear
3	Contact points assembly	9	Rotor	15	Circlip	21	Pin
4	Baseplate	10	Lubrication felt	16	Counterweight	22	Nut
5	Thrust washer	11	Circlip	17	Shaft	23	Washer
6	Thrust washer	12	Cam	18	Spacer	24	Stop plate
						25	Vacuum capsule unit

10 Distributor (Bosch) - reassembly

1 To reassemble, first refit the two centrifugal weight washers onto the cam spindle. Smear a little grease onto the centrifugal weight contact faces and pivots and replace the weights in their original positions (Fig. 4.7).
2 Lubricate the upper end of the spindle with engine oil and slide on the cam. Hook the two springs onto the weight retainers so that they are refitted in their original positions.
3 Position thrust washer and lock ring in the cam. Carefully manipulate the lock ring into position using a screwdriver.
4 Refit the felt pad and thoroughly soak with engine oil.
5 Lubricate the distributor spindle with engine oil and insert it into the housing. The gear may now be tapped into position taking care to line up the lock pin holes in the gear and spindle. Support the spindle whilst performing this operation.
6 Fit a new lock pin to the gear and spindle and make sure that it is symmetrically positioned.
7 Locate the lower breaker plate in the distributor body. Place the distributor cap retaining spring clip and retainer on the outside of the distributor body and secure the retainers and lower breaker plate with the two screws.
8 Position the contact breaker point assembly in the breaker plate in such a manner that the entire lower surface of the assembly contacts the plate. Refit the contact breaker point assembly securing screw but do not fully tighten yet.
9 Hook the diaphragm assembly pull rod into contact with the pivot pin.
10 Secure the diaphragm to the distributor body with the two screws. Also refit the condenser to the terminal side of the

diaphragm bracket securing screw. The condenser must firmly contact its lower stop on the housing.
11 Apply a little grease or petroleum jelly to the cam and to the heel of the breaker lever.
12 Reset the contact breaker points as described in Section 3 and then replace the rotor arm and distributor cap.

11 Distributor (Ford) - reassembly

1 Reassembly is a straightforward reversal of the dismantling process but there are several points which must be noted.
2 Lubricate with the balance weights and other engine oil parts of the mechanical advance mechanism, the distributor shaft and the portion of the shaft on which the cam bears, during assembly. Do not oil excessively, but ensure these parts are adequately lubricated.
3 When fitting the spindle, first replace the thrust washers below the lower breaker plate before inserting into the distributor body. Next fit the wave washer and thrust washer at the lower end and replace the drive gear. Secure it with a new pin.
4 Assemble the upper and lower spindle with the advance stop in the correct slot (the one which was marked) in the mechanical advance plate.
5 After assembling the advance weights and springs, check that they move freely without binding (photo).
6 Before assembling the breaker plates make sure that the nylon bearing studs are correctly located in their holes in the upper breaker plate, and the small earth spring is fitted on the pivot post (photo).

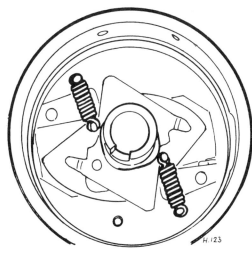
Fig. 4.7. Springs correctly located on centrifugal weights (Bosch) (Sec. 10)

11.5 Mechanical advance mechanism (Ford) Note: different sized springs

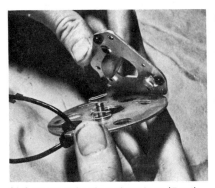
11.6 Reassembly of breaker plates (Ford)

11.7 Breaker plates correctly assembled (Ford)

11.8 Fitting spring clip to breaker plate pivot (Ford)

7 As the upper breaker plate is being refitted pass the holding down stud through the keyhole slot in the lower plate (photo).
8 Hold the upper plate in position and refit the wave washer, flat washer and circlip (photo).
9 When all is assembled reset the contact breaker points as described in Section 2.

---

12 Distributor - installation (crankshaft not moved)

---

1 Provided the crankshaft has not been moved from its static timing (BTDC) position, (see Section 7, paragraph 4), the distributor may be pushed into its recess in the crankcase ensuring that the following two conditions are met:

> *i) The vacuum diaphragm unit will be towards the rear of the engine.*
> *ii) The rotor will turn as the distributor and auxiliary shaft gears mesh and therefore in order to make sure that the contact end of the rotor arm aligns with the No. 1 distributor cap segment, the rotor arm must be turned back about 30° (against normal direction of rotation) before installing the distributor.*

2 When installation is correct, fit the clamp plate and bolt.
3 Reconnect the HT and LT leads and the vacuum pipe (s).

---

13 Distributor - installation (crankshaft position disturbed) and ignition timing

---

1 When a new gear or shaft has been fitted or the engine has been rotated, or if a new assembly is being fitted, it will be necessary to retime the ignition.
2 Look up the initial advance (static) for the particular model in the Specifications at the beginning of this Chapter.
3 Turn the engine until No. 1 piston is coming up to TDC on the compression stroke. This can be checked by removing No. 1 spark plug and feeling the pressure being generated in the cylinder or by removing the oil filler cap and noting when the cam is in the upright position. If this check is not made it is all too easy to set the timing 180° out. The engine can most easily be turned by engaging top gear and edging the car along (except automatic transmission where a spanner will have to be applied to the crankshaft pulley bolt).
4 Continue turning the engine until the appropriate timing mark on the crankshaft pulley is in line with the pointer. This setting must be correct for the initial advance for the engine which has already been looked up.
5 Now with the vacuum advance unit pointing to the rear of the engine and the rotor arm in the same position as was noted before removal, insert the distributor into its location. Notice that the rotor arm rotates as the gears mesh. Lift out the distributor far enough to rotate the shaft one tooth at a time, lowering it home to check the direction of the rotor arm. When it points in the desired direction with the assembly fully home fit the distributor clamp plate, bolt and plain washer. Do not fully tighten yet.
6 Gently turn the distributor body until the contact breaker points are just opening when the rotor is pointing at the contact in the distributor cap which is connected to No. 1 spark plug. A convenient way is to put a mark on the outside of the distributor body in line with the segment in the cover, so that it shows when the cover is removed.
7 If this position cannot be reached check that the drive gear has meshed on the correct tooth by lifting out the distributor once more. If necessary, rotate the drive shaft gear tooth and try again.
  To check the actual moment of opening of the contact points, connect a test bulb between the LT terminal of the points assembly and a good earth. Turn on the ignition switch and as the distributor body is turned, the bulb will light up as the points open.

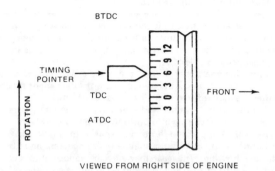

Fig. 4.8. Crankshaft pulley timing marks (2000 cc engine) (Secs. 13 and 14)

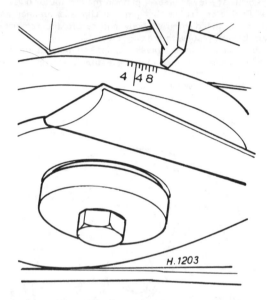

Fig. 4.9. Ignition timing marks (Secs. 13 and 14)

8 Tighten the distributor body clamp bolt.
9 Finally check the ignition timing using a stroboscope as described in Section 14.

---

14 Ignition timing (with stroboscope)

---

1 Mark the appropriate timing mark on the crankshaft pulley (see static advance - Specifications Section) also the pointer with chalk or white paint.
2 The engine should now be brought to normal operating temperature.
3 Disconnect the vacuum pipe(s) from the distributor diaphragm and plug them.
4 Connect a stroboscope in accordance with the maker's instructions (usually interposed between No. 1 spark plug and the end of No. 1 HT lead).
5 Start the engine and let it idle at specified speed, (see Specifications - Chapter 3).
6 Point the stroboscope at the ignition timing marks when they will appear stationary and if the ignition is correctly timed, also in alignment.
7 If the marks are not in alignment, release the distributor clamp plate and turn the distributor until they are.
8 Switch off the ignition, tighten the clamp plate bolt, remove the stroboscope and reconnect the spark plug lead.

15 Ignition resistance wire - testing

To promote longer ignition system life the actual running voltage used in the system is reduced by means of a resistance wire positioned between the ignition switch and the ignition coil.

The circuit is alive when the ignition switch is on in the normal running position but is by-passed while the ignition switch is in the start position thereby applying full battery voltage for easier engine starting.

If the condition exists where the engine will start but will not run with the switch in the running position the resistance wire should be suspect and checked. To carry out this check proceed as follows:

1 Connect up a voltmeter as shown in Fig. 4.11.
2 Fit a jump wire from the distributor terminal of the coil to a good earth.
3 Make sure that all the accessories and lights are switched off.
4 Turn on the ignition.
5 The voltmeter should need between 4.5 and 6.6 volts. If the reading is above or below these limits the resistance wire should be renewed.

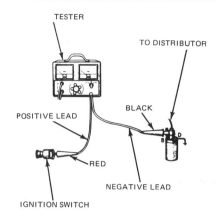

Fig. 4.11. Test circuit for ignition resistance wire (Sec. 15)

16 Distributor vacuum control valve (PVS valve) - description and testing

1 This valve, which is a ported vacuum switch is incorporated in the vacuum line which runs from the retard diaphragm to the intake manifold on dual diaphragm type distributor installations (2000 cc).
2 The engine normally idles with the spark retarded but when the coolant temperature rises above normal, the PVS valve opens the retard side of the distributor vacuum capsule to atmospheric pressure which permits the spark to advance and so increase the engine idling speed. This increased speed continues until the coolant temperature returns to normal.
3 To test the valve if faulty operation is suspected, first make sure that all vacuum hoses are correctly connected.
4 Attach a tachometer to the engine and then run the engine to

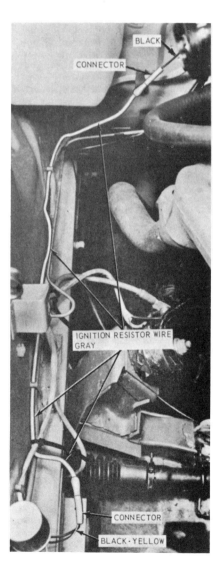

Fig. 4.10. Ignition resistance wire location within engine compartment (Sec. 15)

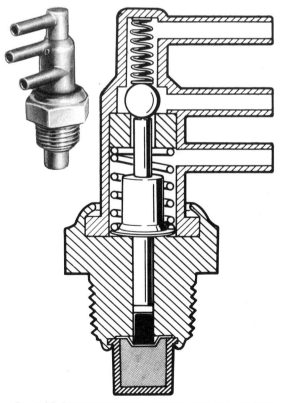

Fig. 4.12. Distributor vacuum control valve with sectional view (Sec. 16)

normal operating temperature and check that the choke valve plate is in the fully open position. Record the engine idling speed shown on the tachometer.

5 Blank off the radiator and run the engine until the coolant temperature indicator lamp comes on or the temperature gauge indicates overheating. Check that the engine speed has increased by at least 100 rpm over the previous idling speed recorded. If this is not the case, the valve must be renewed.

6 To renew the valve, drain about one gallon of coolant into a clean container and then disconnect the vacuum hoses from the PVS valve.

7 Unscrew the valve from the thermostat housing.

8 Installation of the new valve is a reversal of removal but apply jointing compound to the threads of the valve before screwing it in.

17 Spark plugs and HT leads

1 The correct functioning of the spark plugs is vital for the smooth running and efficiency of the engine.

2 At intervals of 6000 miles (9600 km), the plugs should be removed, examined, and cleaned. The condition of the spark plugs will also tell much about the overall condition of the engine. The plugs should be renewed at intervals of 12000 miles (19000 km).

3 If the insulator nose of the spark plug is clean and white, with no deposits, this is indicative of a weak mixture, or too hot a plug (a hot plug transfers heat away from the electrode slowly - a cold plug transfers it away quickly).

4 The plugs fitted as standard are as listed in Specifications at the head of this Chapter. If the tip and insulator nose are covered with hard black looking deposits, then this is indicative that the mixture is too rich. Should the plug be black and oily, then it is likely that the engine is fairly worn, as well as the mixture being too rich.

5 If the insulator nose is covered with light tan or greyish brown deposits, then the mixture is correct and it is likely that the engine is in good condition.

6 If there are any traces of long brown tapering stains on the outside of the white portion of the plug it will have to be renewed, as this shows that there is a faulty joint between the plug body and the insulator, and compression is being allowed to leak away.

7 Plugs should be cleaned by a sand blasting machine which will free them from carbon more thoroughly than cleaning by hand. The machine will also test the condition of the plugs under compression. Any plug that fails to spark at the recommended pressure should be renewed.

8 The spark plug gap is of considerable importance, as, if it is too large or too small, the size of the spark and its efficiency will be seriously impaired. The spark plug gap should be set to the figure given in Specifications at the beginning of this Chapter.

9 To set it, measure the gap with a feeler gauge, and then bend open, or close, the outer plug electrode until the correct gap is achieved. The centre electrode should never be bent as this may crack the insulation and cause plug failure if nothing worse.

10 When replacing the plugs, remember to use new plug washers, and replace the leads from the distributor in the correct firing order, which is 1 3 4 2, No. 1 cylinder being the one nearest the radiator.

11 The plug leads require no routine attention other than being kept clean and wiped over regularly.

12 At intervals of 6000 miles (9600 km) or 3 months, however, pull the leads off the plugs and distributor one at a time and make sure no water has found its way onto the connections. Remove any corrosion from the brass ends, wipe the collars on top of the distributor, and refit the leads.

18 Ignition system - fault diagnosis

There are two main symptoms indicating faults. Either the

engine will not start or fire, or the engine is difficult to start and misfires. If it is a regular misfire, ie; the engine is only running on two or three cylinders, the fault is almost sure to be in the secondary, or high tension circuit. If the misfiring is intermittent, the fault could be in either the high or low tension circuits. If the car stops suddenly or will not start at all, it is likely that the fault is in the low tension circuit. Loss of power and overheating (apart from carburation or emission control system faults - see Chapter 3), are normally due to faults in the distributor or incorrect ignition timing.

Engine fails to start

1 If the engine fails to start and the car was running normally when it was last used, first check there is fuel in the petrol tank. If it turns over normally on the starter motor and the battery is evidently well charged, then the fault may be in either the high or low tension circuits. First check the HT circuit. Note: If the battery is known to be fully charged, the ignition light comes on, and the starter motor fails to turn the engine check the tightness of the leads on the battery terminals and the secureness of the earth lead at its connection to the body. It is quite common for the leads to have worked loose, even if they look and feel secure. If one of the battery terminal posts gets very hot when trying to work the starter motor, this is a sure indication of a faulty connection to that terminal.

2 One of the commonest reasons for bad starting is wet or damp spark plug leads and distributor. Remove the distributor cap. If condensation is visible internally dry the cap with a rag and also wipe over the leads. Replace the cap.

3 If the engine still fails to start, check that current is reaching the plugs, by disconnecting each plug lead in turn at the spark plug end, and holding the end of the cable about 3/16 inch (5 mm) away from the cylinder block. Spin the engine on the starter motor.

4 Sparking between the end of the cable and the block should be fairly strong with a strong regular blue spark. (Hold the lead with rubber to avoid electric shock). If current is reaching the plugs, then remove them and clean and regap them to 0.025 inch (0.64 mm). The engine should now start.

5 If there is no spark at the plug leads take off the HT lead from the centre of the distributor cap and hold it to the block as before. Spin the engine on the starter once more. A rapid succession of blue sparks between the end of the lead and the block indicate that the coil is in order and that the distributor cap is cracked, the rotor arm faulty, or the carbon brush in the top of the distributor cap is not making good contact with the spring on the rotor arm. Possibly, the points are in bad condition. Clean and reset them as described in this Chapter, Section 3 or 4.

6 If there are no sparks from the end of the lead from the coil, check the connections at the coil end of the lead. If it is in order start checking the low tension circuit.

7 Use a 12v voltmeter or a 12v bulb and two lengths of wire. With the ignition switched on and the points open, test between the low tension lead to the coil (it is marked SW BAT or +) and earth. No reading indicates a break in the supply from the ignition switch. Check the connections at the switch to see if any are loose. Refit them and the engine should run. A reading shows a faulty coil or condenser, or broken lead between the coil and the distributor.

8 Take the condenser lead off the points assembly and with the points open test between the moving point and earth. If there now is a reading then the fault is in the condenser. Fit a new one and the fault is cleared.

9 With no reading from the moving point to earth, take a reading between earth and the CB (DIST) terminal of the coil. A reading here shows a broken lead which will need to be replaced between the coil and distributor. No reading confirms that the coil has failed and must be renewed, after which the engine will run once more. Remember to refit the condenser lead to the points assembly. For these tests it is sufficient to separate the points with a piece of dry paper while testing with the points open.

Measuring plug gap. A feeler gauge of the correct size (see ignition system specifications) should have a slight 'drag' when slid between the electrodes. Adjust gap if necessary

Adjusting plug gap. The plug gap is adjusted by bending the earth electrode inwards, or outwards, as necessary until the correct clearance is obtained. Note the use of the correct tool

Normal. Grey-brown deposits, lightly coated core nose. Gap increasing by around 0.001 in (0.025 mm) per 1000 miles (1600 km). Plugs ideally suited to engine, and engine in good condition

Carbon fouling. Dry, black, sooty deposits. Will cause weak spark and eventually misfire. Fault: over-rich fuel mixture. Check: carburettor mixture settings, float level and jet sizes; choke operation and cleanliness of air filter. Plugs can be re-used after cleaning

Oil fouling. Wet, oily deposits. Will cause weak spark and eventually misfire. Fault: worn bores/piston rings or valve guides; sometimes occurs (temporarily) during running-in period. Plugs can be re-used after thorough cleaning

Overheating. Electrodes have glazed appearance, core nose very white – few deposits. Fault: plug overheating. Check: plug value, ignition timing, fuel octane rating (too low) and fuel mixture (too weak). Discard plugs and cure fault immediately

Electrode damage. Electrodes burned away; core nose has burned, glazed appearance. Fault: pre-ignition. Check: as for 'Overheating' but may be more severe. Discard plugs and remedy fault before piston or valve damage occurs

Split core nose (may appear initially as a crack). Damage is self-evident, but cracks will only show after cleaning. Fault: pre-ignition or wrong gap-setting technique. Check: ignition timing, cooling system, fuel octane rating (too low) and fuel mixture (too weak). Discard plugs, rectify fault immediately

Engine misfires

1   If the engine misfires regularly run it at a fast idling speed. Pull off each of the plug caps in turn and listen to the note of the engine. Hold the plug cap in a dry cloth or with a rubber glove as additional protection against a shock from the HT supply.

2   No difference in engine running will be noticed when the lead from the defective circuit is removed. Removing the lead from one of the good cylinders will accentuate the misfire.

3   Remove the plug lead from the end of the defective plug and hold it about 3/16 inch (5 mm) away from the block. Re-start the engine. If the sparking is fairly strong and regular the fault must lie in the spark plug.

4   The plug may be loose, the insulation may be cracked, or the points may have burnt away giving too wide a gap for the spark to jump. Worse still, one of the points may have broken off. Either renew the plug, or clean it, reset the gap, and then test it.

5   If there is no spark at the end of the plug lead, or if it is weak and intermittent, check the ignition lead from the distributor to the plug. If the insulation is cracked or perished, renew the lead. Check the connections at the distributor cap.

6   If there is still no spark, examine the distributor cap carefully for tracking. This can be recognised by a very thin black line running between two or more electrodes, or between an electrode and some other part of the distributor. These lines are paths which now conduct electricity across the cap thus letting it run to earth. The only answer is a new distributor cap.

7   Apart from the ignition being incorrect, other causes of misfiring have already been dealt with under the section dealing with the failure of the engine to start. To recap - these are that:

a)   *The coil may be faulty giving an intermittent misfire;*
b)   *There may be a damaged lead or loose connection in the low tension circuit;*
c)   *The condenser may be short circuiting; or*
d)   *There may be a mechanical fault in the distributor (broken driving spindle or contact breaker spring).*

8   If the ignition timing is too far retarded, it should be noted that the engine will tend to overheat, and there will be a quite noticeable drop in power. If the engine is overheating and the power is down, and the ignition timing is correct, then the carburettor should be checked, as it is likely that this is where the fault lies.

Chapter 5 Clutch

Contents

Specifications

Type	Single dry plate, diaphragm spring
Actuation	Cable
Friction lining outside diameter	8.5 in. (215.9 mm)
Number of torsion springs	6
Free travel (adjuster nut to clutch bellhousing)	0.124 and 0.144 in. (3.15 and 3.65 mm)
Free travel (pedal 'at rest' to back stop)	0.75 in. (19.1 mm)

Torque wrench settings	lb f ft	kg f m
Pressure plate to flywheel bolts	20	2.8
Clutch bellhousing to engine bolts	45	6.2

1 General description

All models covered by this manual are fitted with a 8.45 inch (215.0 mm) single diaphragm spring clutch. The unit comprises a steel cover which is dowelled and bolted to the rear face of the flywheel and contains the pressure plate, diaphragm spring and fulcrum rings.

The clutch disc is free to slide along the splined first motion shaft and is held in position between the flywheel and the pressure plate by the pressure of the pressure plate spring. Friction lining material is riveted to the clutch disc and it has a spring cushion hub to absorb transmission shocks and to help ensure a smooth take off.

The circular diaphragm spring is mounted on shoulder pins and held in place in the cover by two fulcrum rings. The spring is also held to the pressure plate by three spring steel clips which are riveted in position.

The clutch is actuated by a cable controlled by the clutch pedal. The clutch release mechanism consists of a release fork and bearing which are in permanent contact with the release fingers on the pressure plate assembly. There should therefore never be any free-play at the release fork. Wear of the friction material in the clutch is adjusted out by means of a cable adjuster at the lower end of the cable where it passes through the bell housing.

Depressing the clutch pedal actuates the clutch release arm by means of the cable. The release arm pushes the release bearing forward to bear against the release fingers so moving the centre of the diaphragm two annular rings which act as fulcrum points. As the centre of the spring is pushed in, the outside of the spring is pushed out, so moving the pressure plate backward and disengaging the pressure plate from the clutch disc.

When the clutch pedal is released the diaphragm spring forces the pressure plate into contact with the high friction linings on the clutch disc and at the same time pushes the clutch disc a fraction of an inch forward on its splines so engaging the clutch disc with the flywheel. The clutch disc is not firmly sandwiched between the pressure plate and the flywheel so the drive is taken up.

2 Clutch - adjustment

1 Every 6000 miles (9600 km), adjust the clutch operating cable to compensate for wear in the driven plate linings.

2 Release the outer cable locknut at the clutch bellhousing. (Fig. 5.1).

3 Have an assistant pull the clutch pedal up against its stop and then pull the outer cable forward to remove any slack from the cable.

4 Now turn the adjusting nut until there is a clearance between it and the bush in the bellhousing of between 0.124 and 0.144 in (3.15 and 3.65 mm). Use feeler blades to measure this clearance. The pedal will now have a free movement of ¾ in (19.1 mm). (Fig. 5.2).

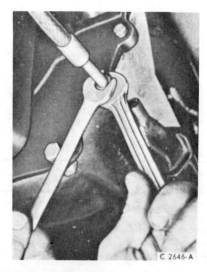

Fig. 5.1. Releasing clutch cable locknut (Sec. 2)

3 Clutch - removal

1   Remove the gearbox as described in Chapter 6.
2   Scribe a mating line from the clutch cover to the flywheel to ensure identical positioning on replacement and then remove the clutch assembly by unscrewing the six bolts holding the cover to the rear face of the flywheel. Unscrew the bolts diagonally half a turn at a time to prevent distortion to the cover flange.
3   With all the bolts and spring washers removed lift the clutch assembly off the locating dowels. The drive plate (clutch disc) may fall out at this stage as it is not attached to either the clutch cover assembly or the flywheel.

4 Clutch - overhaul

1   It is not practical to dismantle the pressure plate assembly and the term 'clutch dismantling and refitting' is a term usually used for simply fitting a new clutch driven plate.
2   If a new clutch driven plate is being fitted it is a false economy not to renew the release bearing at the same time. This will preclude having to replace it at a later date when wear on the clutch linings is very small.
3   If the pressure plate assembly required renewal (see Section 5) an exchange unit must be purchased. This will have been accurately set up and balanced to very fine limits.

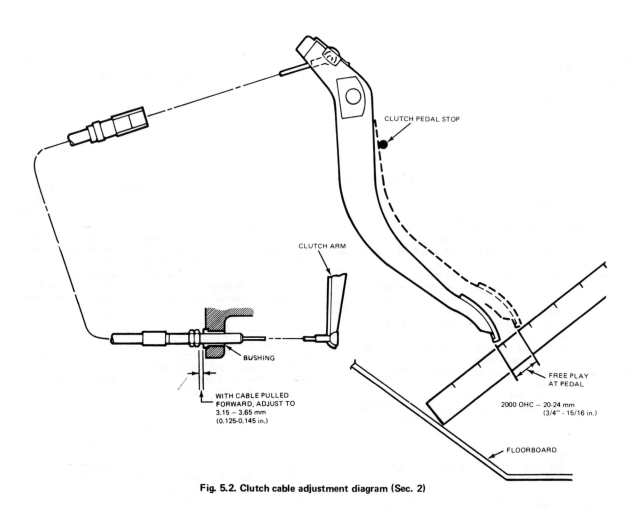

Fig. 5.2. Clutch cable adjustment diagram (Sec. 2)

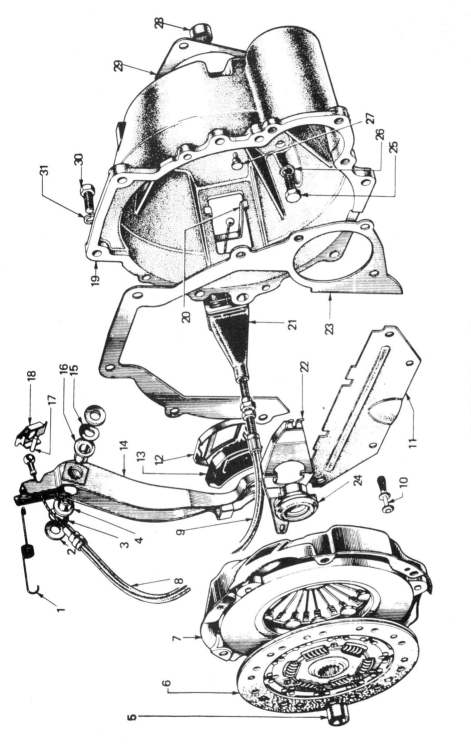

Fig. 5.3. Clutch assembly

1 Spring
2 Washer
3 Washer
4 Bush
5 Bearing
6 Friction plate
7 Pressure plate & diaphragm
    spring assembly

8   Clutch operating cable
9   Clutch operating cable
10 Inspection plate retainer
11 Inspection plate
12 Cover for pedal rubber
13 Pedal rubber
14 Pedal assembly

15 Washer
16 Bush
17 Pin
18 Clip
19 Bellhousing
20 Retaining spring clip
21 Rubber gaiter

22 Clutch release lever
23 Flywheel housing cover
24 Clutch release bearing
    assembly
25 Bolt
26 Spring washer
27 Dowel

28 Bearing
29 Gasket
30 Bolt
31 Spring washer

5 Clutch - inspection

1 Examine the clutch driven plate friction linings for wear and loose rivets and the plate for rim distortion, cracks, broken hub springs, and worn splines. The surface of the friction linings may be highly glazed, but as long as the clutch material pattern can be clearly seen this is satisfactory. Compare the amount of lining wear with a new clutch driven plate at the stores in your local garage, and if the linings are more than three quarters worn renew the driven plate.

2 It is always best to renew the clutch driven plate as an assembly to preclude further trouble, but, if it is wished to merely renew the linings, the rivets should be drilled out and not knocked out with a punch. The manufacturers do not advise that only the linings are renewed and personal experience dictates that it is far more satisfactory to renew the driven plate complete than to try and economise by only fitting new friction linings.

3 Check the machined faces of the flywheel and the pressure plate. If either is grooved it should be machined until smooth or renewed.

4 If the pressure plate is cracked or split it is essential that an exchange unit is fitted, also if the pressure of the diaphragm spring is suspect.

5 Check the release bearing for smoothness of operation. There should be no harshness and no slackness in it. It should spin reasonably freely bearing in mind it has been pre-packed with grease.

6 Clutch - refitting

1 It is important that no oil or grease gets on the clutch driven plate friction linings, or the pressure plate and flywheel faces. It is advisable to replace the clutch with clean hands and to wipe down the pressure plate and flywheel faces with a clean dry rag before reassembly begins.

2 Place the clutch driven plate against the flywheel, ensuring that it is the correct way round. The flywheel side of the clutch driven plate is clearly marked near the centre. If the driven plate is fitted the wrong way round, it will be quite impossible to operate the clutch.

3 Replace the clutch cover assembly loosely on the dowels. Replace the six bolts and spring washers and tighten them finger tight so that the clutch driven plate is gripped but can still be moved.

4 The clutch driven plate must now be centralised so that when the engine and gearbox are mated, the gearbox input shaft splines will pass through the splines in the centre of the driven plate hub.

5 Centralisation can be carried out quite easily by inserting a round bar or long screwdriver through the hole in the centre of the clutch, so that the end of the bar rests in the small hole in the end of the crankshaft containing the input shaft pilot bush. Ideally an old input shaft should be used.

6 Using the input shaft pilot bush as a fulcrum, moving the bar sideways or up and down will move the clutch disc in whichever direction is necessary to achieve centralisation.

7 Centralisation is easily judged by removing the bar and moving the driven plate hub in relation to the hole in the centre of the clutch cover diaphragm spring. When the hub appears exactly in the centre of the hole all is correct. Alternatively the input shaft will fit the bush and centre of the clutch hub exactly obviating the need for visual alignment.

8 Tighten the clutch bolts firmly in a diagonal sequence to ensure that the cover plate is pulled down evenly and without distortion of the flange. Finally tighten the bolts down to the specified torque wrench setting.

7 Clutch release bearing - renewal

1 With the gearbox and engine separated to provide access to the clutch, attention can be given to the release bearing located in the bellhousing, over the input shaft.

2 The release bearing is a relatively inexpensive but important component and unless it is nearly new it is a mistake not to renew it during an overhaul of the clutch.

3 To remove the release bearing first pull off the release arm rubber gaiter.

4 The release arm and bearing assembly can then be withdrawn from the clutch housing.

5 To free the bearing from the release arm simply unhook it, and then with the aid of two blocks of wood and a vice press off the release bearing from its hub.

6 Replacement is a straightforward reversal of these instructions.

8 Clutch cable - renewal

1 Jack-up the front of the car and support securely under the front crossmember.

2 Release the locknut on the outer cable at the bellhousing and back the adjusting nut right off.

3 Prise off the clip (A) from the top of the clutch pedal and then push out pin (B). Withdraw the cable into the engine compartment (Fig. 5.4).

4 Working under the car, pull the flexible bolt clear of the clutch release arm and push the cable towards the rear of the car and release the cable nipple from the outer end of the release arm (Fig. 5.5).

5 Installation of the new cable is a reversal of removal but finally adjust the cable, as described in Section 2, of this Chapter.

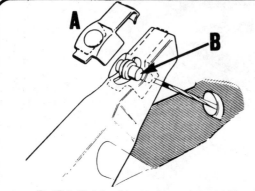

Fig. 5.4. Clutch cable attachment to pedal (Sec. 8)
A Locktab   B Fulcrum pin

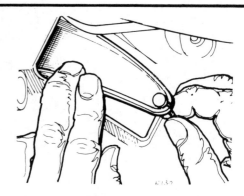

Fig. 5.5. Detaching clutch cable from release fork (Sec. 8)

9 Clutch pedal - removal and refitting

1 The clutch and brake pedals operate on a common cross-shaft.

2 Removal of one pedal will necessitate removal of the other.

3 Disconnect both pedal return springs.

4 Disconnect the clutch cable from the clutch pedal, as described in the preceding Section.

5 Disconnect the vacuum servo unit pushrod from the brake pedal by withdrawing the clevis pin and clip.

6 Extract the circlip from the pedal cross-shaft. This is located between the two pedals adjacent to the mounting bracket.

7 Slowly withdraw the pedal cross-shaft (from the clutch pedal end) taking off the individual components and placing them in order so that they can be refitted in the correct sequence.

8 Apply grease to the cross-shaft and bushes before reassembly and when refitting the brake pushrod, make sure that the yellow paint spot on the pushrod clevis fork is facing the gearbox.

9 Adjust the clutch cable as previously described.

10 Clutch - fault diagnosis

There are four main faults to which the clutch and release mechanism are prone. They may occur by themselves, or in conjunction with any of the other faults. They are clutch squeal, slip, spin and judder.

Clutch squeal - diagnosis and cure

1 If on taking up the drive or when changing gear, the clutch squeals, this is indicative of a badly worn clutch release bearing.

2 As well as regular wear due to normal use, wear of the clutch release bearing is much accentuated if the clutch is ridden or held down for long periods in gear, with the engine running. To minimise wear of this component the car should always be taken out of gear at traffic lights and for similar hold ups.

3 The clutch release bearing is not an expensive item, but difficult to get at.

Clutch slip - diagnosis and cure

1 Clutch slip is a self-evident condition which occurs when the clutch driven plate is badly worn, oil or grease have got onto the flywheel or pressure plate faces, or the pressure plate itself is faulty.

2 The reason for clutch slip is that due to one of the faults above, there is either insufficient pressure from the pressure plate, or insufficient friction from the driven plate to ensure solid drive.

3 If a small amount of oil gets onto the clutch, it will be burnt off under the heat of the clutch engagement, and in the process, gradually darken the linings. Excessive oil on the clutch will burn off leaving a carbon deposit which can cause quite bad slip, or fierceness, spin and judder.

4 If clutch slip is suspected, and confirmation of this condition is required, there are several tests which can be made.

5 With the engine in second or third gear and pulling lightly sudden depression of the accelerator pedal may cause the engine to increase its speed without any increase in road speed. Easing off on the accelerator will then give a definite drop in engine speed without the car slowing.

6 In extreme cases of clutch slip the engine will race under normal acceleration conditions.

7 If slip is due to oil or grease on the linings a temporary cure can sometimes be effected by squirting carbon tetrachloride into the clutch. The permanent cure is, of course, to renew the clutch driven plate and trace and rectify the oil leak.

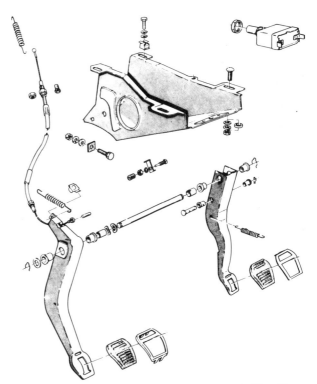

Fig. 5.6. Exploded view of clutch and brake pedals (Sec. 9)

Clutch spin - diagnosis and cure

1 Clutch spin is a condition which occurs when there is an obstruction in the clutch either in the first motion shaft or in the operating lever itself, or oil may have partially burnt off the clutch lining and have left a resinous deposit which is causing the clutch disc to stick to the pressure plate or flywheel.

2 The reason for clutch spin is that due to any, or a combination of, the faults just listed, the clutch pressure plate is not completely freeing from the driven plate even with the clutch pedal fully depressed.

3 If clutch spin is suspected, the condition can be confirmed by extreme difficulty in engaging first gear from rest, difficulty in changing gear, and very sudden take up of the clutch drive at the fully depressed end of the clutch pedal travel as the clutch is released.

4 Check the clutch cable adjustment (Section 2).

5 If these points are checked and found to be in order than the fault lies internally in the clutch, and it will be necessary to remove the clutch for examination.

Clutch judder - diangosis and cure

1 Clutch judder is a self-evident condition which occurs when the gearbox or engine mountings are loose or too flexible. When there is oil in the face on the clutch friction plate, or when the clutch pressure plate has been incorrectly adjusted.

2 The reason for clutch judder is that due to one of the faults just listed, the clutch pressure plate is not freeing smoothly from the driven plate and is snatching.

3 Clutch judder normally occurs when the clutch pedal is released in first or reverse gears, and the whole car shudders as it moves backward or forward.

Chapter 6
Manual gearbox and automatic transmission

Contents

Specifications

Manual gearbox:

Number of gears	4 forward, 1 reverse
Type of gears	Helical, constant mesh
Synchromesh	All forward gears

Ratios:	1600 cc models	2000 cc models
First	2.972 : 1	3.65 : 1
Second	2.010 : 1	1.97 : 1
Third	1.397 : 1	1.37 : 1
Fourth (top)	1.000 : 1	1.00 : 1
Reverse	3.324 : 1	3.66 : 1

Oil capacity:	
1600 cc	1½ pints (0.9 litre)
2000 cc	2.8 US pints

Automatic transmission

Type:	
1600 cc	Borg Warner type 35
2000 cc	Ford type C4
Torque converter ratio range	Infinitely variable between 1 : 1 and 2 : 1

Refill capacity:	
C4*	12.5 US pints
BW 35	11.25 Imp. pints (6.4 litres)
⁺Add	0.6 US pint (0.28 litre) if oil cooler is fitted
Add	1.5 US pints (0.65 litre) if unit is dry

Gear ratios (C4)	
First	2.46 : 1
Second	1.46 : 1
Third	1 : 1
Reverse	2.20 : 1

Gear ratios (BW 35)	
First	2.393 : 1
Second	1.450 : 1
Third	1.000 : 1
Reverse	2.094 : 1

Torque wrench settings

	lb f ft	kg f m
Manual gearbox		
Top cover bolts	14	1.9
Extension housing bolts	36	5.0
Clutch bellhousing to casing	45	6.2
Clutch bellhousing to engine	25	3.5
Automatic transmission (Type C4)		
Torque converter to driveplate bolts	26	3.6
Torque converter to transmission casing	38	5.3
Torque converter drain plug	30	4.1
Oil pan bolts	16	2.2
Torque converter housing to engine	32	4.4
Filler tube nut	40	5.5
Neutral switch locknut	55	7.6
Downshift lever nut	9	1.2
Intermediate band screw	10	1.4
Intermediate band locknut	40	5.5
Low and reverse band screws	10	1.4
Low and reverse band locknuts	40	5.5
Automatic transmission (Type BW 35)		
Torque converter to transmission casing	32	4.4
Torque converter to driveplate bolts	40	5.5
Neutral switch locknut	10	1.4
Oil pan bolts	13	1.8
Oil drain plug	12	1.6
Torque converter housing to engine	26	3.6

1 General description

The manual gearbox fitted to models covered by this manual will be one of two types depending on the engine fitted. It contains four constant mesh helically cut forward gears and one straight cut reverse gear. Synchromesh is fitted between 1st and 2nd, 2nd and 3rd and 3rd and 4th. The individual cast bellhousing, gearbox casing and extension housing are bolted together and contain gear trains of simple design using a minimum number of components. Where close tolerances and limits are required, manufacturing tolerances are compensated for and excessive endfloat or backlash eliminated by the fitting of selective circlips. When overhauling the gearbox always use new circlips, never refit ones that have already been used.

The gear selector mechanism on gearboxes fitted to 1600 cc cars is unusual in that the selector forks are free to slide on one selector rod which also serves as the gearchange shaft. At the gearbox end of this rod lies the selector arm, which, depending on the position of the gearlever, places the appropriate selector fork in the position necessary for the synchroniser sleeve to engage with the dog teeth on the gear selected.

It is impossible to select two gears at once because of an interlock guard plate which pivots on the right-hand side of the gearbox casing. The selector forks when not in use are positively held by the guard plate in their disengaged positions.

Gear selection on 2000 cc models is by means of the remote gearchange lever and operates through three selector rods and levers. The gearchange lever is mounted on the floor of the car and connects with the gear selector levers located on the left-hand side of the gearbox.

Automatic transmission is fitted as a factory option on models covered by this manual. Further information on the unit will be found later in this Chapter.

2 Gearbox (1600 cc models) - removal and installation

1 The gearbox can be removed in unit with the engine from the engine compartment as described in Chapter 1. Alternatively, the gearbox can be separated from the rear of the engine at the bellhousing and the gearbox lowered from under the car. The latter method is easier and quicker than the former.

2 If a hoist or an inspection pit are not available then run the back of the car up on a pair of ramps and jack it up and fit axle stands. Next jack up the front of the car and support on axle stands.

3 Disconnect the battery earth terminal.

4 Working inside the car, push the front seats rearward as far as possible.

5 The centre console must next be removed. The method for the most popular type is given here but the principle is basically the same for all models and versions.

6 Undo and remove the screws securing the parcel tray bolts and lift away the parcel tray. Slide the gaiter up the gearlever (photo).

7 Unlock the lock ring located at the base of the gearchange lever. Unscrew the gearchange lever lock ring and retainer. Lift away the assembly (photos).

8 Undo and remove the centre console and instrument cluster mounting screws.

9 Move the console unit until it is possible to gain access to the rear of the instrument cluster. Make a note of the electrical cable connections and detach from the rear of the instruments.

10 Undo and remove the centre bolts from the handbrake lever compensator and pull the lever handle pulley up. The console unit may now be lifted away from inside the car.

11 Mark the mating flanges of the propeller shaft and final drive so that they may be reconnected in their original positions and undo and remove the four securing bolts.

12 Where a split type propeller shaft is fitted, undo and remove the centre bearing retainer securing bolts, spring and plain washers (photo).

13 Draw the propeller shaft rearward so detaching the front end from the rear of the gearbox and lift away from under the car.

14 Wrap some polythene around the end of the gearbox and secure with string or wire to stop any oil running out. If the gearbox is to be dismantled then drain the oil out now rather than later.

15 Make a note of the cable connections to the starter motor and detach the cables.

16 Undo and remove the two bolts securing the starter motor to the gearbox flange. Lift away the starter motor.

17 Remove the rear engine cover plate and bracket assembly from the clutch housing. Detach the bracket assembly from the cylinder block and swing it back out of the way

18 Pull off the plug attached to the reverse light switch located on the side of the remote control housing.

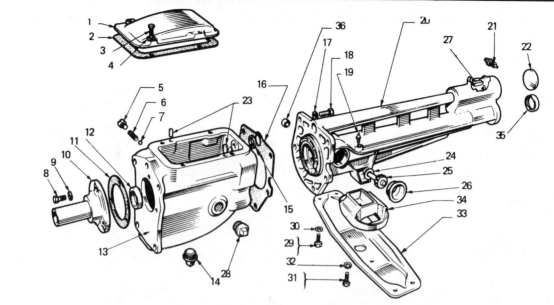

Fig. 6.1A. Exploded view of the gearbox casing and extension (1600 cc models)

1 Gearbox cover	10 Bearing retainer	19 Breather	28 Filler/level plug
2 Gasket	11 Gasket	20 Gearbox extension	29 Bolt
3 Bolt	12 Oil seal	21 Reverse light switch	30 Washer
4 Washer	13 Gearbox casting	22 Plug	31 Bolt
5 Screw	14 Drain plug	23 Dowels	32 Washer
6 Spring *	15 Selector rod seal	24 Circlip	33 Rear crossmember
7 Ball	16 Gasket	25 Speedometer gear	34 Rubber mounting
8 Bolt	17 Washer	26 Plug	35 Oil seal
9 Washer	18 Bolt	27 Gear lever orifice	36 Seal

* Early gearboxes only. On later gearboxes, the spring and ball are in a drilling in the gearbox flange, and are retained by the cover (1)

2.6 Slide gaiter up gear lever

2.7a Bending back lock ring tabs with screwdriver

2.7b Lifting away gear change lever

2.12 Propeller shaft centre bearing retainer securing bolt removal

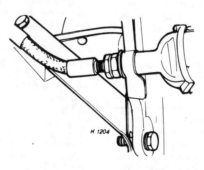

Fig. 6.1B. Location of bracket between engine and clutch housing (Sec. 2)

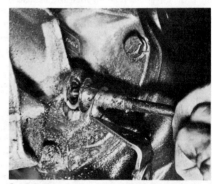

2.19 Speedometer cable retaining circlip removal

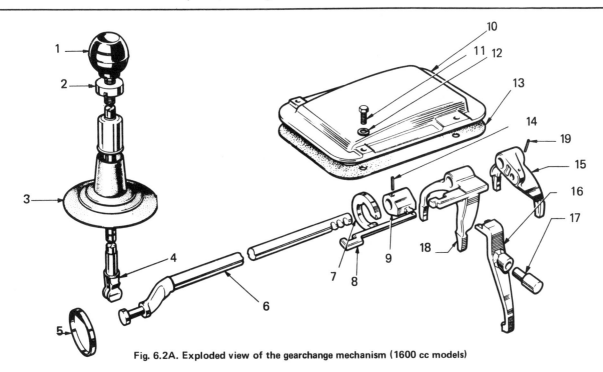

Fig. 6.2A. Exploded view of the gearchange mechanism (1600 cc models)

1 Gearlever knob
2 Knob locknut
3 Gearlever boot
4 Gearlever
5 Plug

6 Gear selector rod
7 Selector interlock plate
8 Third and fourth gearchange
9 Selector arm

10 Gearbox cover
11 Bolt
12 Spring washer
13 Gasket
14 Split locking pin

15 First and second gear selector fork
16 Reverse gear selector fork
17 Fork pivot
18 Third and fourth gear selector fork
19 Pin

19 Using a pair of circlip pliers remove the circlip retaining the speedometer drive cable end to the gearbox extension housing (photo).
20 Pull the speedometer drive cable away from the side of the extension housing.
21 Using a pair of pliers detach the clutch operating cable from the actuating arm protruding from the side of the clutch housing. It will be necessary to pull back the rubber gaiter first.
22 Pull the clutch cable assembly through the locating hole in the flange on the clutch housing.

23 Suitably support the weight of the gearbox by either using a jack or an axle stand. Insert a wooden chock between the sump and engine support so that the engine does not drop when the gearbox is removed.
24 Undo and remove the bolts securing the clutch bellhousing to the rear of the engine.
25 Undo and remove the exhaust pipe securing nuts at the exhaust manifold and the exhaust mounting bracket. Push the assembly away from the gearbox and tie back with string.
26 Undo and remove the one bolt that secures the rubber

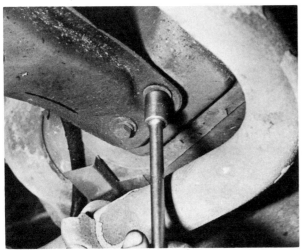

2.27 Gearbox support crossmember to body securing bolt removal

2.28 Crossmember removal

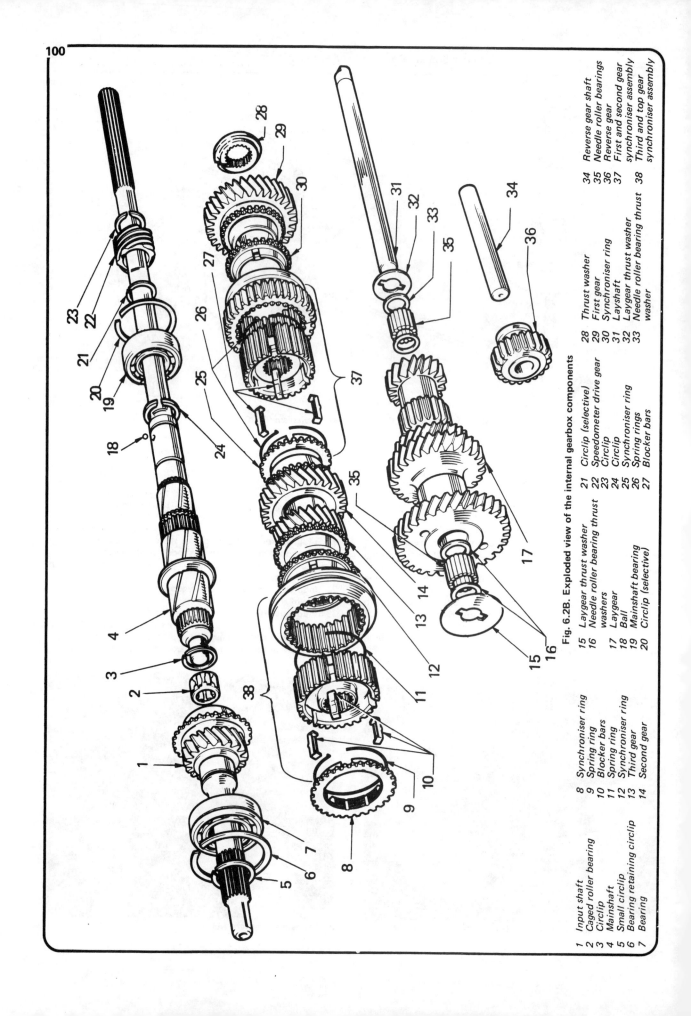

Fig. 6.2B. Exploded view of the internal gearbox components

1 Input shaft
2 Caged roller bearing
3 Circlip
4 Mainshaft
5 Small circlip
6 Bearing retaining circlip
7 Bearing
8 Synchroniser ring
9 Spring ring
10 Blocker bars
11 Spring ring
12 Synchroniser ring
13 Third gear
14 Second gear
15 Laygear thrust washer
16 Needle roller bearing thrust washers
17 Laygear
18 Ball
19 Mainshaft bearing
20 Circlip (selective)
21 Circlip (selective)
22 Speedometer drive gear
23 Circlip
24 Laygear
25 Ball
26 Synchroniser ring
27 Spring rings
27 Blocker bars
28 Thrust washer
29 First gear
30 Synchroniser ring
31 Layshaft
32 Laygear thrust washer
33 Needle roller bearing thrust washer
34 Reverse gear shaft
35 Needle roller bearings
36 Reverse gear
37 First and second gear synchroniser assembly
38 Third and top gear synchroniser assembly

mounting to the gearbox extension housing.

27 Undo and remove the four bolts, spring and plain washers securing the gearbox crossmember to the body (photo).

28 Lift away the crossmember (photo).

29 The assistance of a second person is now required who should be ready to help in taking the weight of the gearbox.

30 **Do not** allow the weight of the gearbox to hang on the input shaft (first motion shaft) as it is easily bent. Carefully separate the gearbox from the engine by sliding it rearwards out of the clutch assembly. It will be necessary to lower the jack or stand to give clearance of the gearbox from the underside of the body.

31 If major work is to be undertaken on the gearbox it is recommended that the exterior be washed with paraffin or water soluble solvent and dried with a non-fluffy rag.

32 Refitting the gearbox is the reverse sequence to removal but the following additional points should be noted:

 a) *Make sure that the engine cover plate gasket is correctly positioned.*
 b) *Adjust the clutch control cable as described in Chapter 5.*
 c) *Before refitting the gearchange lever well grease the fork ends.*
 d) *Do not forget to refill the gearbox with the recommended grade of oil.*

---

3 Gearbox (1600 cc models) - dismantling

Gearbox main assembly

1 Remove the clutch release bearing from the gearbox input shaft (photo).

2 Next lift out the clutch release lever (photo).

3 Undo and remove the four bolts holding the bellhousing to the gearbox (photo).

4 Detach the bellhousing from the gearbox (photo).

5 Slightly loosen the gearbox drain plug and mount the gearbox upright in a vice using the drain plug as a pivot. Make sure the vice is firmly gripping the drain plug so the assembly cannot tilt.

6 Referring to Fig. 6.1A, undo the four bolts holding the gearbox top cover (1) in place (photo A) and remove the cover (photo B). On later gearboxes, the selector spring and detent ball will now be exposed; lift out the spring and remove the ball using a screwdriver with a blob of grease on the end.

7 Prise out the cup shaped oil seal (26) on the side of the gearbox extension (photo).

8 From under this seal pull out the speedometer gear (25) (photo). To start it, it may be necessary to tap it from the other end.

9 From where the gear lever enters the extension housing drive out the rear extension oil seal (22) (photo).

10 On early model gearboxes, remove the plunger screw (5), its spring (6) and the ball (7) from the right-hand side of the gear box casing (photo).

11 Using a small drift drive out the pin holding the selector boss to the central rod (photo).

12 Now withdraw the selector rod (photo A), at the same time holding on to the selector boss and cam (photo B) to prevent them falling into the gearbox.

13 To remove the selector forks, it is necessary to knock the two synchro hubs towards the front of the gearbox, this can be done with a small drift or a screwdriver. Now lift out the selector forks.

14 Turn now to the gearbox extension (20) and remove the bolts (18) and washers (17) which hold it to the gearbox casing.

15 Knock it slightly rearwards with a soft headed hammer then rotate the whole extension until the cut-out on the extension face coincides with the rear end of the layshaft in the lower half of the gearbox casing.

16 Get hold of a metal rod to act as a dummy layshaft 6.13/16 inches long with a diameter of 5/8 inches.

17 Tap the layshaft rearwards with a drift until it is just clear of the front of the gearbox casing then insert the dummy shaft and drive the layshaft out and allow the laygear cluster to drop out of mesh with the mainshaft gears into the bottom of the box.

18 Withdraw the mainshaft and extension assembly from the gearbox casing, pushing the 3rd/top synchronizer hub forward slightly to obtain the necessary clearance. A small roller bearing should come away on the nose of the mainshaft, but if it is not there it will be found in its recess in the input shaft and should be removed.

19 Moving to the front of the gearbox remove the bolts (8) retaining the input shaft cover (10) and take it off the shaft.

20 Remove the large circlip now exposed and then tap on the bearing outer race to remove it, and the input shaft, from inside the gearbox.

21 The laygear can now be withdrawn from the rear of the gearbox together with its thrust washers (one at each end).

22 Remove the mainshaft assembly from the gearbox extension, by taking out the large circlip adjacent to the mainshaft bearing, then tapping the rear of the shaft with a soft headed hammer. Do not discard the circlip at this stage as it is required for setting-up during reassembly.

23 The reverse idler gear can be removed by screwing a suitable bolt into the end of the shaft and then levering the shaft out with the aid of two large open ended spanners (photo).

24 The gearbox is now stripped right out and must be thoroughly cleaned. If there is any quantity of metal chips and fragments in the bottom of the gearbox casing it is obvious that several items will be found to be badly worn. The component parts of the gearbox and laygear should be examined for wear. The input shaft and mainshaft assemblies broken down further as described in the following paragraphs.

3.1 Remove the clutch release bearing

3.2 Lift out the release lever

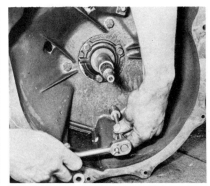
3.3 Remove the bellhousing retaining bolts

3.4 Detach the bellhousing

3.6A Undo the bolts ...

3.6B ... and remove the top cover

3.7 Prise out the cup shaped retainer plug

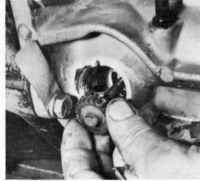
3.8 Remove the speedometer gear

3.9 Drive out the rear extension oil seal

3.10 Remove the plunger screw

3.11 Drive out the selector boss pin

3.12a Withdraw the selector rod ...

3.12b ... whilst holding the selector boss and cam

3.23 Remove the reverse idler shaft

3.35 Remove the large bearing

Input shaft

25 The only reason for dismantling the input shaft is to fit a new ball bearing assembly, or, if the input shaft is being renewed and the old bearing is in excellent condition, then the fitting of a new shaft to an old bearing.

26 With a pair of expanding circlip pliers remove the circlip (5), (Fig. 6.2B) from the input shaft.

27 With a soft-headed hammer gently tap the bearing forward and then remove it from the shaft.

28 The mainshaft has to be dismantled before some of the synchroniser rings can be inspected. For dismantling it is best to mount the plain portion of the shaft between two pieces of wood in a vice.

29 From the forward end of the mainshaft pull off the caged roller bearing (2) and the synchro ring (8). (Fig. 6.2B).

30 With a pair of circlip pliers remove the circlip (3) which holds the third/fourth gear synchroniser hub in place.

31 Ease the hub (38) and third gear (13) forward by gentle leverage with a pair of long nosed pliers.

32 The hub (38) and synchro ring (12) are then removed from the mainshaft.

33 Then slide off third gear. Nothing else can be removed from this end of the mainshaft becaust of the raised lip on the shaft.

34 Move to the other end of the mainshaft and remove the small circlip then slide off the speedometer drive taking care not to loose the ball which located in a groove in the gear and a small recess in the mainshaft.

35 Remove the circlip (21) and then gently lever off the large bearing with the aid of two tyre levers as shown in the photo.

36 The bearing followed by the large thrust washer (28) can then be pulled off. Follow these items by pulling off first gear (29) and the synchroniser ring (30).

37 With a pair of circlip pliers remove the circlip (24) which retains the first and second gear synchroniser assembly in place.

38 The first and second gear synchroniser followed by second gear (14) are then simply slide off the mainshaft. The mainshaft is now completely dismantled.

---

4 Gearbox (1600 cc models) - inspection

1 Carefully clean and then examine all the component parts for general wear, distortion, slackness of fit, and damage to machined faces and threads.

2 Examine the gearwheels for excessive wear and chipping of teeth. Renew them as necessary.

3 Examine the layshaft for signs of wear, where the layshaft needle roller bearings bear. If a small ridge can be felt at either end of the shaft it will be necessary to renew it.

4 The four synchroniser rings (8, 12, 25, 30), (Fig. 6.2B) are bound to be badly worn and it is false economy not to renew them. New rings will improve the smoothness and speed of the gearchange considerably.

5 The needle roller bearing and cage (2) located between the nose of the mainshaft and the annulus in the rear of the input shaft is also liable to wear, and should be renewed as a matter of course.

6 Examine the condition of the two ball bearing assemblies, one on the input shaft (7) and one on the mainshaft (19). Check them for noisy operation, looseness between the inner and outer races, and for general wear. Normally they should be renewed on a gearbox that is being rebuilt.

7 If either of the synchroniser units (37, 38) are worn it will be necessary to buy a complete assembly as the parts are not sold individually.

8 Examine the ends of the selector forks where they rub against the channels in the periphery of the synchroniser units. If possible compare the selector forks with new units to help determine the wear that has occured. Renew them if worn.

9 If the bush bearing in the extension is badly worn it is best to take the extension to your local Ford garage to have the bearing pulled out and a new one fitted.

10 The rear oil seal (35 in Fig. 6.1A) should be renewed as a matter of course. Drive out the old seal with the aid of a drift or broad screwdriver. It will be found that the seal comes out quite easily.

11 With a piece of wood to spread the load evenly, carefully tap a new seal into place ensuring that it enters the bore in the extension squarely.

12 The only point on the mainshaft that is likely to be worn is the nose where it enters the input shaft. However examine it thoroughly for any signs of scoring, picking-up, or flats, and of damage is apparent renew it.

---

5 Gearbox (1600 cc models) - reassembly

Mainshaft

1 If a new synchroniser assembly is being fitted it is necessary to take it to pieces first to clean off all the preservative. These instructions are also pertinent in instances where the outer sleeve has come off the hub accidentally during dismantling.

Fig. 6.3A. The synchronizer assembly alignment marks

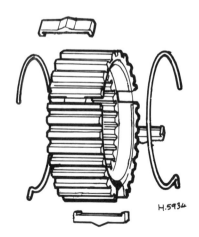

Fig. 6.3B. The synchronizer hub springs must be put on as shown in this illustration

5.5 Refit the second gear and synchronizer ring

5.6a Slide on the first and second gear synchronizer assembly ...

5.6b ... and make sure that the ring fits over the blocker bars

5.7 Refit the circlip

5.9 Slide on the first gear

5.10 Fit the splined thrust washer

5.12 Press the bearing home

5.13 Refit the main bearing selective circlip

5.14 Refit the speedometer drive retaining ball

5.15 Slide on the speedometer drive gear

5.16 Fit the circlip

5.17 Slide on the third gear and synchronizer ring

5.18 Fit the third and fourth gear synchronizer assembly

5.19 Tap the synchronizer fully home

5.20 Fit the securing circlip

2 To dismantle an assembly for cleaning slide the synchroniser sleeve off the splined hub and clean all the preservative from the blocker bars (27), spring rings (26), the hub itself (A), and the sleeve (B).

3 Oil the components lightly and then fit the sleeve (B) to the hub (A) so the lines marked on them (see Fig. 6.3A) are in line. Note the three slots in the hub and fit a blocker bar in each.

4 Fit the two springs (26) one on the front and one on the rear face of the inside of the synchroniser sleeve under the blocker bars with the tagged end of each spring locating in the 'U' section of the same bar. One spring must be put on anticlockwise and one clockwise when viewed from the side (see Fig. 6.3B). When either side of the assembly is viewed face on the direction of rotation of the springs should then appear the same.

5 Prior to reassembling the mainshaft read paragraphs 11 and 13 of this Section, to ensure that the correct thickness of selective circlips can be obtained. Reassembly commences by replacing second gear (14), gear teeth facing the raised lip and its synchronizer ring (25) on the rear portion of the mainshaft (photo).

6 Next slide on the first and second gear synchroniser assembly (37), (photo A) **and make certain** that the cut-outs in the synchroniser ring fit over the blocker bars in synchroniser hub (photo B); that the marks on the mainshaft and hub are in line (where made); and that the reverse gear teeth cut on the synchroniser sleeve periphery are adjacent to second gear.

7 Replace the circlip (24) which holds the synchroniser hub in place (photo).

8 Then fit another synchroniser ring (30) again ensuring that the cut-outs in the ring fit over the blocker bars in the synchroniser hub.

9 Next slide on first gear (29) so the synchronising cone portion lies inside the synchronising ring just fitted (photo).

10 Fit the splined thrust washer (28) to the front of first gear (photo).

11 If a new mainshaft bearing (19) or a new gearbox extension is being used it will now be necessary to select a new large circlip to eliminate endfloat of the mainshaft. To do this, first fit the original circlip in its groove in the gearbox extension and draw it outwards (ie; away from the rear of the extension). Now accurately measure the dimension from the base of the bearing housing to the outer edge of the circlip and record the figure. Also accurately measure the thickness of the bearing outer track and subtract the figure from the depth already recorded. This will give the required shim thickness to give zero endfloat.

12 Loosely fit the selected circlip, lubricate the bearing contact surfaces then press it onto the shaft. To press the bearing home, close the jaws of the vice until they are not quite touching the mainshaft, and with the bearing resting squarely against the side of the vice jaws draw the bearing on by tapping the end of the shaft with a hide or plastic hammer (photo).

13 Replace the small circlip retaining the main bearing in place. This is also a selective circlip and must be such that all endfloat between the bearing inner track and the circlip edge is eliminated (photo).

14 Replace the small ball that retains the speedometer drive in its recess in the mainshaft (photo).

15 Slide on the speedometer drive noting that it can only be fitted one way round as the groove in which the ball fits does not run the whole length of the drive (photo).

16 Now fit the circlip to retain the speedometer drive, (photo). Assembly of this end of the mainshaft is now complete.

17 Moving to the short end of the mainshaft slide on third gear (13) so that the machined gear teeth lie adjacent to second gear, then slide on the synchroniser ring (photo).

18 Fit the third and fourth gear synchroniser assembly (38) (photo) again ensuring that the cut-outs on the ring line up with the blocker bars.

19 With a suitable piece of metal tube over the mainshaft, tap the synchroniser fully home onto the mainshaft (photo).

20 Then fit the securing circlip (3) in place (photo). Apart from the needle roller bearing race which rests on the nose of the mainshaft this completes mainshaft reassembly.

5.27 Fit the laygear needle rollers

5.28 Fit the external washers

5.29 Slide in the dummy layshaft

Input shaft

21 When fitting the new input shaft bearing ensure that the groove cut in the outer periphery faces away from the gear. If the bearing is fitted the wrong way round it will not be possible to fit the large circlip which retains the bearing in the housing.

22 Using the jaws of a vice as a support behind the bearing tap the bearing squarely into place by hitting the rear of the input shaft with a plastic or hide faced hammer.

23 Refit the circlip (5) which holds the bearing to the input shaft.

Gearbox main assembly

24 If removed replace the reverse idler gear and selector lever in the gearbox, by tapping in the shaft (34). Once it is through the casing fit the gearwheel (36) so that 1st gear teeth are facing in towards the main gearbox area.

25 Fit the reverse selector lever in the groove in the idler gear then drive the shaft home with a soft headed hammer until it is flush with the gearbox casing.

26 Slide a retaining washer (16) into either end of the laygear (17) so that they abut the internal machined shoulder.

27 Smear thick grease on the laygear roller bearing surface and fit the needle rollers (35) one at a time (photo) until all are in place. The grease will hold the rollers in position. Build up the needle roller bearings in the other end of the laygear in a similar fashion. There should be 20 at each end.

28 Fit the external washer to each end of the laygear, taking care not to dislodge the roller bearings (photo).

29 Carefully slide in the dummy layshaft used previously for driving out the layshaft (photo).

30 Grease the two thrust washers (15 and 32) and position the larger of the two (15) in the front of the gearbox so the tongues fit into the machined recesses.

31 Fit the smaller of the thrust washers (32) to the rear of the gearbox in the same way (photo).

32 Fit the laygear complete with dummy layshaft in the bottom of the gearbox casing taking care not to dislodge the thrust washers (photo).

33 Now from inside the gearbox slide in the input shaft assembly (1), (photo A) and drive the bearing into place with a suitable drift (photo B).

34 Secure the bearing in position by replacing the circlip (6) (photo).

35 Fit a new gasket to the bearing retainer and smear on some Wellseal or similar sealing compound (photo).

36 Replace the retainer on the input shaft (photo A) ensuring that the oil drain hole is towards the bottom of the gearbox, and tighten down the bolts (photo B).

37 Submerge the gearbox end of the extension housing in hot water for a few minutes, then mount it in a vice and slide in the mainshaft assembly. Take care that the splines do not damage the oil seal (photo).

38 Secure the mainshaft to the gearbox extension by locating the circlip already placed loosely behind the main bearing into its groove in the extension (photo A). Photo B shows the circlip correctly located.

39 Fit a new gasket to the extension housing and then replace the small roller bearing on the nose of the mainshaft. Lubricate the roller bearing with gearbox oil (photo).

40 Slide the combined mainshaft and housing assembly into the rear of the gearbox and mate up the nose of the mainshaft with the rear of the input shaft (photo).

41 Completely invert the gearbox so that the laygear falls into mesh with the mainshaft gears.

42 Turn the extension housing round until the cut-out on it coincides with the hole for the layshaft (photo). It may be necessary to trim the gasket.

43 Push the layshaft into its hole from the rear thereby driving out the dummy shaft at the same time (photo).

44 Tap the layshaft into position so it will fit into its recess in the extension housing flange (photo).

45 Turn the gearbox the right way up again; correctly line up the extension housing, and secure it to the gearbox. Apply a

5.31 Fit the smaller thrust washer at the rear

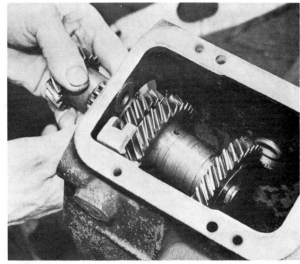

5.32 Fit the laygear carefully

5.33a Slide in the input shaft assembly ...

5.33b ... and drive the bearing into place

5.34 Fit the circlip to retain the bearing

5.35 Apply sealing compound to the bearing retainer

5.36a Refit the input shaft retainer ...

5.36b ... and tighten the bolts

5.37 Slide in the mainshaft assembly

5.38a Locate the circlip in the groove in the extension

5.38b The circlip correctly located

5.39 Refit the mainshaft roller bearing

5.40 Slide the mainshaft and extension housing into the gearbox

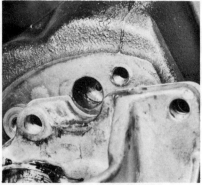
5.42 Turn the extension housing to align the cut-out with the hole for the layshaft

5.43 Push in the layshaft

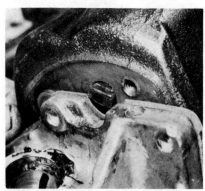
5.44 Ensure that the cut-out in the end of the layshaft is in the horizontal position

5.45 Secure the extension housing to the gearbox

5.46a Push the synchronizer hub fully forward

5.46b Push the synchronizer hub fully forward

5.47a Lower the selector forks into position

5.47b Lower the selector forks into position

non-setting gasket sealant to the bolt threads before fitting them (photo).

46 The selector forks cannot be replaced until the two synchroniser hubs are pushed by means of a screwdriver or drift to their most forward positions (photos A and B).

47 Now lower the selector forks into position (photo A) and it will be found that they will now drop in quite easily (photo B). Now return the synchroniser hubs to their original positions.

48 Slide the gearchange selector rod into place from the rear of the extension and as it comes into the gearbox housing slide onto it the selector boss and 'C' cam, having just made sure that the cam locates in the cut-outs in the selector fork extension arms.

49 Push the selector rod through the boss and the selector forks

until the pin holes on the boss and rail align. Tap the pin into place thereby securing the boss to the selector rod. During this operation ensure that the cut-out on the gearbox end of the selector rail faces to the right.

50 Replace the ball, spring and retaining screw in the top right-hand side of the gearbox casing (early gearboxes only).

51 Apply a small amount of sealer to the blanking plug and gently tap it into position in the rear of the extension behind the selector rail. Peen it with a centre punch in 3 or 4 places to retain it.

52 Insert the detent ball and spring into the drilling on the gearbox top flange (later gearboxes only).

53 Place a new gasket on the gearbox top cover plate, then replace the top cover and tighten down its four retaining bolts.

54 Replace the speedometer drive gear in the extension, smear the edges of its retaining cup with sealing compound and tap the cup into place. Remove the gearbox from the vice and tighten down the drain plug.

55 Refit the bellhousing onto the gearbox, apply a non-setting jointing compound to the bolt threads then fit them.

56 Refit the clutch release fork and bearing.

---

6 Gearbox (2000 cc models) - removal and installation

---

1 Follow the instructions given in Section 2, paragraphs 1 to 3 inclusive.

2 Carefully release the spring retainers and detach the selector rods from the selector levers on the left-hand side of the gearbox.

3 Follow the instructions given in paragraphs 11 to 32, Section 2.

4 When refitting the clutch control cable it should be adjusted as described in Chapter 5.

5 Before reconnecting the selector rods to the selector levers grease the ends of the rods. Also lubricate the ball end of the clutch operating cable.

6 Check the correct operation of the gear selector linkage. If necessary re-adjust as described later in this Chapter.

Fig. 6.4. Correct fitting of the circlip securing the mainshaft rear bearing to the gearbox extension

---

7 Gearbox (2000 cc models) - dismantling

---

1 Remove the clutch release bearing from the gearbox input

shaft.

2 Next remove the clutch release lever.

3 Unscrew and remove the drain plug and allow the oil to drain into a container. Refit the drain plug.

4 Undo and remove the four bolts and spring washers that secure the clutch housing to the gearbox casing. Lightly tap the clutch housing and separate from the gearbox casing. Also remove the three bolts and spring washers securing the input shaft bearing retainer. Lift away the retainer and its gasket.

5 Undo and remove the seven bolts and spring washers that secure the gear change cover. Lift away the cover. Make a note of the location of the selector forks (shift forks). Lift away the

selector forks (Fig. 6.6).

6 Undo and remove the four bolts and spring washers that secure the gearbox extension housing to the gearbox casing.

7 Rotate the extension housing until the end of the countershaft becomes fully visible.

8 Using a suitable diameter drift drive out the countershaft from the front towards the extension housing. Once the counter-shaft is removed the cluster gear may now drop into the bottom of the gearbox casing.

9 Using a soft jawed hammer, gently tap the input shaft from the front of the gearbox casing.

10 The extension housing complete with output shaft may now

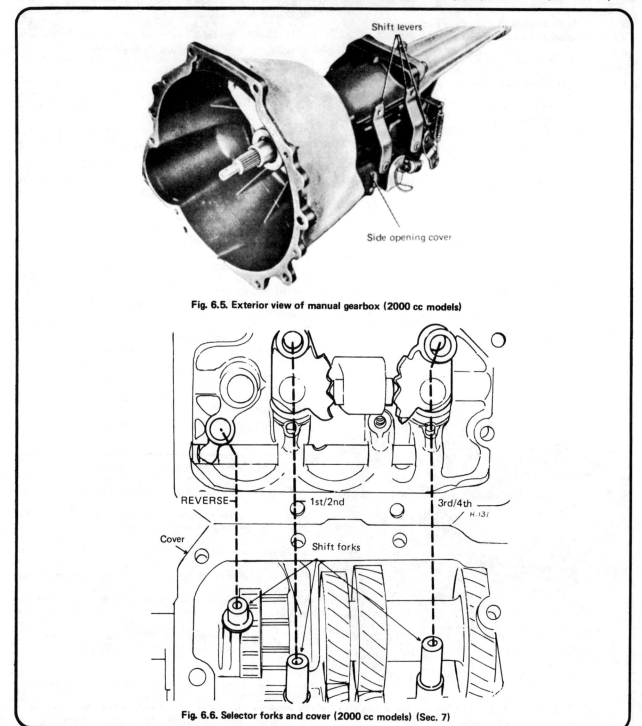

Fig. 6.5. Exterior view of manual gearbox (2000 cc models)

Fig. 6.6. Selector forks and cover (2000 cc models) (Sec. 7)

be drawn rearward from the gearbox casing (Fig. 6.7).
11 Lift out the cluster gear and recover the needle rollers and roller spacers from inside the cluster gear bore.
12 Also lift out the cluster gear thrust washers noting which way round they are fitted.
13 It will now be necessary to make up an offset drift as shown in Fig. 6.8. Using this drift drive out the reverse idler gear shaft towards the rear of the gearbox casing. Do not attempt to remove the shaft by drifting inward.
14 The gear assemblies are now completely stripped from the main casing.
15 Clean out the interior thoroughly and check for dropped needle rollers.
16 The output shaft may now be dismantled.
17 Remove the snap ring located in front of the 3rd/4th gear synchroniser. Withdraw the synchroniser assembly and 3rd gear from the output shaft (Fig. 6.9).
18 Using circlip pliers remove the snap ring and thrust washers located in front of the 2nd gear. Pull off the 2nd gear and blocking ring (Fig. 6.10).
19 Slide off the 1st/2nd gear synchroniser sleeve and synchroniser inserts. It will be observed that the synchroniser hub is splined to the output shaft and cannot be pressed off.
20 Unscrew the speedometer drive retainer and withdraw the

speedometer driven gear and its retainer.
21 A snap ring located behind the 1st gear and extension housing must next be released. This can be a little difficult due to limited working space.
22 The output shaft can now be tapped out of the extension housing using a soft faced hammer.
23 The speedometer drive gear should next be removed. This may be done using a long legged puller or a soft metal drift and hammer (Fig. 6.11).
24 Remove the snap ring located in front of the output shaft bearing. Using a press or bench vice and suitable packing pieces remove the bearing. Note which way round it is fitted (Fig. 6.12).
25 Slide off the spacer and 1st gear including the blocking ring. Remove the insert spring.
26 The input shaft assembly may be dismantled by first removing the circlip using a pair of circlip pliers.
27 Place the input shaft gear on the top of the vice with the outer track of the bearing resting on the vice jaws.
28 Using a soft faced hammer drive the input shaft through the race inner track. The strain placed on the bearing does not matter, as the bearing would not be removed unless it was being renewed. Alternatively use a three legged universal puller.
29 Lift away the race from the input shaft noting the circlip groove on the outer track is offset towards the front.

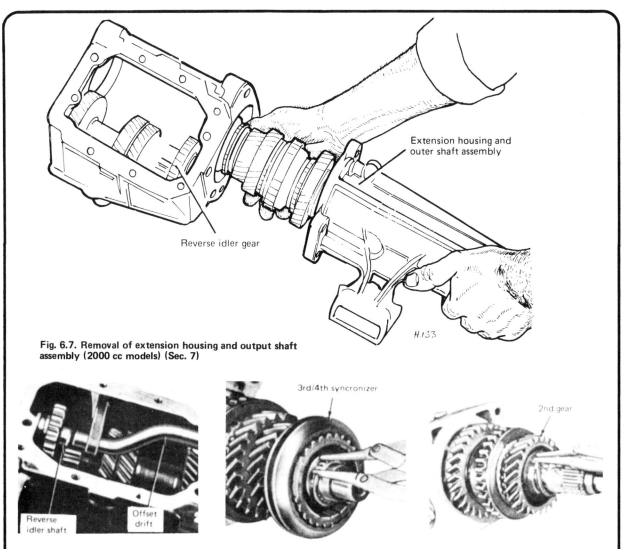

Fig. 6.7. Removal of extension housing and output shaft assembly (2000 cc models) (Sec. 7)

Fig. 6.8. Removal of reverse idler shaft (2000 cc models)

Fig. 6.9. Removal of 3rd gear snap ring (2000 cc models)

Fig. 6.10. Removal of 2nd gear snap ring (2000 cc models)

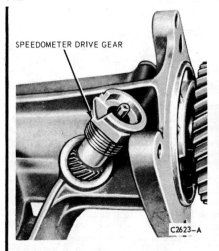

Fig. 6.11. Removal of speedometer drive gear (2000 cc models)

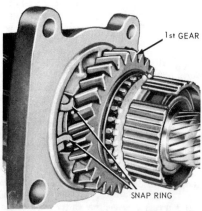

Fig. 6.12. Location of output shaft bearing snap ring (2000 cc models)

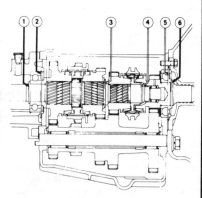

Fig. 6.13. Location of circlips (snap rings) (2000 cc models). Selective circlips are Nos. 1, 2 and 3 (Sec. 8)

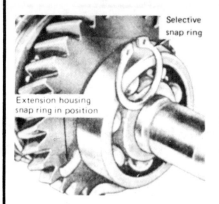

Fig. 6.14. Selecting output shaft bearing snap ring (2000 cc models)

Fig. 6.15. Fitting position of speedometer gear (2000 cc models)

Fig. 6.16. Correct fitting position of insert springs (2000 cc models)

Fig. 6.17. Fitting 2nd gear snap ring (2000 cc models)

Fig. 6.18. Fitting output shaft onto extension housing (2000 cc models)

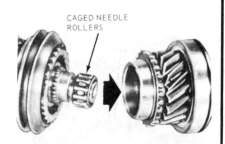

Fig. 6.19. Fitting caged roller bearing to input shaft (2000 cc models)

8 Gearbox (2000 cc models) - inspection

1   Refer to the text contained in Section 4 of this Chapter but note the different locations of the selective circlips in this gearbox, by comparison with those in the 1600 cc type gearbox. (Fig. 6.13).

9 Gearbox (2000 cc models) - reassembly

1   Make sure that all parts are clean and when assembled are well lubricated with gear oil. Where the threads of a securing bolt extend into the gearbox casing or extension housing, apply a little oil resistant sealer to the threads.
2   Slide the insert spring, blocking ring, first gear and spacer onto the rear of the output shaft. The broad side of the spacer must point towards the output shaft bearing.
3   Slide a new extension housing circlip onto the output shaft
4   Carefully press or drift the bearing onto the output shaft and secure it to the output shaft with a new snap ring (Fig. 6.14).
5   If a new bearing or output shaft is being fitted a retaining circlip which fits exactly in the groove must be used.
6   Using a tubular drift drive the speedometer drive gear onto the output shaft. The gear must be accurately positioned as shown in Fig. 6.15. This is very important because there is no locking device for the gear on the shaft.
7   Position the 1st and 2nd gear synchroniser springs offset in the synchroniser but so that their individual tensions oppose each other. This is achieved by placing one end of each spring into the same insert groove (Fig. 6.16).
8   Locate the inserts in their grooves and slide the 1st and 2nd gear synchroniser sleeve onto the synchroniser hub with the selector fork collar facing towards the forward end of the output shaft.
9   Now slide the blocking ring, second gear and thrust washer on the output shaft. Fit the retaining circlip (snap ring) (Fig. 6.17).
10 Obtain a metal bucket or old oil drum of a sufficient size to accommodate the extension housing. Put the extension housing in, place on a stove, fill with water and heat up to near boiling point.
11 Using thick rags remove the extension housing and slide the output shaft and bearing into the extension bore. **Do not** press or drift the output shaft into the extension housing as it will cause the machined bore to become oversize and the bearing outer track will be a loose fit (Fig. 6.18).
12 Fit the snap ring, previously positioned on the output shaft, into the extension housing. This will require a little patience.
13 Position the 3rd and 4th gear synchroniser springs offset in the synchroniser as previously described in paragraph 7.
14 Locate the inserts in their groove and slide the 3rd and 4th

gear synchroniser sleeve onto the synchroniser hub with the narrow shoulder facing rearward.
15 Slide the third gear and third/fourth gear synchroniser assembly on the output shaft. Refit the retaining snap ring.
16 To assemble the input shaft, place the race against soft metal faces (old shell bearings suitably straightened) on the top of the jaws of the vice and, using a drift located in the output spigot bearing hole in the rear of the input shaft, drift the shaft into the bearing. Make quite sure the bearing is the correct way round. Alternatively use a long piece of tube of suitable diameter.
   Refit the circlip that secures the bearing and also the one located in the bearing outer track.
   Fit the input shaft and gear assembly to the gearbox casing and using a soft metal drift on the bearing outer track, make sure it is fully home. Check that the caged roller bearing is correctly located (Fig. 6.19).
17 Inspect the seal in the input shaft bearing retainer and if it shows signs of deterioration prise out with a screwdriver and fit a new one. The lip must face towards the gearbox casing when fitted (Fig. 6.20).
18 Fit the front bearing retainer and a new gasket to the front of the gearbox casing. The oil groove in the retainer must be in line with the main case and the gasket must not cover this passage. Apply a little sealer to the three cover retaining screws and tighten in a progressive manner.
19 Locate the reverse idler gear in the main casing so that the collar for the selector fork faces rearwards. Slide the shaft into position until it is flush with the wall of the main casing.
20 Assemble the cluster gear bearings by first inserting the spacer tube and inner rings into the bore. Apply some thick grease to the needle roller locations and replace the needle rollers. Finally replace the pair of outer rings (Fig. 6.21).
21 Make up a piece of tube the exact length of the cluster gear and the same diameter as the shaft. Slide this into the countershaft bore.
22 Position new cluster gear thrust washers in the main casing retaining with thick grease.
23 Smear a little jointing compound to both faces of the extension housing gasket and fit to the main casing.
24 Slide the extension housing and output shaft assembly into position, taking care not to damage the caged roller bearing on the end of the output shaft.
25 With the extension housing in position and located so that the countershaft can be refitted invert the assembly so that the cluster gear is uppermost. Rotate the input and output shafts until the countershaft can be inserted. The offset lug on the shaft must be correctly positioned at the rear when finally fitted in the main casing. As the shaft is inserted it will eject the dummy shaft (Fig. 6.22).
26 Turn the extension housing until it is the correct way up and secure with the four bolts and spring washers. Apply a little oil resistant sealer to these bolts. Tighten the bolts to the specified

Fig. 6.20. Input shaft bearing retainer - note location of drain slot (2000 cc models)

Fig. 6.21. Components of cluster gear (2000 cc models)

Fig. 6.22. Countershaft lug fitted position (2000 cc models)

torque.

27 Refit the speedometer driven gear to the side of the extension housing.

28 Refer to Fig. 6.23 to identify the selector forks and fit the first/second and third/fourth selector forks with the number stamped on them facing towards the **front** of the gearbox. The reverse selector fork must be fitted with the number facing rearwards. It should be observed that the short leg of the first/second selector fork must be fitted towards the bottom of the gearbox.

29 Apply a little sealer to the gearchange housing gasket and fit to the side of the main casing. Replace the gearchange housing and secure with the bolts and spring washers. These should be tightened to the specified torque wrench setting.

30 Before proceeding further check that all forward gears and the reverse gear can be obtained by operating the two side levers. If one or more gears are unobtainable, remove the housing and investigate the cause.

31 Refit the gearbox bellhousing and secure with the four bolts and spring washers. These should be tightened to the specified torque wrench setting.

32 Replace the clutch release lever, hub and bearing.

33 The gearbox is now ready for refitting. Do not forget to refill with the recommended grade of oil.

---

10 Gearchange linkage (2000 cc models) - removal and refitting

1 Chock the front wheels, jack-up the rear of the car and support on firmly based axle stands.

2 Using a pair of pliers or a screwdriver remove the clips retaining the gearchange rods to the levers. Detach the rods.

3 Working inside the car carefully detach the wood grain panel located at the rear of the console. For this use a strong knife.

4 Undo and remove the two screws securing the plastic cross panel. Slide the plastic cross panel forward and lift away.

5 Ease up the rear corners of the handbrake lever rubber boot which will give access to the two screws. Undo and remove these two screws.

6 Carefully ease up the rear edge of the front wood grain panel and remove the centre retaining screw.

7 Undo and remove the two screws, one each side of the forward lower edge of the console, unscrew the gearchange lever knob and move the console to one side.

8 Undo and remove the three screws that secure the gearchange lever assembly to the floor panel. The gearchange lever assembly may now be lifted up and away from the floor (Fig. 6.25).

9 Should it be necessary to dismantle the assembly, first drive out the pivot pin using a parallel pin punch (Fig. 6.26).

10 Pull the gearchange lever up from the assembly.

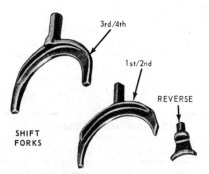

Fig. 6.23. Selector fork identification (2000 cc models) (Sec. 9)

11 Move all three selector levers towards the rear into the horizontal until it is possible for the grooved pin to be moved through the respective cut-outs in the selector levers and shaft retainers.

12 Pull the selector lever shaft out and then drift out the locking pin with a suitable parallel pin punch.

13 Lift away the pressure springs, thrust piece and bushings.

14 To reassemble first smear all sliding surfaces with grease.

15 Position the reverse gear pressure spring on the thrust piece and slide both parts into the main body.

16 Place the bush with the larger diameter facing the change levers.

17 Refit the change levers and vibration dampers (Fig. 6.27).

18 The shaft complete with locking pin and pressure spring may now be inserted into the shaft retainers and change levers. Allow the change levers to swing into the vertical position.

19 Refit the gearchange lever and rubber boot and retain in position with the pivot pin.

20 Refitting the gearchange lever assembly is the reverse sequence to removal. It will however, be necessary to check the adjustment, as described in Section 11.

---

11 Gearchange linkage (2000 cc models) - adjustment

1 Refer to Fig. 6.30 and make up an alignment pin to the dimensions given.

2 Chock the front wheels, jack up the rear of the car and support on firmly based stands.

3 Using a pair of pliers or a screwdriver, remove the clips retaining the gearchange rods to the levers.

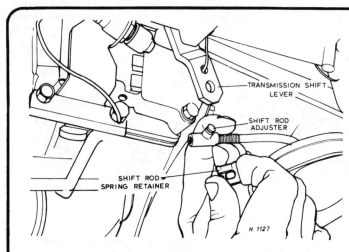

Fig. 6.24. Disconnecting selector rods (2000 cc models) (Sec. 10)

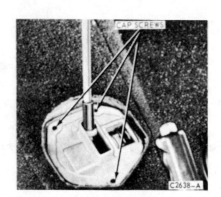

Fig. 6.25. Gearchange lever assembly securing screws (2000 cc models)

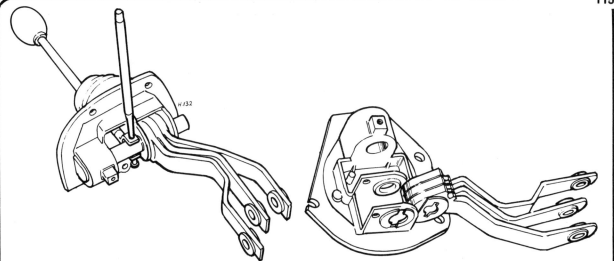

Fig. 6.26. Removal of pivot pin (2000 cc models) (Sec. 10)   **Fig. 6.27. Refitting selector levers to body (2000 cc models) (Sec. 10)**

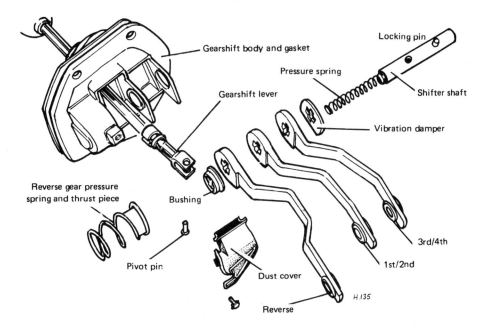

Fig. 6.28. Component parts of remote control gearchange assembly (2000 cc models) (Sec. 10)

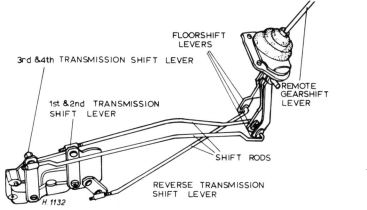

Fig. 6.29. Gearchange lever assembly components (2000 cc models) (Sec. 10) Note shift rod connection to levers

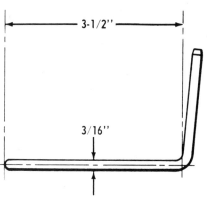

Fig. 6.30. Alignment pin dimensions (2000 cc models) (Sec. 11)

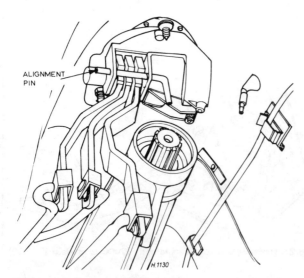

Fig. 6.31. Alignment pin inserted (2000 cc models) (Sec. 11)

4 Insert the previously made alignment pin into the change levers as shown in Fig. 6.31. This ensures that they are accurately positioned.
5 Move the gearbox selector levers to the neutral position.
6 Adjust the length of the selector rods until they fit into the holes in the gearbox selector levers.
7 Refit the selector rods to the gearbox selector levers and retain with the spring retainers. Lubricate the moving parts with a little grease.
8 Remove the alignment pin and lower the car to the ground. Road test to ensure that all gears are easily obtainable.

12 Automatic transmission - general description

An automatic transmission unit may be fitted as a factory option to all models covered by this manual. 2000 cc models are fitted with the Ford C4 three speed automatic transmission unit and 1600 cc models are fitted with the well proven Borg-Warner Type 35.
The system comprises two main components:—
1 A three element hydrokinetic torque converter coupling, capable of torque multiplication at an infinitely variable ratio between 2 : 1 and 1 : 1.
2 A torque/speed responsive and hydraulic epicyclic gearbox comprising a planetary gearset providing three forward ratios and one reverse ratio.
Due to the complexity of the automatic transmission unit, if performance is not up to standard, or overhaul is necessary, it is imperative that this be left to the local dealer who will have the special equipment and knowledge for fault diagnosis and rectification.
The content of the following Sections is therefore confined to supplying general information and any service information and instruction that can be used by the owner.

13 Automatic transmission - special precautions

Towing. If a caravan, boat or trailer is being towed, always select the 'L' position before ascending or descending steep hills to stop overheating of the special transmission fluid, and to receive benefit from engine braking.
Recovery towing. Should it be necessary to have the car towed to a garage it must not be longer than 20 miles (32.19 km) away and the speed should not exceed 30 mph (48.28 kph). Towing is permitted provided the transmission is not damaged and that the

oil level is correct. Put the selector lever in the 'N' position. If there are noises emitting from the transmission, or the towing distance is greater than 20 miles (32.19 km), the propeller shaft should be disconnected and completely removed and the end of the transmission sealed to prevent oil loss and dirt ingress. As an alternative the car can be suspended and towed with the rear wheels off the ground — a steering wheel clamp will be necessary.

14 Automatic transmission - routine maintenance

1 The most important task is to maintain the correct fluid level.

Type C4
2 Have the transmission fluid at normal operating temperature. This can only be achieved by running the car on the road for a minimum distance of five miles (8 km).
3 With the car on level surface and the engine idling, move the speed selector lever through all positions at least three times.
4 Select 'P' and with the engine still idling, wait for a period of between 1 and 2 minutes then withdraw the dipstick. Wipe it clean and then re-insert it. Withdraw it for the second time and read off the fluid level. This should be between the MIN and MAX levels otherwise top-up with fluid of the specified grade.

Borg-Warner 35
5 Ensure that the transmission fluid is at normal operating temperature.
6 With the car on level ground, and the engine idling, move the speed selector lever through all positions at least three times.
7 Select 'P' and switch off the engine. Within one minute of switching off the engine, withdraw the dipstick, wipe it clean, re-insert it and then withdraw it for the second time and read off the fluid level. This should be between the 'MIN' and 'MAX' marks otherwise top-up with fluid of the specified grade.
8 With both types of transmission, always keep the external surfaces of the unit clean to prevent overheating. Keep the air intake grilles clear and make sure that all the checks and adjustments described in this Chapter are regularly carried out.
9 On C4 transmission units, every 12000 miles (19000 km) check and adjust the brake bands, as described in Sections 19 and 20.

15 Automatic transmission unit (Ford type C4) - removal and installation

Although faults should be diagnosed by your dealer while the transmission is still in the car, there is no reason why the unit cannot be removed for repair or a new or exchange transmission installed, by the home mechanic using the following sequence of operations.
1 Open the engine compartment lid and place old blankets over the wings to prevent accidental damage to the paintwork.
2 For safety reasons disconnect the battery earth cable.
3 Raise the car on a hoist or drive over a pit. If neither are available raise the car as high as possible and support on axle stands. Make sure they are very firmly located.
4 Place a suitably large container under the transmission fluid sump. Slacken the sump securing bolts commencing at the rear and working to the front. Allow the fluid to drain out. **Caution:** If the car has just been driven the fluid will be extremely hot and can cause severe burns. Allow to cool down before draining.
5 Make a note of the electrical cable connections to the starter motor. Remove the connectors from their terminals.
6 Undo and remove the three bolts and spring washers which secure the starter motor to the engine. Lift away the starter motor from the converter housing.
7 Undo and remove the bolts and spring washers that secure the access cover to the lower end of the converter housing. Lift

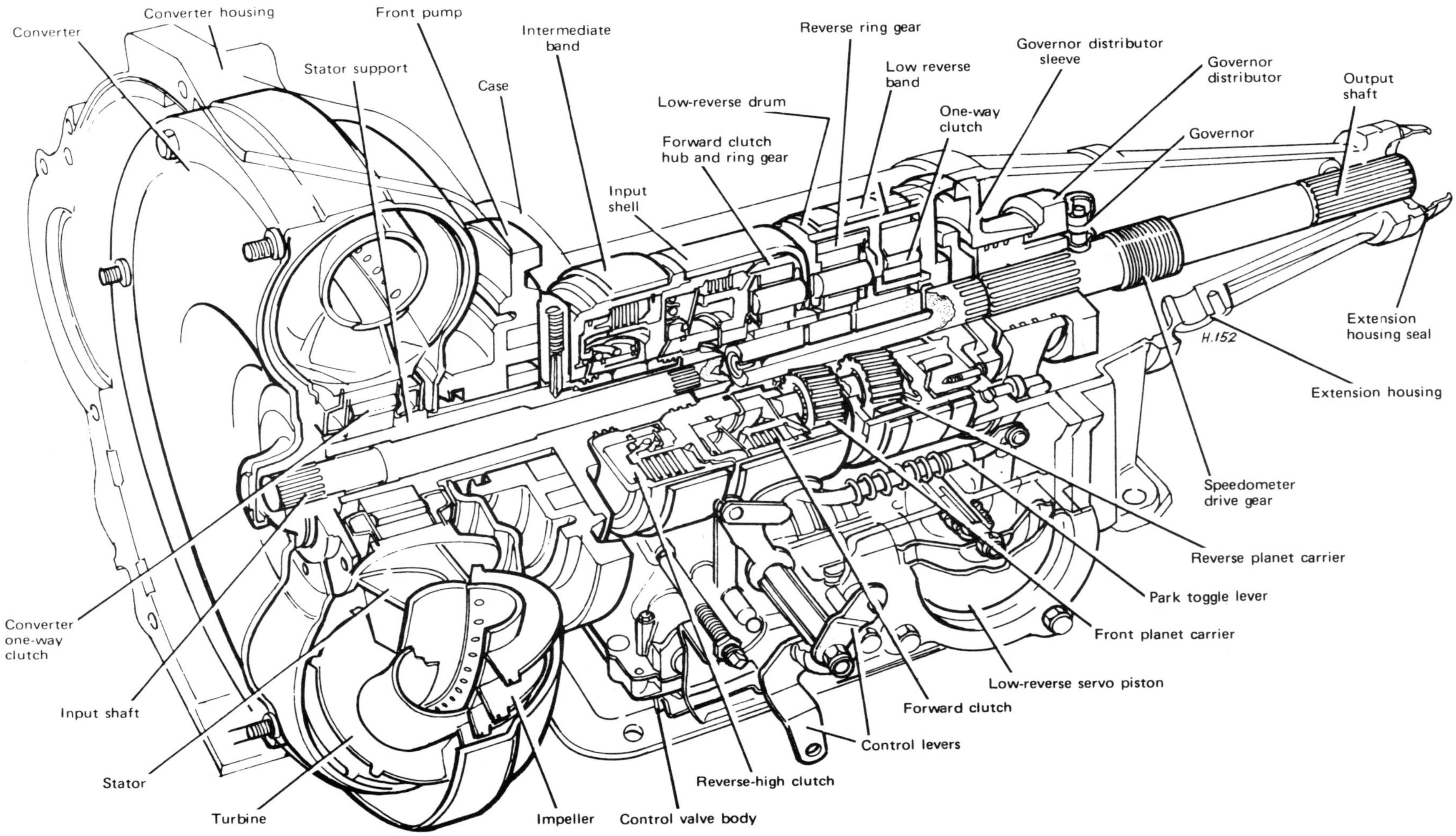

Fig. 6.32 Sectional view of Ford C4 automatic transmission

Output shaft
Extension housing seal
Extension housing
Governor distributor
Governor
Governor distributor sleeve
One-way clutch
Low reverse band
Reverse ring gear
Low-reverse drum
Forward clutch hub and ring gear
Input shell
Intermediate band
Case
Front pump
Stator support
Converter housing
Converter
Converter one-way clutch
Input shaft
Stator
Turbine
Impeller
Control valve body
Reverse-high clutch
Control levers
Forward clutch
Low-reverse servo piston
Front planet carrier
Park toggle lever
Reverse planet carrier
Speedometer drive gear
H.152

away the access cover.

8   Undo and remove the converter to flywheel securing nuts. To do this fit a spanner to the crankshaft pulley securing bolt and turn the crankshaft (therefore the converter) to gain access to these nuts, one at a time.

9   Again turn the converter until the drain plug is accessible. Remove the plug and allow fluid to drain from the converter. Refit the plug once all fluid has drained out.

10   Mark the propeller shaft and rear axle flanges so that they may be reconnected in their original positions. Undo and remove the four securing bolts and lower the rear half of the propeller shaft.

11   Undo and remove the two bolts that secure the centre bearing carrier to its bracket.

12   Carefully lower the front half of the propeller shaft whilst at the same time sliding the front yoke from the rear of the transmission unit.

13   Wrap some rag around the end of the unit to prevent dirt ingress or accidental damage to the splines.

14   Release the speedometer cable from the extension housing.

15   Detach the shift cable from the manual lever at the transmission unit end.

16   Undo and remove the two bolts and spring washers that secure the shift cable bracket to the converter housing. Move the cable and bracket to one side.

17   Detach the downshift cable from the transmission downshift lever bracket.

18   Make a note of the electrical cable connections at the neutral/start switch end and detach the connectors. Disconnect the cables from the support clamps and move out of the way.

19   Detach the vacuum line from the transmission vacuum unit.

20   Using a suitable jack support the weight of the unit and then remove the insulator to extension housing bracket bolt.

21   Undo and remove the crossmember-to-frame securing bolts. Lift away the crossmember.

22   Wipe the ends of the oil cooler pipes at the transmission and detach the pipes. Wrap the ends in rags to stop dirt ingress.

23   Undo and remove the bolt that secures the transmission filler tube to the cylinder block. Lift the tube from the case.

24   Undo and remove the converter housing to engine securing bolts.

25   Check that no cables or securing bolts have been left in position.

26   The assistance of at least one other person is now required because of the weight of the complete unit.

27   Carefully pull the unit rearward and downward. Draw away from under the car.

28   Refitting the unit is the reverse sequence to removal. It will be necessary to adjust the controls and also the inhibitor switch as described later in this Chapter. Do not forget to refill the unit. Do not race the engine for a period of 5 minutes to allow complete circulation of the hydraulic fluid.

16 Speed selector linkage (type C4) - adjustment

1   Move the selector lever to the 'D' position.

2   Chock the front wheels, jack up the rear of the car and support on firmly based stands.

3   Remove the clevis pin and disconnect the cable and bushing from the transmission lever.

4   With the selector lever in the 'D' position, move the transmission lever to the 'D' position, this being the third detent position from the rear of the unit.

5   Adjust the cable length until the clevis pin holes in the manual lever and the end of the cable are in alignment.

6   Reconnect the cable and secure with the clevis pin and clip.

7   Lower the car to the ground and road test to ensure correct operation in all selector lever positions.

17 'Kick-down' cable (type C4) - renewal and adjustment

1   Detach the 'kick-down' cable from the throttle lever bell crank.

2   Slacken the two cable adjustment nuts at the bracket. The cable may now be withdrawn sideways from the bracket.

3   Chock the front wheels, jack up the rear of the car and support on firmly based stands.

4   Working under the car disconnect the 'kick-down' cable from the transmission unit.

5   The cable may now be removed from the car.

6   Refitting the cable is the reverse sequence to removal. It will however be necessary to adjust the linkage.

7   Move the throttle to the wide open position and locate the 'kick-down' cable so that the tang just contacts the throttle shaft. This condition is obtained by repositioning the nuts and then tightening.

18 Neutral start switch (type C4) - removal, refitting and adjustment

1   Detach the downshift cable from the transmission unit downshift lever.

2   Apply some penetrating oil to the downshift lever shaft and nut.

3   Undo and remove the transmission downshift outer lever retaining nut and lever.

4   Undo and remove the two neutral start switch securing bolts.

5   Detach the multi-pin connector from the neutral switch and remove the switch from the transmission unit.

6   To refit the switch, place in position on the transmission unit and replace the two retaining bolts. Do not fully tighten yet.

7   Move the transmission manual lever to the neutral position,

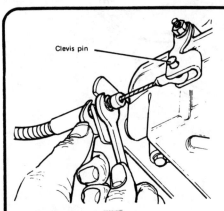

Fig. 6.33. Manual linkage control cable adjustment (C4) (Sec. 16)

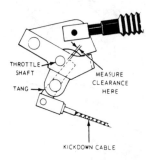

Fig. 6.34. 'Kickdown' linkage adjustment (C4) (Sec. 17)

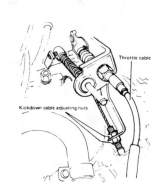

Fig. 6.35. 'Kickdown' linkage adjusting nuts (C4) (Sec. 17)

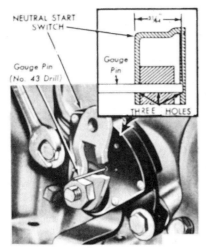
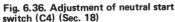

Fig. 6.36. Adjustment of neutral start
switch (C4) (Sec. 18)

Fig. 6.37. Adjusting intermediate band
(C4) (Sec. 19)

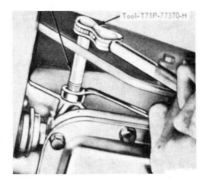

Fig. 6.38. Adjusting low/reverse band
(C4) (Sec. 20)

rotate the switch and insert a No. 43 drill into the gauge pin hole. It must be inserted to a full 31/64 in. (12.0 mm) so that it passes through into the three holes in the switch (Fig. 6.36).

8 Tighten the switch securing bolts to a torque wrench setting of 55 - 57 lb f. ft (7.4 - 7.85 kg fm) and remove the drill.

9 Refit the outer downshift lever and securing nut, which should be tightened to a torque wrench setting of 8 - 9 lb f. ft (1.11 - 1.2 kg fm).

10 Reconnect the downshift cable to the downshift lever.

11 Reconnect the switch wires. Check the operation of the switch in each detent position. The engine should only start when the selector lever is in the 'N' or 'P' position.

19 Intermediate band (C4) - adjustment

1 The intermediate or front band is used to hold the sun gear stationary so as to give the second gear ratio. If it is not correctly adjusted there will be noticeable slip during first to second gearchange or from third to second gearchange. The first symptoms of these conditions will be a very sluggish gearchange instead of the usual crisp action.

2 To adjust the intermediate band, undo and remove the adjustment screw locknut located on the left-hand side of the transmission case (Fig. 6.37).

3 Install a new locknut but leave it unscrewed several turns.

4 Tighten the adjusting screw to a torque wrench setting of 10 lb f ft (1.4 kg fm) and then unscrew it exactly 1¾ turns. Holding the adjusting screw in this position, tighten the locknut to a torque of 40 lb f ft (5.5 kg fm).

20 Low and reverse band (C4) - adjustment

1 The low and reverse band or rear band is in action when 'L' or 'R' position of the selector lever has been obtained to hold the low and reverse pinion carrier stationary. If it is not correctly adjusted, there will be a noticeable malfunction of the automatic transmission unit, whereby there will be no drive with the selector in the 'R' position, also associated with no engine braking on first gear when the selector lever is in the 'L' position.

2 To adjust the rear band, undo and remove the adjusting screw locknut located on the left-hand side of the automatic transmission casing (Fig. 6.38).

3 Install a new locknut but leave it unscrewed several turns.

4 Tighten the adjusting screw to a torque wrench setting of 10 lb f ft (1.4 kg fm) and then unscrew it exactly 3 turns.

5 Tighten the locknut to a torque of 40 lb f ft (5.5 kg fm).

21 Speed selector lever (C4) - removal and refitting

1 Chock the front wheels, jack up the rear of the car and support on firmly based stands.

2 Withdraw the clevis pin and disconnect the selector lever cable and bushing from the selector lever operating arm.

3 Working inside the car carefully detach the wood grain panel at the rear of the console. A strong knife is the best tool to use.

4 Undo and remove the two screws that retain the plastic cross panel. Slide the panel forward and lift away.

5 Lift up the rear corners of the handbrake rubber boot thereby revealing two screws. Undo and remove these screws.

6 Carefully prise up the rear edge of the front wood grain panel and remove the centre retaining screw.

7 Undo and remove the two screws located one each side of the forward lower edge of the console, and move the console to the side.

8 Lift the selector lever indicator bezel upward.

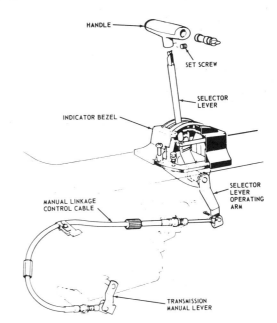

Fig. 6.39. Layout of selector lever assembly and control cable
(C4) (Sec. 21)

9 Undo and remove the three selector lever housing to floor panel securing bolts. Detach the indicator light and remove the selector lever and housing assembly.

10 Slacken the set screw retaining the handle to the selector lever. Fully depress the push button and remove the handle.

11 Remove the plug from the side of the selector housing and remove the retaining nut located at the base of the selector lever.

12 The selector lever and bushings are next removed by lightly tapping the operating arm shaft with a copper drift and hammer.

13 Using a suitable diameter parallel pin punch drift out the cable retaining pin located at the top of the selector lever (Fig. 6.40).

14 Remove the cable adjustment nut from the cable at the lower end of the selector lever and remove the detent plunger, spring and bushing.

15 The cable may now be withdrawn from the selector lever.

16 Reassembly and refitting is the reverse sequence to removal. During reassembly of the selector lever it is necessary to turn the cable adjustment nut until a clearance of 0.005 - 0.010 inch (0.127 - 0.254 mm) is obtained between the bottom of the pawl and detent.

22 Speed selector control cable (C4) - renewal

1 Chock the front wheels, jack up the rear of the car and support on firmly based stands.

2 Withdraw the clevis pin and disconnect the selector lever cable and bushing from the selector lever operating arm.

3 Slacken the cable retaining nut at the body bracket and release the cable from the bracket.

4 Withdraw the clevis pin and disconnect the cable and bushing from the transmission unit.

5 Slacken the cable adjustment nut and locknut at the transmission bracket and lift the cable from the car.

6 Refitting the cable is the reverse sequence to removal. It will be necessary to adjust the cable, as described in Section 16.

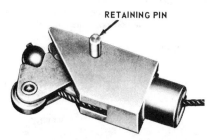

Fig. 6.40. Cable retaining pin (C4) (Sec. 21)

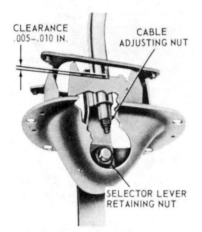

Fig. 6.41. Manual selector lever adjustment (C4) (Sec. 21)

23 Automatic transmission (Borg-Warner type 35) - removal and installation

1 Refer to Section 15, paragraphs 1 to 3 inclusive.

2 Withdraw the transmission unit dipstick and put to one side.

3 Detach the throttle linkage downshift valve control cable.

4 Place a suitable size container under the drain plug, remove the drain plug and allow the fluid to drain out. Refit the plug. **Caution:** If the car has just been driven the fluid will be extremely hot and can cause severe burns. Allow to cool down before draining.

5 Detach the propeller shaft as described in Section 15, paragraphs 10 to 13 inclusive.

6 Disconnect the exhaust pipe bracket from the transmission bracket. Slacken the bracket at the exhaust pipe and rotate it to the side.

7 Using a pair of pliers release the speedometer cable at the transmission extension and withdraw the speedometer cable.

8 Make a note of the cable connections at the starter motor and detach from the terminals. Undo and remove the bolts and spring washers that secure the starter motor to the engine and withdraw from the converter housing.

9 Undo and remove the bolts and spring washers that secure the front lower cover to the converter housing.

10 Undo and remove the four bolts that secure the driveplate to the converter.

11 Detach the manual linkage control from the transmission unit.

12 Make a note of the cable connections to the starter neutral switch terminals. Detach the cable connectors.

13 Support the weight of the transmission unit with a suitable jack.

14 Undo and remove the four bolts that secure the engine support to the underside of the body.

15 Undo and remove the six bolts and spring washers securing the converter housing to the engine.

16 Carefully withdraw the transmission fluid filler tube. Check that all securing bolts and cables have been detached from the unit.

17 The assistance of at least one other person is now required because of the weight of the complete unit.

18 Using a large tyre lever exert pressure between the driveplate and converter so as to prevent the converter becoming disengaged from the transmission unit as it is drawn rearwards. It will also be full of hydraulic fluid.

19 Carefully pull the unit rearwards and lift it away from under the car. Place on wooden blocks so that the selector lever is not damaged or bent.

20 To separate the converter housing from the transmission unit first lift off the converter from the transmission unit, taking suitable precautions to catch the fluid upon separation. Undo and remove the six bolts and spring washers that secure the converter housing to the transmission case. Lift away the converter housing.

21 Refitting the automatic transmission unit is the reverse sequence to removal, but there are several additional points which will assist:

a) *If the torque converter has been removed before refitting it will be necessary to align the front pump drive tangs with the slots in the inner gear and then carefully replace the torque converter. Take extreme precautions not to damage the oil seal.*

b) *Adjust the manual selector linkage, the throttle downshift cable and the inhibitor switch. Full details will be found in this Chapter.*

c) *Do not forget to refill the unit. Do not race the engine for a period of 5 minutes to allow complete circulation of the hydraulic fluid.*

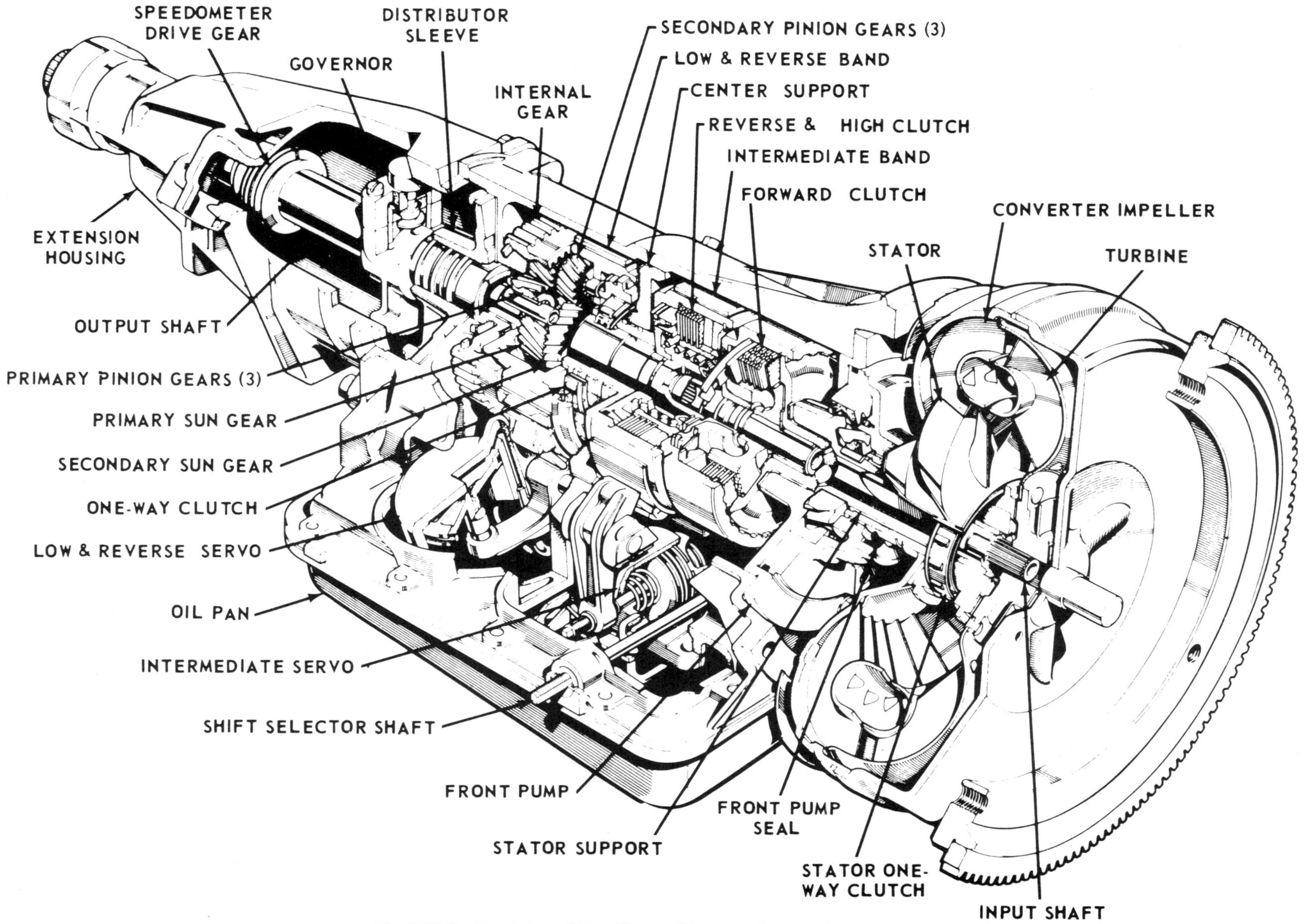
SPEEDOMETER DRIVE GEAR
DISTRIBUTOR SLEEVE
GOVERNOR
INTERNAL GEAR
SECONDARY PINION GEARS (3)
LOW & REVERSE BAND
CENTER SUPPORT
REVERSE & HIGH CLUTCH
INTERMEDIATE BAND
FORWARD CLUTCH
CONVERTER IMPELLER
STATOR
TURBINE
EXTENSION HOUSING
OUTPUT SHAFT
PRIMARY PINION GEARS (3)
PRIMARY SUN GEAR
SECONDARY SUN GEAR
ONE-WAY CLUTCH
LOW & REVERSE SERVO
OIL PAN
INTERMEDIATE SERVO
SHIFT SELECTOR SHAFT
FRONT PUMP
STATOR SUPPORT
FRONT PUMP SEAL
STATOR ONE-WAY CLUTCH
INPUT SHAFT

Fig. 6.42. Sectional view of Borg Warner 35 automatic transmission

24 Neutral start switch (BW 35) - adjustment

1 Select the 'D' position. Make a note of the starter inhibitor and reverse lamp switch cable connections and disconnect the cables from the switch.
2 Connect a test lamp and battery across the smaller starter inhibitor terminals and a further test lamp and battery across the two larger reverse light terminals.
3 Undo the locknut and screw out the switch about two turns. Slowly screw in the switch again until the test lamp connected to the reverse light terminal goes out. Mark the relative position of the switch by putting an alignment mark on the switch body and the transmission casing.
4 Continue screwing in the switch until the test lamp connected to the starter inhibitor terminals lights. Mark the relative position of the switch again.
5 Unscrew the switch until it is half way between the two positions and tighten the locknut.
6 Reconnect the cables and check that the starter motor only operates when the selector lever is in the 'P' or 'N' position. Also check that the reverse light only operates with the selector in the 'R' position. If the switch does not operate it should be renewed.

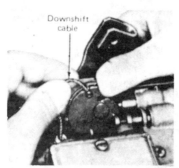

Fig. 6.43. Attaching downshift cable to cam (BW 35) (Sec. 25)

25 Downshift valve control cable (BW 35) - renewal and adjustment

1 Detach the downshift valve control cable from the bell crank assembly.
2 Slacken the cable to bracket retaining nut and withdraw the cable sideways from the bracket.
3 Chock the front wheels, jack up the rear of the car and support on firmly based stands.
4 Wipe the area around the transmission unit drain plug and unscrew. Allow the fluid to drain into a clean container. If the car has just been run take great care as the fluid will be extremely hot and can cause severe burns.
5 Undo and remove the bolts and washers securing the oil pan to the transmission unit body. Lift away the oil pan and its gasket.
6 Rotate the cam sufficiently for the downshift control cable to be detached.
7 Unscrew the outer cable from the transmission body and lift away the cable from the car.
8 To refit the cable first screw the cable into the transmission body and fully tighten.
9 Rotate the cam and connect the downshift control cable to the cam (Fig. 6.43).
10 Connect the downshift cable to the support bracket at the carburettor. Leave the two locknuts slack and adjust them to remove any slack from the inner cable.
11 With the throttle fully released (idling position) check that the cam is as shown in (A) Fig. 6.44.
12 Now depress the accelerator pedal fully to the 'kick-down' position and check that the cam is as shown in (B). Adjust the locknuts as necessary to achieve the correct cam adjustment (Fig. 6.45).
13 If a new cable has been installed, crimp the stop collar (loosely fitted to the cable in production), so that a clearance of 0.030 in. (0.762 mm) is provided between the stop and the end face of the outer cable. This clearance should always be maintained with cable fitted as original equipment (Fig. 6.46).

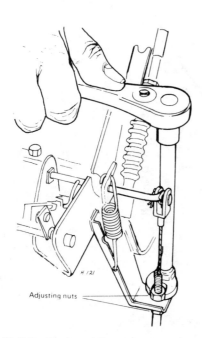

Fig. 6.45. Adjusting downshift cable locknuts (BW 35) (Sec. 25)

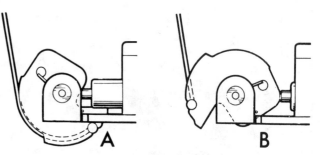

Fig. 6.44. Downshift valve cable adjustment (BW 35) (Sec. 25)

A Idling position

B 'Kickdown' position

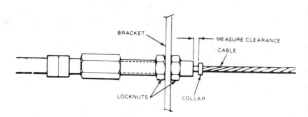

Fig. 6.46. Downshift control cable adjustments (BW 35) (Sec. 25)

26 Fault diagnosis - manual gearbox and automatic transmission

Symptom	Reason/s
Part 1: manual gearbox	
Weak or ineffective synchromesh	Synchronising cones worn, split or damaged
	Baulk ring synchromesh dogs worn, or damaged
Jumps out of gear	Broken gearchange fork rod spring
	Gearbox coupling dogs badly worn
	Selector fork rod groove badly worn
Excessive noise	Incorrect grade of oil in gearbox or oil level too low
	Bush or needle roller bearings worn or damaged
	Gear teeth excessively worn or damaged
	Countershaft thrust washers worn allowing excessive end play
Excessive difficulty in engaging gear	Clutch pedal adjustment incorrect

Note: It is sometimes difficult to decide whether it is worthwhile removing and dismantling the gearbox for a fault which may be nothing more than a minor irritant. Gearboxes which howl, or where the synchromesh can be 'beaten' by a quick gearchange, may continue to perform for a long time in this state. A worn gearbox usually needs a complete rebuild to eliminate noise because the various gears, if re-aligned on new bearings will continue to howl when different wearing surfaces are presented to each other.

The decision to overhaul therefore, must be considered with regard to time and money available, relative to the degree of noise or malfunction that the driver has to suffer.

Part 2: Automatic transmission

As has been mentioned elsewhere in this Chapter no service repair to the automatic transmission unit should be considered by anyone without the specialist knowledge and equipment required to undertake such work. Information is however given on the various adjustments which the author considers may be completed without any difficulty.

Chapter 7 Propeller shaft

Contents

Specifications

Type ... ...   Two piece tubular steel with either three universal joints and rubber mounted centre bearing or two universal joints and centre constant velocity type joint

Length

	Front section	Rear section
Manual gearbox	20.72 in. (526.0 mm)	26.25 in. (666.3 mm)
Automatic transmission	21.89 in. (555.5 mm)	26.25 in. (666.3 mm)

Universal joint spider diameter ... ...   0.63 in. (16.0 mm)

Torque wrench settings

	lb f ft	kg f m
Drive flange bolts	45	6.2
Centre joint bolt	30	4.1

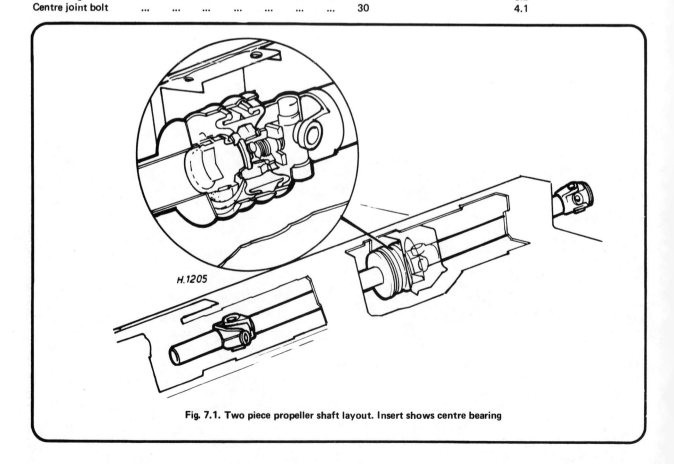

H.1205

Fig. 7.1. Two piece propeller shaft layout. Insert shows centre bearing

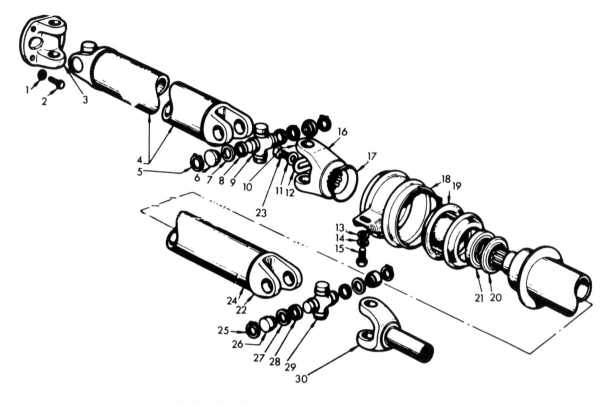

Fig. 7.2. Two piece propeller shaft - component parts

1 Lock washer	9 Spider	17 Bearing cap	25 Circlip
2 Bolt	10 Splined centre yoke	18 Centre bearing housing	26 Needle roller bearing and cap
3 Driveshaft flange yoke	11 Washer	19 Rubber insulator	27 Oil seal
4 Rear section propeller shaft	12 'U' washer	20 Bearing cup	28 Oil seal retainer
5 Circlip	13 Washer	21 Bearing	29 Spider
6 Needle roller bearing & cap	14 Lock washer	22 Front section yoke	30 Splined universal joint
7 Oil seal	15 Bolt	23 Bolt	knuckle
8 Oil seal retainer	16 Yoke	24 Front section propeller shaft	

1 General description

Drive is transmitted from the gearbox to the rear axle by means of a finely balanced tubular propeller shaft split into two halves and supported at the centre by a rubber mounted bearing.

Fitted to the front, centre and rear of the propeller shaft assembly are universal joints which allow vertical movement of the rear axle and slight movement of the complete power unit on its rubber mountings. Each universal joint comprises a four legged centre spider, four needle roller bearings and two yokes.

Fore and aft movement of the rear axle is absorbed by a sliding spline located at the gearbox end. The yoke flange of the rear universal joint is fitted to the rear axle and is secured to the pinion flange by four bolts and lock washers.

The universal joints at the front, centre and rear of the propeller shaft are obtainable as a kit. They are of the sealed type and require no maintenance once assembled.

On some models, a constant velocity type centre joint is used and when this becomes worn, the complete propeller shaft will have to be renewed as an assembly.

2 Propeller shaft - removal and installation

1 Jack-up the rear of the car, or position the rear of the car over a pit or on a ramp.

Fig. 7.3. Propeller shaft with centre constant velocity joint

2 If the rear of the car is jacked-up, supplement the jack with support blocks so that danger is minimised, should the jack collapse.

3 If the rear wheels are off the ground place the car in gear or put the handbrake on to ensure that the propeller shaft does not turn when an attempt is made to loosen the four bolts securing the propeller shaft to the rear axle companion flange.

4 Unscrew and remove the four lock bolts and securing washers which hold the flange on the propeller shaft to the flange on the rear axle.

5 The propeller shaft is carefully balanced to fine limits and it is important that it is replaced in exactly the same position it was in, prior to its removal. Scratch a mark on the propeller shaft and rear axle flanges to ensure accurate mating when the time comes for reassembly (Fig. 7.4).

6 Undo and remove the two bolts holding the centre bearing housing to the underframe.

7 Slightly push the shaft forward to separate the two flanges at the rear, then lower the end of the shaft and pull it rearwards to

disengage it from the gearbox mainshaft splines.

8 Place a large can or tray under the rear of the gearbox extension to catch any oil which is likely to leak through the spline lubricating holes when the propeller shaft is removed.

9 Installation of the two piece propeller shaft is a reversal of the above procedure. Ensure that the mating marks scratched on the propeller shaft and rear axle flanges line up.

10 Note the method of securing the flanges: either nuts and bolts or setscrews according to type of rear axle (Fig. 7.5).

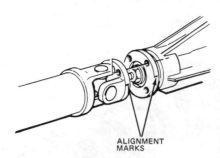

ALIGNMENT
MARKS

Fig. 7.4. Drive flange alignment marks (Sec. 2)

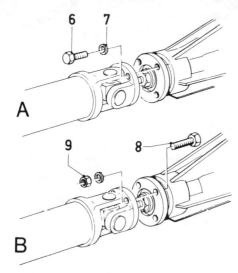

6   7

A

9   8

B

Fig. 7.5. Methods of securing drive flanges. Note position of nuts (Sec. 2)

A Integral type rear axle   6 Setscrew
B Detachable differential   7 Lockwasher
carrier axle   8 Bolt
                                     9 Nut

3 Propeller shaft centre bearing - renewal

1 Prior to removing the centre bearing from the front section of the two piece propeller shaft, carefully scratch marks on the rear yoke and on the shaft just forward of the bearing housing to ensure correct alignment on reassembly.

2 Knock back the tab washer on the centre bolt located in the jaws of the rear yoke. Slacken off the nut and remove the 'U' washer from under it.

3 With the 'U' washer removed the rear yoke can now be drawn off the splines of the front section. The centre bolt and its washer remain attached to the splined front section.

4 Slide the bearing housing with its rubber insulator from the shaft. Bend back the six metal tabs on the housing and remove the rubber insulator.

5 The bearing and its protective caps should now be withdrawn from the splined section of the propeller shaft by careful levering with two large screwdrivers or tyre levers. If a suitable puller tool is available this should always be used in preference to any other method as it is less likely to cause damage to the bearing.

6 To replace the bearing, select a piece of piping or tubing that is just a fraction smaller in diameter than the bearing, place the splined part of the drive shaft upright in a vice, position the bearing on the shaft and using a soft hammer on the end of the piece of tubing, drive the bearing firmly and squarely onto the shaft.

7 Replace the rubber insulator in the bearing housing ensuring that the boss on the insulator is at the top of the housing and will be adjacent to the underframe when the propeller shafts are replaced.

8 When the insulator is correctly positioned bend back the six metal tabs and slide the housing and insulator assembly over the bearing.

9 Slide the splined end of the shaft into the rear yoke ensuring that the previously scribed mating marks are correctly aligned.

10 Replace the 'U' washer under the centre bolt with its smooth surface facing the front section of the propeller shaft. Tighten down the centre bolt to the specified torque and bend up its tab washer to secure it.

4 Universal joints - inspection and repair

1 Wear in the needle roller bearings is characterised by vibration in the transmission, 'clonks' on taking up the drive, and in extreme cases of lack of lubrication, metallic squeaking and ultimately grating and shrieking sounds as the bearings break up.

2 It is easy to check if the needle roller bearings are worn with the propeller shaft in position, by trying to turn the shaft with one hand, the other hand holding the rear axle flange when the rear universal is being checked, and the front half coupling when the front universal is being checked. Any movement between the

7.4 Removing UJ bearing cup circlip

7.6 Pressing out UJ bearing cup

7.7 Removing UJ bearing cup

propeller shaft and the front and the rear half coupling is indicative of considerable wear. If worn, the old bearings and spiders will have to be discarded and a repair kit, comprising new universal joint spiders, bearings, oil seals and retainers purchased. Check also by trying to lift the shaft and noticing any movement in the joints.

3 Examine the propeller shaft splines for wear. If worn it will be necessary to purchase a new front half coupling, or if the yokes are badly worn, an exchange propeller shaft. It is not possible to fit oversize bearings and journals to the trunnion bearing holes.

4 Clean away all traces of dirt and grease from the circlips located on the ends of the bearing cups, and remove the clips by pressing their open ends together with a pair of pliers (photo), and levering them out with a screwdriver.

Note: If they are difficult to remove tap the bearing cup face resting on top of the spider with a mallet which will ease the pressure on the circlip.

5 Take off the bearing cups on the propeller shaft yoke. To do this select two sockets from a socket spanner set, one large enough to fit completely over the bearing cup and the other smaller than the bearing cup.

6 Open the jaws of the vice and with the sockets opposite each other and the universal joint in between, tighten the vice and so force the narrower socket to move the opposite cup partially out of the yoke (photo) into the larger socket.

7 Remove the cup with a pair of pliers (photo). Remove the opposite cup, and then free the yoke from the propeller shaft.

8 Remove the remaining two cups by the same method.

9 Thoroughly clean the yokes and journals.

10 Fit the new oil seals and retainers on the spider journals, place the spider on the propeller shaft yoke and assemble the needle rollers in the bearing races with the assistance of some thin grease. Fill each bearing about a third full with grease and fill the grease holes in the journal spider making sure all air bubbles are eliminated.

11 Again using the vice, press the bearing cups into the yokes making sure that the needles do not get trapped. Use the small socket to fully depress the cups so that the circlips can be inserted in their grooves.

5 Fault diagnosis - propeller shaft

Symptom	Reason/s
Vibration	Wear in sliding sleeve splines
	Worn universal joint bearings
	Propeller shaft out of balance
	Distorted propeller shaft
Knock or 'clunk' when taking up drive	Worn universal joint bearings
	Worn rear axle drive pinion splines
	Loose rear drive flange bolts
	Excessive backlash in rear axle gears

Chapter 8 Rear axle

Contents

Specifications

Type (1600 cc)	Hypoid semi-floating, detachable differential carrier
Ratio (1600 cc)	3.777 : 1
Oil capacity (1600 cc)	2 pints (1.13 litres)
Type (2000 cc)	Hypoid semi-floating, integral differential (Salisbury design)
Ratio (2000 cc)	3.44 : 1
Oil capacity (2000 cc)	2.32 US pints

Torque wrench settings

	lb f ft	kg f m
1600 cc models		
Crownwheel securing bolts	55	7.6
Differential carrier to housing nuts	30	4.1
Differential bearing lockplate bolts	15	2.1
Differential bearing cap bolts	50	6.9
Axle-shaft bearing retainer plate bolts	20	2.8
Drive pinion flange bolts	48	6.6
Radius arm to axle casing	30	4.1
Shock absorber lower mounting	45	6.2
Rear spring 'U' bolts	26	3.6
Pinion self-lock nut (minimum)*	150	20.7
*(see Section 6 for precise preload)		
2000 cc models (with selective lengths pinion spacer)		
Rear axle housing cover plate bolts	30	4.1
Drive pinion self-locking nut	71 to 86	9.8 to 11.9
Other settings as for 1600 cc axle		
2000 cc models (with collapsible type pinion spacer)		
Rear axle housing cover plate bolts	30	4.1
Pinion self-lock nut (minimum)*	150	20.7

*see Section 13
Other settings as for 1600 cc models

1 General description

1 The rear axle is of hypoid semi-floating type and is located by the rear semi-elliptic type leaf road springs in conjunction with two radius arms on pre-1973 models. From 1973 onwards a stabilizer bar is fitted instead of the radius arms.

2 Two types of rear axle may be encountered, according to model and operating territory. One type has a completely detachable differential carrier and the other type is of integral design having only a removable cover plate on the rear face of the axle casing.

3 Unless the necessary tools and gauges are available, it is not recommended that the rear axle is overhauled, although the procedure is described for those who have, later in this Chapter.

4 With detachable differential type axles, it is recommended that the differential unit is either renewed on an exchange basis or the original unit taken to your dealer for reconditioning.

5 On very late models with Salisbury type (integral) rear axles a collapsible pinion bearing spacer is used instead of the fixed, selective length ones previously used (see Sections 13 and 14) in this type of axle.

2 Rear axle (detachable differential) - removal and installation

1 Remove the rear wheel hub caps then loosen the wheel nuts.

2 Raise and support the rear of the body and the differential casing with chocks or jacks so that the rear wheels are clear of the ground. This is most easily done by placing a jack under the centre of the differential, jacking-up the axle and then fitting chocks under the mounting points at the front of the rear springs to support the body.

3 Remove both rear wheels and place the wheel nuts in the hub caps for safe keeping.

4 Mark the propeller shaft and differential drive flanges to ensure replacement in the same relative positions. Undo and remove the nuts and bolts holding the two flanges together.

5 Release the handbrake and by undoing the adjusting nut, disconnect the cable at the pivot point at the rear of the axle casing.

6 Unscrew the union on the brake pipe at the junction on the rear axle and have handy either a jar to catch the hydraulic fluid or a plug to block the end of the pipe.

7 Undo the nuts and bolts holding the shock absorber attachments to the spring seats and remove the bolts thus freeing the shock absorbers. It will probably be necessary to adjust the jack under the axle casing to free the bolts.

8 On pre-1973 cars unscrew the nuts and withdraw the through bolts holding the radius arms to the rear axle casing. On later cars disconnect the anti-roll bar brackets (see Chapter 11).

9 Unscrew the nuts from under the spring retaining plates. These nuts screw onto the ends of the inverted 'U' bolts which retain the axle to the spring.

10 The axle will now be resting free on the jack and can be removed by lifting it through one of the wheel arches.

11 Reassembly is a direct reversal of the removal procedure, but various points must be carefully noted.

12 The nuts on the 'U' bolts must be tightened to the specified torque.

13 The radius arm nuts on the axle casing must not be fully tightened down until the car is resting on its wheels. This also applies to the shock absorber lower mounting bolts. Tighten all bolts to specified torque.

14 Bleed the brakes after reassembly, as described in Chapter 9.

3 Axle-shaft (detachable differential) - removal and installation

1 Raise the rear of the car and support the bodyframe and the axle casing securely.

2 Remove the roadwheel.

3 Remove the brake drum.

4 Remove the four self-locking nuts which retain the bearing retainer plate to the endface of the axle housing. These nuts are accessible through the hole in the axle-shaft flange (Fig. 8.4).

5 A slide hammer must now be attached to the roadwheel studs and the axle-shaft complete with bearing/seal assembly extracted from the axle casing.

6 It is sometimes possible to extract the axle-shaft by bolting an old roadwheel onto the hub and then striking two opposite points on the inner rim simultaneously. A third method is to use two or three bolts placed between the axle-shaft flange and the axle housing end flange. By unscrewing the nuts fitted to the bolts, the effective length of the bolts will be increased and the axle-shaft forced outwards. Unless great care is taken, either of the last two methods can result in a bent axle-shaft.

7 Installation is simply a matter of inserting the shaft into the

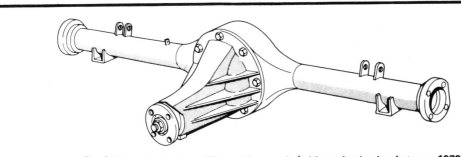

Fig. 8.1. Detachable type differential rear axle (with torsion bar brackets, pre-1973)

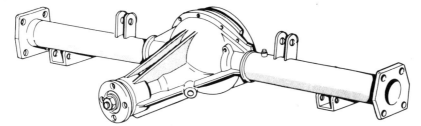

Fig. 8.2. Integral type differential rear axle (with torsion bar brackets, pre-1973)

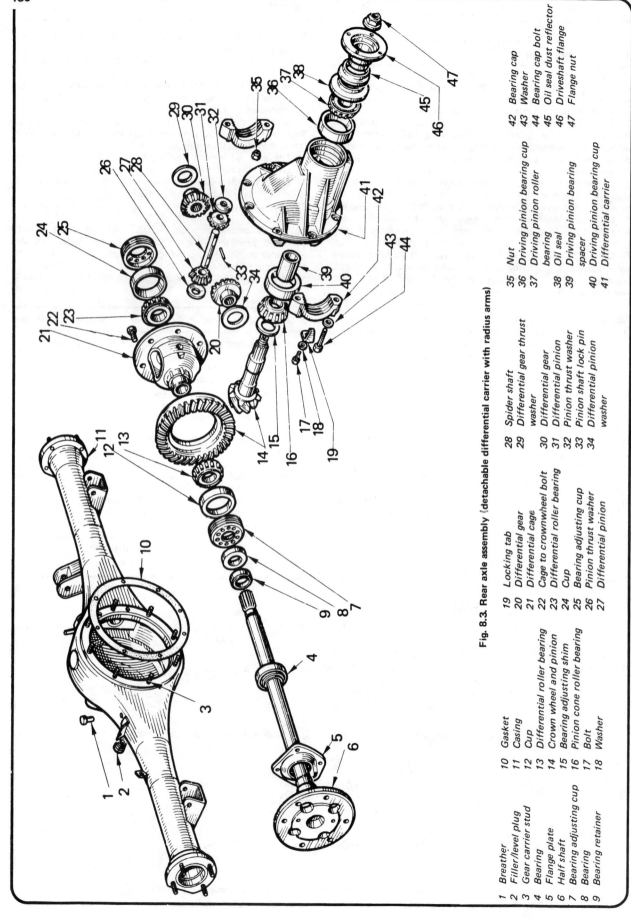

Fig. 8.3. Rear axle assembly (detachable differential carrier with radius arms)

1 Breather	10 Gasket	19 Locking tab	28 Spider shaft	35 Nut	42 Bearing cap
2 Filler/level plug	11 Casing	20 Differential gear	29 Differential gear thrust washer	36 Driving pinion bearing cup	43 Washer
3 Gear carrier stud	12 Cup	21 Differential cage	30 Differential gear	37 Driving pinion roller	44 Bearing cap bolt
4 Bearing	13 Differential roller bearing	22 Cage to crownwheel bolt	31 Differential pinion	38 Oil seal	45 Oil seal dust reflector
5 Flange plate	14 Crown wheel and pinion	23 Differential roller bearing	32 Pinion thrust washer	39 Driving pinion bearing	46 Driveshaft flange
6 Half shaft	15 Bearing adjusting shim	24 Cup	33 Pinion shaft lock pin	40 Driving pinion bearing spacer	47 Flange nut
7 Bearing adjusting cup	16 Pinion cone roller bearing	25 Bearing adjusting cup	34 Differential pinion washer	41 Differential carrier	
8 Bearing	17 Bolt	26 Pinion thrust washer			
9 Bearing retainer	18 Washer	27 Differential pinion			

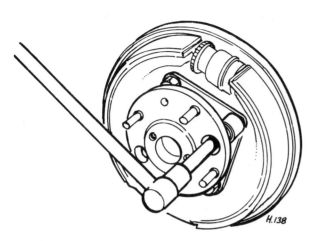

Fig. 8.4. Removal of bearing retainer plate securing bolts (Sec. 3)

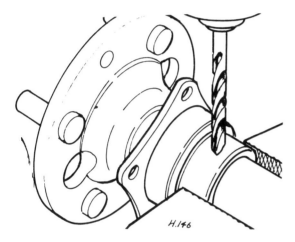

Fig. 8.5. Drilling hole in bearing inner ring prior to cutting with chisel (Sec. 4)

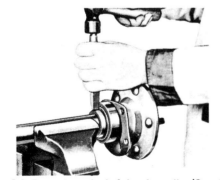

Fig. 8.6. Removing axle shaft bearing collar (Sec. 4)

housing and holding it horizontally until the splines on the shaft can be felt to engage with those of the differential gears. A little grease should be smeared on the outer surface of the hub bearing to prevent future seizure by rust.

4 Axle-shaft bearing/oil seal (detachable differential type axle) - renewal

1 Withdraw the axle-shaft, as described in the preceding Section.
2 Secure the assembly in a vice, the jaws of which have been

fitted with soft metal protectors.
3 Drill a hole in the bearing securing collar and then remove the collar by splitting it with a cold chisel. Take care not to damage the shaft during these operations (Figs. 8.5 and 8.6).
4 Using a suitable press, draw off the combined bearing/oil seal.
5 To the axle-shaft, install the bearing retainer plate, the new bearing (seal side towards differential) and a new bearing collar.
6 Applying pressure to the collar only, using a press or bearing puller, seat the components against the shoulder of the axle-shaft flange.
7 Install the axle-shaft as described in the preceding Section.

5 Differential carrier - removal and installation

1 To remove the differential carrier assembly, drain the oil from the axle by removing the drain plug in the base of the banjo casing, (if fitted), jack up the rear of the vehicle, remove both roadwheels and brake drums and then partially withdraw both axle-shafts as described in Section 3.
2 Disconnect the propeller shaft at the rear end as described in Chapter 7.
3 Undo the eight self-locking nuts holding the differential carrier assembly to the axle casing. If an oil drain plug has not been fitted, pull the assembly slightly forward and allow the oil to drain in a suitable tray or bowl. The carrier complete with the crownwheel can now be lifted clear with the gasket.
4 Before replacement, carefully clean the mating surfaces of the carrier and the axle casing and always fit a new gasket. Replacement is then a direct reversal of the above instructions. The eight nuts retaining the differential carrier assembly to the axle casing should be tightened to the specified torque.

6 Detachable type differential - overhaul

Most professional garages will prefer to renew the complete differential carrier assembly as a unit if it is worn, rather than to dismantle the unit to renew any damaged or worn parts. To do the job correctly "according to the book" requires the use of special and expensive tools which the majority of garages do not have.
The primary object of these special tools is to enable the mesh of the crownwheel to the pinion to be very accurately set and thus ensure that noise is kept to a minimum. If any increase in noise cannot be tolerated (provided that the rear axle is not already noisy due to a defective part) then it is best to purchase an exchange built up differential unit. The differential assembly should be stripped as follows:
1 Remove the differential assembly from the rear axle, as described in Section 5.
2 With the differential assembly on the bench begin dismantling the unit.
3 Undo and remove the bolts, spring washers and lock plates securing the adjustment cups to the bearing caps.
4 Release the tension on the bearing cap bolts and unscrew the differential bearing adjustment cups. Note from which side each cup originated and mark with a punch or scriber.
5 Unscrew the bearing cap bolts and spring washers. Ensure that the caps are marked so that they may be fitted in their original positions upon reassembly (Fig. 8.7).
6 Pull off the caps and then lever out the differential unit complete with crownwheel and differential gears.
7 Recover the differential bearing outer tracks and inspect the bearings for wear or damage. If evident the bearings will have to be renewed.
8 Using a universal puller and suitable thrust block draw off the old bearings.
9 Undo and remove the bolts and washers that secure the crownwheel to the differential cage. Mark the relative positions of the cage and crownwheel if new parts are not to be fitted and lift off the crownwheel.

Fig. 8.7. Differential bearing cap mating marks (detachable type differential rear axle) (Sec. 6)

Fig. 8.8. Removing pinion, bearing and spacer from detachable type differential carrier (Sec. 6)

10 Clamp the pinion flange in a vice and then undo the nut. Any damage caused to the edge of the flange by the vice should be carefully filed smooth.

11 With the nut removed pull off the splined pinion flange. Tap the end of the pinion shaft if the flange appears to be stuck.

12 The pinion complete with spacer and rear bearing cone may now be extracted from the rear of the housing (Fig. 8.8).

13 Using a drift carefully tap out the pinion front bearing and oil seal.

14 Check the bearings for sign of wear and if evident the outer tracks must be removed using a suitable soft metal drift.

15 To dismantle the pinion assembly detach the bearing spacer and remove the rear bearing cone using a universal puller. Recover any shims found between the rear bearing and pinion head.

16 Tap out the differential pinion shaft locking pin which is tapered at one end and must be pushed out from the crownwheel side of the case.

17 Push the differential pinion shaft out of the case and rotate the pinions around the differential gears, so that they may be extracted through the apertures in the case. Cupped thrust washers are fitted between the pinions and the case and may be extracted after the pinions have been removed.

18 Remove the differential gears and thrust washers from the differential case.

19 Wash all parts and wipe dry with a clean non-fluffy rag.

20 Again check all bearings for signs of wear or pitting. If evident a new set of bearings should be obtained.

21 Examine the teeth of the crownwheel and pinion for pitting, score marks, chipping and general wear. If a crownwheel and pinion is required a mated crownwheel and pinion must be fitted and under no circumstances may only one part of the two be renewed.

22 Inspect the differential pinions and side gears for signs of pitting, score marks, chipping and general wear. Obtain new gears as necessary.

23 Inspect the thrust washers for signs of wear or deep scoring. Obtain new thrust washers as necessary.

24 Once the pinion oil seal has been disturbed it must be discarded and a new one obtained.

25 Commence reassembly by lubricating the differential gear thrust washers and then positioning a flat washer on each differential side gear. Position the two gears in the case.

26 Positon the cupped thrust washers on the machined faces in

Fig. 8.9. Inserting spider shaft into differential case (detachable type differential) (Sec. 6)

the case and retain in position with a smear of grease.

27 Locate the pinion gears in the case diametrically opposite each other and rotate the gears to move the pinion gears in line with the holes in the shaft.

28 Check that the thrust washers are still in place and push the spider shaft through the case, thrust washers and pinions. If the pinions do not line up they are not diametrically opposite each other, and should be extracted and repositioned (Fig. 8.9).

29 Insert the locking pin (tapered end first) and lightly peen the case to prevent the pin working out.

30 Examine the bearing journals on the differential case for burrs, and refit the differential bearing cones onto the differential case using a suitable diameter tubular drift. Make sure they are fitted the correct way round.

31 Examine the crownwheel and differential case for burrs, score marks and dirt. Clean as necessary and then refit the

crownwheel. Take care to line up the bolt holes and any previously made marks if the original parts are being refitted.

32 Refit the crownwheel to differential case securing bolts and tighten in a diagonal manner to the specified torque wrench setting.

33 Using a suitable diameter drift carefully drift the pinion bearing cups into position in the final drive housing. Make sure they are the correct way round.

34 Slide the shim onto the pinion shaft and locate behind the pinion head and then fit the inner cone and race of the rear bearing. It is quite satisfactory to drift the rear bearing on with a piece of tubing 12 to 14 inches long with sufficient internal diameter to just fit over the pinion shaft. With one end of the tube bearing agingt the race, tap the top end of the tube with a hammer, so driving the bearing squarely down the shaft and hard up against the underside of the thrust washer.

35 Slide a new collapsible type spacer over the pinion shaft and insert the assembly into the differential carrier.

36 Fit the pinion front bearing outer track and race followed by a new pinion oil seal.

37 Fit the pinion drive flange and screw on the pinion self-locking nut until a pinion endfloat exists of between 0.002 and 0.005 in (0.05 and 0.13 mm). Tighten the nut only a fraction at a time and check the pinion turning torque after each tightening, using either a suitable torque gauge or a spring balance and length of cord wrapped round the pinion drive flange. The correct pinion turning torque should be:

Original bearings
Torque wrench	12 to 18 lb in (0.14 to 0.216 kg/m)
Pull on spring balance	12 to 18 lb (5 to 8 kg)

New bearings
Torque wrench	20 to 26 lb in (0.24 to 0.31 kg/m)
Pull on spring balance	20 to 26 lb (9 to 11 kg)

38 To the foregoing figures, add 3 lb. in (0.035 kg/m) if a new pinion oil seal has been fitted.

39 Throughout the nut tightening process, hold the pinion flange quite still with a suitable tool.

40 If the pinion nut is overtightened, the nut cannot be un-screwed to correct the adjustment as the pinion spacer will have been over compressed and the assembly will have to be dismantled and a new collapsible type spacer fitted.

41 Fit the differential cage to the differential carrier and refit the two bearing caps, locating them in their original positions.

42 Tighten the bearing cap bolts finger tight and then screw in the two adjustment cups.

43 It is now necessary to position the crownwheel relative to the pinion. If possible mount a dial indicator gauge, with the probe resting on one of the teeth of the crownwheel to determine the backlash. Backlash may be varied by moving the whole differential assembly using the two adjustment cups until the required setting is obtained.

44 Tighten the bearing cap securing bolts and recheck the back-lash setting.

45 The best check the D-I-Y motorist can make to ascertain the correct meshing of the crownwheel and pinion is to smear a little engineers blue onto the crownwheel and then rotate the pinion. The contact mark should appear right in the middle of the crownwheel teeth. If the mark appears on the toe or the heel of the crownwheel teeth then the crownwheel must be moved either nearer or further away from the pinion. The various tooth patterns that may be obtained are illustrated in Fig. 8.10.

46 When the correct meshing between the crownwheel and pinion has been obtained refit the adjustment cup lock plates, bolts and spring washers.

47 The differential unit can now be refitted to the axle casing.

7 Pinion oil seal - renewal with detachable type differential in position in car

1 Jack-up the rear of the car and secure on stands both under the bodyframe and axle casing.

2 Remove the roadwheels and brake drums.

3 Disconnect the propeller shaft from the pinion drive flange.

4 Using either a spring balance and a length of cord wrapped round the drive pinion or a torque wrench (lb/in) check and record the turning torque of the pinion.

5 Hold the drive pinion quite still with a suitable tool and unscrew and remove the pinion self-locking nut.

6 Remove the washer, drive flange, dust deflector and then prise out the oil seal. Do not damage or lever against the pinion shaft splines during this operation.

7 Tap in the new oil seal using a piece of tubing as a drift. Do not inadvertently knock the end of the pinion shaft.

8 Repeat the operations described in paragraphs 37 to 40 of Section 6, but ensuring that the final pinion turning torque figure agrees with that recorded before diamantling.

9 Refit the brake drums, propeller shaft and roadwheels and lower the car.

8 Rear axle (integral type differential) - removal and installation

1 The procedure is similar to that described in Section 2.

9 Axle-shaft (integral type differential) - removal and installation

1 The procedure is similar to that described in Section 3.

10 Axle-shaft bearing/oil seal (integral type differential) - renewal

1 The procedure is similar to that described in Section 4.

11 Rear cover (integral type differential axle) - removal and refitting

1 Wipe down the rear of the final drive housing to prevent the possibility of dirt entering the rear axle.

2 Release the handbrake cross cable from the rear of each brake backplate by pulling out the small spring clips and with-drawing the clevis pins.

3 To give more room to work in, release the handbrake return spring from its brackets on the axle casing and then detach the operating lever from the casing.

4 Place a container of at least 3 Imp. pints (3.6 US pints, 1.7 litres) capacity under the rear axle casing to catch the oil as the rear cover is released.

5 Undo and remove the ten bolts and spring washers that secure the rear cover to the final drive housing. Lift away the rear cover and its gasket.

6 Before refitting the rear cover make sure that the mating faces are free of the old gasket or jointing compound.

7 Fit a new gasket and then the rear cover and secure with the ten bolts and spring washers. The cover bolts protrude into the final drive housing so it is important that a suitable oil resistance sealing compound is smeared onto the threads of each bolt before it is fitted.

8 Tighten the cover securing bolts to the specified torque wrench setting.

9 Reconnect the handbrake operating lever, cross cable and return spring.

10 Do not forget to refill with the correct grade of oil.

134

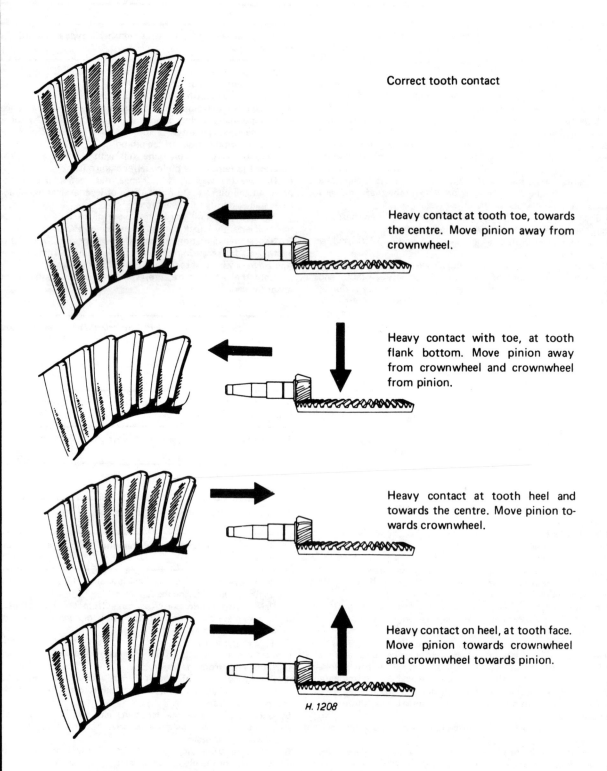

Correct tooth contact

Heavy contact at tooth toe, towards the centre. Move pinion away from crownwheel.

Heavy contact with toe, at tooth flank bottom. Move pinion away from crownwheel and crownwheel from pinion.

Heavy contact at tooth heel and towards the centre. Move pinion towards crownwheel.

Heavy contact on heel, at tooth face. Move pinion towards crownwheel and crownwheel towards pinion.

H. 1208

Fig. 8.10. Correct meshing of crownwheel and pinion, and repositioning guide for incorrect tooth marking (Sec. 6)

12 Pinion oil seal (integral differential - early models) - renewal

1 This operation may be performed with the rear axle in position or on the bench.

2 Undo and remove the two bolts, spring and plain washers that secure the centre bearing support to the underside of the body.

3 With a scriber or file mark a line across the propeller shaft and pinion driving flanges so that they may be refitted together in their original positions.

4 Undo and remove the four bolts and spring washers securing the propeller shaft and pinion driving flanges and carefully lower the propeller shaft to the floor.

5 Carefully clean the front of the final drive housing as there will probably be a considerable amount of dirt and oil if the seal has been leaking for a while.

6 Using a suitable long handled tool or large wrench, grip the drive pinion flange and with a socket undo and remove the pinion flange retaining self locking nut. This nut must be discarded and a new one obtained ready for reassembly.

7 Place a container under the front of the final drive housing to catch any oil that may issue once the oil seal has been removed.

8 Using a universal puller and suitable thrust pad pull off the drive pinion flange from the drive pinion.

9 Using a screwdriver or small chisel carefully remove the old oil seal. It will probably be necessary to partially destroy it. Note the correct way round it is fitted with the lip facing inwards.

10 Before fitting a new seal apply some grease to the inner face between the two lips of the seal.

11 Apply a little jointing compound to the outer face of the seal.

12 Using a tubular drift of suitable diameter carefully drive the oil seal into the final drive housing. Make quite sure that it is fitted squarely into the housing.

13 Replace the drive pinion flange and once again hold squarely with the tool or large wrench. Fit a new self locking nut and tighten to a torque wrench setting of 71 to 86 lb f ft (10 to 12 kg f m).

14 Reconnect the propeller shaft aligning the previously made marks on the flanges, and refit the bolts with new spring washers. Tighten to the specified torque wrench setting.

15 Refit the centre bearing support securing bolts, spring and plain washers and tighten to the specified torque wrench setting.

16 Finally check the oil level in the rear axle and top-up if necessary.

13 Pinion oil seal (integral differential - late models) - renewal

1 Late model rear axles are fitted with a collapsible type spacer on the pinion shaft. The procedure for renewing the oil seal is similar to that described in Section 7.

14 Integral type differential - overhaul

1 It is recommended that for complete overhaul the rear axle be removed from the car as described in Section 8. Before commencing work refer to the introduction to Section 6. In this case it would be better to look for a secondhand rear axle instead of just the differential unit.

2 Refer to Section 11 and remove the rear cover and then to Section 9 and withdraw the half shafts by about 6 inches (152.4 mm).

3 Working inside the axle casing undo and remove the four bolts that hold the two 'U' shaped differential bearing caps in the casing (Fig. 8.17).

4 With a scriber mark the relative positions of the two bearing caps as they must be refitted in their original positions. Lift away the two end caps; there may already be mating numbers as shown in Fig. 8.11.

5 Obtain two pieces of 2 inch (50 mm) square wood at least 12 inches (304.8 mm) long and with a sharp knife, taper the ends along a length of 6 inches (154.4 mm) (Fig. 8.12).

6 Place the tapered ends of the wood levers in the two cutaways of the differential casing and using the rear cover face of the final drive housing as a fulcrum carefully lever the differential assembly from the final drive housing.

7 If it is necessary to remove the two differential case bearings these may be removed next using a universal two legged puller and suitable thrust pad. Carefully ease each bearing from its location. Recover the shim packs from behind each bearing noting from which side they came (Fig. 8.13).

8 Using a scriber mark the relative positions of the crownwheel and differential housing so that the crownwheel may be refitted in its original position, unless of course, it is to be renewed.

9 Undo and remove the eight bolts that secure the crownwheel to the differential housing. Using a soft faced hammer tap the crownwheel from its location on the differential housing.

10 Using a suitable diameter parallel pin punch, tap out the pin that locks the differential pinion gear shaft to the differential housing. Note: The hole into which the peg fits is slightly

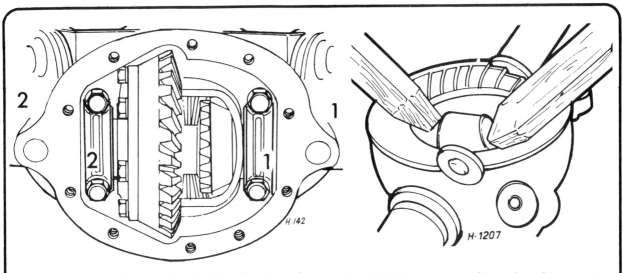

Fig. 8.11. Differential casing and end cap identification marks (integral type differential) (Sec. 14)

Fig. 8.12. Using two pieces of tapered wood to ease out differential assembly (integral type differential) (Sec. 14)

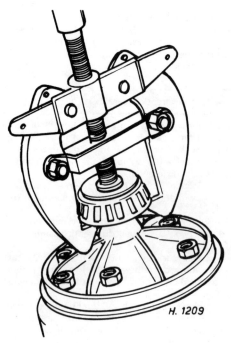

Fig. 8.13. Using universal puller to remove differential case taper roller bearing cone (integral type differential) (Sec. 14)

Fig. 8.14. Removing differential pinion gear shaft locking pin (integral type differential) (Sec. 14)

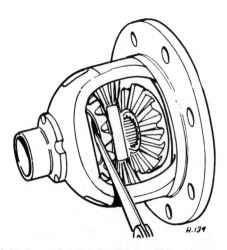

Fig. 8.15. Determination of side gear endfloat (integral type differential) (Sec. 14)

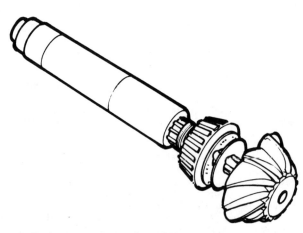

Fig. 8.16. Using suitable diameter tube to refit pinion taper roller bearing (integral type differential) (Sec. 14)

14 The pinion shaft may now be removed from the final drive housing. Carefully inspect the large taper roller bearing behind the pinion gear and if it shows signs of wear or pitting on the rollers or cage the bearing must be renewed.

15 Using a universal two legged puller and suitable thrust pad draw the bearing from the pinion shaft.

16 The smaller taper roller bearing and oil seal may next be removed from the final drive housing   pinion drive flange end. To do this use a soft metal drift with a tapered end or suitable diameter tube and working inside the housing tap the bearing circumference outwards so releasing first the oil seal and then the bearing.

17 Again using the soft metal drift and working inside the housing drift out the bearing cups. These must not be used with new bearings.

18 The final drive assembly is now dismantled and should be washed and dried with a clean non-fluffy rag ready for inspection.

19 Carefully inspect the parts as described in Section 6.

20 When new parts have been obtained as required, reassembly can begin. First fit the thrust washers to the side gears and place them in position in the differential housing.

21 Place the thrust washers behind the differential pinion gears and mesh these two gears with the side gears through the two

tapered, and the opposite end may be lightly peened over and should be cleaned with a suitable diameter drill (Fig. 8.14).

11 Using a soft metal drift tap out the differential pinion gear shaft. Lift away the differential pinion gears, side gears and thrust washers taking care to ensure that the thrust washers are left with their relative gears.

12 Professional fitters at the dealers use a special tool for holding the pinion drive flange stationary whilst the nut in the centre of the flange is unscrewed. As it is tightened to a torque wrench setting of 71 to 86 lb f ft (10 to 12 kg f m) it will require some force to undo it. The average owner will not normally have the use of this special tool so, as an alternative method clamp the pinion flange in a vice and then undo the nut. Any damage caused to the edge of the flange by the vice should be carefully filed smooth. This nut must not be used again so a new one will be required during reassembly.

13 Using a universal two legged puller and suitable thrust pad draw the pinion drive flange from the end of the pinion shaft.

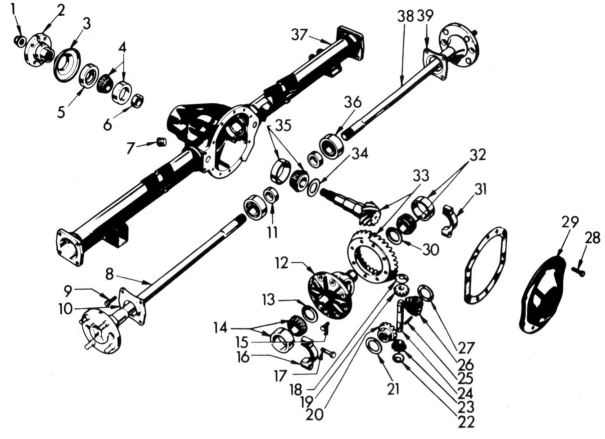

Fig. 8.17. Rear axle assembly (integral differential)

1	Pinion nut	11	Retainer ring	21	Selective spacer	31	Bearing cap

1   Pinion nut
2   Flange
3   Deflector
4   Bearing assembly
5   Seal
6   Selective spacer
7   Filler/level plug
8   Half shaft
9   Bolt
10 Bearing retainer

11 Retainer ring
12 Differential housing
13 Selective spacer
14 Bearing assembly
15 Bolt
16 Bearing cap
17 Bolt
18 Pinion thrust washer
19 Differential pinion
20 Differential gear

21 Selective spacer
22 Pinion thrust washer
23 Differential pinion
24 Spider shaft
25 Pinion shaft lock pin
26 Differential gear
27 Selective spacer
28 Bolt
29 Rear axle housing cover
30 Selective spacer

31 Bearing cap
32 Bearing assembly
33 Crownwheel and pinion
    assembly
34 Selective spacer
35 Bearing assembly
36 Half shaft bearing
37 Axle housing
38 Half shaft
39 Bearing retainer

apertures in the differential housing. Make sure they are diametrically opposite to each other. Rotate the differential pinion
gears through 10° so bringing them into line with the pinion gear
shaft bore in the housing.
22 Insert the pinion gear shaft with the locking pin hole in line
with the pin hole.
23 Using feeler gauges measure the endfloat of each side gear.
The correct clearance is 0.006 inch (0.15 mm) and if this figure
is exceeded new thrust washers must be obtained. Dismantle the
assembly again and fit new thrust washers (Fig. 8.15).
24 Lock the pinion gear shaft using the pin which should be
tapped fully home using a suitable diameter parallel pin punch.
Peen over the end of the pin hole to stop the pin working its way
out.
25 The crownwheel may next be refitted. Wipe the mating faces
of the crownwheel and differential housing and if original parts
are being used place the crownwheel into position with the previously made marks aligned. Refit the eight bolts that secure the
crownwheel and tighten these in a progressive and diagonal
manner to a final torque wrench setting of 57 to 62 lb f ft (8 to
8.7 kg f m).
26 Place the shim packs back in their original fitted position on
the differential housing bearing location. Using a piece of

suitable diameter tube very carefully fit the differential housing
bearings with the smaller diameter of the taper outwards. The
bearing cage must not in any way be damaged.
27 Place the shims behind the head of the pinion gear and using
a suitable diameter tube carefully fit the larger taper roller
bearing onto the pinion shaft. The larger diameter of the bearing
must be next to the pinion head.
28 Using suitable diameter tubes fit the two taper roller bearing
cones into the final drive housing making sure that they are
fitted the correct way round (Fig. 8.16).
29 Slide the shim and spacer onto the pinion shaft and insert
into the final drive housing.
30 Refit the second and smaller diameter taper roller bearing
onto the end of the pinion shaft and follow this with a new oil
seal. Before the seal is actually fitted apply some grease to the
inner face between the two lips of the seal.
31 Apply a little jointing compound to the outer face of the
seal.
32 Using a tubular drift of suitable diameter carefully drive the
oil seal into the final housing. Make quite sure that it is fitted
squarely into the housing.
33 Replace the drive pinion flange and hold securely in a bench
vice. On early models tighten the pinion nut to a torque wrench

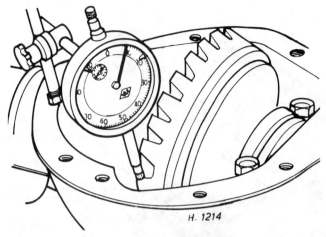

Fig. 8.18. Using dial gauge to determine crownwheel/pinion backlash (Sec. 14)

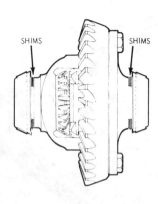

Fig. 8.19. Location of side shim packs (integral type differential) (Sec. 14)

setting of between 71 and 86 lb f ft (10 and 12 kg f m). On later models with a collapsible spacer, tighten the nut and check the preload as described in Section 13.

34 Fit the bearing cones to the differential housing bearings and carefully ease the housing into position in the final drive housing.

35 Replace the bearing caps in their original positions. Smear a little jointing compound on the threads of each cap securing bolt and fit into position. When all four bolts have been replaced tighten these up in a diagonal and progressive manner to a final torque wrench setting of 43 to 44 lb f ft (6 to 6.8 kg f m).

36 If possible mount a dial indicator gauge so that the probe is resting on one of the teeth of the crownwheel and determine the backlash between the crownwheel and pinion. The backlash may be varied by decreasing the thickness of the shims behind one bearing and increasing the thickness of shims behind the other thus moving the crownwheel into or out of mesh as required. The total thickness of the shims must not be changed (Figs. 8.18 and 8.19).

37 The best check the do-it-yourself owner can make to ascertain the correct meshing of the crownwheel and pinion is to

smear a little engineer's blue onto the crownwheel and pinion and then rotate the pinion. The contact mark should appear right in the middle of the crownwheel teeth. Refer to Fig. 8.10 where the correct tooth pattern is shown. Also shown are incorrect tooth patterns and the method of obtaining the correct pattern. Obviously this will take time and further dismantling but will be worth it.

38 Before refitting the rear cover make sure that the mating faces are free from traces of the old gasket or jointing compound.

39 Fit a new gasket and then the rear cover and secure with the ten bolts and spring washers. The cover bolts protrude into the final drive housing so it is important that a suitable oil resistant sealing compound is smeared onto the threads of each bolt before it is fitted.

40 Tighten the cover securing bolts to the specified torque setting.

41 Refit the halfshafts and then the complete rear axle assembly.

42 Do not forget to refill with correct grade oil.

15 Fault diagnosis - rear axle

Symptom	Reason/s
Vibration	Worn axleshaft bearings
	Loose drive flange bolts
	Out of balance propeller shaft
	Tyres require balancing
Noise	Insufficient lubricant
	Worn gears and differential components generally
'Clunk' on acceleration or deceleration	Incorrect crownwheel and pinion mesh
	Excessive backlash due to wear in crownwheel and pinion teeth
	Worn axleshaft or differential side gear splines
	Loose drive flange bolts
	Worn drive pinion flange splines
Oil leakage	Faulty pinion or axleshaft oil seals
	May be caused by blocked axle housing breather

Chapter 9 Braking system

Contents

Specifications

Type of system	...	...	...	...	...	...	...	Disc at front, drum at rear
Footbrake	...	...	...	...	...	...	...	Hydraulic on all four wheels
Handbrake	...	...	...	...	...	...	...	Mechanical to rear wheels only
Front brake layout	...	...	...	...	...	...	Trailing calipers
Hydraulic system	...	...	...	...	...	...	Dual line, tandem master cylinder and servo assisted

Brake dimensions
Front:

Disc diameter	...	...	...	...	...	...	...	9.625 in. (24.45 cm)
Disc thickness	...	...	...	...	...	...	...	0.50 in. (12.70 mm)
Disc runout	...	...	...	...	...	...	...	0.0035 in. (0.089 mm)
Pad swept area	...	...	...	...	...	...	189.5 sq. in. (1.230 sq. cm)
Cylinder diameter	...	...	...	...	...	...	2.125 in. (5.39 cm)

Rear:

Drum diameter	...	...	...	...	...	...	...	9.0 in. (22.9 cm)
Lining width	...	...	...	...	...	...	...	1.75 in. (44.5 mm)
Lining thickness	...	...	...	...	...	...	0.188 in. (4.78 mm)
Total swept area	...	...	...	...	...	...	99.0 sq. in. (639.0 sq. cm)
Cylinder diameter	...	...	...	...	...	...	0.75 in. (19.05 cm)

Vacuum servo unit

Boost ratio	...	...	...	...	...	...	...	2.2 : 1
Diaphragm area	...	...	...	...	...	...	...	38 sq. in. (245.161 sq. cm)

Torque wrench settings

	lb f ft	kg f m
Caliper securing bolts	50	6.9
Disc to hub bolts	34	4.7
Rear backplate to axle housing	18	2.5
Roadwheel nuts	55	7.6

1 General description

Disc brakes are fitted to the front wheels of all models together with single leading shoe drum brakes at the rear. The mechanically operated handbrake works on the rear wheels only.

The brakes fitted to the front wheels are of the rotating disc and static caliper type, with one caliper per disc, each caliper containing two piston operated friction pads, which on application of the footbrake pinch the disc rotating between them. The front brakes are of the trailing caliper type to minimise the entry of water.

Application of the footbrake creates hydraulic pressure in the master cylinder and fluid from the cylinder travels via steel and flexible pipes to the cylinders in each half of the calipers, thus pushing the pistons, to which are attached the friction pads, into contact with either side of the disc.

Two seals are fitted to the operating cylinders, the outer seal prevents moisture and dirt entering the cylinder, while the inner seal which is retained in a groove inside the cylinder, prevents fluid leakage.

As the friction pads wear so the pistons move further out of

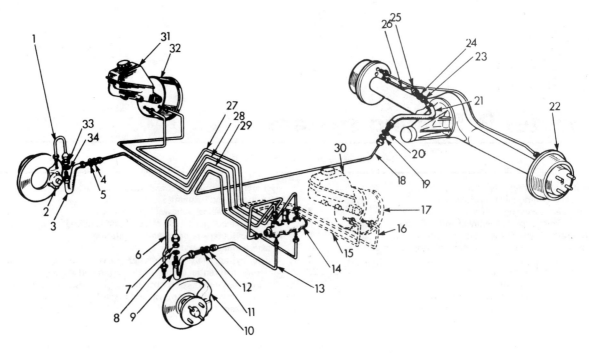

Fig. 9.1. Brake hydraulic system (rhd)

1 Pipe	10 Brake caliper	19 Nut	28 Pipe
2 Caliper	11 Washer	20 Washer	29 Pipe
3 Flexible hose	12 Nut	21 Flexible hose	30 Master cylinder (lhd)
4 Nut	13 Pipe	22 Brake drum	31 Master cylinder
5 Washer	14 Pressure differential valve	23 Washer	32 Servo
6 Pipe	15 Pipe	24 Nut	33 Nut
7 Nut	16 Pipe	25 Pipe	34 Washer
8 Washer	17 Servo (lhd)	26 Pipe	
9 Flexible hose	18 Pipe	27 Pipe	

the cylinders and the level of fluid in the hydraulic reservoir drops. Disc pad wear is therefore taken up automatically and eliminates the need for periodic adjustment by the owner.

All models use a floor mounted handbrake lever located between the front seats.

A single cable runs from the lever to a compensator mechanism on the back of the rear axle casing. From the compensator a single cable runs to the rear brake drums. As the rear brake shoes wear the handbrake cables operate a self adjusting mechanism in the rear brake drums thus doing away with the necessity for the owner to adjust the brakes on each rear wheel individually. The only adjustment required is on the handbrake compensator mechanism, due to wear in the linkage. All models have the dual line braking system with a separate hydraulic system for the front and rear brakes so that if failure of the hydraulic pipes to the front or rear brakes occurs half the braking system still operates. Servo assistance in this condition is still available. A warning light is fitted on the facia which illuminates should either circuit fail. The bulb is connected to a pressure differential switch in the hydraulic line (see Section 16).

---

2 Front disc pads - inspection and renewal

---

1 Apply the handbrake, remove the front wheel trim, slacken the wheel nuts, jack up the front of the car and place on firmly based axle stands. Remove the front wheel.

2 Inspect the amount of friction material left on the pads. The pads must be renewed when the thickness of the friction material has been reduced to a minimum of 0.12 inches (3.00 mm).

3 If the fluid level in the master cylinder reservoir is high, when

the pistons are moved into their respective bores to accommodate new pads the level could rise sufficiently for the fluid to overflow. Place absorbent cloth around the reservoir or syphon a little fluid out so preventing paintwork damage being caused by the hydraulic fluid.

4 Using a pair of long nosed pliers, extract the two small clips that hold the main retaining pins in place (Fig. 9.2).

5 Remove the main retaining pins which run through the caliper and the metal backing of the pads and the shims.

6 The friction pads can now be removed from the caliper. If they prove difficult to remove by hand a pair of long nosed pliers can be used. Lift away the shims and tension springs (where fitted) (Fig. 9.3).

7 Carefully clean the recesses in the caliper in which the friction pads and shims lie, and the exposed faces of each piston from all traces of dirt or rust.

8 Using a piece of wood carefully retract the pistons.

9 Place the brake pad tension springs on the brake pads and shims and locate in the caliper. Insert the main pad retaining pins making sure that the tangs of the tension springs are under the retaining pins. Secure the pins with the small wire clips.

10 Refit the roadwheel and lower the car. Tighten the wheel nuts securely and replace the wheel trim.

11 To correctly seat the pistons pump the brake pedal several times and finally top up the hydraulic fluid level in the master cylinder reservoir as necessary.

---

3 Front brake caliper - removal and refitting

---

1 Apply the handbrake, remove the front wheel trim, slacken the wheel nuts, jack-up the front of the car and place on firmly

Fig. 9.2. Brake pad retaining pins and clips (Sec. 2)

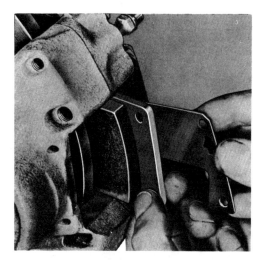

Fig. 9.3. Withdrawing pad and shim (Sec. 2)
Note: 1   *Pad colour coding on edge*
            2   *Arrow in shim*

Fig. 9.4. Caliper mounting bolts (Sec. 3)

based axle stands. Remove the front wheel.
2 Wipe the top of the master cylinder reservoir and unscrew the cap. Place a piece of polythene sheet over the top of the reservoir and refit the cap.
3 Remove the friction pads, as described in Section 2.
4 If it is intended to fit new caliper pistons and/or the seals, depress the brake pedal to bring the pistons into contact with the disc and assist subsequent removal of the pistons.
5 Wipe the area clean around the flexible hose bracket and

detach the pipe as described in Section 12. Tape up the end of the pipe to stop the possibility of dirt ingress.
6 Using a screwdriver or chisel bend back the tabs on the locking plate and undo the two caliper body mounting bolts. Lift away the caliper from its mounting flange on the suspension leg (Fig. 9.4).
7 To refit the caliper, position it over the disc and move it until the mounting bolt holes are in line with the two front holes in the suspension leg mounting flange.
8 Fit the caliper retaining bolts through the two holes in a new locking plate and insert the bolts through the caliper body. Tighten the bolts to the specified torque wrench setting.
9 Using a screwdriver, pliers or chisel bend up the locking plate tabs so as to lock the bolts.
10 Remove the tape from the end of the flexible hydraulic pipe and reconnect it to the union on the hose bracket. Be careful not to cross the thread of the union nut during the initial turns. The union nut should be tightened securely using a spanner of short length.
11 Push the pistons into their respective bores so as to accommodate the pads. Watch the level of hydraulic fluid in the master cylinder reservoir as it can overflow if too high whilst the pistons are being retracted. Place absorbent cloth around the reservoir or syphon a little fluid out so preventing paintwork damage.
12 Fit the pads, shims and tension springs, as described in Section 2.
13 Bleed the hydraulic system, as described in Section 13. Replace the roadwheel and lower the car.

4 Disc caliper - servicing

1 The pistons should be removed first. To do this half withdraw one piston from its bore in the caliper body (Fig. 9.5).
2 Carefully remove the securing circlip and extract the sealing bellows from its location in the lower part of the piston skirt. Completely remove the piston.
3 If difficulty is experienced in withdrawing the pistons use a jet of compressed air or foot pump to move it out of its bore.
4 Remove the sealing bellows from its location in the annular ring which is machined in the cylinder bore.
5 Remove the piston sealing ring from the cylinder bore using a small screwdriver but do take care not to scratch the fine finish of the bore.
6 To remove the second piston repeat the operations in paragraphs 1 to 5 inclusive.
7 It is important that the two halves of the caliper are not separated under any circumstances. If hydraulic fluid leaks are evident from the joint, the caliper must be renewed complete.
8 Thoroughly wash all parts in methylated spirits or clean hydraulic fluid. During reassembly new rubber seals must be fitted, these should be well lubricated with clean hydraulic fluid.
9 Inspect the pistons and bores for signs of wear, score marks or damage, and, if evident new parts should be obtained ready for fitting or a new caliper obtained.
10 To reassemble, fit one of the piston seals into the annular groove in the cylinder bore.
11 Fit the rubber bellows to the cylinder bore groove so that the lip is turned outward.
12 Lubricate the seal and rubber bellows with correct hydraulic fluid. Push the piston, crown first, through the rubber sealing bellows and then into the cylinder bore. Take care as it is easy for the piston to damage the rubber bellows.
13 With the piston half inserted into the cylinder bore fit the inner edge of the bellows into the annular groove in the piston skirt.
14 Push the piston down the bore as far as it will go. Secure the rubber bellows to the caliper with the circlip.
15 Repeat the operations in paragraphs 10 to 14 inclusive for the second piston.
16 The caliper is now ready for refitting. It is recommended that

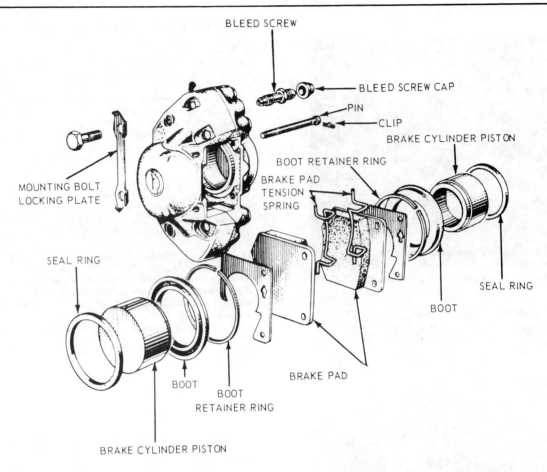

Fig. 9.5. Component parts of caliper (Sec. 4)

the hydraulic pipe end is temporarily plugged to stop any dirt entering whilst it is being refitted, before the pipe connection is made.

5   Front disc and hub - removal and installation

1   After jacking up the car and removing the front wheel, remove the caliper as described in Section 4.
2   Tap off the dust cap from the centre of the hub.
3   Remove the split pin from the nut retainer and lift away the adjusting nut retainer.
4   Unscrew the adjusting nut and lift away the thrust washer and outer taper bearing.
5   Pull off the complete hub and disc assembly from the stub axle.
6   From the back of the hub assembly carefully prise out the grease seal and lift away the inner tapered bearing.
7   Carefully clean out the hub and wash the bearings with petrol making sure that no grease or oil is allowed to get onto the brake disc.
8   Should it be necessary to separate the disc from the hub for renewal or regrinding, first bend back the locking tabs and undo the four securing bolts. With a scriber mark the relative positions of the hub and disc to ensure refitting in their original positions and separate the disc from the hub.
9   Thoroughly clean the disc and inspect for signs of deep scoring, cracks or excessive corrosion. If these are evident, the disc may be reground but no more than a maximum total of 0.060 inch (1.524 mm) may be removed. It is however, desirable to fit a new disc if at all possible.
10 To reassemble make quite sure that the mating faces of the disc and hub are very clean and place the disc on the hub, lining

Fig. 9.6. Front hub bearing and components (Sec. 5)

up any previously made marks.
11 Fit the four securing bolts and two new tab washers and tighten the bolts in a progressive and diagonal manner to the specified torque wrench setting. Bend up the locking tabs.
12 Work some grease well into the bearing, fully pack the bearing cages and rollers. **Note:** leave the hub and grease seal empty to allow for subsequent expansion of the grease.
13 To reassemble the hub, first fit the inner bearing and then gently tap the grease seal into the hub. A new seal must always be fitted as, during removal, it was probably damaged or distorted. The lip must face inwards to the hub.
14 Replace the hub and disc assembly onto the stub axle and slide in the outer bearing and thrust washer.
15 Refit the adjusting nut and tighten it to a torque wrench setting of 27 lb f ft (3.7 kg f m) whilst rotating the hub and disc to ensure free movement and centralisation of the bearings.

Slacken the nut back by 90° which will give the required end-float of 0.001 - 0.005 in (0.03 - 0.13 mm). Fit the nut retainer and a new split pin, but at this stage do not lock the split pin.

16 If a dial indicator gauge is available, it is advisable to check the disc for run-out. The measurement should be taken as near to the edge of the worn yet smooth part of the disc as possible, and must not exceed 0.002 in (0.05 mm). If the figure obtained is found to be excessive, check the mating surfaces of the disc and hub for dirt or damage and check the bearing and cups for excessive wear or damage.

17 If a dial indicator gauge is not available the run-out can be checked by means of a feeler gauge placed between the casting of the caliper and the disc. Establish a reasonably tight fit with the feeler gauge between the top of the casting and the disc and rotate the disc and hub. Any high or low spots will immediately become obvious by extra tightness or looseness of the fit of the feeler gauge. The amount of run-out can be checked by adding or subtracting feeler gauges as necessary.

18 Once the disc run-out has been checked and found to be correct bend the ends of the split pin back and replace the dust cap.

19 Reconnect the brake hydraulic pipe and bleed the brakes as described in Section 13 of this Chapter.

6 Drum brake shoes - inspection and renewal

After high mileages, it will be necessary to fit replacement shoes with new linings. Refitting new brake linings to shoes is not considered economic, or possible without the use of special equipment. However, if the services of a local garage or workshop having brake relining equipment are available then there is no reason why the original shoes should not be relined successfully. Ensure that the correct specification linings are fitted to the shoes.

1 Chock the front wheels, jack up the rear of the car and place on firmly based axle stands. Remove the roadwheel.

2 Release the brake drum retaining screw, and using a soft faced hammer on the outer circumference of the brake drum remove the brake drum.

3 The brake linings should be renewed if they are so worn that the rivet heads are flush with the surface of the lining. If bonded linings are fitted, they must be renewed when the lining material has worn down to 0.6 inches (1.52 mm) at its thinnest part.

4 Depress each shoe holding down spring and rotate the spring retaining washer through 90° to disengage it from the pinion secured to the backplate. Lift away the washer and spring.

5 Ease each shoe from its location slot in the fixed pivot and then detach the other end of each shoe from the wheel cylinder.

6 Note which way round and into which holes in the shoes the two retracting springs fit and detach the retracting springs.

7 Lift away the two brake shoes and retracting springs.

8 If the shoes are to be left off for a while, place a warning on the steering wheel. Also place an elastic band around the wheel cylinder to stop the piston falling out.

9 Withdraw the ratchet wheel assembly from the wheel cylinder and rotate the wheel until it abuts the slot head bolt shoulder. If this is not done difficulty will arise in refitting the brake drum.

10 Thoroughly clean all traces of dust from the shoes, backplates and brake drums using a stiff brush. It is recommended that compressed air is not used as it blows up dust which should not be inhaled. Brake dust can cause judder, or squeal and, therefore, it is important to clean out as described.

11 Check that the piston is free in the cylinder, that the rubber dust covers are undamaged and in position, and that there are no hydraulic leaks.

12 Prior to reassembly smear a trace of brake grease on the shoe support pads, brake shoe pivots and on the ratchet wheel face and threads.

13 To reassemble first fit the retracting springs to the shoe webs in the same position as was noted during removal.

14 Fit the shoe assembly to the backplate by first positioning the rear shoe in its location on the fixed pivot and over the parking brake link. Follow this with the front shoe.

15 Secure each shoe to the backplate with the spring and dished washer, disc facing inwards and turning through 90° to lock in position. Make sure that each shoe is firmly seated on the backplate.

16 Refit the brake drum and push it up the studs as far as it will go. Secure with the retaining screw.

17 The shoes must next be centralised by the brake pedal being depressed firmly several times.

18 Pull on and then release the handbrake several times until it is no longer possible to hear the clicking noise of the ratchet being turned by the ratchet arms. It is important to note that with the ratchet wheel in the fully off adjustment position, it is possible for the indexing lever on the parking brake link to over-ride the ratchet and stay in this position. When operating the link lever it is necessary to ensure that it always returns to the fully off position each time.

19 Refit the roadwheel and lower the car. Road test to ensure correct operation of the brakes.

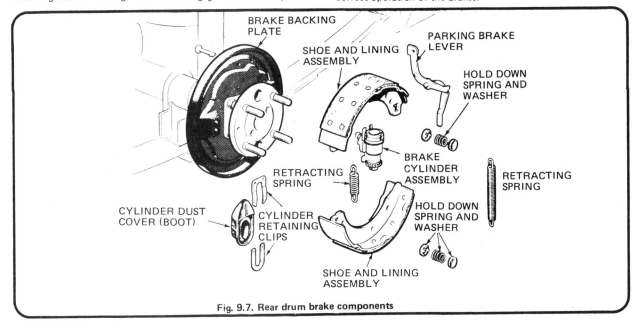

Fig. 9.7. Rear drum brake components

7 Drum brake wheel cylinder - removal, inspection and overhaul

If hydraulic fluid is leaking from the brake wheel cylinder, it will be necessary to dismantle it and renew the seal. Should brake fluid be found running down the side of the wheel, or if it is noticed that a pool of liquid forms alongside one wheel or the level of fluid in the master cylinder drops it is also indicative of failed seals.

1   Refer to Section 6 and remove the brake drum and shoes. Clean down the rear of the backplate using a stiff brush. Place a quantity of rag under the backplate to catch any hydraulic fluid that may issue from the open pipe or wheel cylinder.

2   Wipe the top of the brake master cylinder reservoir and un-screw the cap. Place a piece of polythene sheet over the top of the reservoir and replace the cap.

3   Using an open ended spanner carefully unscrew the hydraulic pipe connection union at the rear of the wheel cylinder. To prevent dirt entering tape over the end of the pipe.

4   Withdraw the split pin and clevis pin from the handbrake lever at the rear of the backplate.

5   Using a screwdriver carefully ease the rubber dust cover from the rear of the backplate and lift away.

6   Pull off the two 'U' shaped retainers holding the wheel cylinder to the backplate noting that the spring retainer is fitted from the handbrake link end of the wheel cylinder and the flat retainer from the other end, the flat retainer being located between the spring retainer and the wheel cylinder (Fig. 9.8).

7   The wheel cylinder and handbrake link can now be removed from the brake backplate.

8   To dismantle the wheel cylinder first remove the small metal clip holding the rubber dust cap in place then prise off the dust cap (Fig. 9.9).

9   Take the piston complete with its seal out of the cylinder bore and then withdraw the spring. Should the piston and seal prove difficult to remove gentle pressure will push it out of the bore.

10 Inspect the cylinder bore for score marks caused by impurities in hydraulic fluid. If any are found the cylinder and piston will require renewal together as a replacement unit.

11 If the cylinder bore is sound thoroughly clean it out with fresh hydraulic fluid.

12 The old rubber seal will probably be visibly worn or swollen. Detach it from the piston, smear a new rubber seal with hydraulic fluid and assemble it to the piston with the flat face of the seal next to the piston rear shoulder.

13 Reassembly is a direct reversal of the dismantling procedure. If the rubber dust cap appears to be worn or damaged it should also be renewed.

14 Before commencing refitting smear the area where the cylinder slides on the backplate and the brake shoe support pads, brake shoe pivots, ratchet wheel face and threads with brake grease.

15 Replacement is a straightforward reversal of the removal sequence but the following parts should be checked with extra care.

16 After fitting the rubber boot, check that the wheel cylinder can slide freely in the backplate and that the handbrake link operates the self adjusting mechanism correctly.

17 It is important to note that the self adjusting ratchet mechanism on the right-hand rear brake is right-hand threaded and the mechanism on the left-hand rear brake is left-hand threaded.

18 When replacement is complete bleed the braking system as described in Section 13.

8 Drum brake backplate - removal and refitting

1   To remove the backplate refer to Chapter 8 and remove the halfshaft.

2   Detach the handbrake cable from the handbrake relay lever on the backplate.

3   Wipe the top of the brake master cylinder reservoir and unscrew the cap. Place a piece of polythene sheet over the top of the reservoir and replace the cap.

4   Using an open ended spanner, carefully unscrew the hydraulic pipe connection union to the rear of the wheel cylinder. To prevent dirt entering tape over the pipe ends.

5   The brake backplate may now be lifted away.

Fig. 9.8. Withdrawing rear wheel cylinder retaining plate (Sec. 7)

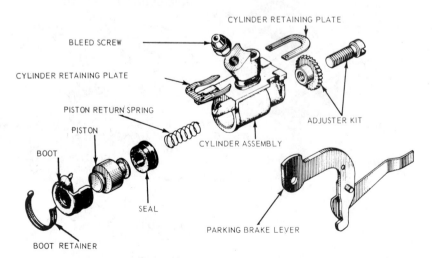

BLEED SCREW

CYLINDER RETAINING PLATE

CYLINDER RETAINING PLATE

PISTON RETURN SPRING

PISTON

BOOT

SEAL

BOOT RETAINER

CYLINDER ASSEMBLY

ADJUSTER KIT

PARKING BRAKE LEVER

Fig. 9.9. Exploded view of rear wheel cylinder (Sec. 7)

6 Refitting is the reverse sequence to removal. It will be necessary to bleed the brake hydraulic system, as described in Section 13.

9 Master cylinder - removal and installation

1 Apply the handbrake and chock the front wheels. Drain the fluid from the master cylinder reservoir and master cylinder by attaching a plastic bleed tube to one of the front brake bleed screws. Undo the screw one turn and then pump the fluid out into a clean glass container by means of the brake pedal. Hold the brake pedal against the floor at the end of each stroke and tighten the bleed screw. When the pedal has returned to its normal position loosen the bleed screw and repeat the process. The above sequence should now be carried out on one of the rear brake bleed screws.
2 Wipe the area around the two union nuts on the side of the master cylinder body and using an open ended spanner undo the two union nuts. Tape over the ends of the pipes to stop dirt entering (Fig. 9.10).
3 Undo and remove the two nuts and spring washers that secure the master cylinder to the rear of the servo unit. Lift away the master cylinder taking care not to damage the servo unit seal and ensure that no hydraulic fluid is allowed to drop onto the paintwork.
4 Refitting the master cylinder is the reverse sequence to removal. Always start the union nut before finally tightening the master cylinder nuts. It will be necessary to bleed the complete hydraulic system: full details will be found in Section 13.

10 Master cylinder - servicing

If a replacement master cylinder is to be fitted, it will be necessary to lubricate the seals before fitting to the car as they have a protective coating when originally assembled. Remove the blanking plugs from the hydraulic pipe union seatings. Inject clean hydraulic fluid into the master cylinder and operate the primary piston several times so that the fluid spreads over all the internal working surfaces.

If the master cylinder is to be dismantled after removal proceed as follows:
1 The component parts are shown in Fig. 9.11.
2 Prior to dismantling wipe the exterior of the master cylinder clean.
3 Using a clean metal rod of suitable diameter depress the primary piston until it reaches the stop so that the pressure of the intermediate piston is removed from the stop screw.
4 Unscrew the stop screw and remove the sealing washer. Release the pressure on the piston.
5 Lightly depress the primary piston again to relieve the pressure on the circlip located in the bore at the flanged end of the cylinder. With a pair of pointed pliers remove the circlip taking care not to scratch the finely finished bore.
6 Lift away the stop washer, and withdraw the primary piston assembly.
7 Undo and remove the connection screw and withdraw the deep spring retainer, spring, flat spring retainer, seal retainer, primary seal, seal, seal protector and secondary seal from the piston.
8 The intermediate piston assembly may now be removed by lightly tapping on the master cylinder against a wooden base.
9 Withdraw the spring, spring retainer, seal retainer, primary cup seal, seal protector and the two secondary seals from the piston.
10 Thoroughly wash all parts in either methylated spirits or clean approved hydraulic fluid and place in order ready for inspection.
11 Examine the bores of the master cylinder carefully for any signs of scoring, ridges or corrosion and, if it is found to be smooth all over, new seals can be fitted. If there is any doubt as to the condition of the bore, then a new assembly must be

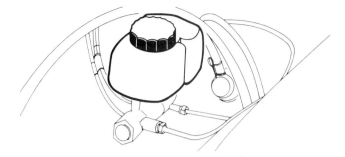

Fig. 9.10. Location of master cylinder

obtained.
12 If examination of the seals shows them to be apparently oversize or very loose on their seats, suspect oil contamination in the system. Oil will swell these rubber seals, and if one is found to be swollen it is reasonable to assume that all seals in the braking system will require attention.
13 Before reassembly again wash all parts in methylated spirits or clean approved hydraulic fluid. **Do not** use any other type of oil or cleaning fluid or the seals will be damaged.
14 Reassemble according to the piston assembly diagram (Fig. 9.11) noting the following points:
   Dip all seals in clean hydraulic fluid before fitting.
   Secondary seals are identified by a silver band.
   Tighten the stop screw to the specified torque setting.

11 Master cylinder (alternative type) - servicing

1 Refer to the introduction in Section 10.
2 The component parts are shown in Fig. 9.12.
3 Prior to dismantling wipe the exterior of the master cylinder clean.
4 Undo and remove the two screws and spring washers holding the reservoir to the master cylinder body. Lift away the reservoir. Using an Allen key, or wrench unscrew the tipping valve nut and lift away the seal. Using a suitable diameter rod push the primary plunger down the bore, this operation enabling the tipping valve to be withdrawn.
5 Using a compressed air jet, very carefully applied to the rear outlet connection, blow out all the master cylinder internal components. Alternatively, shake out the parts. Take care that adequate precautions are taken to ensure all parts are caught as they emerge.
6 Separate the primary and secondary plungers from the intermediate spring. Use the fingers to remove the gland seal from the primary plunger.
7 The secondary plunger assembly should be separated by lifting the thimble leaf over the shouldered end of the plunger. Using the fingers, remove the seal from the secondary plunger.
8 Depress the secondary spring, allowing the valve stem to slide through the keyhole in the thimble, thus releasing the tension on the spring.
9 Detach the valve spacer, taking care of the spring washer which will be found located under the valve head.
10 For information on inspection refer to Section 10, paragraphs 10 to 14 inclusive.
11 All components should be assembled wet by dipping in clean brake fluid. Using fingers only, fit new seals to the primary and secondary plungers ensuring that they are the correct way round. Place the dished washer with the dome against the underside of the valve seat. Hold it in position with the valve spacer ensuring that the legs face towards the valve seal.
12 Replace the plunger return spring centrally on the spacer insert the thimble into the spring, and depress until the valve stem engages in the keyhole of the thimble.
13 Insert the reduced end of the plunger into the thimble until

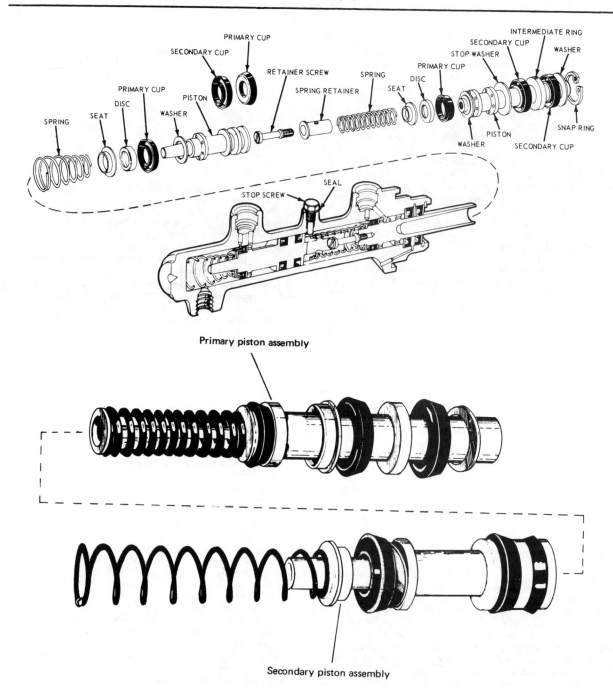

Fig. 9.11. Tandem master cylinder - component parts (Sec. 10)

the thimble engages under the shoulder of the plunger, and press home the thimble leaf. Replace the intermediate spring between the primary and secondary plungers.

14 Check that the master cylinder bore is clean and smear with clean brake fluid. With the complete assembly suitably wetted with brake fluid, carefully insert the assembly into the bore. Ease the lips of the piston seals into the bore taking care that they do not roll over. Push the assembly fully home.

15 Refit the tipping valve assembly, and seal, to the cylinder bore and tighten the securing nut to a torque wrench setting of 27 - 35 lb f ft (4.8 - 6.22 kg f m).

16 Using a clean screwdriver push the primary piston in and out checking that the recuperating valve opens when the screwdriver

is withdrawn and closes again when it is pushed it.

17 Check the condition of the front and rear reservoir gaskets and if there is any doubt as to their condition they must be renewed.

18 Replace the hydraulic fluid reservoir and tighten the two retaining screws.

19 The master cylinder is now ready for refitting to the servo unit. Bleed the complete hydraulic system and road test the car.

---

12 Flexible hose - inspection, removal and refitting

1   Inspect the condition of the flexible hydraulic hoses leading

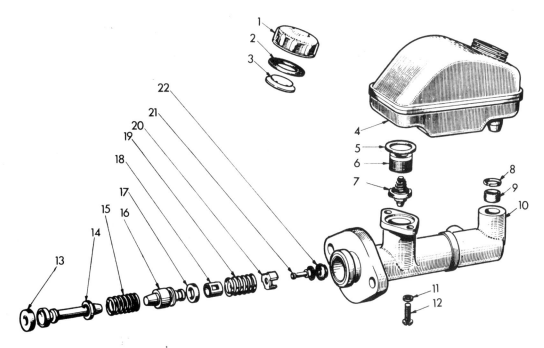

Fig. 9.12. Exploded view of alternative type master cylinder (Sec. 11)

1 Reservoir cap	7 Tipping valve	13 Seal	19 Spring
2 Cap seal	8 Circlip	14 Primary piston	20 Spring retainer
3 Seal retainer	9 Gasket	15 Spring	21 Valve
4 Reservoir	10 Master cylinder body	16 Secondary piston	22 Seal
5 Sealing ring	11 Washer	17 Seal	
6 Tipping valve retainer	12 Screw	18 Spring retainer	

from under the front wings to the brackets on the front suspension units, and also the single hose on the rear axle casing. If they are swollen, damaged or chafed, they must be renewed.

2 Undo the locknuts at both ends of the flexible hoses and then holding the hexagon nut on the flexible hose steady undo the other union nut and remove the flexible hose and washer.

3 Replacement is a reversal of the removal procedure, but carefully check that all the securing brackets are in a sound condition and that the locknuts are tight.

13 Bleeding the hydraulic system

1 Removal of all the air from the hydraulic system is essential to the correct working of the braking system, and before undertaking this, examine the fluid reservoir cap to ensure that both vent holes, one on top and the second underneath but not in line, are clear; check the level of fluid and top up if required.

2 Check all brake line unions and connections for possible seepage, and at the same time check the conditon of the rubber hoes, which may be perished.

3 If the condition of the wheel cylinders is in doubt, check for possible signs of fluid leakage.

4 If there is any possibility of incorrect fluid having been put into the system, drain all the fluid out and flush through with methylated spirits. Renew all piston seals and cups since these will be affected and could possibly fail under pressure.

5 Gather together a clean jar, a 9 inch length of tubing which fits tightly over the bleed nipples, and a tin of the correct brake fluid.

6 Centralise the piston in the pressure differential valve (see Section 14). To do this, modify the blade of a screwdriver as shown and after removing the rubber cover from the base of the valve insert the screwdriver and wedge it to hold the piston centralised (Fig. 9.13).

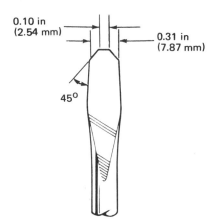

0.10 in
(2.54 mm)

0.31 in
(7.87 mm)

45°

Fig. 9.13. Pressure differential switch piston centralising tool (Sec. 13)

7 Clean the dirt from around the front caliper bleed nipple which is furthest from the master cylinder.

8 Open the bleed valve with a spanner and then have an assistant quickly depress the brake pedal. After slowly releasing the pedal, pause for a moment to allow the fluid to recoup in the master cylinder and then depress again. This will force air from the system. Continue until no more air bubbles can be seen coming from the tube. At intervals make certain that the reservoir is kept topped up, otherwise air will enter at this point again.

9 Repeat this operation on the other front brake and the rear brakes. When completed, check the level of the fluid in the reservoir and then check the feel of the brake pedal, which

should be firm and free from any 'spongy' action, which is normally associated with air in the system.

14 Pressure differential switch - description and servicing

1   This device is incorporated in the hydraulic circuit and is a switch in which a piston is kept 'in balance' when the hydraulic pressures in the independent front and rear hydraulic brake circuits are equal. In the event of a drop in pressure in either circuit, the piston is displaced and makes an electrical contact to illuminate a warning light on the instrument panel. To dismantle the switch, first disconnect the hydraulic pipes at their unions on the switch body. To prevent a loss of hydraulic fluid either place a piece of polythene under the cap of the master cylinder and screw it down tightly or plug the ends of the two pipes leading from the master cylinder
2   Referring to Fig. 9.14 disconnect the wiring from the switch assembly.
3   Undo the single bolt holding the assembly to the rear of the engine compartment and remove it from the car.
4   To dismantle the assembly start by undoing the end plug and discarding the copper gasket. Then undo the adaptor and also discard its copper gasket as they must be renewed.
5   Unscrew the switch assembly from the top of the unit then push the small and large pistons out of their bores taking extreme care not to damage the bores during this operation.
6   Take the small seals from their pistons making a careful note that the seals are slightly tapered and that the large diameter on each seal is fitted to the slotted end of the pistons. Discard the seals as they must not be reused.
7   Pull the dust cover off the bottom of the unit and also discard this component.
8   Carefully examine the pistons and the bore of the actuator for score marks scratches or damage; if any are found the complete unit must be exchanged for a new one.

15 Vacuum servo unit - description

1   A vacuum servo unit is fitted into the brake hydraulic circuit in serles with the master cylinder, to provide assistance to the driver when the brake pedal is depressed. This reduces the effort required by the driver to operate the brakes under all braking conditons.
2   The unit operates by vacuum obtained from the induction manifold and comprises basically a booster diaphragm and check valve. The servo unit and hydraulic master cylinder are connected together so that the servo unit piston rod acts as the master cylinder pushrod. The driver's braking effort is transmitted through another pushrod to the servo unit piston and its built-in control system. The servo unit piston does not fit tightly into the cylinder but has a strong diaphragm to keep its edges in constant contact with the cylinder wall, so assuring an air tight seal between the two parts. The forward chamber is held under vacuum conditions created in the inlet manifold of the engine and, during periods when the brake pedal is not in use, the controls open a passage to the rear chamber so placing it under vacuum conditions as well. When the brake pedal is depressed, the vacuum passage to the rear chamber is cut off and the chamber exposed to atmospheric pressure. The consequent rush of air pushes the servo piston forward in the vacuum chamber and operates the main pushrod to the master cylinder.
3   The controls are designed so that assistance is given under all conditions and, when the brakes are not required, vacuum in the rear chamber is established when the brake pedal is released. All air from the atmosphere entering the rear chamber is passed through a small air filter.
4   Under normal operating conditions the vacuum servo unit is very reliable and does not require overhaul except at very high mileages. In this case it is far better to obtain a service exchange unit, rather than repair the original unit.

16 Vacuum servo unit - removal and installation

1   Slacken the clip securing the vacuum hose to the servo unit; carefully draw the hose from its union.
2   Refer to Section 11 and remove the master cylinder.
3   Using a pair of pliers remove the spring clip in the end of the brake pedal to pushrod clevis pin. Lift away the clevis pin and the bushes.
4   Undo and remove the nuts and spring washers securing the servo unit mounting bracket to the bulkhead. Lift away the

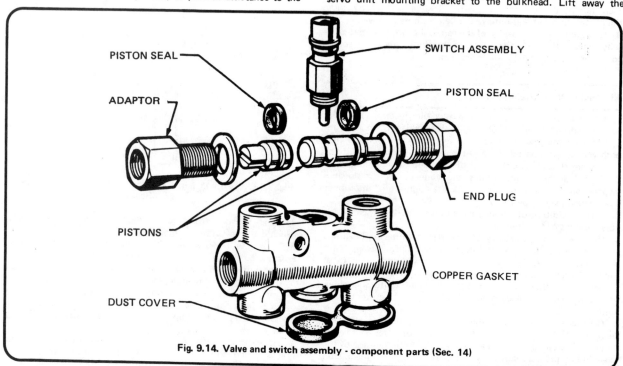

Fig. 9.14. Valve and switch assembly - component parts (Sec. 14)

servo unit and bracket.

5 Undo and remove the four nuts and spring washers that secure the bracket to the servo unit.

6 Refitting the servo unit is the reverse sequence to removal. It will be necessary to bleed the brake hydraulic system as described in Section 15.

17 Vacuum servo unit - servicing

Thoroughly clean the outside of the unit using a stiff brush and wipe with a non-fluffy rag. It cannot be too strongly emphasised that cleanliness is important when working on the servo. Before any attempt be made to dismantle, refer to Fig. 9.15 where it will be seen that two items of equipment are required. Firstly, a base plate must be made to enable the unit to be safely held in a vice. Secondly, a lever must be made similar to the form shown. Without these items it is impossible to dismantle satisfactorily.

To dismantle the unit proceed as follows:

1 Refer to Fig. 9.15 and, using a file or scriber make a line across the two halves of the unit to act as a datum for alignment.

2 Fit the previously made base plate into a firm vice and attach the unit to the plate using the master cylinder studs.

3 Fit the lever to the four studs on the rear shell as shown.

4 Use a piece of long rubber hose and connect one end to the adaptor on the engine inlet manifold and the other end to the non return valve. Start the engine and this will create a vacuum in the unit so drawing the two halves together.

5 Rotate the lever in an anticlockwise direction until the front shell indentations are in line with the recesses in the rim of the rear shell. Then press the lever assembly down firmly whilst an assistant stops the engine and quickly removes the vacuum pipe from the inlet manifold connector. Depress the operating rod so

as to release the vacuum, whereupon the front and rear halves should part. If necessary, use a soft faced hammer and lightly tap the front half to break the bond.

6 Lift away the rear shell followed by the diaphragm return spring, the dust cap, end cap and the filter. Also withdraw the diaphragm. Press down the valve rod and shake out the valve retaining plate. Then separate the valve rod assembly from the diaphragm plate (Fig. 9.16).

7 Gently ease the spring washer from the diaphragm plate and withdraw the pushrod and reaction disc.

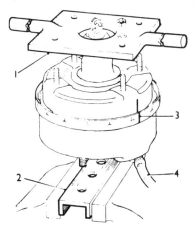

Fig. 9.15. Special tools required to dismantle servo unit (Sec. 17)

1 Lever	3 Scribe line
2 Base plate	4 Vacuum applied

Fig. 9.16. Servo unit - component parts (Sec. 17)

1 Bolt	7 Dished washer	13 Stop key	19 Diaphragm
2 Seat assembly	8 Brake servo pushrod	14 Seal	20 Diaphragm plate
3 Front shell	9 Reaction disc	15 Piston guide	21 Spring
4 Seal	10 Washer	16 Filter retainer	
5 Valve assembly	11 Filter	17 Dust cover	
6 Pushrod assembly	12 Castellated washer	18 Rear shell	

8 The seal and plate assembly in the end of the front shell are a press fit. It is recommended that, unless the seal is to be renewed, they be left in-situ.

9 Thoroughly clean all parts. Inspect them for signs of damage, stripped threads etc., and obtain new ones as necessary. All seals should be renewed and for this a 'Major Repair Kit' should be purchased. This kit will also contain two separate greases which must be used as directed and not interchanged.

10 To reassemble first smear the seal and bearing with Ford grease numbered '64949008 EM - 1C - 14' and refit the rear shell positioning it such that the flat face of the seal is towards the bearing. Press into position and refit the retainer.

11 Lightly smear the disc and hydraulic pushrod with Ford grease number '64949008 EM - 1C - 14'. Refit the reaction disc and pushrod to the diaphragm plate and press in the large spring washer. The small spring washer supplied in the 'Major Repair Kit' is not required. It is important that the length of the pushrod is not altered in any way and any attempt to move the adjustment bolt will strip the threads. If a new hydraulic pushrod has been required, the length will have to be reset. Details of this operation are given at the end of this Section.

12 Lightly smear the outer diameter of the diaphragm plate neck and the bearing surfaces of the valve plunger with Ford grease number '64949008 EM - 1C - 14'. Carefully fit the valve rod assembly into the neck of the diaphragm and fix with the retaining plate.

13 Fit the diaphragm into position and the non-return valve to the front shell. Next smear the seal and plate assembly with Ford grease numbered '64949008 EM - 1C - 15' and press into the front shell with the plate facing inwards.

14 Fit the front shell to the base plate and the lever to the rear shell. Reconnect the vacuum hose to the non-return valve and the adaptor on the engine inlet manifold. Position the diaphragm return spring in the front shell. Lightly smear the outer bead of the diaphragm with Ford grease numbered '64949008 EM - 1C - 14' and locate the diaphragm assembly in the rear shell. Position the rear shell assembly on the return spring and line up the previously made scribe marks.

15 The assistant should start the engine. Watching one's fingers very carefully, press the two halves of the unit together and, using the lever tool, turn clockwise to lock the two halves together. Stop the engine and disconnect the hose.

16 Press a new filter into the neck of the diaphragm plate, refit the end cap and position the dust cover onto the special lugs of the rear shell.

17 Hydraulic pushrod adjustment only applies if a new pushrod has been fitted. It will be seen from Fig. 9.17 that there is a bolt screwed into the end of the pushrod. The amount of protrusion has to be adjusted in the following manner: Remove the bolt and coat the threaded portion with Loctite Grade B. Reconnect the vacuum hose to the adaptor on the inlet valve and non return valve. Start the engine and screw the prepared bolt into the end of the pushrod. Adjust the position of the bolt head so that it is 0.011 to 0.016 inch (0.28 to 0.40 mm) below the face of the front shell as shown by dimension A in Fig. 9.17. Leave the unit for a minimum of 24 hours to allow the Loctite to set hard.

18 Refit the servo unit to the car as described in the previous section. To test the servo unit for correct operation after overhaul first start the engine and run for a period of two minutes and then switch off. Wait for ten minutes and apply the footbrake very carefully, listening to hear the rush of air into the servo unit. This will indicate that vacuum was retained and, therefore operating correctly.

---

18 Handbrake - adjustment

Adjustment of the handbrake is normally automatically carried out by the action of the rear brake automatic adjusters. When new components have been fitted or the handbrake cable has stretched, then the following operations should be carried out.

1 Chock the front wheels, jack up the rear of the car and

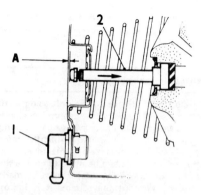

Fig. 9.17. Pushrod setting (Sec. 17)

A *Pushrod setting 0.011 - 0.016 in. (0.28 - 0.40 mm)*
1 *Vacuum applied*
2 *Pushrod against reaction disc*

support on firmly based axle stands located under the rear axle. Release the handbrake.

2 Slide under the car and check that the primary cable follows its correct run and is correctly in its guide. The cable guides must be kept well greased at all times.

3 First adjust the effective length of the primary cable by slackening the locknut (A) on the end of the cable adjacent to the relay lever on the rear axle (Fig. 9.18).

4 Adjust the nut until the primary cable has no slack in it and the relay lever is just clear of the slot in the banjo casing. Retighten the locknut.

5 Slacken the locknut (B) on the end of the transverse cable adjacent to the right-hand rear brake. Check that the parking brake operating levers are in the fully 'off' position, that is back on their stops, and adjust the cable so that there is no slack. Check that the operating levers are still on their stops and tighten the locknut.

---

19 Handbrake control lever - removal and refitting

1 Chock the front wheels, jack-up the rear of the car and support on firmly based axle stands. Release the handbrake.

2 Working inside the car remove the carpeting from around the area of the handbrake lever.

3 Models fitted with a console: refer to Chapter 12 and remove the console.

4 Remove the split pin and withdraw the clevis pin that connects the primary cable to the lower end of the handbrake lever. This protrudes under the floor panels (Fig. 9.19).

5 Undo and remove the six self-tapping screws which secure the handbrake lever rubber boot to the floor. Draw the rubber boot up the lever.

6 Undo and remove the two bolts that secure the handbrake lever assembly to the floor. Lift away the lever assembly.

7 Refitting the lever assembly is the reverse sequence to removal. The following additional points should be noted:
   a) Apply some grease to the primary cable clevis pin.
   b) Adjust the primary cable as described in Section 20.

---

20 Handbrake cables - renewal

Primary cable

1 Chock the front wheels, jack up the rear of the car and support on firmly based axle stands. Release the handbrake.

2 Working under the car unscrew and remove the nuts that

Fig. 9.18. Handbrake linkage adjustment points (Sec. 18)

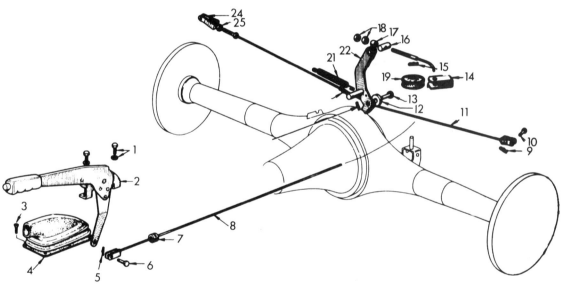

Fig. 9.19. Handbrake assembly

1 Bolt and washer	8 Cable	15 Retainer pin	22 Retaining pin
2 Handbrake lever	9 Retaining pin	16 Pin	23 Retaining pin
3 Screw	10 Clevis pin	17 Spacer	24 Clevis
4 Dust cover	11 Transverse cable	18 Adjusting & locknuts	25 Adjusting nut
5 Retaining pin	12 Cable pulley	19 Pulley	
6 Clevis pin	13 Clevis pin	20 Compensator	
7 Cable guide	14 Pulley retainer	21 Spring	

secure the end of the primary cable to the relay lever located at the rear of the axle casing.

3   Detach the primary cable from the end of the handbrake lever by removing the split pin and withdrawing the clevis pin.

4   Detach the cable from its underbody guides and lift away.

5   Refitting the primary cable is the reverse sequence to removal but the following additional points should be noted:

　　a) Apply some grease to the cable guides and insert the cable. Also lubricate the front clevis pin.

　　b) Refer to Section 18 and adjust the primary cable.

Transverse cable

1   Chock the front wheels, jack up the front of the car and

support on firmly based axle stands. Release the handbrake.

2   Working under the car remove the split pin and withdraw the clevis pin that secures the transverse cable to the left-hand backplate.

3   Detach the cable from the right-hand rear backplate by removing the locknut and unscrewing the cable from the clevis.

4   Remove the pulley pins, split pin and withdraw the pulley pin. Lift away the little pulley wheel and transverse cable.

5   Refitting the transverse cable is the reverse sequence to removal but the following additional points should be noted:

　　a) Apply some grease to the pulley and pivot pin, the threaded end of the cable and the clevis pin.

　　b) Adjust the transverse cable as described in Section 18.

21 Brake pedal - removal and refitting

1   The brake and clutch pedals operate on a common cross shaft

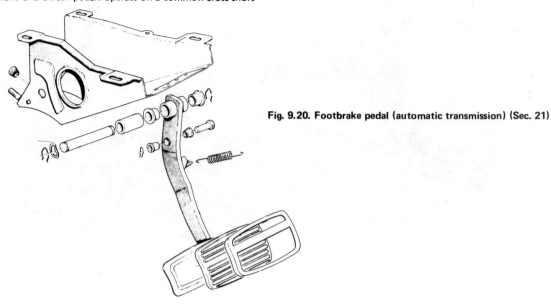

and dismantling is fully described in Section 9 of Chapter 5.
2   On vehicles equipped with automatic transmission, components of the single foot pedal are shown in Fig. 9.20.

Fig. 9.20. Footbrake pedal (automatic transmission) (Sec. 21)

22 Fault diagnosis - braking system

Before diagnosing faults from the following chart, check that any braking irregularities are not caused by:
1   Uneven and incorrect tyre pressures.
2   Incorrect 'mix' of radial and crossply tyres.
3   Wear in the steering mechanism.
4   Defects in the suspension and dampers.
5   Misalignment of the body frame.

Symptom	Reason/s
Pedal travels a long way before the brakes operate	Brake shoes set too far from the drums (auto. adjusters seized)
Stopping ability poor, even though pedal pressure is firm	Linings discs or drums badly worn or scored One or more wheel hydraulic cylinders seized, resulting in some brake shoes not pressing against the drums (or pads against discs) Brake linings contaminated with oil Wrong type of linings fitted (too hard) Brake shoes wrongly assembled Servo unit not functioning
Car veers to one side when the brakes are applied	Brake pads or linings on one side are contaminated with oil Hydraulic wheel cylinder(s) on one side partially or fully seized A mixture of lining materials fitted between sides Unequal wear between sides caused by partially seized wheel cylinders
Pedal feels spongy when the brakes are applied	Air is present in the hydraulic system
Pedal feels springy when the brakes are applied	Brake linings not bedded into the drums (after fitting new ones) Master cylinder or brake backplate mounting bolts loose Severe wear in brake drums causing distortion when brakes are applied. Discs out of true.
Pedal travels right down with little or no resistance and brakes are virtually non-operative	Leak in hydraulic system resulting in lack of pressure for operating wheel cylinders If no signs of leakage are apparent the master cylinder internal seals are failing to sustain pressure
Binding, juddering, overheating	One or a combination of causes given in the foregoing sections

Chapter 10 Electrical system

Contents

Specifications

System type ... ...   12 volt, negative earth

Battery
Type ... ...   Lead acid
Capacity at 20 hr. rate ... ...   38, 57 or 66 amp/hr.
Plates per cell ... ...   9, 11 or 13
Specific gravity charged ... ...   1.275 to 1.290
Electrolyte capacity ... ...   7.7 Imp pints (9.3 US pints, 4.3 litres)

Alternator
Lucas: ... ...   Type 15 ACR
   Maximum charge ... ...   28 amps
   Speed (ratio to engine) ... ...   1.88 to 1
Bosch: ... ...   Type K1
   Maximum charge ... ...   35 amps
   Speed (ratio to engine) ... ...   1.88 to 1

Regulator
Operating speed ... ...   5000 rpm
Alternator output ... ...   Not exceeding 10 amps
Voltage setting ... ...   14.1 to 14.4 volts

Starter motor (Lucas)

Type	Pre-engaged
Number of teeth on pinion	11
Number of teeth on ring gear	132
Gear ratio	12 : 1
Maximum brush length	0.375 inch (9.52 mm)
Brush spring pressure	28 oz (0.805 kg)
Minimum commutator thickness	0.8 in. (2.05 mm)
Lock torque	7 lb f ft (0.97 kg f m) with 350 - 370 amps
Torque at 1000 rpm	4.4 lb f ft (0.61 kg f m) with 260 - 375 amps
Light running current	65 amp at 8,000 - 10,000 rpm
Maximum armature endfloat	0.010 in. (0.25 mm)
Solenoid:	
Closing (Series) winding resistance	0.21 to 0.025 ohms
Hold-on (Shunt) winding resistance	0.9 to 1.1 ohms

Starter motor (Bosch)

Type	Pre-engaged
Teeth on pinion	10
Teeth on ring gear	135
Ratio	13.5 : 1
Number of brushes	4
Minimum brush length	0.375 in. (9.52 mm)
Brush spring pressure	42.3 oz (1.190 kg)
Current draw (mounted on engine)	100 - 130 amps at 68°F (20°C)
Engine cranking speed	180 rpm (approx)

Fuses

No.	Rating	Circuit protected 1600 cc	2000 cc
1	16 Amp	Interior lamp, hazard flashers, cigar lighter	Interior lamp, clock, cigar lighter
2	8 A	LH side, tail lamps and instrument lights	Rear licence plate, instrument illumination
3	8 A	RH side, tail lamps, licence plate	RH parking and tail lamp
4	8 A	High beam	LH parking and tail lamp
5	16 A	Low beam	Horn, heater blower
6	16 A	Stop lamps, heater, direction indicator, gauges, reverse lamps	Wiper motor, reverse lamps
7	16 A	Wiper motor	Direction indicator lamps and stop lamps

One additional 16 A fuse is located behind the instrument panel for the protection of the heated rear window. Two fuses are mounted in conjunction with the headlamp relay within the engine compartment.

Bulbs

		1600 cc	2000 cc
Reverse light		21 CP	21 CP
Clock		1.2 CP	1.2 CP
Cluster illumination		2 CP	2.2 CP
Courtesy light		10 watt	6 CP
Front direction indicator		21 watt	32/4 CP
Headlights (high beam)		—	37.5 watts
Headlight (high and low beam)		40/45 watt	40 and 50 watts
Indicator lights		2 CP	1.0 CP
Number plate lights		4 CP	5 CP
Rear direction indicator		21 watt	32 CP
Tail and stop light		21/5 watt	32/4 CP
Front side light		4 watt	4 watt

Torque wrench settings

		lb f ft	kg f m
Starter motor bolts		25	3.5
Alternator mounting bolts		18	2.5
Alternator mounting bracket		25	3.5
Alternator pulley nut		25	3.5

1 General description

The major components of the 12 volt negative earth system comprise a 12 volt battery, an alternator (driven from the crankshaft pulley), and a starter motor.

The battery supplies a steady amount of current for the ignition, lighting and other electrical circuits and provides a reserve of electricity when the current consumed by the electrical equipment exceeds that being produced by the alternator.

The alternator has its own integral regulator which ensures a high output if the battery is in a low state of charge and the demand from the electrical equipment is high, and a low output if the battery is fully charged and there is little demand for the electrical equipment.

When fitting electrical accessories to cars with a negative earth system it is important, if they contain silicone diodes or transistors, that they are connected correctly, otherwise serious damage may result to the components concerned. Items such as radios, tape recorders, electric ignition systems, electric tachometer, automatic dipping etc, should all be checked for correct polarity.

It is important that the battery positive lead is always disconnected if the battery is to be boost charged, also if the body repairs are to be carried out using electronic welding equipment - the alternator must be disconnected otherwise serious damage can be caused. Whenever the battery has to be disconnected it must always be reconnected with the negative terminal earthed.

2 Battery - removal and installation

1 The battery is on a carrier fitted to the left-hand wing valance of the engine compartment. It should be removed once every three months for cleaning and testing. Disconnect the positive and then the negative leads from the battery terminals by undoing and removing the plated nuts and bolts. Note that two cables are attached to the positive terminal.

2 Unscrew and remove the bolt, and plain washer that secures the battery clamp plate to the carrier. Lift away the clamp plate. Carefully lift the battery from its carrier holding it vertically to ensure that none of the electrolyte is spilled.

3 Replacement is a direct reversal of this procedure. **Note:** Replace the negative lead before the position lead and smear the terminals with petroleum jelly to prevent corrosion. **Never** use an ordinary grease.

3 Battery - maintenance and inspection

1 Normal weekly battery maintenance consists of checking the electrolyte level of each cell to ensure that the separators are covered by ¼ inch (6.35 mm) of electrolyte. If the level has fallen top up the battery using distilled water only. Do not over-fill. If a battery is overfilled or any electrolyte spilled, immediately wipe away and neutralize as electrolyte attacks and corrodes any metal it comes into contact with very rapidly.

2 If the battery has the Auto-fil device fitted, a special topping up sequence is required. The white balls in the Auto-fil battery are part of the automatic topping up device which ensures correct electrolyte level. The vent chamber should remain in position at all times except when topping up or taking specific gravity readings. If the electrolyte level in any of the cells is below the bottom of the filling tube top up as follows:

   a) *Lift off the vent chamber cover.*
   b) *With the battery level, pour distilled water into the trough until all the filling tubes and trough are full.*
   c) *Immediately replace the cover to allow the water in the trough and tubes to flow into the cells. Each cell will automatically receive the correct amount of water.*

3 As well as keeping the terminals clean and covered with petroleum jelly, the top of the battery, and especially the top of the cells, should be kept clean and dry. This helps prevent corrosion and ensures that the battery does not become partially discharged by leakage through dampness and dirt.

4 Once every three months remove the battery and inspect the battery securing bolts, the battery clamp plate, tray and battery leads for corrosion (white fluffy deposits on the metal which are brittle to touch). If any corrosion is found, clean off the deposits with ammonia and paint over the clean metal with an anti-rust/anti-acid paint.

5 At the same time inspect the battery case for cracks. If a crack is found, clean and plug it with one of the proprietary compounds marketed for this purpose. If leakage through the crack has been excessive then it will be necessary to refill the appropriate cell with fresh electrolyte as detailed later. Cracks are frequently caused to the top of the battery case by pouring in distilled water in the middle of winter *after* instead of *before* a run. This gives the water no chance to mix with the electrolyte and so the former freezes and splits the battery case.

6 If topping-up the battery becomes excessive and the case has been inspected for cracks that could cause leakage, but none are found, the battery is being overcharged and the voltage regulator

will have to be checked and reset.

7 With the battery on the bench at the three monthly interval check, measure the specific gravity with a hydrometer to determine the state of charge and condition of the electrolyte. There should be very little variation between the different cells and if a variation in excess of 0.025 is present it will be due to either:

   a) *Loss of electrolyte from the battery at sometime caused by spillage or a leak resulting in a drop in the specific gravity of the electrolyte, when the deficiency was replaced with distilled water instead of fresh electrolyte.*
   b) *An internal short circuit caused by buckling of the plates or a similar malady pointing to the likelihood of total battery failure in the near future.*

8 The specific gravity of the electrolyte for fully charged conditions at the electrolyte temperature indicated, is listed in Table A. The specific gravity of a fully discharged battery at different temperatures of the electrolyte is given in Table B.

Table A
Specific Gravity - Battery Fully Charged

1.268 at 100°F or 38°C electrolyte temperature
1.272 at 90°F or 32°C electrolyte temperature
1.276 at 80°F or 27°C electrolyte temperature
1.280 at 70°F or 21°C electrolyte temperature
1.284 at 60°F or 16°C electrolyte temperature
1.288 at 50°F or 10°C electrolyte temperature
1.292 at 40°F or 4°C electrolyte temperature
1.296 at 30°F or -1.5°C electrolyte temperature

Table B
Specific Gravity - Battery Fully Discharged

1.098 at 100°F or 38°C electrolyte temperature
1.102 at 90°F or 32°C electrolyte temperature
1.106 at 80°F or 27°C electrolyte temperature
1.110 at 70°F or 21°C electrolyte temperature
1.114 at 60°F or 16°C electrolyte temperature
1.118 at 50°F or 10°C electrolyte temperature
1.122 at 40°F or 4°C electrolyte temperature
1.126 at 30°F or -1.5°C electrolyte temperature

4 Battery - electrolyte replenishment

1 If the battery is in a fully charged state and one of the cells maintains a specific gravity reading which is 0.025 or more lower than the others, and a check of each cell has been made with a voltmeter to check for short circuits (a four to seven second test should give a steady reading of between 12 to 18 volts) then it is likely that electrolyte has been lost from the cell with the low reading.

2 Top-up the cell with a solution of 1 part sulphuric acid to 2.5 parts of water. If the cell is already fully topped-up draw some electrolyte out of it with a pipette.

3 When mixing the sulphuric acid and water **never add water to sulphuric acid** - always pour the acid slowly onto the water in a glass container. **If water is added to sulphuric acid it will explode.**

4 Continue to top-up the cell with the freshly made electrolyte and then recharge the battery and check the hydrometer readings.

5 Battery charging

1 In winter time when heavy demand is placed upon the battery, such as when starting from cold, and much electrical equipment is continually in use, it is a good idea to occasionally have the battery fully charged from an external source at the rate of 3.5 to 4 amps.

2 Continue to charge the battery at this rate until no further rise in specific gravity is noted over a four hour period.

3 Alternatively, a trickle charger charging at the rate of 1.5

amps can be safely used overnight.

4 Specially rapid 'boost' charges which are claimed to restore the power of the battery in 1 to 2 hours are most dangerous as they can cause serious damage to the battery plates through over-heating.

5 While charging the battery, note that the temperature of the electrolyte should never exceed 100°F (37.8°C).

6 Alternator - general description

The alternator may be of Lucas or Bosch type according to engine capacity or date of production.

The main advantage of the alternator lies in its ability to provide a high charge at low revolutions. Driving slowly in heavy traffic with a dynamo invariably means no charge is reaching the battery. In similar conditions even with the wiper, heater, lights and perhaps radio switched on the alternator will ensure a charge reaches the battery.

7 Alternator - routine maintenance

1 The equipment has been designed for the minimum amount of maintenance in service, the only items subject to wear being the brushes and bearings.

2 Brushes should be examined after about 75,000 miles (120,000 km) and renewed if necessary. The bearings are pre-packed with grease for life, and should not require further attention.

3 Check the fan belt every 3,000 miles (5,000 km) for correct adjustment which should be 0.5 inch (13 mm) total movement at the centre of the run between the alternator and water pump pulleys.

8 Alternator - special procedures

Whenever the electrical system of the car is being attended to, and external means of starting the engine is used, there are certain precautions that must be taken otherwise serious and expensive damage can result.

1 Always make sure that the negative terminal of the battery is earthed. If the terminal connections are accidentally reversed or if the battery has been reverse charged the alternator diodes will be damaged.

2 The output terminal on the alternator marked 'BAT' or 'B+' must never be earthed but should always be connected directly to the positive terminal of the battery.

3 Whenever the alternator is to be removed or when disconnecting the terminals of the alternator circuit, always disconnect the battery earth terminal first.

4 The alternator must never be operated without the battery to alternator cable connected.

5 It the battery is to be charged by external means always disconnect both battery cables before the external charger is connected.

6 Should it be necessary to use a booster charger or booster battery to start the engine always double check that the negative cable is connected to negative terminal and the positive cable to positive terminal.

9 Alternator - removal and refitting

1 Disconnect the battery leads.

2 Note the terminal connections at the rear of the alternator and disconnect the plug or multi pin connector.

3 Undo and remove the alternator adjustment arm bolt, slacken the alternator mounting bolts and push the alternator inward towards the engine. Lift away the fan belt from the pulley.

4 Remove the remaining two mounting bolts and carefully lift the alternator away from the car.

5 Take care not to knock or drop the alternator otherwise this can cause irreparable damage.

6 Refitting the alternator is the reverse sequence to removal.

7 Adjust the fan belt so that it has 0.5 inch (13 mm) total movement at the centre of the run between the alternator and water pump pulleys.

10 Alternator - fault finding and repair

Due to the specialist knowledge and equipment required to test or service an alternator it is recommended that if the performance is suspect, the car be taken to an automobile electrician who will have the facilities for such work. Because of this recommendation, information is limited to the inspection and renewal of the brushes. Should the alternator not charge or the system be suspect the following points may be checked before seeking further assistance:

1 Check the fanbelt tension, as described in Section 7.
2 Check the battery, as described in Section 3.
3 Check all electrical cable connections for cleanliness and security.

11 Alternator brushes (Lucas) - inspection, removal and refitting

1 Undo and remove the two screws and washers securing the end cover (Fig. 10.1).

2 To inspect the brushes correctly the brush holder moulding should be removed complete by undoing the two bolts and disconnecting the 'Lucar' connection to the diode plates.

3 With the brush holder moulding removed and the brush assemblies still in position check that they protrude from the face of the moulding by at least 0.2 inches (5 mm). Also check that when depressed, the spring pressure is 7 - 10 ozs. when the end of the brush is flush with the face of the brush moulding. To be done with any accuracy this requires a push type spring gauge.

4 Should either of the foregoing requirements not be fulfilled the spring assemblies should be replaced.

5 This can be done by simply renewing the holding screws of each assembly and replacing them.

6 With the brush holder moulding removed the slip rings on the face end of the rotor are exposed. These can be cleaned with a petrol soaked cloth and any signs of burning may be removed very carefully with fine glass paper. On no account should any other abrasive be used or any attempt at machining be made.

7 When the brushes are refitted they should slide smoothly in their holders. Any sticking tendency may first be rectified by wiping with a petrol soaked cloth or, if this fails, by carefully polishing with a very fine file where any binding marks may appear.

8 Reassemble in the reverse order of dismantling. Ensure that leads which may have been connected to any of the screws are reconnected correcty. Note:

1 If the charging system is suspect, first check the fan belt tension and condition - refer to Section 7 for details.
2 Check the battery - refer to Section 3 for details.
3 With an alternator the ignition warning light control feed comes from the centre point of a pair of diodes in the alternator via a control unit similar in appearance to an indicator flasher unit. Should the warning light indicate lack of charge, check this unit and if suspect replace it.
4 Should all the above prove negative then proceed to check the alternator.

12 Alternator brushes (Bosch) - inspection, removal and refitting

1 Undo and remove the two screws, spring and plain washers that secure the brush box to the rear of the brush end housing. Lift away the brush box (Fig. 10.2).

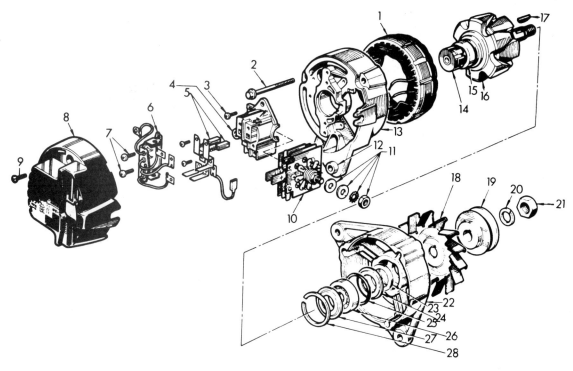

Fig. 10.1. Lucas alternator - component parts (Sec. 11)

1 Stator	8 End cover	15 Bearing	22 Casing
2 Through bolt	9 Screws	16 Rotor	23 Seal
3 Screw	10 Rectifier	17 Woodruff key	24 Bearing cup
4 Washer	11 Nut and washers	18 Fan	25 Seal
5 Brushes	12 Spacer	19 Pulley wheel	26 Bearing
6 Regulator	13 Stator body	20 Washer	27 Bearing cup
7 Screws	14 Slip ring	21 Nut	28 Circlip

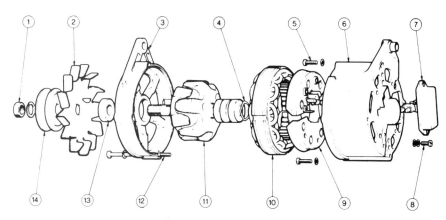

Fig. 10.2. Bosch alternator - component parts (Sec. 12)

1 Nut	4 Washer	7 Brush box	11 Rotor
2 Fan	5 Retaining screw	8 Brush box retaining screw	12 Through bolt
3 Drive end bracket	6 Brush end housing	9 Diode support	13 Bearing
		10 Stator	14 Pulley

2 Check that the carbon brushes are able to slide smoothly in their guides without any sign of binding.

3 Measure the length of the brushes and if they have worn down to 0.35 inch (9 mm) or less, they must be renewed.

4 Hold the brush wire with a pair of engineer's pliers and unsolder it from the brush box. Lift away the two brushes.

5 Insert the new brushes and check to make sure that they are free to move in their guides. If they bind, lightly polish with a very fine file.

6 Solder the brush wire ends to the brush box taking care that solder is allowed to pass to the standed wire.

7 Whenever new brushes are fitted new springs should also be fitted.

8 Refitting the brush box is the reverse sequence to removal.

13 Starter motor - general description

The starter motor is of the pre-engaged type and is of either Lucas or Bosch manufacture. The motor assembly comprises a solenoid, a lever, starter drive gear and motor. It can be seen that the solenoid is fitted to the top of the motor. The plunger inside the solenoid is connected to a centre pivoting lever, the other end of which is in contact with the drive sleeve and drive gear.

When the starter motor switch is operated, the solenoid is energised causing the plunger to move into the solenoid and the pinion to move into mesh with the starter ring gear on the flywheel (manual gearbox) or drive plate ring gear (automatic transmission). Upon the pinion bearing engaging with the ring gear, heavy duty contacts in the rear of the solenoid are closed and full current is supplied to the motor.

Once the engine has started, the starter switch is released and, under spring action, the plunger is moved from the centre of the solenoid and by means of the pivoting lever, the pinion is moved out of mesh with the ring gear.

14 Starter motor - testing on engine

1 If the starter motor fails to operate then check the condition of the battery by turning on the headlamps. If they glow brightly for several seconds and then gradually dim, the battery is in a discharged condition.
2 If the headlamps continue to glow brightly and it is obvious that the battery is in good condition, check tightness of the earth lead from the battery terminal to its connection on the body frame. Make a general check for faulty connections. Check the tightness of the connections at the rear of the solenoid. Check the wiring with a voltmeter for breaks or short circuits.
3 If the battery is fully charged, the wiring in order and the motor electrical circuit checked for continuity, and it still fails to operate then it will have to be removed from the car for examination. Before this is done, however, ensure that the pinion gear has not jammed in mesh with the flywheel due either to a broken solenoid spring or dirty pinion gear splines. To release the pinion, engage a low gear and with the ignition switched off, rock the car backwards and forwards which should release the pinion mesh with the ring gear. If the pinion still remains jammed, the starter motor must be removed for further examination.

15 Starter motor - removal and installation

1 Chock the rear wheels, apply the handbrake, and jack-up the front of the car. Support on firmly based axle stands.
2 Disconnect the two battery terminals.
3 Make a note of the electrical connections at the rear of the solenoid and disconnect the top heavy duty cable. Also release the two Lucar terminals situated below the heavy duty cable. There is no need to undo the lower heavy duty cable at the rear of the solenoid.
4 Undo and remove the two bolts which hold the starter motor in place and lift away upward through the engine compartment.
5 Generally, replacement is a straightforward reversal of the removal sequence. Check that the electrical cable connections are clean and firmly attached to their respective terminals.

16 Starter motor (Lucas) - dismantling, overhaul and reassembly

1 Detach the heavy duty cable linking the solenoid 'STA' terminal to the starter motor terminal, by undoing and removing the securing nuts and washers (Fig. 10.3).
2 Undo and remove the two nuts and spring washers securing the solenoid to the drive end bracket.
3 Carefully withdraw the solenoid coil unit from the drive end bracket.

4 Lift off the solenoid plunger and return spring from the engagement lever.
5 Remove the rubber sealing block from the drive end bracket.
6 Remove the retaining ring (spire nut) from the engagement lever pivot pin and withdraw the pin.
7 Unscrew and remove the two drive end bracket securing nuts and spring washers and withdraw the bracket.
8 Lift away the engagement lever from the drive operating plate.
9 Extract the split pin from the end of the armature and remove the shim washers and thrust plate from the commutator end of the armature shaft.
10 Remove the armature together with its internal thrust washer.
11 Withdraw the thrust washer from the armature.
12 Undo and remove the two screws securing the commutator end bracket to the starter motor body yoke.
13 Carefully detach the end bracket from the yoke, at the same time disengaging the field brushes gear. Lift away the end bracket.
14 Move the thrust collar clear of the jump ring and then remove the jump ring. Withdraw the drive assembly from the armature shaft.
15 At this stage if the brushes are renewed, their flexible connectors must be unsoldered and the connectors of new brushes soldered in their place. Check that the new brushes move freely in their holders as detailed above. If cleaning the commutator with petrol fails to remove all the burnt areas and spots, then wrap a piece of glass paper around the commutator and rotate the armature.
16 If the commutator is very badly worn, remove the drive gear. Then mount the armature in a lathe and, with the lathe turning at high speed, take a very fine cut out off the commutator and finish the surface by polishing with glass paper. **Do not undercut the mica insulators between the commutator segments.**
17 With the starter motor dismantled, test the four field coils for an open circuit. Connect a 12 volt battery with a 12 volt bulb in one of the leads between the field terminal post and the tapping point of the field coils to which the brushes are connected. An open circuit is proved by the bulb not lighting.
18 If the bulb lights, it does not necessarily mean that the field coils are in order, as there is a possibility that one of the coils will be earthed to the starter yoke or pole shoes. To check this, remove the lead from the brush connector and place it against a clean portion of the starter yoke. If the bulb lights, the field coils are earthing. Replacement of the field coils calls for the use of a wheel operated screwdriver, a soldering iron, caulking and riveting operations, and is beyond the scope of the majority of owners. The starter yoke should be taken to a reputable electrical engineering works for new field coils to be fitted. Alternatively purchase an exchange Lucas starter motor.
19 If the armature is damaged this will be evident on inspection. Look for signs of burning, discolouration and for conductors that have lifted away from the commutator. Reassembly is a straightfoward reversal of the dismantling procedure.
20 If a bearing is worn so allowing excessive side play of the armature shaft, the bearing bush must be renewed. Drift out the old bush with a piece of suitable diameter rod, preferably with a shoulder on it to stop the bush collapsing.
21 Soak a new bush in engine oil for 24 hours, or if time does not permit, heat in an oil bath at 100°C (212°F) for two hours prior to fitting.
22 As new bushes must not be reamed after fitting, it must be pressed into position using a small mandrel of the same internal diameter as the bush and with a shoulder on it. Place the bush on the mandrel and press into position using a bench vice.
23 Use a test lamp and battery to test the continuity of the coil windings between terminal 'STA' and a good earth point on the solenoid body. If the light fails to light, the solenoid should be renewed.
24 To test the solenoid contacts for correct opening and closing, connect a 12 volt battery and a 60 watt test lamp between the main unmarked Lucar terminal and the 'STA' terminal. The

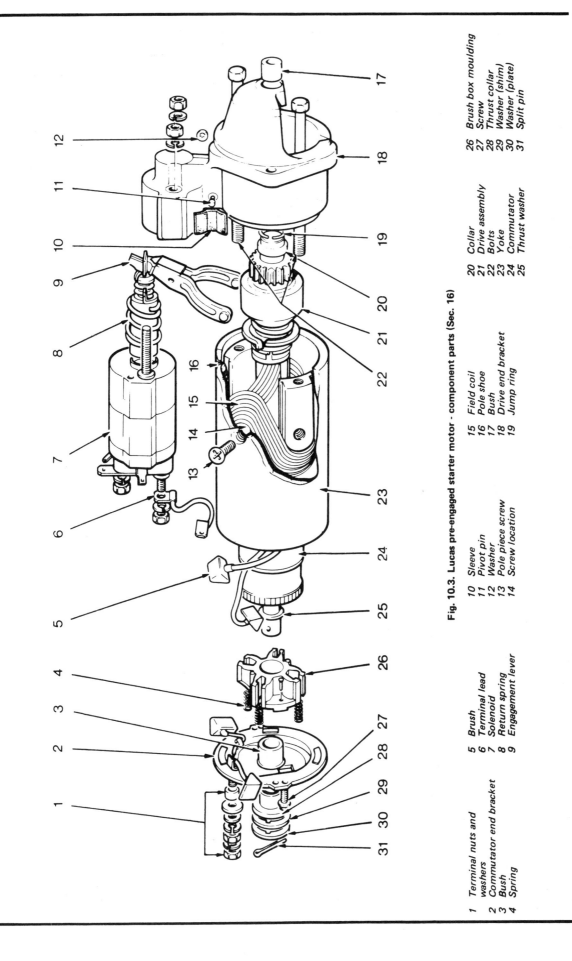

Fig. 10.3. Lucas pre-engaged starter motor - component parts (Sec. 16)

1 Terminal nuts and washers
2 Commutator end bracket
3 Bush
4 Spring
5 Brush
6 Terminal lead
7 Solenoid
8 Return spring
9 Engagement lever
10 Sleeve
11 Pivot pin
12 Washer
13 Pole piece screw
14 Screw location
15 Field coil
16 Pole shoe
17 Bush
18 Drive end bracket
19 Jump ring
20 Collar
21 Drive assembly
22 Bolts
23 Yoke
24 Commutator
25 Thrust washer
26 Brush box moulding
27 Screw
28 Thrust collar
29 Washer (shim)
30 Washer (plate)
31 Split pin

lamp should not light.

25 Energise the solenoid with a separate 12 volt supply connected to the small unmarked Lucar terminal and a good earth on the solenoid body.

26 As the coil is energised the solenoid should be heard to operate and the test lamp should light with full brilliance.

27 The contacts may only be renewed as a set; ie; moving and fixed contacts. The fixed contacts are part of the moulded cover.

28 To fit a new set of contacts, first undo and remove the moulded cover securing screws.

29 Unsolder the coil connections from the cover terminals.

30 Lift away the cover and moving contact assembly.

31 Fit a new cover and moving contact assembly, soldering the connections to the cover terminals.

32 Refit the moulded cover securing screws.

33 Whilst the motor is apart, check the operation of the drive clutch. It must provide instantaneous take up of the drive in one direction and rotate easily and smoothly in the opposite direction.

34 Make sure that the drive moves freely on the armature shaft splines wihtout binding or sticking.

35 To reassemble the starter motor is the reverse sequence to dismantling. The following additional points should be noted:

  a) *When assembling the drive always use a new retaining ring (spire nut) to secure the engagement lever pivot pin.*
  b) *Make sure that the internal thrust washer is fitted to the commutator end of the armature shaft before the armature is fitted.*
  c) *Make sure that the thrust washers and plate are assembled in the correct order and are prevented from rotating separately, by engaging the collar pin with the locking piece on the thrust plate.*

17 Starter motor (Bosch) - dismantling, overhaul and reassembly

The procedure is similar to that described in the preceding Section but refer to Fig. 10.4 for detail differences in component design.

18 Headlamp - bulb renewal

1 Open the bonnet and prop it with its stay.

2 Remove the crosshead screw from the headlamp retaining clip (Fig. 10.5).

3 Depress the clip and pull the headlamp forward and up.

4 Unscrew and remove the four screws (2) which retain the bezel. Do not touch the adjustment screws (1) (Fig. 10.6).

5 Withdraw the bezel and then remove the bulb after releasing the spring clip that holds the bulb to the reflector.

6 Refitting is a reversal of removal.

19 Headlamp sealed beam unit - renewal

1 Remove the two securing screws from the top of the outer headlamp bezel (Fig. 10.7).

2 Withdraw the bezel but take care not to break the bottom two retaining tongues.

3 Release the screws which retain the lamp unit retaining ring and pull the components forward.

4 Disconnect the connecting plug at the rear of the lamp unit.

5 Installation of the new lamp unit is a reversal of removal and provided the adjustment screws have not been touched then the lamp will not require beam alignment.

20 Headlamp - beam alignment

1 This should be carried out by a service station using optical beam setting equipment.

21 Headlamp switches - removal and refitting

Dip switch

1 The switch is part of the combination switch mounted on the steering column controlling the direction indicator switch and

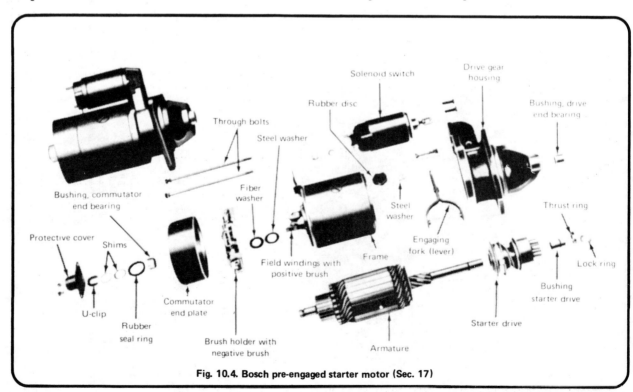

Fig. 10.4. Bosch pre-engaged starter motor (Sec. 17)

Fig. 10.5. Bulb type headlamp (1600 cc)

1   Retaining screw 2   Spring clip

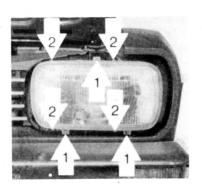

Fig. 10.6. Bulb type headlamp adjusting screws (1) and bezel screws (2)

Fig. 10.7. Removing headlamp sealed-beam unit

Fig. 10.8. Removing sidelamp bulb from headlamp assembly (1600 cc)

1   Headlamp reflector
2   Connecting plug
3   Side lamp bulb

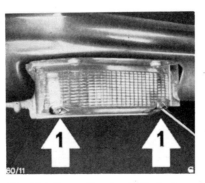

Fig. 10.9. Front direction indicator lamp lens screw (1) - 1600 cc

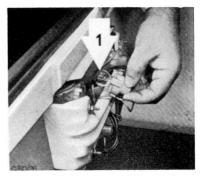

Fig. 10.10. Removing reverse lamp bulb from within the luggage boot (1600 cc)

horn button.

2 Disconnect the battery.

3 Undo and remove the bolts that secure the steering column to the underside of the instrument panel. Lower the steering column.

4 Undo and remove the two screws that secure the steering column half shrouds and lift away the two parts. It may be necessary to use a knife to separate the two halves before removal.

5 Undo and remove the two screws and shakeproof washers located on the lever side of the switch and detach the switch assembly from the steering column.

6 Disconnect the multi pin plug from the switch cable harness and lift away the switch.

7 Refitting the switch is the reverse sequence to removal. Before the shroud is refitted check that the switch and self cancel system operates correctly. For this the battery will have to be reconnected.

On/off switch

1 Disconnect the battery.

2 Working behind the instrument panel detach the multi-pin connector from the rear of the headlight switch.

3 Depress the two switch retaining clips and push the switch out of the panel.

4 To refit the switch push into the panel until the clips spring out thereby retaining it. Reconnect the multi-pin connector and finally the battery.

---

22 Front and rear lamps (1600 cc) - bulb renewal

Front parking light

The front parking (sidelight) bulb is fitted into the rear of the headlamp reflector and lens assembly. To renew a bulb first detach the headlight unit as described in Section 18 and then pull the parking bulb holder out of the reflector and lens assembly. The bulb may then be pulled from the holder. Refitting is the reverse sequence to removal (Fig. 10.8).

Front direction indicator light

Undo and remove the two crosshead screws and lift away the lens from below the bumper. To remove the bulb gently depress and turn in an anti-clockwise direction to release the bayonet fitting. Refitting the bulb is the reverse sequence to removal. Ensure that the seal is properly seated to prevent entry of dust and water (Fig. 10.9).

Rear, stop reverse and direction indicator lights

Open the luggage compartment lid and unscrew the four locknuts retaining the protection shroud. Lift away the shroud. Pull the relevant bulb holder from the rear of its reflector and remove the bulb by gently depressing and turning in an anticlockwise direction to release the bayonet fitting. Refitting the bulb holder and shroud is the reverse sequence to removal (Fig. 10.10).

---

23 Front and rear lamps (2000 cc) - bulb renewal

Front parking and direction indicator

Unscrew and remove the two lens securing screws. Gently depress the bulb and turn it anticlockwise and then release it from its bayonet type holder. Refitting is the reverse sequence to removal (Fig. 10.11).

Front side marker lamps

Reach under the front wing and peel back the rubber cover from the bulb holder. Turn the bulb holder anticlockwise and

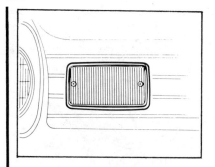

Fig. 10.11. Parking and front direction indicator lamp (2000 cc)

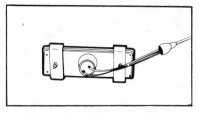

Fig. 10.12. Front side marker lamp (rear view) - 2000 cc

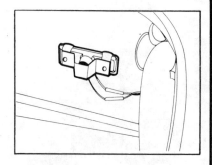

Fig. 10.13. Rear side marker lamp, viewed from within luggage boot (2000 cc)

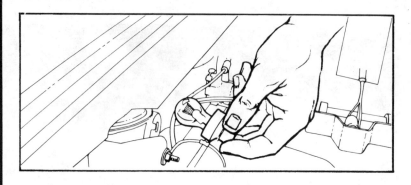

Fig. 10.14. Removing lamp holder from within luggage boot (2000 cc)

Fig. 10.15. Removing rear licence plate lamp (1600 cc)

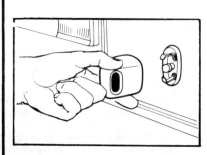

Fig. 10.16. Removing rear licence plate lamp lens (2000 cc)

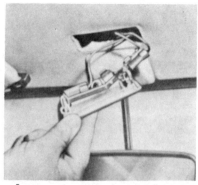

Fig. 10.17. Removing interior courtesy lamp

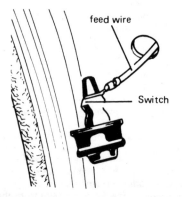

feed wire

Switch

Fig. 10.18. Courtesy lamp switch removed from door pillar

Fig. 10.19. Location of map light

Fig. 10.20. Location of hazard warning switch

pull the holder from the lamp body. The bulb can now be extracted (without twisting) from the holder. Refitting is the reverse of removal (Fig. 10.12).

Rear side marker lamps

Open the luggage boot and remove the lamp protective cover which is retained by two nuts. Turn the bulb holder anti-clockwise and pull it from the lamp body. The bulb can now be extracted (without twisting) from the holder. Refitting is the reverse of removal (Figs. 10.13 and 10.14).

Rear, stop, direction indicator and reverse lamps

Open the luggage boot, remove the protective shield from the lamp assembly. Pull the appropriate bulb holder from the lamp body. Remove the bulb from the holder by depressing it and then twisting it anticlockwise. Refitting is the reverse of removal.

---

24 Rear licence plate lamp - bulb renewal

1600 cc models

Press the two lamp retaining lugs together and pull the lamp from the bumper bar. Remove the lens securing screws and pull the bulb from the holder (Fig. 10.15).

2000 cc models

Remove the two lens securing screws and extract the bulb from its holder. Refitting in both cases is a reversal of removal (Fig. 10.16).

---

25 Reverse lamp switch (manual gearbox) - adjustment

The angular switch bracket is held to the gearchange lever housing by one screw. If it is necessary to adjust the position of the switch first slacken the screw and move the gearchange lever into the reverse position.

Carefully move the switch towards the gearchange lever until the lamps light. Tighten the retaining screw.

---

26 Courtesy light and map light - removal and refitting

Courtesy light bulb or switch

To gain access to the bulb or switch carefully ease the lamp from the roof. Remove the bulb or switch as applicable. If the switch is to be removed it is recommended that the battery earth cable be detached as a safety precaution (Fig. 10.17).

Courtesy light door pillar switch

1 Disconnect the battery earth terminal.
2 Using a screwdriver carefully ease the switch from the aperture in the body (Fig. 10.18).
3 Detach the terminal from the back of the switch and lift away the switch.
4 Refitting is the reverse sequence to removal.

Map light bulb

To renew the bulb, push the housing back carefully and remove the bulb. Fit the new bulb and housing (Fig. 10.19).

Map light switch

1 Disconnect the battery earth terminal.
2 Undo and remove the two screws that secure the switch to the panel.
3 Draw the switch from the panel and detach the two leads.
4 Refitting is the reverse sequence to removal.

---

27 Hazard warning switch - removal and refitting

---

1 The switch can be removed from the facia panel by reaching

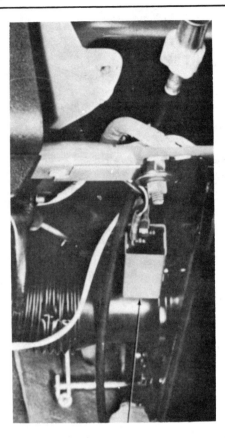

Fig. 10.21. Location of direction indicator flasher unit (behind facia) (Sec. 28)

up behind the panel and depressing the two switch retaining clips (Fig. 10.20).
2 The leads can now be disconnected from the switch.
3 Refitting and reconnection are reversals of removal.

---

28 Relays and flasher units

---

1 Various relays and flasher units are fitted according to date of vehicle production.
2 They are located either behind the instrument panel (access to them is gained after drawing the panel forward, according to type, as described in later Sections of this Chapter) or within the engine compartment.
3 In the event of failure of a particular piece of equipment always check the connecting wiring, bulbs and fuses before assuming that it is the relay or flasher unit that is at fault. Take the relay or flasher unit to your dealer for testing or check the circuit by substituting a new component.

---

29 Instrument panel (1600 cc and 2000 cc) - removal and refitting

---

1 Disconnect the battery earth terminal.
2 Undo and remove the two bolts that secure the steering column to the underside to the dash panel. Carefully lower the column.
3 Undo and remove the five Phillips lead screws that secure the cluster and pad assembly to the instrument panel (Fig. 10.23).
4 Carefully draw the cluster and pad assembly forward by a sufficient amount to gain access to the connections at the rear of the panel.
5 Make a note of the cable connections at the rear of the gauges and switches and then detach the cables.

Fig. 10.22. Horn and headlamp relays (within engine compartment) (Sec. 28)

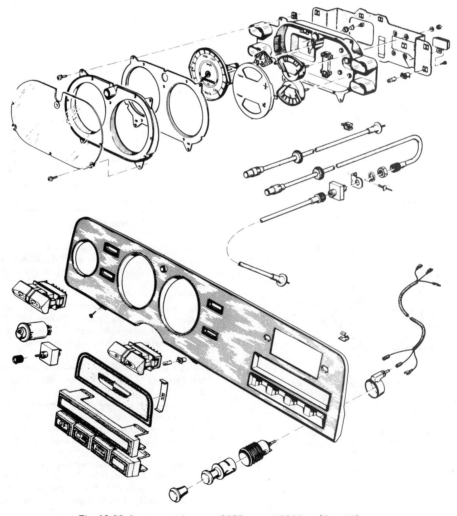

Fig. 10.23. Instrument layout - 1600 cc and 2000 cc (Sec. 29)

6   Disconnect the speedometer cable from the rear of the instrument.

7   The cluster and pad assembly may now be removed from the car.

8   Undo and remove the four screws that secure the cluster to the pad and lift away the cluster assembly.

9   Refitting the cluster and pad is the reverse sequence to removal.

30 Instrument panel (1600 cc GT early models and 2000 cc option) - removal and refitting

1   Disconnect the battery earth terminal.

2   Detach the two heater control knobs.

3   Undo and remove the four screws that secure the access cover at the right of the instrument panel. Lift away the cover.

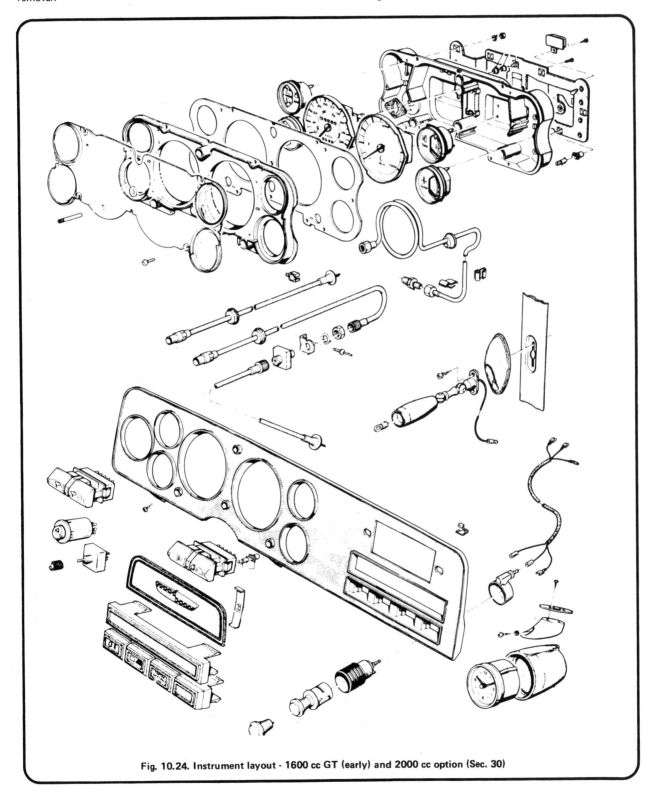

Fig. 10.24. Instrument layout - 1600 cc GT (early) and 2000 cc option (Sec. 30)

4 Undo and remove the three screws and **only slacken** the one
nut securing the instrument cluster and pad assembly to the
instrument panel.

5 Carefully pull the cluster and pad assembly rearward by a
sufficient amount to gain access to the connections at the rear of
the panel.

6 Make a note of the cable connections at the rear of the
gauges and switches and then detach the cables.

7 Disconnect the speedometer cable from the rear of the instrument.

8 Disconnect the oil pressure gauge tube at the rear of the
gauge. It is very important that the tube is not bent or twisted.

9 The cluster and pad assembly may now be removed from the
car.

10 Undo and remove the four screws that secure the cluster to
the pad and lift away the cluster assembly.

11 Refitting the cluster and pad is the reverse sequence to
removal.

31 Instrument panel (1600 GT and 2000 cc - late models) - removal and refitting

1 The procedure is similar to that described in the preceding
Section.

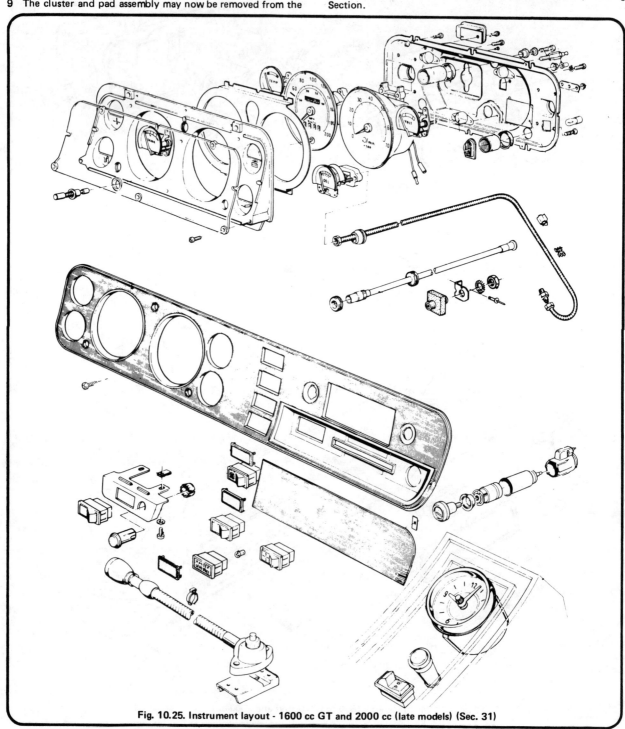

Fig. 10.25. Instrument layout - 1600 cc GT and 2000 cc (late models) (Sec. 31)

Fig. 10.26. Ignition warning buzzer (2000 cc) - behind instrument panel (Sec. 36)

32 Speedometer cable - renewal

1 Chock the front wheels, jack up the rear of the car and support on firmly based stands.
2 Working under the car carefully remove the snap ring that secures the speedometer cable to the transmission. Detach the cable.
3 Now working in the engine compartment remove the speedometer cable clip located on the engine bulkhead.
4 Ease the speedometer cable rubber grommet from the engine bulkhead.
5 Refer to Sections 29, 30 or 31 as applicable and move the instrument cluster rearwards by a sufficient amount to gain access to the rear of the speedometer.
6 Detach the cable from the rear of the speedometer.
7 Refitting is the reverse sequence to removal. For reliable operation it is very important that there are no sharp bends in the cable run.

33 Clock (console mounted) - removal and refitting

1 Disconnect the lead from the battery negative terminal.
2 With a small screwdriver or knife carefully prise the wood grain panel and clock assembly away from the console.
3 Detach the electric cables and bulb socket from the rear of the instrument.
4 To release the clock from the panel depress the three retaining clips and withdraw the clock.
5 Should adjustment be necessary, rotate the adjustment screw in the required direction.
6 Refitting the clock is the reverse sequence to removal.

34 Instrument illumination and warning lamp bulbs - renewal

1 Reach up behind the instrument panel and release the bulb holder from its socket.
2 Extract the bulb from its holder.
3 Refitting is a reversal of removal.

35 Instrument voltage regulator - removal and refitting

1 Remove the instrument panel according to type.
2 Unscrew and remove the single screw that retains the instrument voltage regulator to the rear of the instrument panel and withdraw the regulator.
3 Refitting is a reversal of removal.

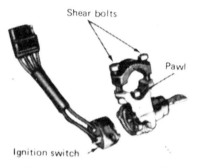

Fig. 10.27. Ignition switch and steering lock (Secs. 36 and 37)

36 Ignition switch - removal and refitting

1 Disconnect the battery earth terminal.
2 Undo and remove the two steering column shroud securing screws and lift away the two parts. It may be necessary to use a knife to separate the two halves before removal.
3 Set the ignition key to the 'O' position.
4 Note the location of the cables at the ignition switch and then detach the cables.
5 Undo and remove the two screws that secure the ignition switch to the lock. Lift away the switch.
6 Refitting the ignition switch is the reverse sequence to removal.
7 On 2000 cc models, an ignition warning buzzer is installed as a part of the anti-theft circuit (Fig. 10.26).

37 Steering column lock - removal and refitting

1 Disconnect the battery earth terminal.
2 Undo and remove the two steering column shroud securing screws and lift away the two parts. It may be necessary to use a knife to separate the two halves before removal.
3 Undo and remove the two screws that secure the upper steering column support bracket.
4 Turn the column until it is possible to gain access to the headless bolts.
5 Note the location of the cables to the ignition switch terminals and lock body and then detach the cables.
6 Using a suitable diameter drill remove the headless bolts that clamp the lock to the steering column. Alternatively use a centre punch to rotate the bolts.
7 Lift away the lock assembly and clamp bracket.

8 Refitting the lock assembly is the reverse sequence to removal. Make sure that the pawl enters the steering shaft. It will be necessary to use new shear bolts which must be tightened equally before the heads are separated from the shank.

38 Fuses

1 If a fuse blows, always trace and rectify the cause before renewing it with one of the same rating.
2 The fuse block is located within the engine compartment on the side apron (Fig. 10.28).
3 The fuse ratings and circuits protected vary according to model and reference should be made to Specifications Section at the front of this Chapter.
4 Two separate fuses are mounted integral with the headlamp relay and where a heated rear screen is fitted, an additional fuse is located behind the instrument panel.

39 Horn - fault tracing and rectification

1 If the horn works badly or fails completely, check the wiring leading to the horn plug located on the body panel next to the horn itself. Also check that the plug is properly pushed home and is in a clean condition free from corrosion etc.
2 Check that the horn is secure on its mounting and that there is nothing lying on the horn body.
3 If the fault is not an external one, remove the horn cover and check the leads inside the horn. If they are sound, check the contact breaker contacts. If these are burnt or dirty clean them with a fine file and wipe all traces of dirt and dust away with a petrol moistened rag.

40 Windscreen wiper blades - renewal

1 Lift the wiper arm away from the windscreen and remove the old blade by turning it in towards the arm and then disengage the arm from the slot in the blade.
2 To fit a new blade, slide the end of the wiper arm into the slotted spring fastening in the centre of the blade. Push the blade firmly onto the arm until the raised portion of the arm is fully home in the hole in the blade.

41 Windscreen wiper arm - removal and refitting

1 Before removing a wiper arm, turn the windscreen wiper switch on and off to ensure the arms are in their normal parked position parallel with the bottom of the windscreen.
2 To remove an arm, pivot the arm back and pull the wiper arm head off the splined drive. If the arm proves difficult to remove, a screwdriver with a wide blade, can be used to lever the wiper arm head off the splines. Care must be taken not to damage the splines.
3 When replacing an arm position it so it is in the correct relative parked position and then press the arm head onto the splined drive until it is fully home on the splines.

42 Windscreen wiper mechanism - fault diagnosis and rectification

1 Should the windscreen wipers fail, or work very slowly, then check the terminals on the motor for loose connections, and make sure the insulation of all the wiring is not cracked or broken thus causing a short circuit. If this is in order then check the current the motor is taking by connecting an ammeter in the circuit and turning on the wiper switch. Consumption should be between 2.3 and 3.1 amps.
2 If no current is passing through the motor, check that the switch is operating correctly.

Fig. 10.28. Location of fuse block on side of engine compartment (Sec. 38)

3 If the wiper motor takes a very high current check the wiper blades for freedom of movement. If this is satisfactory check the gearbox cover and gear assembly for damage.
4 If the motor takes a very low current ensure that the battery is fully charged. Check the brush gear and ensure the brushes are bearing on the commutator. If not, check the brushes for freedom of movement and, if necessary, renew the tension springs. If the brushes are very worn they should be replaced with new ones. Check the armature by substitution if this unit is suspect.

43 Windscreen wiper motor and linkage - removal and refitting

1 Disconnect the battery by removing the negative earth lead and then remove the wiper blades and arms, as described in the previous Sections.
2 Undo and remove the two nuts holding the wiper spindles to the bodywork in front of the windscreen.
3 Remove the parcel shelf by taking off the two spring clips at either end and by undoing the single screw on the driver's side and the two screws on the passenger's side.
4 To gain better access to the wiper motor disconnect the flexible hoses from the heater to the demister vents above the dash, also the aeroflow flexible pipes.
5 Disconnect the two control cables on the heater at the heater end, making a careful note of their correct fitting in relation to the positions of the heater controls on the facia. Tuck the cables out of the way under the facia.
6 Remove the single screw holding the wiper motor to its mounting bracket and lower the motor and linkage just enough to be able to see the leads running to the motor.
7 Disconnect the leads at thier connectors on the motor making a note of their relative positions for reassembly purposes.
8 Now lower the complete wiper motor and linkage assembly down in front of the heater and remove it from the car (Fig. 10.30).
9 Reassembly is a direct reversal of the removal procedure, but the screw securing the wiper motor to its mounting bracket should not be fully tighened down until the wiper spindle nuts have been replaced thus ensuring correct alignment of the linkage.

44 Windscreen wiper motor - dismantling, inspection and re-assembly

1 Start by removing the linkage mechanism from the motor. Carefully prise the short wiper link off the motor operating arm and remove the plastic pivot bush.
2 Undo the three screws which hold the linkage to the wiper motor and separate the two.
3 Unscrew the two bolts holding the motor case to the gearbox housing and withdraw the motor case complete with the armature.

169

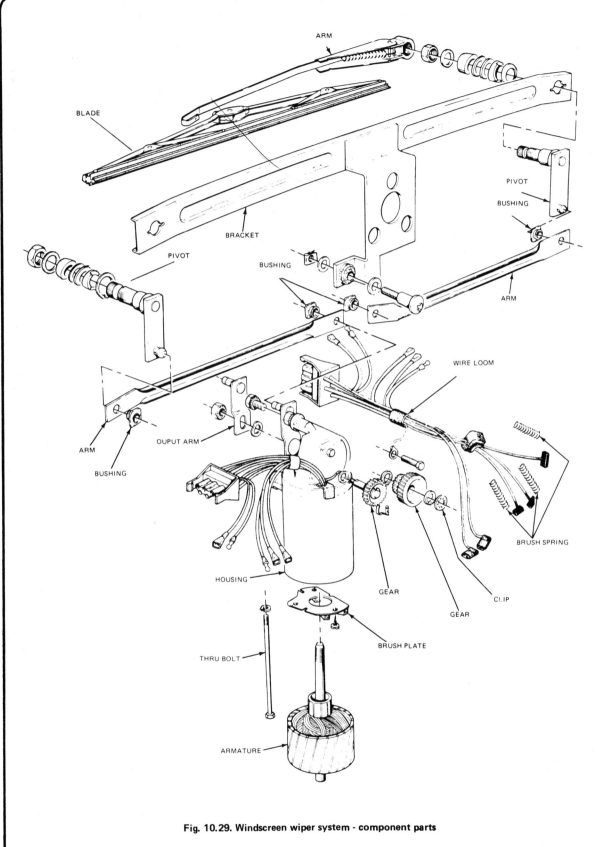

Fig. 10.29. Windscreen wiper system - component parts

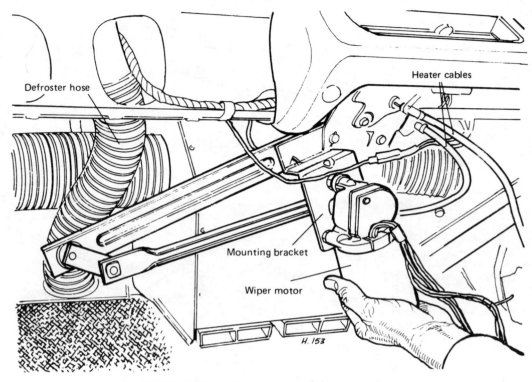

Fig. 10.30. Windscreen wiper motor and linkage removal
(Sec. 43)

4 Take the brushes out of their holders and remove the brush springs.
5 Undo the three screws which hold the brush mounting plate to the wiper gearbox and withdraw the brush mounting plate.
6 Remove the earth wire on the gearbox cover plate by undoing the screw nearest the motor case. Undo the other screw on the gearbox cover plate and remove the cover plate and switch assembly.
7 Pull the spring steel armature stop out of the gearbox casing. Then remove the spring clip and washer which retain the wiper pinion gear in place and withdraw the gear and washer.
8 Undo the nut securing the wiper motor operating arm and remove the lockwasher, arm, wave washer and flat washer in that order.
9 Having removed the operating arm withdraw the output gear, park switch and washer from the gearbox casing.
10 Carefully examine all parts for signs of wear or damage and renew as necessary.
11 Reassembly is a direct reversal of the above procedure.

45 Radios and tape players - fitting (general)

A radio or tape player is an expensive item to buy, and will only give its best performance if fitted properly. It is useless to expect concert hall performance from a unit that is suspended from the dashpanel on string with its speaker resting on the back seat or parcel shelf! If you do not wish to do the installation yourself there are many in-car entertainment specialists' who can do the fitting for you.
Make sure the unit purchased is of the same polarity as the car, and ensure that units with adjustable polarity are correctly set before commencing installation.
It is difficult to give specific information with regard to fitting, as final positioning of the radio/tape player, speakers and aerial is entirely a matter of personal preference. However, the following paragraphs give guidelines to follow, which are relevant to all installations.

Radios

Most radios are a standardised size of 7 inches wide, by 2 inches deep - this ensures that they will fit into the radio aperture provided in most cars. If your car does not have such an aperture, then the radio must be fitted in a suitable position either in, or beneath the dashpanel. Alternatively, a special console can be purchased which will fit between the dashpanel and the floor, or on the transmission tunnel. These consoles can also be used for additional switches and instrumentation if required. Where no radio aperture is provided, the following points should be borne in mind before deciding exactly where to fit the unit.

a) *The unit must be within easy reach of the driver wearing a seat belt.*
b) *The unit must not be mounted in close proximity to an electric tachometer, the ignition switch and its wiring, or the flasher unit and associated wiring.*
c) *The unit must be mounted within reach of the aerial lead, and in such a place that the aerial lead will not have to be routed near the components detailed in the preceding paragraph 'b'.*
d) *The unit should not be positioned in a place where it might cause injury to the car occupants in an accident; for instance, under the dashpanel above the driver's or passengers' legs.*
e) *The unit must be fitted really securely.*

Some radios will have mounting brackets provided together with instructions: others will need to be fitted using drilled and slotted metal strips, bent to form mounting brackets - these strips are available from most accessory shops. The unit must be properly earthed, by fitting a separate earthing lead between the casing of the radio and the vehicle frame.
Use the radio manufacturer's instructions when wiring the radio into the vehicle's electrical system. If no instructions are available refer to the relevent wiring diagram to find the location of the radio 'feed' connection in the vehicle's wiring circuit. A 1-2 amp 'in-line' fuse must be fitted in the radio's 'feed' wire - a

choke may also be necessary (see next Section).

The type of aerial used, and its fitted position is a matter of personal preference. In general the taller the aerial, the better the reception. It is best to fit a fully retractable aerial - especially, if a mechanical car-wash is used or if you live in an area where cars tend to be vandalised. In this respect electric aerials which are raised and lowered automatically when switching the radio on or off are convenient, but are more likely to give trouble than the manual type.

When choosing a site for the aerial the following points should be considered:

a) *The aerial lead should be as short as possible - this means that the aerial should be mounted at the front of the car.*

b) *The aerial must be mounted as far away from the distributor and HT leads as possible.*

c) *The part of the aerial which protrudes beneath the mounting point must not foul the roadwheels, or anything else.*

d) *If possible the aerial should be positioned so that the coaxial lead does not have to be routed through the engine compartment.*

e) *The plane of the panel on which the aerial is mounted should not be so steeply angled that the aerial cannot be mounted vertically (in relation to the 'end-on' aspect of the car). Most aerials have a small amount of adjustment available.*

Having decided on a mounting position, a relatively large hole will have to be made in the panel. The exact size of the hole will depend upon the specific aerial being fitted, although, generally, the hole required is of ¾ inch diameter. On metal bodied cars, a 'tank-cutter' of the relevent diameter is the best tool to use for making the hole. This tool needs a small diameter pilot hole drilled through the panel, through which, the metal clamping bolt is inserted. On GRP bodied cars, a 'hole-saw' is the best tool to use. Again, this tool will require the drilling of a small pilot hole. When the hole has been made the raw edges should be de-burred with a file and then painted, to prevent corrosion.

Fit the aerial according to the manufacturer's instructions. If the aerial is very tall, or if it protrudes beneath the mounting panel for a considerable distance it is a good idea to fit a stay between the aerial and the vehicle frame. This stay can be manufactured from the slotted and drilled metal strips previously mentioned. The stay should be securely screwed or bolted in place. For best reception it is advisable to fit an earth lead between the aerial body and the vehicle frame - this is essential for GRP bodied cars.

It will probably be necessary to drill one or two holes through bodywork panels in order to feed the aerial lead into the interior of the car. Where this is the case ensure that the holes are fitted with rubber grommets to protect the cable, and to stop possible entry of water.

Positioning and fitting of the speaker depends mainly on its type. Generally, the speaker is designed to fit directly into the aperture already provided in the car (usually in the shelf behind the rear seats, or in the top of the dashpanel). Where this is the case, fitting the speaker is just a matter of removing the protective grille from the aperture and screwing or bolting the speaker in place. Take great care not to damage the speaker diaphragm whilst doing this. It is a good idea to fit a 'gasket' between the speaker frame and the mounting panel, in order to prevent vibration - some speakers will already have such a gasket fitted.

If a 'pod' type speaker was supplied with the radio, the best acoustic results will normally be obtained by mounting it on the shelf behind the rear seat. The pod can be secured to the mounting panel with self-tapping screws.

When connecting a rear mounted speaker to the radio, the wires should be routed through the vehicle beneath the carpets or floor mats - preferably through the middle, or along the side of the floorpan, where they will not be trodden on by passengers. Make the relevant connections as directed by the radio manufacturer.

By now you will have several yards of additional wiring in the car, use PVC tape to secure this wiring out of harm's way. Do not leave electrical leads dangling. Ensure that all new electrical connections are properly made (wires twisted together will not do) and completely secure.

The radio should now be working, but before you pack away your tools it will be necessary to 'trim' the radio to the aerial. If specific instructions are not provided by the radio manufacturer, proceed as follows. Find a station with a low signal strength on the medium-wave band. Slowly, turn the trim screw of the radio in, or out, until the loudest reception of the selected station is obtained - the set is then 'trimmed' to the aerial.

Tape players

Fitting instructions for both cartridge and cassette stereo tape players are the same and in general the same rules apply as when fitting a radio. Tape players are not usually prone to electrical interfernece like radio - although it can occur - so positioning is not so critical. If possible the player should be mounted on an 'even-keel'. Also, it must be possible for a driver wearing a seat belt to reach the unit in order to change, or turn over, tapes.

For the best results from speakers designed to be recessed into a panel, mount them so that the back of the speaker protrudes into an enclosed chamber within the car (eg; door interiors or the boot cavity).

To fit recessed type speakers in the front doors first check that there is sufficient room to mount the speaker in each door without it fouling the latch or window winding mechanism. Hold the speaker against the skin of the door, and draw a line, around the periphery of the speaker. With the speaker removed draw a second 'cutting' line, within the first, to allow enough room for the entry of the speaker back, but at the same time providing a broad seat for the speaker flange. When you are sure that the cutting-line' is correct, drill a series of holes around its periphery. Pass a hacksaw blade through one of the holes and then cut through the metal between the holes until the centre section of the panel falls out.

De-burr the edges of the hole and then paint the raw metal to prevent corrosion. Cut a corresponding hole in the door trim panel - ensuring that it will be completely covered by the speaker grille. Now drill a hole in the door edge and a corresponding hole in the door surround. These holes are to feed the speaker leads through - so fit grommets. Pass the speaker leads through the door trim, door skin and out through the holes in the side of the door and door surround. Refit the door trim panel and then secure the speaker to the door using self-tapping screws. Note: if the speaker is fitted with a shield to prevent water dripping on it, ensure that this shield is at the top.

Pod type speakers can be fastened to the shelf behind the rear seat, or anywhere else offering a corresponding mounting point on each side of the car. If the pod speakers are mounted on each side of the shelf behind the rear seat, it is a good idea to drill several large diameter holes through to the boot cavity beneath each speaker - this will improve the sound reproduction. Pod speakers sometimes offer a better reproduction quality if they face the rear window - which then acts as a reflector - so it is worthwhile to do a little experimenting before finally fixing the speaker.

46 Radios and tape players - suppression of interference (general)

To eliminate buzzes and other unwanted noises, costs very little and is not as difficult as sometimes thought. With a modicum of common sense and patience and following the instructions in the following paragraphs, interference can be virtually eliminated.

The first cause for concern is the generator. The noise this makes over the radio is like an electric mixer and the noise speeds up when you rev up (if you wish to prove the point, you

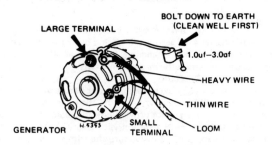

Fig. 10.31. The correct way to connect capacitor to the generator (Sec. 46)

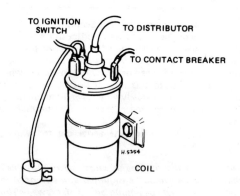

Fig. 10.32. The capacitor must be connected to the ignition switch side of the coil (Sec. 46)

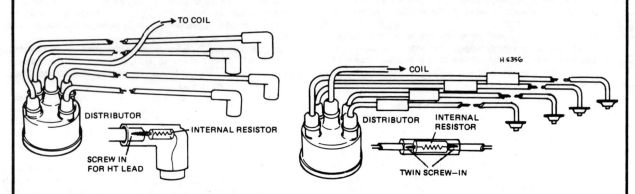

Resistive spark plug caps

Fig. 10.33. Ignition HT lead suppressors (Sec. 46)

'In-line' suppressors

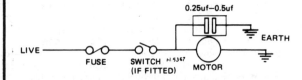

Fig. 10.34. Correct method of suppressing electric motors (Sec. 46)

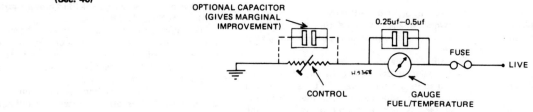

Fig. 10.35. Method of suppressing gauges and their control units (Sec. 46)

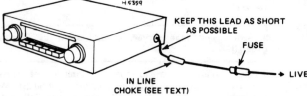

Fig. 10.36. An 'in-line' choke should be fitted into the live supply lead as close to the unit as possible (Sec. 46)

can remove the drivebelt and try it). The remedy for this is simple; connect a 1.0 uf - 3.0 uf capacitor between earth, probably the bolt that holds down the generator base, and the *large* terminal on the dynamo or alternator. This is most important, for if you connect it to the small terminal, you will probably damage the generator permanently (see Fig. 10.31).

A second common cause of electrical interference is the ignition system. Here a 1.0 ohm capacitor must be connected between earth and the SW or + terminal on the coil (see Fig. 10.32). This may stop the tick-tick-tick sound that comes over the speaker. Next comes the spark itself.

There are several ways of curing interference from the ignition HT system. One is to use carbon film HT leads but these have a tendency to "snap" inside and you don't know then, why you are firing on only half your cylinders. So the second, and more successful method is to use resistive spark plug caps (Fig. 10.33) of about 10,000 ohm to 15,000 ohm resistance. If, due to lack of room, these cannot be used, an alternative is to use 'in-line' suppressors (Fig. 10.33) - if the interference is not too bad, you may get away with only one suppressor in the coil to distributor line. If the interference does continue (a "clacking" noise) then doctor all HT leads.

At this stage it is advisable to check that the radio is well earthed, also the aerial, and to see that the aerial plug is pushed well into the set and that the radio is properly trimmed (see preceding Section). In addition, check that the wire which supplies the power to the set is as short as possible and does not wander all over the car. At this stage it is a good idea to check that the fuse is of the correct rating. For most sets this will be about 1 to 2 amps.

At this point the more usual causes of interference have been suppressed. If the problem still exists, a look at the causes of interfernece may help to pinpoint the component generating the stray electrical discharges.

The radio picks up electromagnetic waves in the air; now some are made by radio stations and other broadcasters and some, not wanted, are made by the car. The home made signals are produced by stray electrical discharges floating around the car. Common producers of these signs are electric motors; ie; the windshield wipers, electric screen washers, electric window winders, heater fan or an electric aerial if fitted. Other sources of interference are electric fuel pumps, flashing turn signals, and instruments. The remedy for these cases is shown in Fig. 10.34 for an electric motor whose interference is not too bad and Fig. 10.35 for instrument suppression. Turn signals are not normally suppressed. In recent years, radio manufacturer's have included in the line (live) of the radio, in addition to the fuse, an 'in-line' choke. If your installation lacks one of these, put one in as shown in Fig. 10.36.

All the foregoing components are available from radio shops or accessory shops. For a transistor radio, a 2A choke should be adequate. If you have an electric clock fitted this should be suppressed by connecting a 0.5 uf capacitor directly across it as shown for a motor in Fig. 10.34.

If after all this, you are still experiencing radio interference, first assess how bad it is, for the human ear can filter out unobtrusive unwanted noises quite easily. But if you are still adamant about eradicating the noise, then continue.

As a first step, a few "experts" seem to favour a screen between the radio and the engine. This is OK as far as it goes - literally! - for the whole set is screened and if interference can get past that then a small piece of aluminium is not going to stop it.

A more sensible way of screening is to discover if interference is coming down the wires. First, take the live lead; interference can get between the set and the choke (hence the reason for keeping the wires short). One remedy here is to screen the wire and this is done by buying screened wire and fitting that. The loudspeaker lead could be screened also to prevent 'pick-up' getting back to the radio - although this is unlikely.

Without doubt, the worst source of radio interference comes from the ignition HT leads, even if they have been suppressed. The ideal way of suppressing these is to slide screening tubes over the leads themselves. As this is impractical, we can place an aluminium shield over the majority of the lead areas. In a vee- or twin-cam engine this is relatively easy but for a straight engine, the results are not particularly good.

Now for the really impossible cases, here are a few tips to try out. Where metal comes into contact with metal, an electrical disturbance is caused which is why good clean screening connections are essential. To remove interference due to overlapping or butting panels you must bridge the join with a wide braided earth strap (like that from the frame to the engine/transmission). The most common moving parts that could create noise and should be strapped are, in order of importance:

a) *Silencer to frame*
b) *Exhaust pipe to engine block and frame*
c) *Air cleaner to frame*
d) *Front and rear bumpers to frame*
e) *Steering column to frame*
f) *Hood and trunk lids to frame*
g) *Hood frame to frame on soft tops*

These faults are most pronounced when (1) the engine is idling, (2) labouring under load. Although the moving parts are already connected with nuts, bolts, etc, these do tend to rust and corrode, thus creating a high resistance interference source.

If you have a "ragged" sounding pulse when mobile, this could be wheel or tyre static. This can be cured by buying some anti-static powder and sprinkling it liberally inside the tyres.

If the interference takes the shape of a high pitched screeching noise that changes its note when the car is in motion and only comes now and then, this could be related to the aerial, especially if it is of the telescopic or whip type. This source can be cured quite simply by pushing a small rubber ball on top of the aerial (yes, really) as this breaks the electric field before it can form; but it would be much better to buy yourself a new aerial of a reputable brand. If, on the other hand, you are getting a loud rushing sound every time you brake, then this is brake static. This effect is most prominent on hot dry days and is cured only by fitting a special kit, which is quite expensive.

In conclusion, it is pointed out that it is relatively easy, and therefore cheap, to eliminate 95 per cent of all noise, but to eliminate the final 5 per cent is time and money consuming. It is up to the individual to decide if it is worth it. Please remember also, that you will not get Concert Hall performance from a cheap radio.

Finally, at the beginning of this Section are mentioned tape players; these are not usually affected by interference but in a very bad case, the best remedies are the first three suggestions plus using a 3 - 5 amp choke in the "live" line and in incurable cases screen the live and speaker wires.

Note: if your car is fitted with electronic ignition, then it is not recommended that either the spark plug resistors or the ignition coil capacitor be fitted as these may damage the system. Most electronic ignition units have built-in suppression and should, therefore, not cause interfernece.

See pages 174 and 175 for 'Fault diagnosis - electrical system'.

47 Fault diagnosis - electrical system

Symptom	Reason(s)
No electricity at starter motor	Battery discharged Battery defective internally Battery terminal leads loose or earth lead not securely attached to body Loose or broken connections in starter motor circuit Starter motor switch or solenoid faulty
Electricity at starter motor: faulty motor	Starter motor pinion jammed in mesh with flywheel gear ring Starter brushes badly worn, sticking, or brush wires loose Commutator dirty, worn or burnt Starter motor armature faulty Field coils earthed
Electrical defects	Battery in discharged condition Starter brushes badly worn, sticking or brush wires loose. Loose wires in starter motor cicuit
Dirt or oil on drive gear	Starter motor pinion sticking on the screwed sleeve
Mechanical damage	Pinion or flywheel gear teeth broken or worn
Lack of attention or mechanical damage	Pinion or flywheel gear teeth broken or worn Starter drive main spring broken Starter motor retaining bolts loose
Wear or damage	Battery defective internally Electrolyte level too low or electrolyte too weak due to leakage Plate separators no longer fully effective Battery plates severely sulphated
Insufficient current flow to keep battery charged	Fan belt slipping Battery terminal connections loose or corroded Alternator not charging properly Short in lighting circuit causing continual battery drain Regulator unit not working correctly
Alternator not charging*	Fan belt loose and slipping, or broken Brushes worn, sticking, broken or dirty Brush springs weak or broken

If all appears to be well but the alternator is still not charging, take the car to an automobile electrician for checking of the alternator and regulator.

Battery will not hold charge for more than a few days	Battery defective internally Electrolyte level too low or electrolyte too weak due to leakage Plate separators no longer fully effective Battery plates severely sulphated Fan/alternator belt slipping Battery terminal connections loose or corroded Alternator not charging properly Short in lighting circuit causing continual battery drain Regulator unit not working correctly
Ignition light fails to go out, battery runs flat in a few days	Fan belt loose and slipping or broken Alternator faulty

Failure of individual electrical equipment to function correctly is dealt with alphabetically, below.

Fuel gauge gives no reading	Fuel tank empty! Electric cable between tank sender unit and gauge earthed or loose Fuel gauge case not earthed Fuel gauge supply cable interrupted Fuel gauge unit broken
Fuel gauge registers full all the time	Electric cable between tank unit and gauge broken or disconnected

Symptom	Reason(s)
Horn operates all the time	Horn push either earthed or stuck down Horn cable to horn push earthed
Horn fails to operate	Blown fuse Cable or cable connection loose, broken or disconnected Horn has an internal fault
Horn emits intermittent or unsatisfactory noise	Cable connections loose Horn incorrectly adjusted
Lights do not come on	If engine not running, battery discharged Light bulb filament burnt out or bulbs broken Wire connections loose, disconnected or broken Light switch shorting or otherwise faulty
Lights come on but fade out	If engine not running battery discharged
Lights give very poor illumination	Lamp glasses dirty Reflector tarnished or dirty Lamps badly out of adjustment Incorrect bulb with too low wattage fitted Existing bulbs old and badly discoloured Electrical wiring too thin not allowing full current to pass
Lights work erratically - flashing on and off, especially over bumps	Battery terminals or earth connections loose Lights not earthing properly Contacts in light switch faulty
Wiper motor fails to work	Blown fuse Wire connections loose, disconnected or broken Brushes badly worn Armature worn or faulty Field coils faulty
Wiper motor works very slowly and takes excessive current	Commutator dirty, greasy or burnt Drive to spindles too bent or unlubricated Drive spindle binding or damaged Armature bearings dry or unaligned Armature badly worn or faulty
Wiper motor works slowly and takes little current	Brushes badly worn Commutator dirty, greasy, or burnt Armature badly worn or faulty
Wiper motor works but wiper blades remain static	Linkage disengaged or faulty Drive spindle damaged or worn Wiper motor gearbox parts badly worn

176

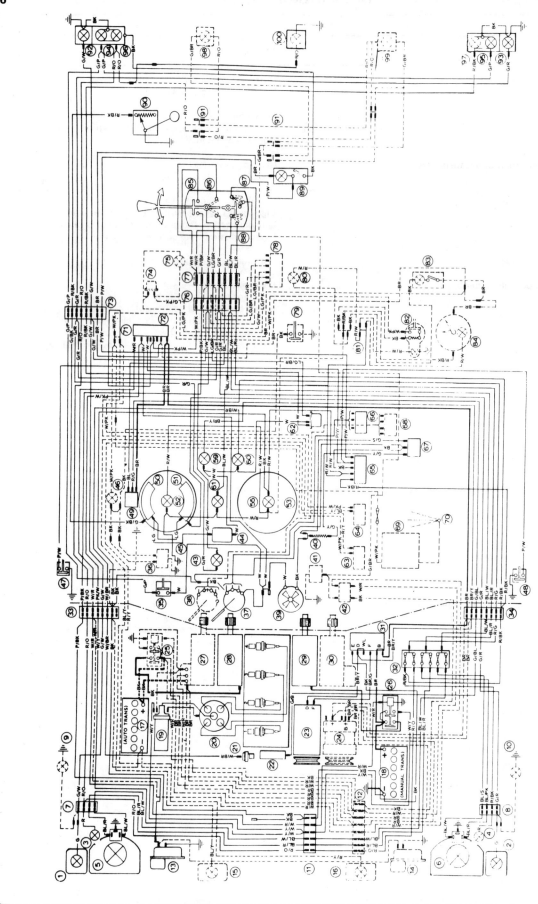

Wiring diagram for early 1600 cc models

Colour code and key for Wiring Diagram early 1600 cc and 1600 cc GT models

Code	Wiring colour		Code	Wiring colour
R	Red		Y	Yellow
Bk	Black		LG	Light Green
Bl	Black		P	Purple
W	White		O	Orange
Br	Brown		Pk	Pink
G	Green			

Code	Item		Code	Item
1	RH turn signal lamp (front)		52	Instrument illumination lamp
2	LH turn signal lamp (front)		53	Speedometer
3	RH side lamp (front)		54	Tachometer
4	LH side lamp (front)		55	Speedometer illumination lamp
5	RH headlamp		56	Tachometer illumination lamp
6	LH headlamp		57	Battery condition indicator
7	RH front loom connector		58	Oil pressure gauge
8	LH front loom connector		59	Generator warning lamp
9	RH side flasher (R.P.O.)		60	Oil pressure warning lamp
10	LH side flasher (R.P.O.)		61	Main beam warning lamp
11	Engine compartment loom connector		62	Turn signal flasher unit
12	Engine compartment loom connector (R.P.O.)		63	Fog lamp switch (R.P.O.
13	Horn		64	Road lamp switch (R.P.O.)
14	Dual horn (R.P.O.)		65	Interior lamp & panel illumination switch
15	Road lamp (R.P.O.)		66	Windscreen wiper switch
16	Fog lamp (R.P.O.)		67	Heater switch
17	Battery (L.H.D.)		68	Windscreen wiper switch - 2 speed (R.P.O.)
18	Battery (R.H.D.)		69	Radio (R.P.O.)
19	Ignition coil		70	Radio aerial (R.P.O.
20	Distributor		71	Accessory connector
21	Oil pressure switch		72	Ignition switch
22	Temperature sender unit		73	Rear wiring loom connector
23	Generator		74	Emergency flasher unit (R.P.O.)
24	Alternator (R.P.O.)		75	Emergency flasher indicator lamp (R.P.O.)
25	Starter solenoid (automatic transmission)		76	Steering column connector
26	Starter solenoid (manual transmission)		77	Steering column connector (R.P.O.)
27	Pre-engaged starter motor - automatic transmission (R.P.O.)		78	Emergency flasher switch (R.P.O.)
28	Inertia starter motor - automatic transmission		79	Parking brake warning switch (R.P.O.)
29	Inertia starter motor - manual transmission		80	Transmission selector illumination lamp (R.P.O.)
30	Pre-engaged starter motor - manual transmission (R.P.O.)		81	Accessory illumination connector
31	Regulator		82	Cigar lighter (R.P.O.)
32	Fuse block		83	Map reading lamp (R.P.O.)
33	RH bulkhead wiring connector		84	Clock (R.P.O.)
34	LH bulkhead wiring connector		85	Horn switch
35	Stop lamp switch		86	Direction indicator switch
36	Brake fluid low pressure switch (R.P.O.)		87	Column dip switch
37	Windscreen wiper motor		88	Headlamp flasher switch
38	Windscreen wiper motor - 2 speed (R.P.O.)		89	Interior light
39	Heater motor		90	Fuel gauge sender unit
40	Heater resistance		91	R.P.O. connectors
41	Reversing lamp switch - manual transmission (R.P.O.)		92	RH turn signal lamp (Rear)
42	Reversing lamp and park inhibitor switch - automatic transmission (R.P.O.)		93	LH turn signal lamp (Rear)
			94	RH stop lamp
43	Turn signal warning lamp		95	LH stop lamp
44	Instrument voltage regulator		96	RH side lamp (Rear)
45	Instrument panel earth		97	LH side lamp (Rear)
46	Brake fluid low pressure warning lamp (R.P.O.)		98	RH reversing lamp
47	RH courtesy switch		99	LH reversing lamp
48	LH courtesy switch		100	Licence plate lamp
49	Side/head lamp switch		101	Clock
50	Fuel gauge		102	Cigar lighter
51	Temperature gauge		103	Headlamp flasher relay (R.P.O.)

178

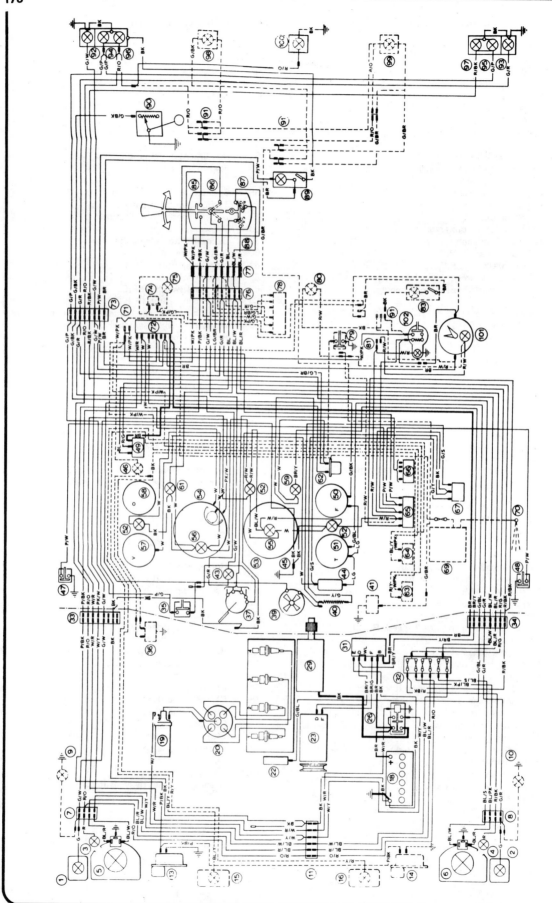

Wiring diagram for early 1600 cc GT models
(see page 177 for colour code and key)

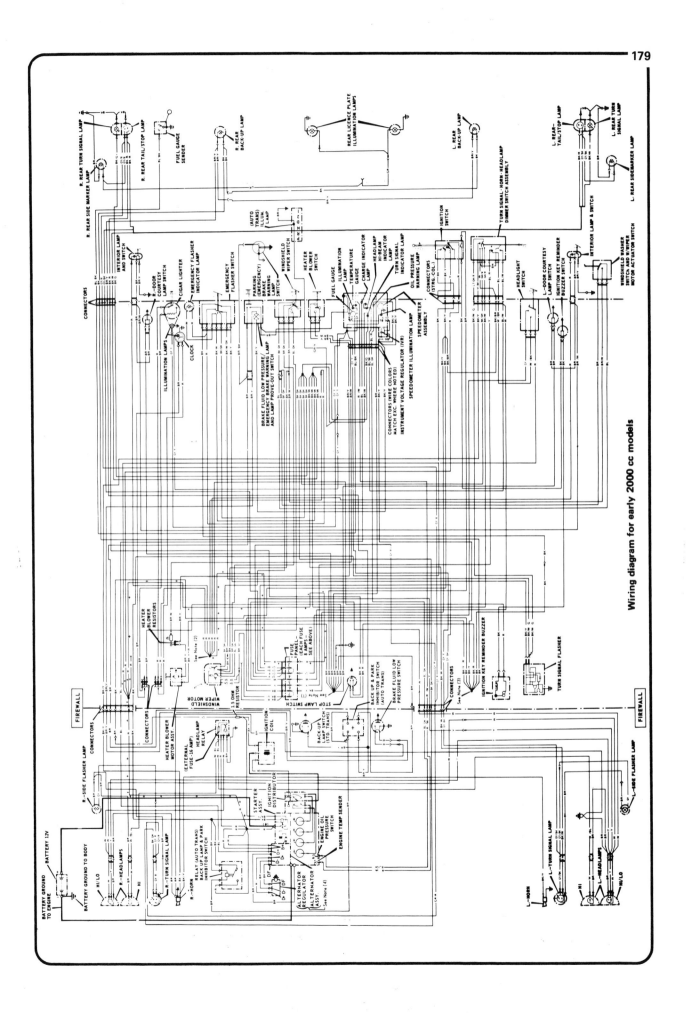

Wiring diagram for early 2000 cc models

Wiring diagram for later 2000 cc models
(see page 184 for colour code and key)

181

Wiring diagram for 2000 cc (later models) - continued
(see page 184 for colour code and key)

Wiring diagram for 2000 cc (later models) - continued
(see page 184 for colour code and key)

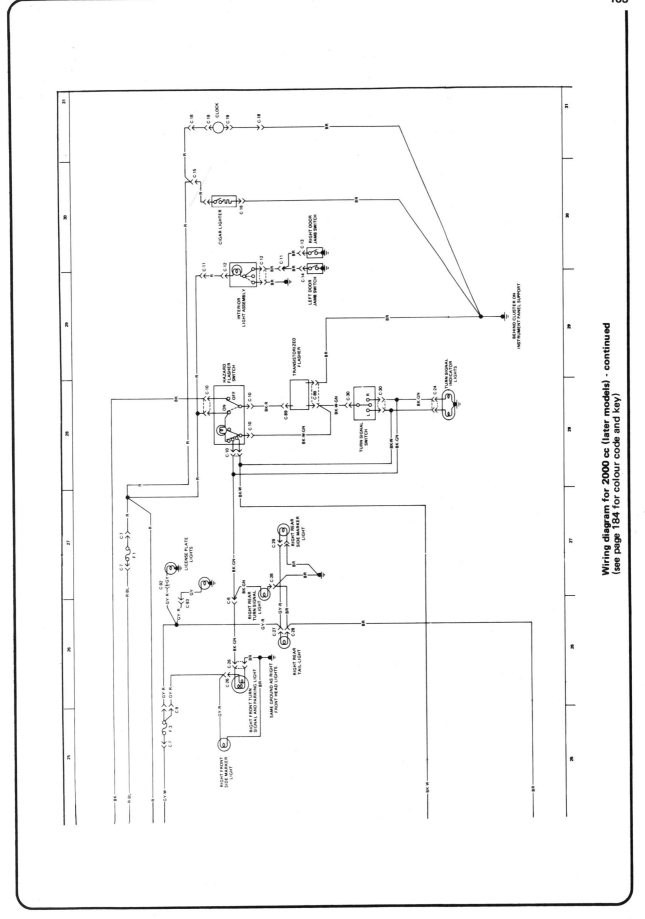

**Wiring diagram for 2000 cc (later models) - continued
(see page 184 for colour code and key)**

Key to Wiring Diagram for later 2000 cc models

Component	Location	Component	Location
Air conditioner clutch	F-7	Stop lights	
Alternator	B-1	Left	C-14
Alternator regulator	C-1	Right	C-14
Battery	A-1	Tail lights	
Buzzers		Left	E-23
Key reminder	B-4	Right	C-26
Seat belt	C-4	Rear turn signal	
Cigar lighter	B-30	Left	E-24
Clock	B-31	Right	C-27
Constant voltage regulator	B-12	Motors	
Distributor	E-5	A/C blower	F-8
Flashers		Heater blower	D-7
Hazard flasher	C-28	Starter	D-1
Turn signal	E-28	Windshield wiper	B-9
Gauges		Radio	B-4
Ammeter	A-2	Relays	
Fuel	C-12	Air conditioning	C-8
Tachometer	C-11	Automatic transmission	D-2
Temperature	C-13	Dimmer	D-18
Heated backlight	C-16	Heated backlight	C-16
Heater blower motor	D-7	Starter motor	D-1
Heater blower motor resistor	E-7	Starter override switch	C-3
Horns	D-6, D-7	Two-tone horn	C-7
Ignition coil	D-5	Seat belt logic box	D-4
Ignition resistor wire	D-5	Senders	
Illumination lights		Fuel gauge	C-12
Ammeter and oil pressure gauge	D-20	Water temperature gauge	C-13
Blower switch	D-23	Switches	
Cigar lighter	C-19	A/C blower	D-8
Clock	D-20	A/C control	E-7
Dome	B-29	Dimmer	
Fuel gauge	C-12	Instrument panel illumination	C-21
Glove box	D-6	High beam	C-18
Hazard flasher	D-22	Door jamb	
Lighting switch	D-21	Driver's	B-5, C-29
Map	E-21	Passenger's	C-30
PRND 12	C-24	Door jamb - key buzzer	B-4
Tachometer	C-11	Dual brake warning	D-12
Temperature gauge	C-13	Gear	E-3
Windshield wiper switch	D-22	Glove box lamp	D-6
Indicator lights		Hazard flasher	B-28
Alternator	C-11	Heated backlight	E-15
Brake warning	C-12	Heater blower	F-7
Heated backlight	E-16	Horn	C-6
High beam	E-19	Ignition	B-3
Seat belt	C-4	Lighting	C-18
Turn signal	E-28	Neutral start	E-2
Exterior lights		Parking brake	D-12
Back-up	E-13	Seat belt retractor	
Headlights		Driver's	E-5
Left	E-17	Passenger's	F-4
Right	E-18	Turn signal	D-28
License plate	B-27	Seat sensor	
Park and turn signal		Driver's	F-3
Left	E-23	Passenger's	F-4
Right	B-26	Starter override	C-3
Side marker		Stoplight	B-10
Left front	E-23	Windshield wiper	C-9
Left rear	E-24	Foot switch	D-10
Right front	B-25		
Right rear	C-27		

Wiring colour code

BK	Black	BL	Blue	GY	Grey	V	Violet
R	Red	W	White	BR	Brown	O	Orange
Y	Yellow	GN	Green				

Chapter 11 Suspension and steering

Contents

Specifications

Front suspension	...	...	...	...	...	...	Independent, MacPherson strut

Rear suspension

Cars up to Sept. 1972 ...	...	...	...	...	...	...	Semi-elliptic leaf springs, radius arms and telescopic shock absorbers
Cars after Sept. 1972 ...	...	...	...	...	...	...	Semi-elliptic leaf springs, stabiliser bar and telescopic shock absorbers

Steering gear

Type ...	...	...	...	...	...	...	...	Rack and pinion
Number of turns (lock-to-lock)	...	...	...	...	...			3.7
Turning circle ...	...	...	...	...	...	...	...	32 ft (9.75 m)

	Standard suspension	Heavy duty suspension
Camber	-0° 30' to 0° 30'	-0° 10' to 0° 50'
Castor	0° 30' to 1° 30'	
	Standard suspension	Heavy duty suspension
Steering axis inclination	7° 30' to 8° 30'	7° 10' to 8° 10'
Toe-in	0 to 0.25 in (0 to 6.4 mm)	
Track (front)	53.3 in (135.3 cm)	
Track (rear)	52.3 in (132.7 cm)	

Wheels

Type and size ...	...	...	...	...	...	...	...	Pressed steel, 5.00J x 13

Tyres

							1600 cc	2000 cc
Standard size ...	...	...	...	...	...	...	165 SR 13 radial	165 SR 13 radial
Optional size ...	...	...	...	...	...	...	—	185-70 SR 13 radial

								1600 cc (up to 3 people no luggage)	1600 cc (full load)
Pressures*:									
Front ...	...	...	...	...	...	...	...	24 p.s.i. (1.7 kg/cm^2)	27 p.s.i. (1.9 kg/cm^2)
Rear ...	...	...	...	...	...	...	...	27 p.s.i. (1.9 kg/cm^2)	31 p.s.i. (2.2 kg/cm^2)

For 2000 cc tyre pressures, consult glovebox sticker

Torque wrench settings
Front suspension

						lb f ft	kg f m
Suspension strut upper mounting bolts	...	...	...	...	20	2.8
Suspension strut piston rod nut	...	...	...	...	32	4.4
Track control arm ball stud ...	...	...	...	...	35	4.8
Front stabiliser bar clamp bolts	...	...	...	...	20	2.8
Stabiliser bar to track control arm	...	...	...	...	30	4.1
Track control arm inner pivot bolt	...	...	...	...	27	3.7
Track control ball stud nut ...	...	...	...	...	35	4.8

	lb f ft	kg f m
Steering arm to suspension strut	34	4.7
Wheel nuts	55	7.6
Disc to hub bolts	34	4.7
Front crossmember to body side frame	30	4.1
Rear suspension		
Radius arms to axle housing (pre. '73)	30	4.1
Radius arms to body frame (pre. '73)	30	4.1
Shock absorber lower mounting	45	6.2
Shock absorber upper mounting	20	2.8
Stabiliser bar to rear axle (1973 on)	36	5.0
Stabiliser bar to bodyframe (1973 on)	36	5.0
Locknuts to stabiliser bar end fittings	30	4.1
Rear spring 'U' bolts	30	4.1
Rear spring front hanger	32	4.4
Rear spring rear shackle nuts	10	1.4
Steering		
Steering gear to crossmember	20	2.8
Trackrod-end ball stud	25	3.5
Trackrod-end locknut	20	2.8
Flexible coupling pinch bolt	15	2.1
Steering wheel nut	25	3.5

1 General description

Each of the independent front suspension MacPherson strut units consists of a vertical strut enclosing a double acting damper surrounded by a coil spring.

The upper end of each strut is secured to the top of the wing valance under the bonnet by rubber mountings.

The wheel spindle carrying the brake assembly and wheel hub is forged integrally with the suspension unit foot.

The steering arms are connected to each unit which is in turn connected to trackrods and thence to the rack and pinion steering gear.

The lower end of each suspension unit is located by a track control arm. A stabilising torsion bar is fitted between the outer ends of each track control arm and secured at the front to mountings on the body front member.

A rubber rebound stop is fitted inside each suspension unit thus preventing the spring becoming over-extended and jumping out of its mounting plates. Upward movement of the wheel is limited by the spring becoming fully compressed but this is damped by the addition of a rubber bump stop fitted around the suspension unit piston rod which comes into operation before the spring is fully compressed.

Whenever repairs have been carried out on a suspension unit it is essential to check the wheel alignment as the linkage could be altered which will affect the correct front wheel settings.

Every time the car goes over a bump vertical movement of a front wheel pushes the damper body upward against the combined resistance of the coil spring and the damper piston.

Hydraulic fluid in the damper is displaced and forced through the compression valve into the space between the inner and outer cylinder. On the downward movement of the suspension, the road spring forces the damper body downward against the pressure of the hydraulic fluid which is forced back again through the rebound valve. In this way the natural oscillations of the spring are damped out and a comfortable ride is obtained.

On the front uprights it is worth noting that there is a shroud inside the coil spring which protects the machined surface of the piston rod from road dirt.

The steering gear is of the rack and pinion type and is located on the front crossmember by two 'U' shaped clamps. The pinion is connected to the steering column by a flexible coupling. Above the flexible coupling the steering column is split by a universal joint designed to collapse on impact thus minimising injury to the driver in the event of an accident.

Turning the steering wheel causes the rack to move in a lateral direction and the trackrods attached to each end of the rack pass this movement to the steering arms on the suspension/axle nuts thereby moving the roadwheels.

Two adjustments are possible on the steering gear, namely rack damper adjustment and pinion bearing pre-load adjustment, but the steering gear must be removed from the car to carry out these adjustments. Both adjustments are made by varying the thickness of shim-packs.

At the rear, the axle is located by two inverted 'U' bolts at each end of the casing to underslung semi-elliptic leaf springs which provide both lateral and longitudinal location.

On cars built up to late 1972, lateral movement of the rear axle is further controlled by two radius arms connected between the top of the axle casing and the body. On cars built after this date, a stabiliser bar is substituted for the radius arms.

Double acting telescopic shock absorbers are fitted between the spring plates on the rear axle and reinforced mountings in the boot of the car. These shock absorbers work on the same principle as the front shock absorbers.

In the interests of lessening noise and vibration the spring and dampers are mounted on rubber bushes. A rubber spacer is also incorporated between the axle and the springs.

2 Front hub bearings - maintenance and adjustment

1 *Every 12000 miles (19000 km)* check the front hub bearings for correct adjustment.

2 To check the condition of the hub bearings, jack-up the front end of the car remove the disc pads (Chapter 9) and grasp the roadwheel at two opposite points to check for any rocking movement in the wheel hub. Watch carefully for any movement in the steering gear, which can easily be mistaken for hub movement.

3 If a front wheel hub has excessive movement, this is adjusted by removing the hub cap and then levering off the small dust cap. Remove the split pin through the stub axle and take off the adjusting nut retainer.

4 If a torque wrench is available tighten the centre adjusting nut down to a torque of 27 lb f ft (3.37 kg f m) and then slacken it off 90° and replace the nut retainer and a new split pin.

5 Assuming a torque wrench is not available however, tighten up the centre nut until a slight drag is felt on rotating the wheel. Then loosen the nut very slowly until the wheel turns freely again and there is just a perceptible endfloat.

6 Now replace the nut retainer, a new split pin and the dust cap.

7 Refit the disc pads, the roadwheel and lower the car.

8 *Every 36000 miles (58000 km),* jack-up the front of the car

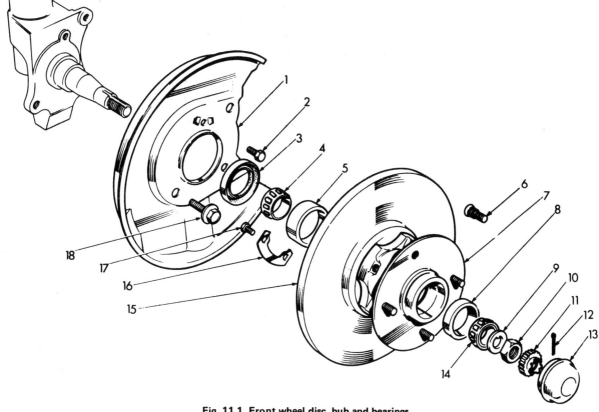

Fig. 11.1. Front wheel disc, hub and bearings

1 Brake backplate	5 Bearing cup	9 Washer	14 Bearing
2 Bolt	6 Wheel stud	10 Nut	15 Brake disc
3 Seal	7 Hub	11 Nut retainer	16 Locking tab
4 Bearing	8 Bearing cup	12 Split pin	17 Bolt
		13 Dust cap	18 Bolt

and remove the roadwheels, then disconnect the hydraulic brake pipe at the union on the suspension unit and either plug the open ends of the pipes, or have a jar handy to catch the escaping fluid.

9   Bend back the locking tabs on the two bolts holding the brake caliper to the suspension unit, undo the bolts and remove the caliper.

10 By judicious tapping and levering remove the dust cap from the centre of the hub.

11 Remove the split pin from the nut retainer and undo the larger adjusting nut from the stub axle.

12 Withdraw the thrust washer and the outer tapered bearing.

13 Pull off the complete hub and disc assembly from the stub axle.

14 Carefully prise out the grease seal from the back of the hub assembly and remove the inner tapered bearing.

15 Carefully clean out the hub and wash the bearings with petrol making sure that no grease or oil is allowed to get onto the brake disc.

16 Working the grease well into the bearings fully pack the bearing cages and rollers with wheel bearing grease. **Note:** Leave the hub cavity half empty to allow for subsequent expansion of the grease.

17 To reassemble the hub assembly first fit the inner bearing and then gently tap the grease seal back into the hub. If the seal was at all damaged during removal a new one must be fitted.

18 Replace the hub and disc assembly on the stub axle and slide on the outer bearing and the thrust washer.

19 Adjust the hub bearings, as described in earlier paragraphs of

this Section, refit the caliper and connect the hydraulic brake line.

20 Bleed the brakes, as described in Chapter 9.

3   Front hub - dismantling and bearing renewal

1   Remove the hub/disc assembly, as described in Section 2.

2   Remove the oil seal and roller bearing races.

3   Using a brass drift or bearing puller, remove the bearing tracks from the ends of the hub.

4   If the disc is to be renewed because of scoring or distortion (see Chapter 9), bend down the lockplate tabs and unscrew and remove the bolts which connect the hub and disc.

5   Reassembly is a reversal of removal but if all front wheel bearings are being renewed, take care not to mix up the bearings and their tracks but keep them in their boxes until required as matched sets.

6   Use new locking plates under the disc to hub bolts and tighten all bolts to specification.

7   Pack the bearings with grease and adjust them, as described in Section 2.

4   Front suspension strut - removal and installation

1   It is difficult to work on the front suspension of the Capri without one or two special tools, the most important of which is a set of adjustable spring clips which is Ford tool No. **P.5045**

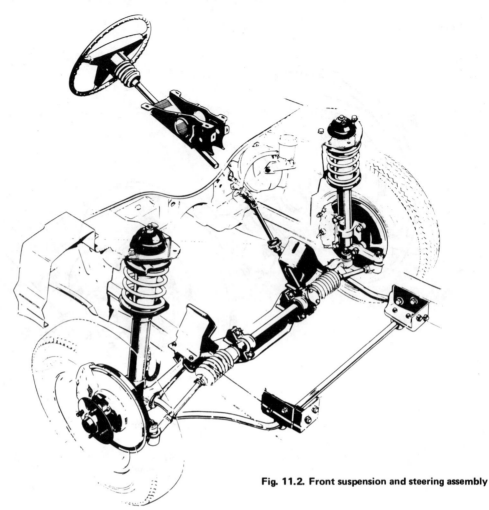

Fig. 11.2. Front suspension and steering assembly

(USA tool number T70P-5045). This tool, or similar clips or compressors are vital and any attempt to dismantle the units without them may result in personal injury (Fig. 11.3).

2   Get someone to sit on the wing of the car and with the spring partially compressed in this way, securely fit the spring clips.

3   Jack-up the car and remove the roadwheel, then disconnect the brake pipe at the bracket on the suspension leg and plug the pipes or have a jar handy to catch the escaping hydraulic fluid.

4   Disconnect the trackrod from the steering arm by pulling out the split pin and undoing the castellated nut, thus leaving the steering arm attached to the suspension unit.

5   Remove the outer end of the track control arm from the base of the suspension strut by pulling out the split pin and undoing the castellated nut.

6   Working under the bonnet undo the three bolts holding the top end of the suspension strut to the side panel and lower the unit complete with the brake caliper away from the car.

7   Replacement is a direct reversal of the removal sequence, but remember to use new split pins on the steering arm to trackrod nut and also on the track control arm to suspension unit nut.

8   The top suspension unit mounting bolts should be tightened to the specified torque, the track control arm to suspension strut nut and the steering arm to trackrod end nut also to the specified torque.

---

5   Front coil spring - removal and refitting

---

1   Get someone to sit on the front wing of the car and with the spring partially compressed in this way securely fit spring clips or

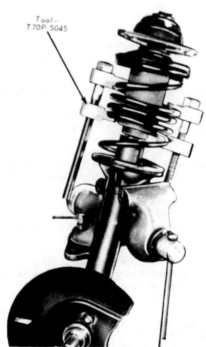

Fig. 11.3. Front suspension coil spring compressed (Secs. 4 & 5)

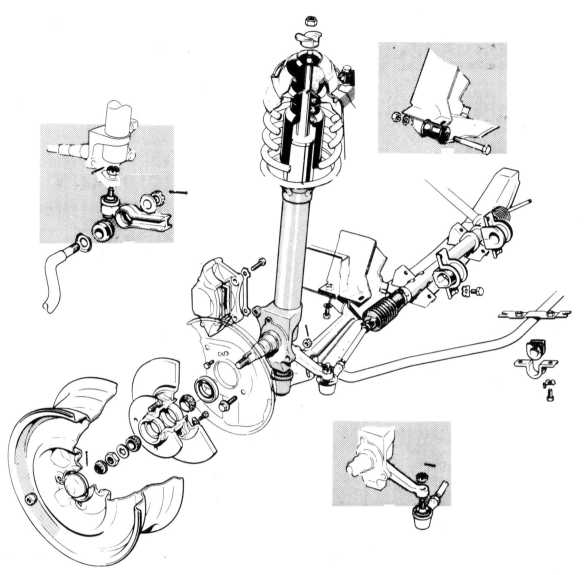

Fig. 11.4. Partly exploded view of one side of the front suspension

a roadspring compressor.

2   Jack-up the front of the car, fit stands and remove the road-wheel.

3   Working under the bonnet, remove the piston nut and the cranked retainer.

4   Undo and remove the three bolts securing the top of the suspension unit to the side panel.

5   Push the piston rod downwards as far as it will go. It should now be possible to remove the top mounting assembly the dished washer and the upper spring seat from the top of the spring.

6   The spring can now be lifted off its bottom seat and removed over the piston assembly.

7   If a new spring is being fitted check extremely carefully that it is of the same rating as the spring on the other side of the car. The colour coding of the springs can be found in the Specifications at the beginning of this Chapter.

8   Before fitting a new spring it must be compressed with the adjustable restrainers and make sure that the clips are placed on the same number of coils, and in the same position as on the

9   Place the new spring over the piston and locate it on its bottom seat, then pull the piston and fit the upper spring seat so that it locates correctly on the flats cut on the piston rod.

10 Fit the dished washer to the piston rod ensuring that the convex side faces upward.

11 Now fit the top mounting assembly. With the steering in the straight-ahead position, fit the cranked retainer so that the ear on the retainer faces inwards and is at 90° to the centre line of the car. Later models have retainers which incorporate two ears. Screw on the piston rod nut having previously applied Loctite or a similar compound to the threads. Do not fully tighten the piston nut at this stage (Fig. 11.5).

12 If necessary pull the top end of the unit upward until it is possible to locate correctly the top mount bracket and fit the three retaining bolts from under the bonnet. These nuts must be tightened down to the specified torque.

13 Remove the spring clips, fit the roadwheel and lower the car to the ground.

14 Finally slacken off the piston rod nut, get an assistant to hold the upper spring seat to prevent it turning and retighten the nut to a torque of 28 to 30 lb f ft (3.9 to 4.4 kg f m).

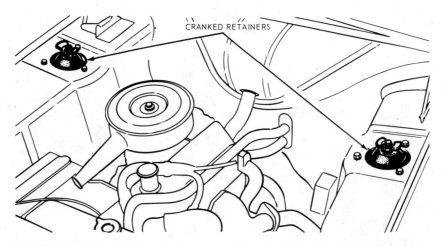

Fig. 11.5. Correct position of cranked retainers on suspension upper mountings (Sec. 5)

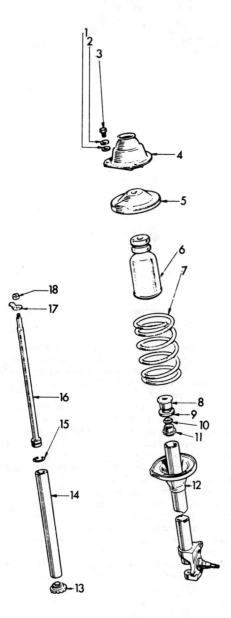

6 Front stabiliser bar - removal and refitting

1   Jack-up the front of the car, support the car on suitable stands and remove both front roadwheels.
2   Working under the car at the front, knock back the locking tabs on the four bolts securing the two front clamps that hold the stabiliser bar to the frame and then undo the four bolts and remove the clamps and rubber insulators.
3   Remove the split pins from the castellated nuts retaining the stabiliser bar to the track control arms then undo the nuts and pull off the large washers, carefully noting the way in which they are fitted.
4   Pull the stabiliser bar forward out of the two track control arms and remove it from the car.
5   With the stabiliser bar out of the car remove the sleeve and large washer from each end of the bar again noting the correct fitting positions.
6   Reassembly is a reversal of the above procedure, but new locking tabs must be used on the front clamp bolts and new split pins on the castellated nuts. The nuts on the clamps and the castellated nuts on each end of the stabiliser bar must be fully tightened down until the car is resting on its wheels.
7   Once the car is on its wheels the castellated nuts on the ends of the stabiliser bar should be tightened down to the specified torque and the new split pins fitted. The four clamp bolts on the front mounting points must be tightened down to the specified torque and the locking tabs knocked up.

7 Track control arm - removal and refitting

1   Jack-up the front of the car, support the car on suitable stands and remove the front wheel.
2   Working under the car remove the split pin and unscrew the castellated nut that secures the track control arm to the stabiliser bar.

Fig. 11.6. Front suspension unit - component parts

1	Washer	10 Rod gland
2	Spring washer	11 Rod bush and guide
3	Bolt	12 Tube & spindle assembly
4	Upper mounting	13 Compression valve
5	Upper spring seat	14 Cylinder
6	Bump stop	15 Ring
7	Coil spring	16 Piston
8	Piston rod gland cap	17 Cranked retainer
9	Oil seal ring	18 Nut

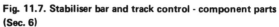

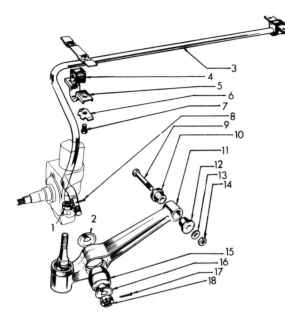

Fig. 11.7. Stabiliser bar and track control - component parts
(Sec. 6)

1 Castellated nut
2 Dished washer
3 Stabiliser bar
4 Rubber bush
5 'U' clamp
6 Locking tab
7 Bolt
8 Split pin
9 Bolt
10 Bush
11 Track control arm
12 Bush
13 Washer
14 Nut
15 Bush
16 Dished washer
17 Split pin
18 Castellated nut

3 Lift away the large dished washer noting which way round it is fitted.

4 Remove the self lock nut and flat washer from the back of the track control arm pivot bolt. Release the inner end of the track control arm.

5 Withdraw the split pin and unscrew the nut securing the track control arm balljoint to the base of the suspension unit. Separate the joint.

6 To refit the track control arm first assemble the track control arm ball stud to the base of the suspension unit.

7 Refit the nut and tighten to the specified torque. Secure with a new split pin.

8 Place the track control arm so that it correctly locates over the stabiliser bar and then secure the inner end.

9 Slide the pivot bolt into position from the front and secure with the flat washer and a new self-locking nut. The nut must be to the rear. Tighten the nut to the specified torque when the car is on the ground.

10 Fit the dished washer to the end of the stabiliser bar making sure it is the correct way round and secure with the castellated nut. This must be tightened, when the car is on the ground, to the specified torque. Lock the castellated nut with a new split pin.

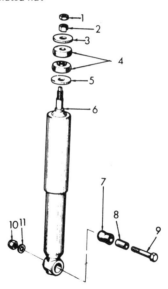

Fig. 11.8. Rear shock absorber mountings (Sec. 8)

1 Locknut		7 Bush	
2 Nut		8 Insert	
3 Washer		9 Bolt	
4 Rubber bushes		10 Shakeproof washer	
5 Washer		11 Nut	
6 Shock absorber			

8 Rear shock absorber - removal and refitting

1 Chock the front wheels to prevent the car moving, then jack up the rear of the car and for convenience sake remove the roadwheels.

2 Working inside the boot, hold the top of the shock absorber piston to prevent it turning by holding a small spanner (¼ inch A/F) across the flats provided and then with an open-ended spanner remove the locknut and main nut from the piston rod.

3 Lift off the large steel washer and the rubber bush.

4 Working under the car, remove the nut, lock washer and bolt that retain the lower end of the shock absorber to the axle casing.

5 Lower the shock absorber from the car, then remove the further rubber bush and steel washer from the top of the piston rod.

6 Replacement is a reversal of the above procedure.

7 The nut on the bolt securing the lower end of the shock absorber must be tightend down to the speicified torque.

8 Tighten the top mounting nut to specified torque while

holding the piston rod from turning by means of its flats. Tighten the locknut.

9 Rear leaf spring - removal and refitting

1 Chock the front wheels to prevent the car moving, then jack-up the rear of the car and support it on suitable stands. To make the springs more accessible remove the roadwheels.

2 Then place a trolley jack underneath the differential housing to support the rear axle assembly when the springs are removed. Do not raise the jack under the differential housing so that the

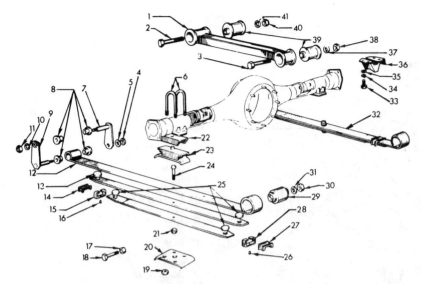

Fig. 11.9. Rear spring and radius arm assemblies - component parts

1 Radius arm	12 Spring leaf	23 Insulator	34 Spring washer
2 Bolt	13 Spacer	24 Centre bolt	35 Washer
3 Bolt	14 Clamp insulator	25 Spacers	36 Plate
4 Nut	15 Clamp	26 Rivet	37 Washer
5 Washer	16 Pin	27 Clamp insulator	38 Nut
6 'U' bolts	17 Bush	28 Clamp	39 Bush
7 Shackle plate and bolt	18 Bolt	29 Bush	40 Bolt
8 Bushes	19 Nut	30 Nut	41 Washer
9 Shackle plate and bolt	20 'U' bolt plate	31 Washer	
10 Spring washer	21 Bolt	32 Spring assembly	
11 Nut	22 Plate	33 Bolt	

springs are flattened, but raise it just enough to take the full weight of the axle with the springs fully extended.

3 Undo the rear shackle nuts and remove the combined shackle bolt and plate assemblies. Then remove the rubber bushes.

4 Undo the nut from the front mounting and take out the bolt running through the mounting.

5 Undo the nuts on the ends of the four 'U' bolts and remove the 'U' bolts together with the attachment plate and rubber spring insulators.

6 Replacement is a direct reversal of the above procedure. The nuts on the 'U' bolts, spring front mounting and rear shackles must be torqued down to the figures given in the Specifications at the beginning of this Chapter, only after the car has been lowered onto its wheels.

10 Rear radius arm (cars up to Sept '72) - removal and refitting

1 Chock the front wheels to prevent the car moving, then jack-up the rear of the car and support it on suitable stands.

2 Undo the nut and remove the bolt holding the rear end of the radius arm to the axle casing.

3 To take the tension off the radius arm it may be necessary to slightly raise the axle casing with a jack.

4 Repeat this procedure on the front mounting nut and bolt and remove the radius arm from the car bodyframe.

5 Replacement is a reversal of the above procedure but the nuts should be torqued down to the figures given in the Specifications at the beginning of this Chapter, after the car has been lowered onto its wheels.

11 Rear stabiliser bar (cars after Sept '72) - removal and refitting

1 The rear stabiliser bar fitted to these cars is in place of the two

radius arms fitted to earlier models (Fig. 11.11).

2 To remove the bar, first disconnect the primary handbrake cable from the lever on the rear of the differential unit and withdraw the cable from the pulley.

3 Unbolt both stabiliser bar brackets from the rear axle casing. This will first necessitate using a suitable lever to prise the bar to the rear in order to relieve the bolts of any preload.

4 Disconnect the stabiliser bar end mountings from the bodyframe and then lift the bar away.

5 Before installing the rear stabiliser bar, the setting of the end fittings must be checked, particularly if they have been removed for renewal of their flexible bushes (see Section 12). Screw on the end fittings to obtain the dimension shown (A) (Fig. 11.10) and then tighten the locknuts with the end fittings in the correct attitude.

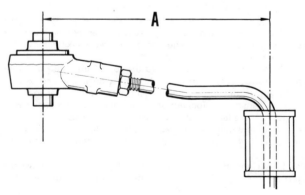

Fig. 11.10. Rear stabiliser bar end fitting setting diagram (Sec. 11)

A = 10.14 to 10.34 in. (259.5 to 264.5 mm)

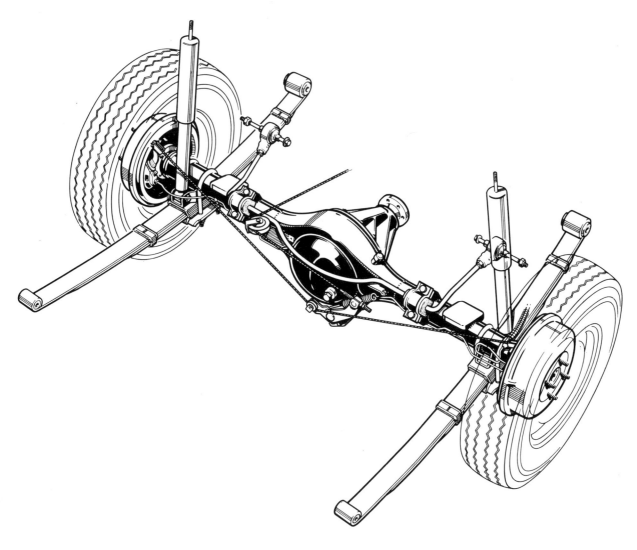

Fig. 11.11. Rear stabiliser bar (cars after September 1972)
(Sec. 11)

6   The bolts which secure the end fittings to the bodyframe
must be fitted so that their heads are nearer the centre of the
car. Do not tighten these bolts until the weight of the car is again
on the roadwheels (Fig. 11.12).
7   Using the lever, prise the stabiliser bar forward so that the
brackets can be bolted to the axle casing.
8   Reconnect the handbrake cable and adjust as described in
Chapter 9.
9   Lower the car to the ground and then tighten the end fitting
bolts to the specified torque.

12 Flexible bushes - renewal

1   The flexible bushes used in the road-spring eyes, the radius
arms and the stabiliser bar end fittings can all be removed and
refitted by using a press, a vice or length of studding and suitable
pieces of tubing as distance pieces (Fig. 11.13).
2   The application of some glycerine or brake fluid will
facilitate installation of the new bushes.
3   When pressing in the stabiliser bar end fitting bushes insert
the chamfered side first and locate the semi-circular recesses as
shown in Fig. 11.14.

Fig. 11.12. Inserting rear stabiliser bar end fitting bolts (Sec. 11)

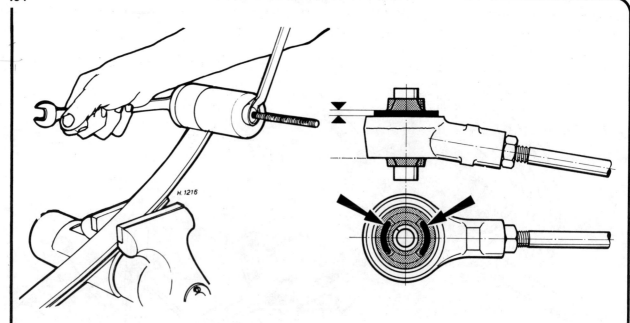

Fig. 11.13. Alternative method of removing spring bushes
(Sec. 12)

Fig. 11.14. Correct installation of rear stabiliser bar end fitting
bushes (Sec. 12)

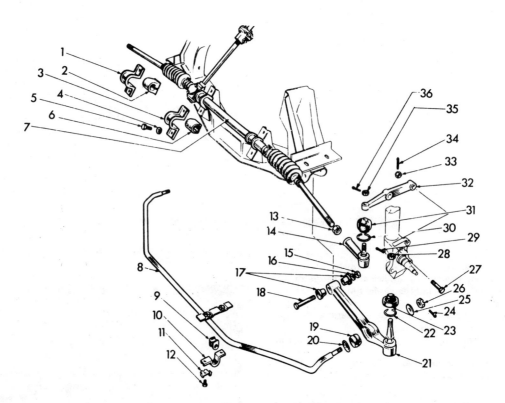

Fig. 11.15. Steering and track control assemblies

1 'U' clamp	10 Clamp	19 Bush	28 Castellated nut
2 Rubber bush	11 Locking tab	20 Washer	29 Split pin
3 'U' clamp	12 Bolt	21 Track control arm	30 Ring
4 Washer	13 Locknut	22 Ring	31 Bush
5 Bolt	14 Track rod end	23 Seal	32 Steering arm
6 Bush	15 Nut	24 Split pin	33 Nut
7 Rack housing	16 Washer	25 Washer	34 Split pin
8 Stabiliser bar	17 Bush	26 Castellated nut	35 Castellated nut
9 Rubber bush	18 Bolt	27 Bolt	36 Split pin

13 Steering gear - removal and installation

1 Before starting this job, set the front wheels in the straight-ahead position. Then jack-up the front of the car and place blocks under the wheels; lower the car slightly on the jack so that the trackrods are in a near horizontal position.

2 Remove the nut and bolt from the clamp at the front of the flexible coupling on the steering column. This clamp holds the coupling to the pinion splines.

3 Working on the front crossmember knock back the locking tabs on the two nuts on each rack housing 'U' clamp, undo the nut and remove the locking tabs and clamps.

4 Remove the split pins and castellated nuts from the ends of each track rod when they join the steering arms. Separate the track rods from the steering arms using a ball joint separator or wedges and lower the steering gear downwards out of the car.

5 Before replacing the steering gear make sure that the wheels have remained in the straight-ahead position. Also check the condition of the mounting rubbers round the housing and if they appear worn or damaged renew them.

6 Check that the steering gear is also in the straight-ahead position. This can be done by ensuring that the distances between the ends of both track rods and the steering gear housing on both sides are the same.

7 Place the steering gear in its location on the crossmember and at the same time mate up the splines on the pinion with the splines in the clamp on the steering column flexible coupling. (Fig. 11.16).

8 Replace the two 'U' clamps using new locking tabs under the bolts, tighten down the bolts to the specified torque.

9 Refit the trackrod ends into the steering arms, replace the castellated nuts and tighten them to the specified torque. Use new split pins to retain the nuts.

10 Tighten the clamp bolt on the steering column flexible coupling to the specified torque, having first made sure that the pinion is correctly located in the splines.

11 Jack-up the car, remove the blocks from under the wheels and lower the car to the ground. It is advisable at this stage to take the car to your local dealer and have the toe-in checked (see also Section 19).

14 Steering gear - adjustments

1 For the steering gear to function correctly, two adjustments are necessary. These are pinion bearing preload and rack damper adjustment.

2 To carry out these adjustments, remove the steering gear from the car as described in the previous Section, then mount the steering gear in a soft jawed vice so that the pinion is in a horizontal position and the rack damper cover plate to the top.

3 Remove the rack damper cover plate by undoing the two retaining bolts, then take off the gasket and shims from under the plate. Also remove the small springs and the recessed yoke which bears on the rack.

4 Now remove the pinion bearing preload cover plate from the base of the pinion, by undoing the two bolts. Then take off the gasket and shim pack.

5 To correctly set the pinion bearing preload, replace the cover plate without the gasket and shims and tighten down the bolts evenly until the cover plate is just touching the pinion bearing.

6 Using feeler gauges, measure the gap between the cover plate and the steering gear casing. To be sure that the cover plate has been evenly tightened, take a reading adjacent to each bolt. These readings should be the same. If they are not, loosen the cover plate and retighten it more evenly.

7 Assemble a shim pack including a gasket, which must be fitted next to the cover plate on refitting, which is 0.002 to 0.004 inch (0.05 to 0.10 mm) less than the measured gap. Shim thicknesses available are listed below:

Fig. 11.16. Steering column universal joint and flexible coupling (Sec. 13)

Material	Thickness
Steel	0.010 in. (0.254 mm)
Steel	0.005 in. (0.127 mm)
Steel	0.002 in. (0.051 mm)
Paper	0.005 in. (0.127 mm)

8 Remove the cover plate again, fit the assembled shim pack and gasket, with the gasket next to the cover plate, refit the cover plate and having applied Loctite or similar sealer on the threads of the bolts, tighten them down to a torque of 6 to 8 lb f ft (0.9 to 1.1 kg f m).

9 To set the rack damper adjustment, replace the yoke in its location on the rack and make sure it is fully home. Then measure the distance between the bottom of the recess in the yoke and the top of the steering gear casing.

10 Assemble a shim pack with a gasket on each side of the shims which is between 0.0005 to 0.0035 inch (0.0127 to 0.0775 mm) greater than the dimension measured in the previous paragraph. Shim thicknesses available are as listed below:

Material	Thickness
Steel	0.010 in. (0.254 mm)
Steel	0.005 in. (0.127 mm)
Steel	0.002 in. (0.051 mm)
Paper	0.005 in. (0.127 mm)

11 Refit the spring into its recess in the yoke and fit the shim pack and gaskets. Replace the cover plate having first applied Loctite or similar sealing compound to the bolt threads. Then tighten down the bolts to a torque of 6 to 8 lb f ft (0.9 to 1.1 kg f m).

15 Steering gear - dismantling and reassembly

1 Remove the steering gear from the car as previously described.

2 Unscrew the ball joints and locknuts from the end of each trackrod, having previously marked the threads to ensure correct positioning on reassembly. Alternatively, the number of turns required to undo the ball joint can be counted and noted.

3 Slacken off the clips securing the rubber bellows to each trackrod and the steering gear housing then pull off the bellows. Have a quantity of rag handy to catch the oil which will escape when the bellows are removed.

4 To dismantle the steering gear, it is only necessary to remove

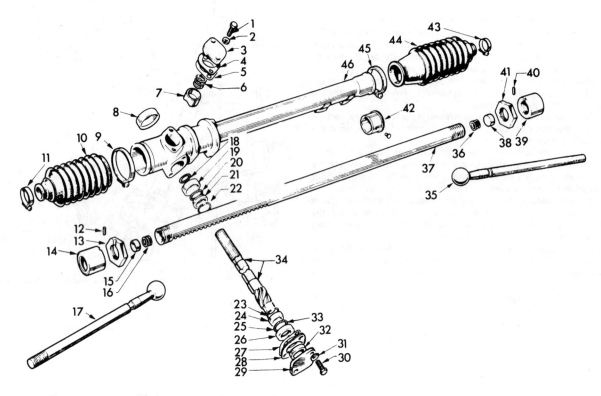

Fig. 11.17. Rack and pinion assembly (Sec. 15)

1	Bolt	13	Nut	25	Balls	37	Rack
2	Washer	14	Ball joint housing	26	Bearing	38	Bearing
3	Cover	15	Bearing	27	Shim	39	Ball joint housing
4	Gasket	16	Spring	28	Gasket	40	Pin
5	Shim	17	Track rod	29	Cover	41	Nut
6	Spring	18	Oil seal	30	Bolt	42	Bush
7	Rack slipper	19	Bearing	31	Washer	43	Clip
8	Seal	20	Balls	32	Spacer	44	Bellows
9	Clip	21	Race	33	Balls	45	Clip
10	Bellows	22	Circlip	34	Pinion	46	Rack housing
11	Clip	23	Circlip	35	Track rod		
12	Pin	24	Race	36	Spring		

the trackrod which is furthest away from the pinion both right and left-hand drive cars.

5   To remove the trackrod place the steering gear in a soft jawed vice. Working on the trackrod ball joint carefully drill out the pin that locks the ball housing to the locknut. Great care must be taken not to drill too deeply or you will drill into the threads on the rack thus causing irreparable damage. The hole should be about 3/8th inch (9.5 mm) deep.

6   Hold the locknut with a spanner, then grip the ball housing with a mole wrench and undo it from the threads on the rack.

7   Take out the spring and ball seat from the recess in the end of the rack and then unscrew the locknut from the threads on the rack. The spring and ball seat must be replaced by new components on reassembly.

8   Carefully prise out the pinion dust seal then withdraw the pinion together with the bearing assembly nearest the flexible coupling. As the bearings use bearing tracks and loose balls (14 in each bearing) care must be taken not to lose any of the balls or drop them into the steering gear on reassembly.

9   With the pinion removed, withdraw the complete rack assembly with one trackrod still attached from the pinion end of the casing, having first removed the rack damper cover, gasket, shims, spring and yoke, as described in Section 14, paragraph 3.

10 Now remove the remaining pinion bearing assembly from the rack casing.

11 It is always advisable to withdraw the rack from the pinion end of the casing. This avoids passing the rack teeth through the bush at the other end of the casing and causing possible damage.

12 Carefully examine all parts for signs of wear or damage. Check the condition of the rack support bush at the opposite end of the casing from the pinion. If this is worn renew it. If the rack or pinion teeth are in any way damaged a completely new steering gear will have to be fitted.

13 Take the pinion oil seal off the top of the casing and replace it with a new seal.

14 To commence reassembly fit the lower pinion bearing and thrust washer into their recess in the casing. The loose balls can be held in place by a small amount of grease.

15 Replace the rack in the casing from the pinion end and position it in the straight-ahead position by equalising the amount it protrudes at either end of the casing.

16 Replace the remaining pinion bearing and thrust washer onto the pinion and fit the pinion into the casing so that the large master spline on the pinion shaft is parallel to the rack and on the right-hand side of the pinion. This applies to both right and left-hand drive cars.

17 Replace the rack damper yoke, springs, shims, gasket and cover plate.

18 To replace the trackrod which has been removed, start by fitting a new spring and ball seat to the recess in the end of the rack shaft and replace the locknut onto the threads of the rack.
19 Lubricate the ball, ball seat and ball housing with a small amount of SAE 90 EP oil. Then slide the ball housing over the trackrod and screw the housing onto the rack threads keeping the trackrod in the horizontal position until the trackrod starts to become stiff to move.
20 Using a normal spring balance hook it round the trackrod half an inch from the end and check the effort required to move it from the horizontal position.
21 By adjusting the tightness of the ball housing on the rack threads the effort required to move the trackrod must be set at 5 lbs (2.8 kg).
22 Tighten the locknut up to the housing and then recheck that the effort required to move the trackrod is still correct at 5 lb (2.8 kg).
23 On the line where the locknut and ball housing meet, drill a 1/8th inch (3.18 mm) diameter hole which must be 3/8th inch (9.5 mm) deep. Even if the two halves of the old hole previously drilled out align, a new hole must be drilled.
24 Tap a new retaining pin into the hole and peen the end over to secure it.
25 Replace the rubber bellows and the trackrod ends ensuring that they are replaced in exactly the same position from which they were removed.
26 Remove the rack damper cover plate and pour in 0.25 Imp. pint (0.3 US pints, 0.15 litre) of SAE 90 EP oil. Then carry out both steering gear adjustments, as detailed in Section 14.
27 After replacing the steering gear on the car as described in Section 13 it is strongly recommended that you take the car to your nearest Ford dealer and have the toe-in correctly adjusted (see also Section 19).

16 Steering wheel - removal and refitting

1 Set the roadwheels in the straight-ahead position.
2 Prise out the motif from the centre of the steering wheel.
3 Hold the wheel quite still and unscrew (two or three turns only) the steering wheel retaining nut.
4 Place the thumbs on the end of the loosened nut and grip the hub with the fingers. The wheel should now slide off the splines.
5 If it does not come off, do not strike the rear of the wheel as damage to the column may result. The column shrouds will have to be removed, as described in the next Section and a suitable puller used which will exert pressure on the end of the steering shaft.

6 When the wheel is released, remove the securing nut completely and observe the alignment marks under the nut. Withdraw the steering wheel.
7 Installation is a reversal of removal but make sure that the roadwheels are in the straight-ahead position, that the wheel to shaft alignment marks are opposite each other and then tighten the securing nut to the specified torque wrench setting.

17 Steering column - removal and installation

1 Set the roadwheels in the straight-ahead position.
2 Disconnect the lead from the battery negative terminal.
3 Working within the engine compartment, remove the pinch bolt from the steering shaft flexible coupling.
4 Remove the steering wheel, as described in the preceding Section.
5 Remove the securing screws and withdraw the steering column shrouds (Fig. 11.18).
6 Lift the direction indicator cancelling cam and its spring from the shaft, noting their relative positions.
7 Disconnect the direction indicator switch and ignition switch lead plugs and then withdraw the direction indicator switch from the top of the steering column after removing the two retaining screws.
8 Withdraw the column assembly into the car interior.
9 Installation is a reversal of removal but tighten all bolts and nuts to the specified torque.
10 Correct alignment of the segmented type rubber steering column coupling is very important. On models produced from 1973 onwards, one of the steering column bearings is spring loaded and this permits a slight movement of the steering shaft when the steering wheel is pulled towards the driver. This condition is normal but if the steering wheel can be pushed in a downward direction by a small amount then this condition is incorrect and will almost certainly be caused by misalignment of the steering column flexible coupling.

18 Steering column - dismantling and reassembly

1 If the column must be dismantled due to wear in the bearings, first check that individual components are obtainable.
2 Remove the assembly, as described in the preceding Section.
3 Extract the lower bearing circlip and retaining washer and pull the lower bearing from the steering shaft.
4 Withdraw the shaft upwards from the column tube making sure that the steering column lock is in the released (ignition key

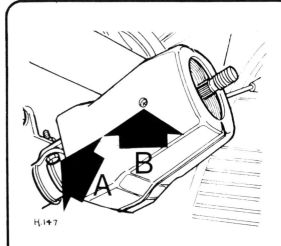 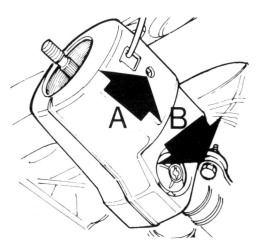

Fig. 11.18. Steering column shroud screws (A) and steering column support bolts (B) (early type cars) (Sec. 17)

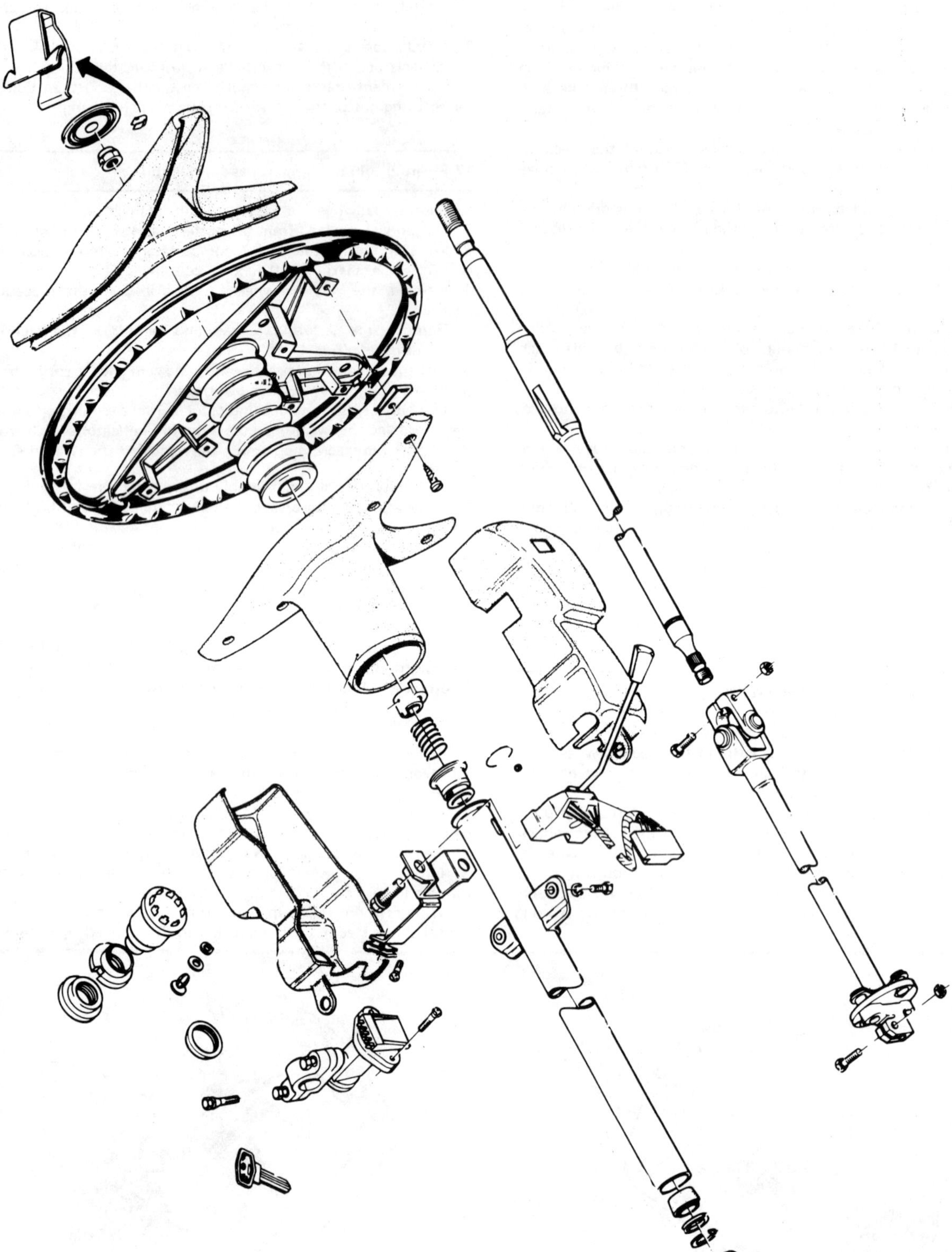

Fig. 11.19. Exploded view of steering column assembly (late type steering column shroud and steering wheel spoke cover) (Sec. 18)

turned on) position.

5 The upper bearing can now be removed from the column tube.

6 Reassembly is a reversal of dismantling but install the new upper bearing so that it is flush with the end of the column. Use a new circlip at the bottom of the column.

19 Steering angles and front wheel alignment

1 Accurate front wheel alignment is essential for good steering and tyre wear. Before considering the steering angle, check that the tyres are correctly inflated, that the front wheels are not buckled, the hub bearings are not worn or incorrectly adjusted and that the steering linkage is in good order, without slackness or wear at the joints.

2 Wheel alignment consists of four factors:

Camber, which is the angle at which the front wheels are set from the vertical when viewed from the front of the car. Positive camber is the amount (in degrees) that the wheels are tilted outwards at the top from the vertical.

Castor, is the angle between the steering axis and a vertical line when viewed from each side of the car. Positive castor is when the steering axis is inclined rearward.

Steering axis inclination is the angle, when viewed from the front of the car, between the vertical and an imaginary line drawn between the upper and lower suspension strut pivots.

Toe-in is the amount by which the distance between the *front* inside edges of the roadwheels (measured at hub height) is less than the distance measured between the *rear* inside edges.

3 The angles for Camber, Castor and Steering axis are set in production and are not adjustable.

4 Front wheel alignment (toe-in) checks are best carried out with modern setting equipment but a reasonably accurate alternative is by means of the following procedure.

5 Place the car on level ground with the wheels in the straight-ahead position.

6 Obtain or make a toe-in gauge. One may easily be made from a length of rod or tubing, cranked to clear the sump or bell housing and having a setscrew and locknut at one end.

7 With the gauge, measure the distance between the two inner wheel rims at hub height at the front of the wheel.

8 Rotate the roadwheel through 180° (half a turn) by pushing or pulling the car and then measure the distance again at hub height between the inner wheel rims at the rear of the roadwheel. This measurement should either be the same as the one just taken or greater by not more than ¼ inch (6.4 mm).

9 Where the toe-in is found to be incorrect slacken the locknuts on each trackrod, also the flexible bellows clips and rotate each trackrod by an equal amount until the correct toe-in is obtained.

Tighten the trackrod-end locknuts while the ball joints are held in the centre of their arcs of travel. It is imperative that the lengths of the trackrods are always equal otherwise the wheel angles on turns will be incorrect. If new components have been fitted, set the roadwheels in the straight-ahead position and also centralise the steering wheel. Now adjust the lengths of the trackrods by turning them so that the trackrod end ball joint studs will drop easily into the eyes of the steering arms. Measure the distances between the centres of the ball joints and the grooves on the inner ends of the trackrods and adjust if necessary so that they are equal. This is an initial setting only and precise adjustment must be carried out as described in earlier paragraphs of this Section.

20 Wheels and tyres

1 Check the tyre pressures weekly.

2 Frequently inspect the tyre walls and treads for damage and pick out any large stones which have become trapped in the tread pattern.

3 If the wheels and tyres have been balanced on the car then they should not be moved to a different axle position. If they have been balanced off the car then, in the interests of extending tread life, they can be moved between front and rear on the same side of the car and the spare incorporated in the rotational pattern.

4 Never mix tyres of different construction or very dissimilar tread pattern.

5 Always keep the roadwheels tightened to the specified torque wrench setting and if the bolt holes become elongated or flattened, renew the wheel.

6 Occasionally, clean the inner faces of the roadwheels and if there is any sign of rust, paint them with metal preservative paint.

7 Before removing a roadwheel which has been balanced on the car, always mark one wheel stud and bolt hole so that the roadwheel may be refitted in the same relative position to maintain the balance.

21 Modifications to later models

1 On very late model cars, the front suspension strut lower swivels are fitted with grease plugs.

2 Every 36000 miles (58000 km) these plugs should be unscrewed and removed and a nipple substituted. Pump grease into the swivel until the rubber dust excluder can be felt to expand.

3 Remove the nipple and refit the plug.

See next page for 'Fault diagnosis - suspension and steering'

22 Fault diagnosis - suspension and steering

Before diagnosing faults from the following chart, check that any irregularities are not caused by:
1   Binding brakes.
2   Incorrect 'mix' of radial and crossply tyres.
3   Incorrect tyre pressures.
4   Misalignment of the body frame.

Symptom	Reason(s)
Steering wheel can be moved considerably before any sign of movement of the roadwheels is apparent	Wear in the steering linkage, gear and column coupling.
Vehicle difficult to steer in a consistent straight line - wandering	As above. Wheel alignment incorrect (indicated by excessive or uneven tyre wear). Front wheel hub bearings loose or worn. Worn ball joints.
Steering stiff and heavy	Incorrect wheel alignment (indicated by excessive or uneven tyre wear). Excessive wear or seizure in one or more of the joints in the steering linkage or suspension. Excessive wear in the steering gear unit.
Wheel wobble and vibration	Roadwheels out of balance. Roadwheels buckled. Wheel alignment incorrect. Wear in the steering linkage, suspension ball joints or track control arm pivot. Broken front spring.
Excessive pitching and rolling on corners and during braking	Defective shock absorber and/or broken spring.
Knocking noise from front suspension top mounts	Fit modified top mount.
Excessive endplay in steering shaft	Misaligned steering coupling.

Chapter 12 Bodywork and fittings

Contents

1 General description

The combined body and underframe is of all steel welded construction. This makes a very strong and torsionally rigid shell.

The Capri is only available in two door form. The door hinges are welded to the doors and securely bolted to the body. To prevent the doors opening too wide and causing damage check straps are fitted.

The Capri uses an through-flow ventilation system. Air being drawn in through a grille on the scuttle can either be heated or pass straight into the car. Used air passes out through a grille at the base of the rear window.

All models are fitted with bucket type front seats with seat belts as standard. The rear seats are also fitted with anchor points for belts which can be obtained as an optional extra.

An air conditioning system can be optionally fitted.

2 Maintenance - bodywork and underframe

1 The condition of your car's bodywork is of considerable importance as it is on this that the secondhand value of the car will mainly depend. It is very much more difficult to repair neglected bodywork than to renew mechanical assemblies. The hidden portions of the body, such as the wheels arches and the underframe and the engine compartment are equally important though obviously not requiring such frequent attention as the immediately visible paintwork.

2 Once a year or every 12,000 miles (19,000 km) it is a sound scheme to visit your local main agent and have the underside of the body steam cleaned. This will take about 1½ hours. All traces of dirt and oil will be removed and the underside can then be inspected carefully for rust, damaged hydraulic pipes, frayed electrical wiring and similar maladies.

3 At the same time the engine compartment should be cleaned in the same manner. If steam cleaning facilities are not available then brush a water soluble cleanser over the whole engine and engine compartment with a stiff paintbrush, working it well in where there is an accumulation of oil and dirt. Do not paint the ignition system but protect it with oily rags when the cleanser is washed off. As the cleanser is washed away it will take with it all traces of oil and dirt, leaving the engine looking clean and bright.

4 The wheel arches should be given particular attention as undersealing can easily come away here and stones and dirt thrown up from the road wheels can soon cause the paint to chip and flake and so allow rust to set it. If rust is found, clean down to the bare metal with wet and dry paper, paint on an anti-corrosive coating and renew the paintwork and undercoating.

5 The bodywork should be washed once a week or when dirty. Thoroughly wet the car to soften the dirt and then wash the car down with a soft sponge and plenty of clean water. If the surplus dirt is not washed off very gently, in time it will wear the paint down as surely as wet and dry paper. It is best to use a hose if this is available. Give the car a final wash down and then dry with a soft chamois leather to prevent the formation of spots.

6 Spots of tar and grease thrown up from the road can be removed with a rag dampened with petrol.

7 Once every six months, or every three months, if wished, give the bodywork and chromium trim a thoroughly good wax polish. If a chromium cleaner is used to remove rust on any of the car's plated parts remember that the cleaner also removes part of the chromium so use sparingly.

3 Maintenance - upholstery and carpets

1 Remove the carpets and thoroughly vacuum clean the interior of the car every three months or more frequently if necessary.

2 Beat out the carpets and vacuum clean them if they are very dirty. If the heading or upholstery is soiled apply an upholstery cleaner with a damp sponge and wipe off with a clean dry cloth.

4 Maintenance - PVC external roof covering

Under no circumstances try to clean any external PVC roof

covering with detergents, caustic soaps or spirit cleaners. Plain soap and water is all that is required with a soft brush to clean dirt that may be ingrained. Wash the covering as frequently as the rest of the car.

---

5 Minor body damage - repair

The photo sequence on pages 206 and 207 illustrate the operations detailed in the following sub-Sections.

Repair of minor scratches in the car's bodywork

If the scratch is very superficial, and does not penetrate to the metal of the bodywork, repair is very simple. Lightly rub the area of the scratch with a paintwork renovator (eg; T-Cut), or a very fine cutting paste, to remove loose paint from the scratch and to clear the surrounding bodywork of wax polish. Rinse the area with clean water.

Apply touch-up paint to the scratch using a thin paint brush, continue to apply thin layers of paint until the surface of the paint in the scratch is level with the surrounding paintwork. Allow the new paint at least two weeks to harden; then blend it into the surrounding paintwork by rubbing the paintwork in the scratch area with a paintwork renovator (eg; T-Cut), or a very fine cutting paste. Finally apply wax polish.

An alternative to painting over the scratch is to use Holts "Scratch-Patch". Use the same preparation for the affected area; then simply pick a patch of a suitable size to cover the scratch completely. Hold the patch against the scratch and burnish its backing paper; the patch will adhere to the paintwork, freeing itself from the backing paper at the same time. Polish the affected area to blend the patch into the surrounding paintwork. Where the scratch has penetrated right through to the metal of the bodywork, causing the metal to rust, a different repair technique is required. Remove any loose rust from the bottom of the scratch with a penknife, then apply rust inhibiting paint (eg: Kurust) to prevent the formation of rust in the future. Using a rubber nylon applicator fill the scratch with bodystopper paste. If required, this paste can be mixed with cellulose thinners to provide a very thin paste which is ideal for filling narrow scratches. Before the stopper-paste in the scratch hardens, wrap a piece of smooth cotton rag around the top of a finger. Dip the finger in cellulose thinners and then quickly sweep it across the surface of the stopper-paste in the scratch; this will ensure that the surface of the stopper-paste is slightly hollowed. The scratch can now be painted over as described earlier in this Section.

Repair of dents in the car's bodywork

When deep denting of the car's bodywork has taken place, the first task is to pull the dent out, until the affected bodywork almost attains its original shape. There is little point in trying to restore the original shape completely, as the metal in the damaged area will have stretched on impact and cannot be re-shaped fully to its original contour. It is better to bring the level of the dent up to a point which is about 1/8 inch (3 mm) below the level of the surrounding bodywork. In cases where the dent is very shallow anyway, it is not worth trying to pull it out at all.

If the underside of the dent is accessible, it can be hammered out gently from behind, using a mallet with a wooden or plastic head. Whilst doing this, hold a suitable block of wood firmly against the impact from the hammer blows and thus prevent a large area of bodywork from being 'belled-out'.

Should the dent be in a section of the bodywork which has a double skin or some other factor making it inaccessible from behind, a different technique is called for. Drill several small holes through the metal inside the dent area - particularly in the deeper sections. Then screw long self-tapping screws into the holes just sufficiently for them to gain a good purchase in the metal. Now the dent can be pulled out by pulling on the protruding heads of the screws with a pair of pliers.

The next stage of the repair is the removal of the paint from the damaged area, and from an inch or so of the surrounding 'sound' bodywork. This is accomplished most easily by using a wire brush or abrasive pad on a power drill, although it can be done just as effectively by hand using sheets of abrasive paper. To complete the preparations for filling, score the surface of the bare metal with a screwdriver or the tang of a file, or alternatively, drill small holes in the affected area. This will provide a really good 'key' for filler paste.

To complete the repair see the Section on filling and respraying.

Repair of rust holes or gashes in the car's bodywork

Remove all paint from the affected area and from an inch or so of the surrounding 'sound' bodywork, using an abrasive pad or a wire brush on a power drill. If these are not available a few sheets of abrasive paper will do the job just as effectively. With the paint removed you will be able to gauge the severity of the corrosion and therefore decide whether to replace the whole panel (if this is possible) or to repair the affected area. Replacement body panels are not as expensive as most people think and it is often quicker and more satisfactory to fit a new panel then to attempt to repair large areas of corrosion.

Remove all fittings from the affected area except those which will act as a guide to the original shape of the damaged bodywork (eg; headlamp shells etc.,). Then, using tin snips or a hacksaw blade, remove all loose metal and any other metal badly affected by corrosion. Hammer the edges of the hole inwards in order to create a slight depression for the filler paste.

Wire brush the affected area to remove the powdery rust from the surface of the remaining metal. Paint the affected area with rust inhibiting paint (eg; Kurust); if the back of the rusted area is accessible treat this also.

Before filling can take place it will be necessary to block the hole in some way. This can be achieved by the use of one of the following materials: Zinc gauze, Aluminium tape or Polyurethane foam.

Zinc gauge is probably the best material to use for a large hole. Cut a piece to the approximate size and shape of the hole to be filled, then position it in the hole so that its edges are below the level of the surrounding bodywork. It can be retained in position by several blobs of filler paste around its periphery.

Aluminium tape should be used for small or very narrow holes. Pull a piece off the roll and trim it to the approximate size and shape required, then pull off the backing paper (if used) and stick the tape over the hole; it can be overlapped if the thickness of one piece is insufficient. Burnish down the edges of the tape with the handle of a screwdriver or similar, to ensure that the tape is securely attached to the metal underneath.

Polyurethane foam is best used where the hole is situated in a section of bodywork of complex shape, backed by a small box section (eg; where the sill panel meets the rear wheel arch - most cars). The unusual mixing procedure for this foam is as follows: Put equal amounts of fluid from each of the two cans provided in the kit, into one container. Stir until the mixture begins to thicken, then quickly pour this mixture into the hole, and hold a piece of cardboard over the larger apertures. Almost immediately the polyurethane will begin to expand, gushing frantically out of any small holes left unblocked. When the foam hardens it can be cut back to just below the level of the surrounding bodywork with a hacksaw blade.

Bodywork repairs - filling and re-spraying

Before using this Section, see the Sections on dent, deep scratch, rust hole and gash repairs.

Many types of bodyfiller are available, but generally speaking those proprietary kits which contain a tin of filler paste and a tube of resin hardener (eg; Holts Cataloy) are best for this type of repair. A wide, flexible plastic or nylon applicator will be found invaluable for imparting a smooth and well contoured finished to the surface of the filler.

Mix up a little filler on a clean piece of card or board - use the hardener sparingly (follow the maker's instructions on the packet) otherwise the filler will set very rapidly.

Using the applicator, apply the filler paste to the prepared area; draw the applicator across the surface of the filler to achieve the correct contour and to level the filler surface. As soon as a contour that approximates to the correct one is achieved, stop working the paste - if you carry on too long the paste will become sticky and begin to 'pick-up' on the applicator. Continue to add thin layers of filler paste at twenty-minute intervals until the level of the filler is just 'proud' of the surrounding bodywork.

Once the filler has hardened, excess can be removed using a Surform plane or Dreadnought file. From then on, progressively finer grades of abrasive paper should be used, starting with a 40 grade production paper and finishing with 400 grade 'wet-and-dry' paper. Always wrap the abrasive paper around a flat rubber, cork or wooden block - otherwise the surface of the filler will not be completely flat. During the smoothing of the filler surface the 'wet-and-dry' paper should be periodically rinsed in water. This will ensure that a very smooth finish is imparted to the filler at the final stage.

At this stage the 'dent' should be surrounded by a ring of bare metal, which in turn should be encircled by the finely 'feathered' edge of the good paintwork. Rinse the repair area with clean water, until all of the dust produced by the rubbing-down operation is gone.

Spray the whole repair area with a light coat of grey primer - this will show up any imperfections in the surface of the filler. Repair these imperfections with fresh filler paste or body-stopper, and once more smooth the surface with abrasive paper. If bodystopper is used, it can be mixed with cellulose thinners to form a really thin paste which is ideal for filling small holes.

Repeat this spray and repair procedure until you are satisfied that the surface of the filler and the feathered edge of the paint-work are perfect. Clean the repair area with clean water and allow to dry fully.

The repair area is now ready for spraying. Paint spraying must be carried out in a warm, dry, windless and dust free atmosphere. This condition can be created artificially if you have access to a large indoor working area, but if you are forced to work in the open, you will have to pick your day very carefully. If you are working indoors, dousing the floor in the work area with water will 'lay' the dust which would otherwise be in the atmosphere. If the repair area is confined to one body panel, mask off the surrounding panels; this will help to minimise the effects of a slight mis-match in paint colours. Bodywork fittings (eg; chrome strips, door handles etc) will also need to be masked off. Use genuine masking tape and several thicknesses of newspaper for the masking operation.

Before commencing to spray, agitate the aerosol can thoroughly, then spray a test area (an old tin, or similar) until the technique is mastered. Cover the repair area with a thick coat of primer; the thickness should be built up using several thin layers of paint rather than one thick one. Using 400 grade 'wet-and-dry' paper, rub down the surface of the primer until it is really smooth. While doing this, the work area should be thoroughly doused with water, and the 'wet-and-dry' paper periodically rinsed in water. Allow to dry before spraying on more paint.

Spray on the top coat, again building up the thickness by using several thin layers of paint. Start spraying in the centre of

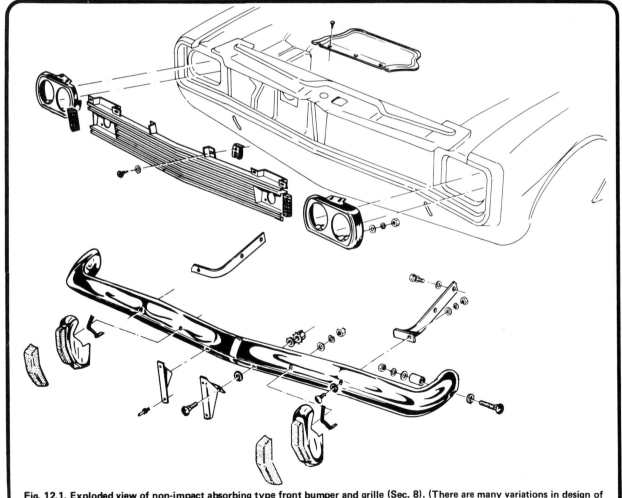

Fig. 12.1. Exploded view of non-impact absorbing type front bumper and grille (Sec. 8). (There are many variations in design of components according to car model and date of production)

the repair area and then, using a circular motion, work outwards until the whole repair area and about 2 inches of the surrounding original paintwork is covered. Remove all masking material 10 to 15 minutes after spraying on the final coat of paint.

Allow the new paint at least 2 weeks to harden fully; then, using a paintwork renovator (eg; T-Cut) or a very fine cutting paste, blend the edges of the new paint into the existing paintwork. Finally, apply wax polish.

6 Major body damage - repair

1 Because the body is built on the unitary principle and is integral with the underframe, major damage must be repaired by competent mechanics with the necessary welding and hydraulic straightening equipment.
2 If the damage has been serious it is vital that the body is checked for correct alignment as otherwise the handling of the car will suffer and many other faults such as excessive tyre wear and wear in the transmission and steering may occur. A special alignment jig is available to Ford dealers and to ensure that all is correct a repaired car should always be checked on this jig.

7 Maintenance - locks and hinges

Once every six months or 6,000 miles (10,000 km) the door, bonnet and boot hinges should be oiled with a few drops of engine oil. The door striker plate can be given a thin smear of grease to reduce wear and ensure free movement.

8 Bumpers (non-impact absorbing type) - removal and refitting

1 The bumpers are removable after unscrewing the end bolts which are accessible under the front wings.
2 Unscrew the bolts which secure the bumper bar to the support brackets and lift the bumper away from the car.
3 The overriders may be unbolted from the bumper either before or after removing the bumper bar.
4 Refitting is a reversal of removal but adjust the setting of the bumper bar before fully tightening the securing bolts.
5 The rear licence plate lamp leads must be disconnected before the rear bumper is removed.

9 Bumpers (impact absorbing type) - removal and refitting

1 On late model cars built for operation in North America, special moulded urethane impact absorbing bumpers are fitted to front and rear.
2 The bumpers have a full length steel reinforcement bar which itself is rigidly mounted to the body by means of support arms.
3 Removal and dismantling of these bumpers is simply a matter of unscrewing the securing bolts.

10 Windscreen - removal and refitting

1 If you are unfortunate enough to have a windscreen shatter, or should you wish to renew your present windscreen, fitting a replacement is one of the few jobs which the average owner is advised to leave to a professional. For the owner who wished to attempt the job himself however, the following instructions are given.
2 Cover the bonnet with a blanket or cloth to prevent accidental damage and remove the windscreen wiper blades and arms as detailed in Chapter 10.
3 Put on a pair of lightweight shoes and get into one of the front seats. With a piece of soft cloth between the soles of your shoes and the windscreen glass, place both feet in one top corner of the windscreen and push firmly (Fig. 12.2).
4 When the weatherstrip has freed itself from the body flange in that area repeat the process at frequent intervals along the top edge of the windscreen, until from outside the car the glass and weatherstrip can be removed together.
5 If you are having to replace your windscreen due to a shattered screen, remove all traces of sealing compound and broken glass from the weatherstrip and body flange.
6 Move the heater controls to 'HOT' and 'DEFROST' and switch on the blower motor. This will remove any glass fragments in the ducting. Be careful about flying glass so take necessary precautions.
7 Gently prise out the clip which covers the joint of the chromium finisher strip and pull the finisher out of the weatherstrip. Then remove the weatherstrip from the glass or if it is still on the car, as in the case of a shattered screen, remove it from the body flange.
8 To fit a new windscreen start by fitting the weatherstrip around the new windscreen glass.
9 Apply a suitable sealer to the weatherstrip to body groove. In this groove then fit a fine but strong piece of cord right the way round the groove allowing an overlap of about six inches at the joint.
10 From outside the car place the windscreen in its correct position making sure that the loose end of the cord is inside the car.
11 With an assistance pressing firmly on the outside of the windscreen get into the car and slowly pull out the cord thus drawing the weatherstrip over the body flange (Fig. 12.3).

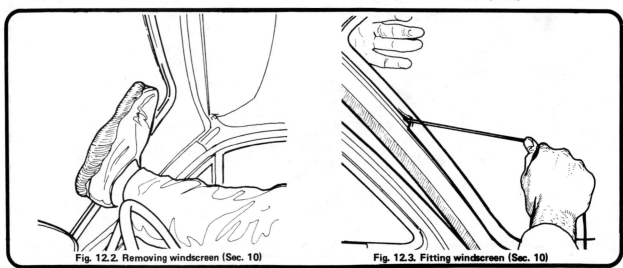

Fig. 12.2. Removing windscreen (Sec. 10)   Fig. 12.3. Fitting windscreen (Sec. 10)

12 Apply a further layer of sealer to the underside of rubber to glass groove from outside the car.

13 Replace the chromium finisher strip into its groove in the weatherstrip and replace the clip which covers its joint.

14 Carefully clean off any surplus sealer from the windscreen glass before it has a chance to harden and then replace the windscreen wiper arms and blades.

11 Door rattles - tracing and rectification

1 The most common cause of door rattles is a misaligned loose, or worn striker plate, however other causes may be:
    a) *Loose door or window winder handles.*
    b) *Loose, or misaligned door lock components.*
    c) *Loose or worn remote control mechanism.*

2 It is quite possible for door rattles to be the result of a combination of the above faults so a careful examination should be made to determine the exact cause of the rattle.

3 If striker plate wear or misalignment is the cause of the rattle the plate should be renewed or adjusted as necessary. The procedures for these tasks are detailed in Section 12.

4 Should the window winder handle rattle, this can be easily rectified by inserting a rubber washer between the escutcheon and door trim panel.

5 If the rattle is found to be emanating from the door lock it will in all probability mean that the lock is worn and therefore

should be replaced with a new unit as described in Section 14.

6 Lastly, if it is worn hinge pins causing the rattle they should be renewed. This is not a d-i-y job as a special tool is required for their removal and replacement

12 Door striker plate - removal, refitting and adjustment

1 Striker plate removal and adjustment are not really d-i-y tasks as a special tool is required to turn the plate retaining screws. However, if the tool can be hired or borrowed from your local Ford dealers, proceed as follows:

2 If it is wished to renew a worn striker plate mark its position on the door pillar with a pencil. This will enable the new plate to be fitted in exactly the same position.

3 To remove the plate, simply undo the four special screws which hold the plate and anti-slip shim in position. Replacement is equally straightforward.

4 To adjust the striker plate slacken the retaining screws until the plate can just be moved, gently close the door, with the outside push button depressed, to the fully closed position. Release the button.

5 Move the door in and out until it is flush with the surrounding bodywork. Then fully depress the button and gently open the door.

6 Check that the striker plate is vertical and tighten down the four special screws. Adjustment is now completed.

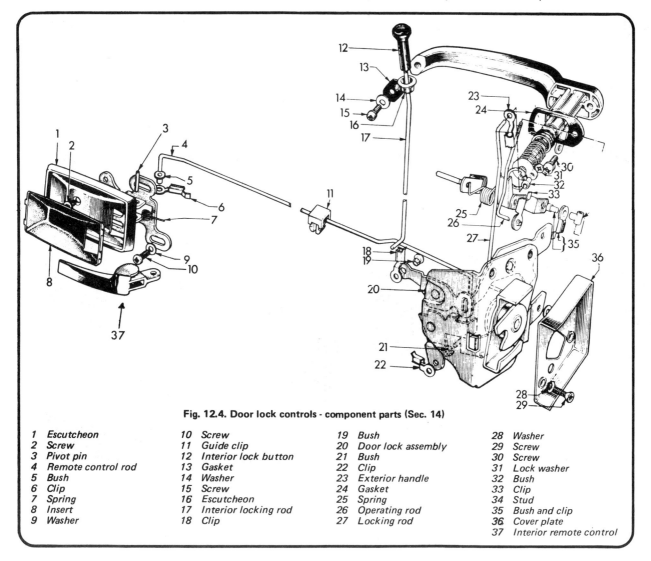

Fig. 12.4. Door lock controls - component parts (Sec. 14)

1	Escutcheon	10	Screw	19	Bush	28	Washer
2	Screw	11	Guide clip	20	Door lock assembly	29	Screw
3	Pivot pin	12	Interior lock button	21	Bush	30	Screw
4	Remote control rod	13	Gasket	22	Clip	31	Lock washer
5	Bush	14	Washer	23	Exterior handle	32	Bush
6	Clip	15	Screw	24	Gasket	33	Clip
7	Spring	16	Escutcheon	25	Spring	34	Stud
8	Insert	17	Interior locking rod	26	Operating rod	35	Bush and clip
9	Washer	18	Clip	27	Locking rod	36	Cover plate
						37	Interior remote control

This sequence of photographs deals with the repair of the dent and paintwork damage shown in this photo. The procedure will be similar for the repair of a hole. It should be noted that the procedures given here are simplified — more explicit instructions will be found in the text

In the case of a dent the first job — after removing surrounding trim — is to hammer out the dent where access is possible. This will minimise filling. Here, the large dent having been hammered out, the damaged area is being made slightly concave

Now all paint must be removed from the damaged area, by rubbing with coarse abrasive paper. Alternatively, a wire brush or abrasive pad can be used in a power drill. Where the repair area meets good paintwork, the edge of the paintwork should be 'feathered', using a finer grade of abrasive paper

In the case of a hole caused by rusting, all damaged sheet-metal should be cut away before proceeding to this stage. Here, the damaged area is being treated with rust remover and inhibitor before being filled

Mix the body filler according to its manufacturer's instructions. In the case of corrosion damage, it will be necessary to block off any large holes before filling — this can be done with aluminium or plastic mesh, or aluminium tape. Make sure the area is absolutely clean before ...

... applying the filler. Filler should be applied with a flexible applicator, as shown, for best results; the wooden spatula being used for confined areas. Apply thin layers of filler at 20-minute intervals, until the surface of the filler is slightly proud of the surrounding bodywork

Initial shaping can be done with a Surform plane or Dreadnought file. Then, using progressively finer grades of wet-and-dry paper, wrapped around a sanding block, and copious amounts of clean water, rub down the filler until really smooth and flat. Again, feather the edges of adjoining paintwork

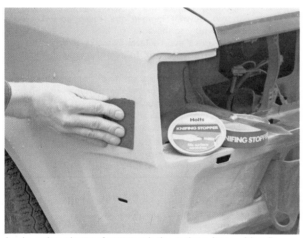

Again, using plenty of water, rub down the primer with a fine grade wet-and-dry paper (400 grade is probably best) until it is really smooth and well blended into the surrounding paintwork. Any remaining imperfections can now be filled by carefully applied knifing stopper paste

The top coat can now be applied. When working out of doors, pick a dry, warm and wind-free day. Ensure surrounding areas are protected from over-spray. Agitate the aerosol thoroughly, then spray the centre of the repair area, working outwards with a circular motion. Apply the paint as several thin coats

The whole repair area can now be sprayed or brush-painted with primer. If spraying, ensure adjoining areas are protected from over-spray. Note that at least one inch of the surrounding sound paintwork should be coated with primer. Primer has a 'thick' consistency, so will find small imperfections

When the stopper has hardened, rub down the repair area again before applying the final coat of primer. Before rubbing down this last coat of primer, ensure the repair area is blemish-free — use more stopper if necessary. To ensure that the surface of the primer is really smooth use some finishing compound

After a period of about two weeks, which the paint needs to harden fully, the surface of the repaired area can be 'cut' with a mild cutting compound prior to wax polishing. When carrying out bodywork repairs, remember that the quality of the finished job is proportional to the time and effort expended

13 Door interior trim - removal and refitting

1 Carefully prise the black plastic trim from its recess in the window winder handle. This will expose the handle retaining screws. Remove the screw, handle and escutcheon.
2 Prise the black plastic trim out of the recess in the escutcheon of the interior lock release handle. Unscrew the screw securing the escutcheon in position. Remove the escutcheon.
3 Unscrew and remove the black plastic knob on the interior door lock. Carefully prise the escutcheon beneath it out of the trim.
4 Remove the two screws securing the lower part of the armrest. Move the armrest towards the top front corner of the door. This will release the retaining lug. Remove the armrest complete.
5 Insert a thin strip of metal with all the sharp edges removed (a six inch steel rule is ideal) between the door and the recessed trim panel. This will release one or two of the panel retaining clips without damaging the trim. The panel can now be gently eased off by hand. Removal is now complete.
6 Replacement is generally a reversal of the removal procedure. **Note:** When replacing the panel ensure that each of the panel retaining clips is firmly located in its hole by sharply striking the panel in the approximate area of each clip with the palm of the hand. This will eliminate the possibility of the trim rattling.

14 Door lock assembly - removal and refitting

1 Remove the door trim panel, as described in Section 13.
2 Temporarily replace the window winder handle and wind the window up. Remove the polythene sheet covering the interior of the door by cutting through the adhesive around its periphery with a sharp blade.
3 Disconnect the remote control rod by freeing it from the clip at the remote handle end.
4 Disconnect the push button rod, exterior operating rod and locking rod from the lock by releasing their clips.
5 Unscrew and remove the two screws securing the window channel.
6 Remove the three screws securing the lock to the door. The lock can now be withdrawn. Remove the four rod connecting clips from the lock. Removal is now complete.
7 *Replacement:* Replace the four rod connecting clips on the lock.
8 Reposition the lock assembly in the door recess and secure it with the three screws. Replace the two window channel retaining screws.
9 Reconnect all operating rods, and check the operation of the lock.
10 Replace the polythene sheet over the door aperture, using a suitable adhesive, followed by the door trim panel and fitments.

15 Door lock interior remote control handle - removal and refitting

1 Remove the door trim panel, as described in Section 13 followed by the polythene sheet covering the door apertures.
2 Disconnect the spring clip securing the remote control operating rod to the lock mechanism.
3 Remove the three screws securing the remote control assembly to the door inner panel. Push out the anti-rattle clip around the remote control operating rod and remove the remote control assembly through the door access hole. Removal is now complete (Fig. 12.5).
4 Replacement is a straightforward reversal of the removal procedure.

16 Window regulator - removal and refitting

1 Remove the door trim panel, as described in Section 13. Carefully peel off the polythene sheet over the door apertures.
2 Temporarily replace the window regulator handle and wind the window down. Remove the seven screws securing the regulator assembly to the door.
3 Carefully draw the regulator assembly towards the rear of the door, this will disengage it from the runner in the base of the window glass.
4 Push the window glass up and support it in the raised position with a wedge. The regulator assembly can now be withdrawn through the access hole in the door (Fig. 12.6).
5 Refitting the regulator is the reverse sequence to removal. Lubricate all moving parts.

17 Door glass - removal and refitting

1 First remove the door trim panel and window regulator assembly, as described in Sections 13 and 16 respectively.
2 The window glass can now be rotated through 90° and removed through the top of the door (Fig. 12.8).
3 Replacement is a straightforward reversal of the removal procedure.

18 Door glass weatherstrip - renewal

1 Wind the window down to its fullest extent. Carefully prise the weatherstrip out of the groove in the door outer bright metal finish moulding.
2 *Replacement:* Correctly position the weatherstrip over its groove. With the thumbs, carefully press the strip fully into the groove.
3 Wind the window up and check that the weatherstrip is

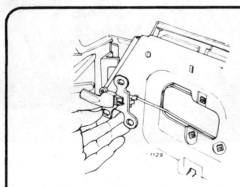

Fig. 12.5. Removal of remote control handle from door frame (Sec. 15)

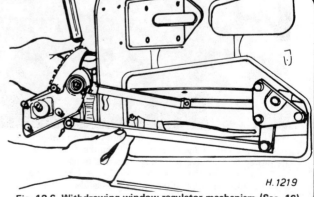

H.1219

Fig. 12.6. Withdrawing window regulator mechanism (Sec. 16)

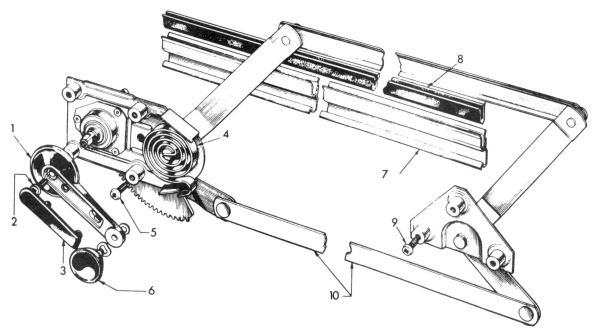

Fig. 12.7. Window regulator assembly (Sec. 16)

1	Handle	4	Spring
2	Retaining screw	5	Screw
3	Insert	6	Knob

7	Channel	10	Regulator
8	Sealing strip		assembly
9	Screw		

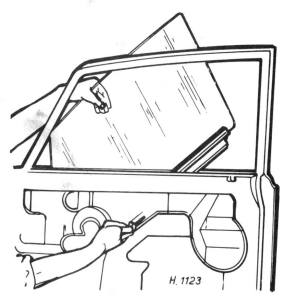

Fig. 12.8. Removal of door window glass (Sec. 17)

correctly fitted.

19 Bonnet - removal and refitting

1   Open the bonnet lid and prop it in the open position with its stay.
2   Using a suitable sharp implement, scribe a line around the exterior of the hinges on the underside of the bonnet. Unscrew and remove the two nuts and washers on each side, followed by the bolt plates. With the help of an assistant the bonnet can now be lifted off, after releasing the stay.

3   Replacement is a reversal of the removal procedure. However, before finally tightening the nuts which secure the bonnet ensure that the hinges are correctly aligned with the scribed lines. This will ensure correct bonnet/body alignment.

20 Luggage boot lid - removal and refitting

1   Open the boot lid to its fullest extent. Using a suitable implement scribe a line around the exterior of the hinges on the underside of the lid.
2   Remove the two bolts and washers on each side securing the boot lid to its hinges. With assistance the boot lid can now be lifted off.
3   Replacement is a reversal of the removal procedure. However, before fully tightening the boot lid securing bolts ensure that the hinges are aligned with the scribed marks in the lid. This will ensure correct boot lid/body alignment.
4   Should it be necessary to remove the boot lid counter-balancing torsion rods, use a large adjustable wrench to disengage the cranked end of the rod from its retaining bracket (Fig. 12.12).
5   Now disconnect the double cranked end from the hinge and withdraw the torsion rod complete.
6   Repeat these operations to remove the opposite rod.
7   Installation is a reversal of removal.

21 Front seat - removal and installation

1   Undo and remove the two bolts and spring washers that secure the front ends of the seat mounting brackets to the box member on the front panel.
2   Release the seat locking catch and tip the seat forward. Undo and remove the two bolts and washers that secure the rear ends of the seats mounting brackets to the floor panel.
3   Carefully lift away the seat and mounting brackets.
4   Refitting the front seat is the reverse sequence to removal. Lubricate all moving parts to ensure ease of operation.

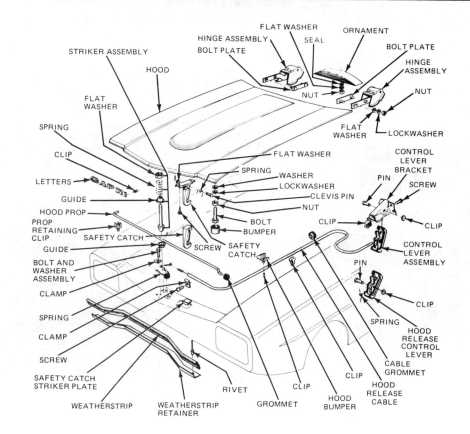

FLAT WASHER
HINGE ASSEMBLY
SEAL
ORNAMENT
BOLT PLATE
BOLT PLATE
HINGE ASSEMBLY
STRIKER ASSEMBLY
HOOD
NUT
NUT
FLAT WASHER
FLAT WASHER
LOCKWASHER
SPRING
CLIP
FLAT WASHER
CONTROL LEVER BRACKET
LETTERS
SPRING
WASHER
PIN
SCREW
GUIDE
LOCKWASHER
CLEVIS PIN
NUT
CLIP
HOOD PROP
PROP RETAINING CLIP
BOLT
BUMPER
CLIP
CONTROL LEVER ASSEMBLY
SAFETY CATCH
SCREW
SAFETY CATCH
GUIDE
PIN
BOLT AND WASHER ASSEMBLY
CLIP
CLAMP
SPRING
SPRING
HOOD RELEASE CONTROL LEVER
CLAMP
CABLE GROMMET
SCREW
CLIP
HOOD RELEASE CABLE
SAFETY CATCH STRIKER PLATE
CLIP
HOOD BUMPER
WEATHERSTRIP
WEATHERSTRIP RETAINER
RIVET
GROMMET

Fig. 12.9. Bonnet lid components (2000 cc model shown) (Sec. 20)

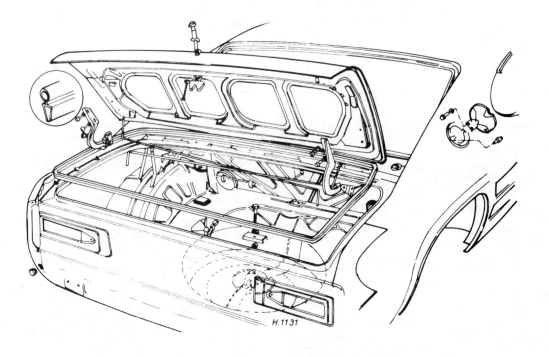

H.1131

Fig. 12.10. Luggage compartment - component parts

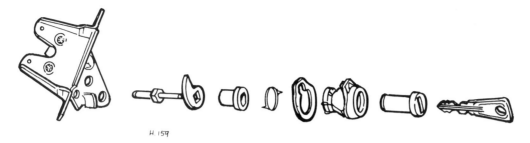

Fig. 12.11. Boot lid lock assembly (Sec. 20)

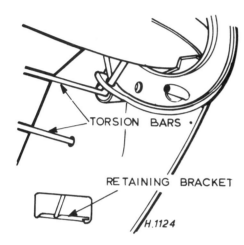

Fig. 12.12. Boot lid torsion rod attachment (Sec. 20)

Fig. 12.13. Rear seat cushion retaining screw (Sec. 22)

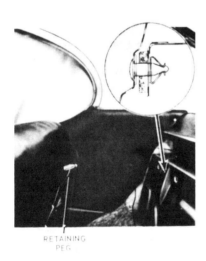

Fig. 12.14. Rear seat back retaining peg (Sec. 22)

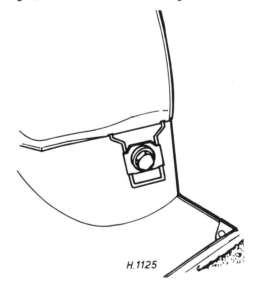

Fig. 12.15. Rear seat securing bolt (Sec. 22)

22 Rear seat - removal and installation

1 Unscrew and remove the two crosshead screws located at the lower edge of the cushion. Lift away the cushion.
2 Open the boot lid and from inside the boot compartment turn the seat pegs with a screwdriver so as to release them from the two spring clips that secure the top of the rear backrest.
3 Unscrew the two bolts located one each side at the lower corner and lift away the bracket from inside the car.
4 Refitting the rear seat backrest and cushion is the reverse sequence to removal.

23 Front parcels shelf - removal and refitting

1 Undo and remove the two screws and two nuts and washers that secure the parcel shelf in the area around the bonnet release catch handle.
2 Undo and remove the two screws and washers securing the fuse panel and carefully move to one side.
3 Undo and remove the four access trim panel attaching screws and washers and also the map light retaining clip.
4 Undo and remove the two screws that secure the map light.
5 Undo and remove the two screws securing the map light

bracket.

6   Undo and remove the nut and washer located on the right-hand side of the parcel shelf compartment.

7   Release the two plastic pins each side of the parcel shelf and then lift away the parcel shelf from inside the car.

8   Refitting the parcel shelf is the reverse sequence to removal.

___

24 Centre console - removal and refitting

1   Using a small screwdriver ease up the wood grain panel in front of the handbrake lever. Lift away the panel.

2   Undo and remove the two screws securing the forward end of the console to the floor.

3   Carefully lift the gearchange lever rubber boot up and remove the two screws at the rear end.

4   With a screwdriver ease up the rear panel and remove the two screws.

5   Carefully prise up the clock wood grain panel and disconnect the two electrical connectors and one illumination bulb.

6   Undo and remove the main securing screw at the rear end under the clock panel.

7   Slide the plastic brace below the handbrake lever forwards and remove it. The console may now be lifted away from inside the car.

8   Refitting the console is the reverse sequence to removal.

___

25 Glovebox - removal and refitting

1   Remove the steering column shroud and the ashtray.

2   Remove the direction indicator switch screws and let the

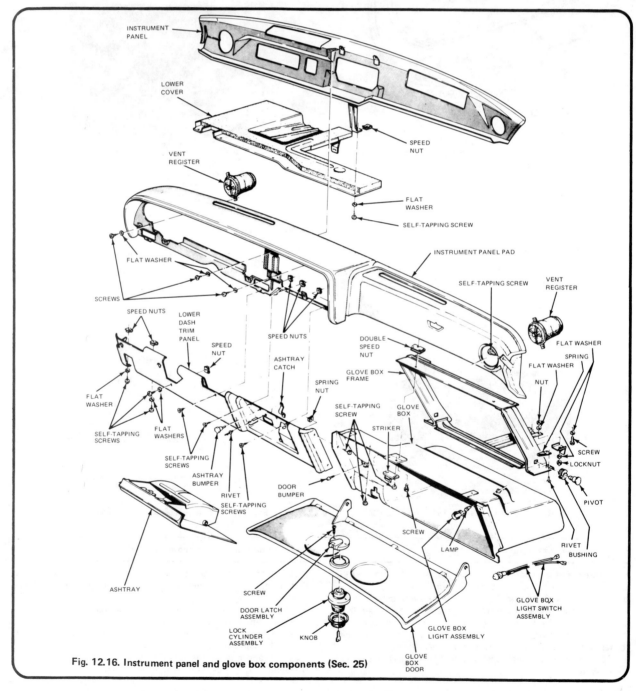

Fig. 12.16. Instrument panel and glove box components (Sec. 25)

213

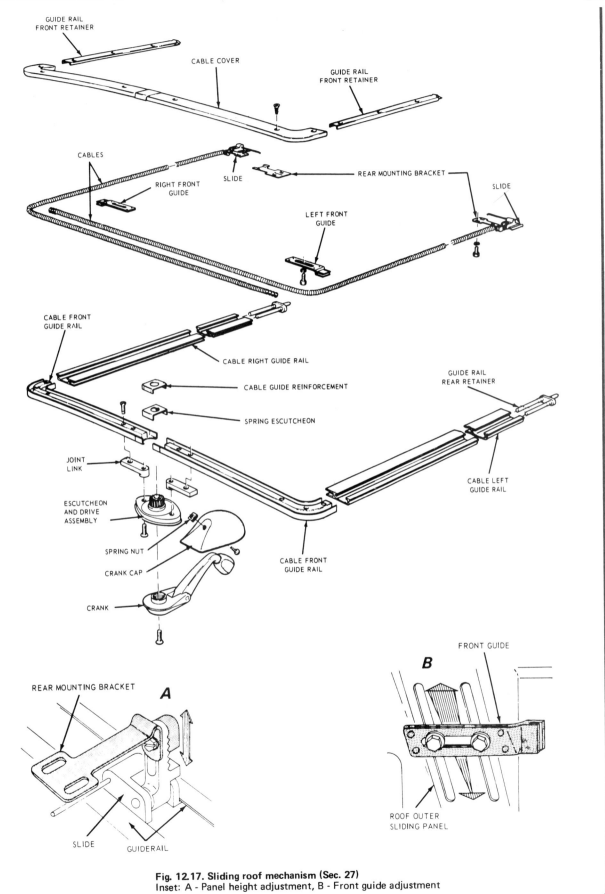

Fig. 12.17. Sliding roof mechanism (Sec. 27)
Inset: A - Panel height adjustment, B - Front guide adjustment

switch hang by its electrical leads.
3   Remove the lower dash trim panel securing screws, pull the
panel forward and downward so that the cigar lighter and clock
lead connectors can be disconnected and then remove the trim
panel completely.
4   Remove the upper and lower glovebox retaining screws and
pull the glovebox forward so that the glovebox lamp lead
connector can be disconnected.
5   Remove the glovebox.
6   Installation is a reversal of removal.

26 Instrument panel crash pad - removal and refitting

Not all the operations in this Section apply to all cars but are
dependent upon model and year of manufacture.
1   Disconnect the lead from the battery negative terminal.
2   Remove the steering column shroud and ashtray.
3   Disconnect the hazard warning switch and remove it.
4   Release the direction indicator switch and leave it hanging by
its electrical leads.
5   Remove the lower dash trim panel, as described in paragraph
3 of the preceding Section.
6   Pull off the instrument panel illumination control knob.
7   Remove the instrument cluster bezel (two screws) and disconnect the seat belt warning lamp lead.
8   Disconnect the oil pressure gauge tube.
9   Remove the instrument cluster, as described in Chapter 10,
according to type.
10 Remove the heater control panel bezel.
11 Working behind the instrument panel, push the lighting and
wiper switches from their recesses.
12 Disconnect the flexible pipes from the defroster and vent
outlets.
13 Remove the left and right-hand pillar trim.
14 The instrument panel crash pad can now be removed after
withdrawing the securing screws.

27 Sliding roof - adjustment

1   Adjustment of the optionally specified sliding roof may be
carried out by carefully following this procedure.
2   Open the sliding roof to the halfway position.
3   Unclip the sliding roof interior panel at its front edge and
then fully close the sliding roof leaving the interior panel in its
partly open position. Working inside the car, slide the interior
trim panel as far as possible to the rear.
4   With the sliding roof closed, loosen the front and rear
adjusting clamps. Adjust the front height of the roof panel by
moving the front mounting slide forwards or backwards as
necessary. Adjust the rear height of the roof panel by raising or
lowering the rear section as required. Fully tighten the two
clamps.
5   Working inside the car, with the sliding roof closed, remove
one screw and withdraw the handle.
6   Remove the two retaining screws and drop out the winder
gear mechanism (Fig. 12.18).
7   Wind back the gear until it is hard against its internal lock-
stop. Refit the mechanism and the handle.
8   Check the sliding roof for correct operation and then with
the roof panel partially open, slide the interior trim panel
forward and clip it into position.

28 Seat belt - starter interlock system

1   This sytem is installed on North American cars (not Canada)
and is designed to prevent operation of the car unless the front
seat belts have been fastened.
2   If either of the front seats is occupied and the safety belts
have not been fastened, then as the ignition key is turned to the
'II' (ignition on) position a warning lamp will flash and a buzzer

Fig. 12.18. Removing sliding roof winder gear (Sec. 27)

will sound.
3   If the warning is ignored, further turning of the key to the
start position will not actuate the starter motor.
4   In an emergency and in the event of a failure in the system,
an override switch is located under the bonnet on the left-hand
valance. One depression of the switch will permit one starting
sequence of the engine without the front seat belts being
fastened.
5   If a fault develops in the system, first check the fuse and then
the security of all leads and connections.

29 Heater - removal and installation

1   Remove the earth terminal connection from the battery.
Remove the radiator cap, open the cooling system drain taps and
allow all of the coolant to drain. **Note:** If the coolant contains
anti-freeze drain it into a suitable container, this will allow the
coolant to be re-used.
2   Next remove the seven crosshead screws securing the under-
dash cowl panel, followed by the four parcel shelf securing trim
clips, two each side. Remove the two screws on the passenger
side, and one on the driver's side, and withdraw the parcel shelf.
3   Slacken the two wire clips and disconnect the two heater
pipes from their unions on the bulkhead. This is done from
inside the engine compartment.
4   Still in the engine compartment, remove the two screws
holding the heater pipe plate and sealing gasket to the bulkhead. Detach the plate and gasket from the bulkhead.
5   Remove the ashtray and pull off the heater control knobs.
Detach the heater control quadrant from the dashboard, by removing its two securing screws. Withdraw the control quadrant
from beneath the dashboard.
6   Remove the temperature control and direction control outer
cable clips from the quadrant plate and detach the two inner
cables from the control levers.
7   Note the wiring positions and detach the wires from the
heater blower motor.
8   Working under the facia pull the air supply pipe from the
face level vent. Remove the belt rail finishing strip by unscrewing
the three securing screws. The face level vent assembly can then
be removed after undoing its three securing screws. To gain
access to one of the mounting screws at the left side of the
heater assembly the windscreen wiper motor must be removed.
Refer to Chapter 10.
9   If a seat belt warning buzzer is fitted, remove the buzzer
securing screws and let it hang by its electrical leads. If a floor
console is fitted this must next be removed.
10 Using a small screwdriver ease up the wood grain panel in
front of the handbrake lever. Lift away the panel. Undo and
remove the screws securing the forward end of the console to the
floor.

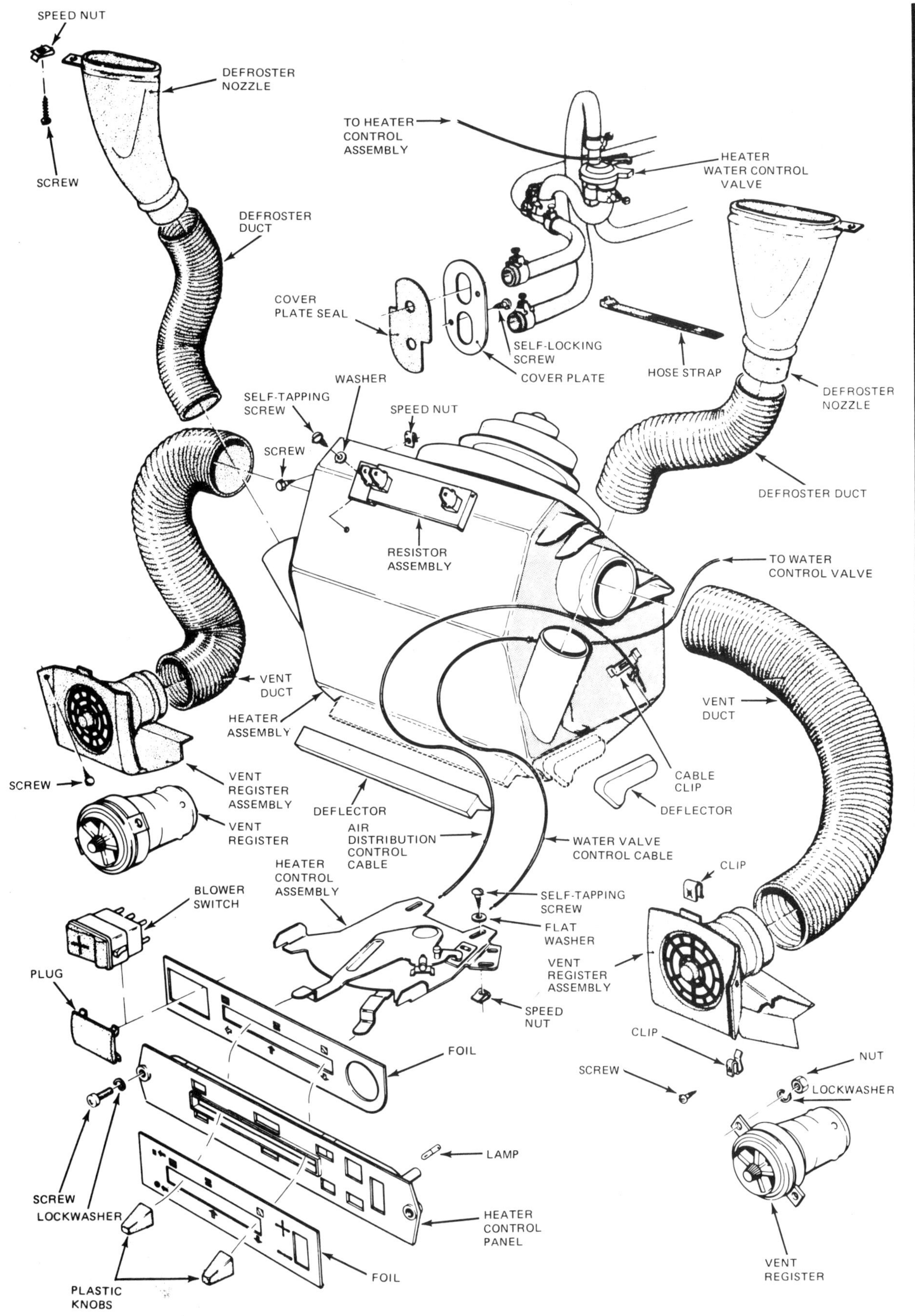

SPEED NUT

DEFROSTER NOZZLE

SCREW

DEFROSTER DUCT

TO HEATER CONTROL ASSEMBLY

HEATER WATER CONTROL VALVE

COVER PLATE SEAL

SELF-LOCKING SCREW

COVER PLATE

HOSE STRAP

DEFROSTER NOZZLE

DEFROSTER DUCT

WASHER

SELF-TAPPING SCREW

SPEED NUT

SCREW

RESISTOR ASSEMBLY

TO WATER CONTROL VALVE

VENT DUCT

HEATER ASSEMBLY

VENT DUCT

SCREW

VENT REGISTER ASSEMBLY

VENT REGISTER

DEFLECTOR

AIR DISTRIBUTION CONTROL CABLE

WATER VALVE CONTROL CABLE

CABLE CLIP

DEFLECTOR

HEATER CONTROL ASSEMBLY

BLOWER SWITCH

SELF-TAPPING SCREW

FLAT WASHER

VENT REGISTER ASSEMBLY

CLIP

PLUG

SPEED NUT

CLIP

FOIL

SCREW

NUT

LOCKWASHER

SCREW

LOCKWASHER

LAMP

HEATER CONTROL PANEL

PLASTIC KNOBS

FOIL

VENT REGISTER

Fig. 12.19. Exploded view of the heater unit (Secs. 29 and 30)

11 Carefully lift the gearchange lever rubber boot up and remove the two screws at the rear end.
12 With a screwdriver ease up the rear panel and remove the two screws.
13 Carefully prise up the clock wood grain panel and disconnect the two electrical connectors and one light bulb.
14 Undo and remove the main securing screw at the rear end under the clock panel.
15 Slide the plastic brace below the handbrake lever forwards and remove it. The console may now be lifted away from inside the car.
16 Finally remove the four retaining bolts and withdraw the heater assembly.
17 Replacement is generally a reversal of the removal procedure.
Note: when the heater assembly is reinstalled it will probably be necessary to adjust the heater control cables as detailed in Section 31.

30 Heater - dismantling and reassembly

1 With the heater unit removed, as described in the preceding Section, release the eight clips which hold the two halves of the assembly together.
2 Release the clips from the temperature control flap shaft and withdraw the shaft.
3 Lift away the heater radiator tube gasket.
4 Disconnect the leads from the resistor pack.
5 Disconnect the motor leads and release the clips which secure the motor to the centre hub.
6 Withdraw the motor and fan assembly (Fig. 12.20).
7 The heater matrix can now be removed from the lower half of the heater casing (Fig. 12.21).
8 It is not recommended that the motor or matrix be repaired but rather new components be fitted. This is due to the fact that any heat used in soldering leaks in the matrix or leads to the motor must be localised to prevent damage to adjacent parts.

31 Heater control cables - adjustment

1 Control cable adjustment should be carried out whenever the control cables have been disconnected from the heater, or if the heater cannot be operated correctly.
2 Move the lower control lever to the extreme left position and

release the spring clip that secures the direction control cable to the heater body (Figs. 12.22 and 12.23).
3 Move the floor-defrost door to the off position by rotating the lever up to the end of its travel.
4 Slide the end of the outer cable to the floor defrost lever and secure to the heater body with the spring clip.
5 To adjust the temperature control cable move the upper control lever to the extreme left position.
6 Release the spring clip that secures the temperature control cable to the heater.
7 Move the temperature blend door firmly to the maximum heat position by rotating the door lever up to the end of its

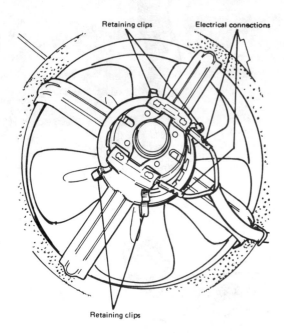
Fig. 12.20. Heater motor and fan assembly (Sec. 30)

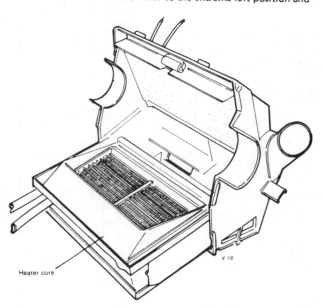
Fig. 12.21. Removal of heater unit matrix (Sec. 30)

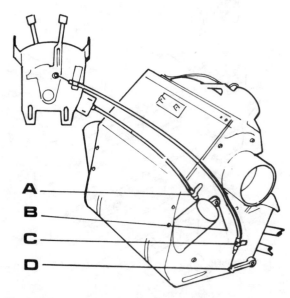
Fig. 12.22. Heater control components identification (Sec. 31)

A Spring clip
B Mixer valve lever
C Spring clip
D Distributor valve lever

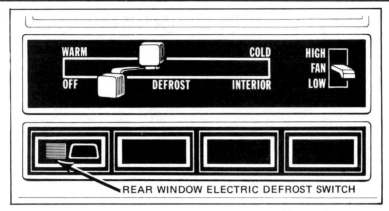

Fig. 12.24. Air conditioner control panel (Sec. 32)

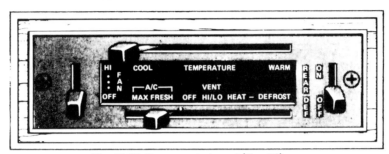

Fig. 12.23. Heater control panel (Sec. 31)

travel.

8 Slide the end of the outer cable to the temperature blend door lever and secure to the heater body with the spring clip.

32 Air-conditioning system

1 Where the car is equipped with an air-conditioning system, the checks and maintenance operations must be limited to the following items. No part of the system must be disconnected due to the danger from the refrigerant which will be released. Your Ford dealer or a refrigeration engineer must be employed if the system has to be evacuated or recharged.

2 Regularly check the condition of the system hoses and connections.

3 Inspect the fins of the condenser (located ahead of the radiator) and brush away accumulations of flies and dirt.

4 Check the compressor drivebelt adjustment. There should be a total deflection of ½ in. (12.7 mm) at the centre of the longest run of the belt. Where adjustment is required, move the position of the idler pulley.

5 Keep the air conditioner drain tube clear. This expels condensation produced within the unit to a point under the car.

6 When the system is not in use, move the controls to the 'OFF' position. During the winter period operate the unit for a few minutes every three or four weeks to keep the compressor in good order.

7 Every six months, have your Ford dealer check the refrigerant level in the system.

33 Fault diagnosis - heating system

Symptom	Reason
Insufficient heat	Faulty coolant reservoir cap
	Faulty cooling system thermostat
	Kink in heater hose
	Faulty control lever or cable
	Heater matrix blocked
	Blower fuse blown
	Low coolant level
Inadequate defrosting or general heat circulation	Incorrect setting of deflector doors
	Disconnected ducts
	Carpet obstructing airflow outlet

Supplementary wiring diagrams

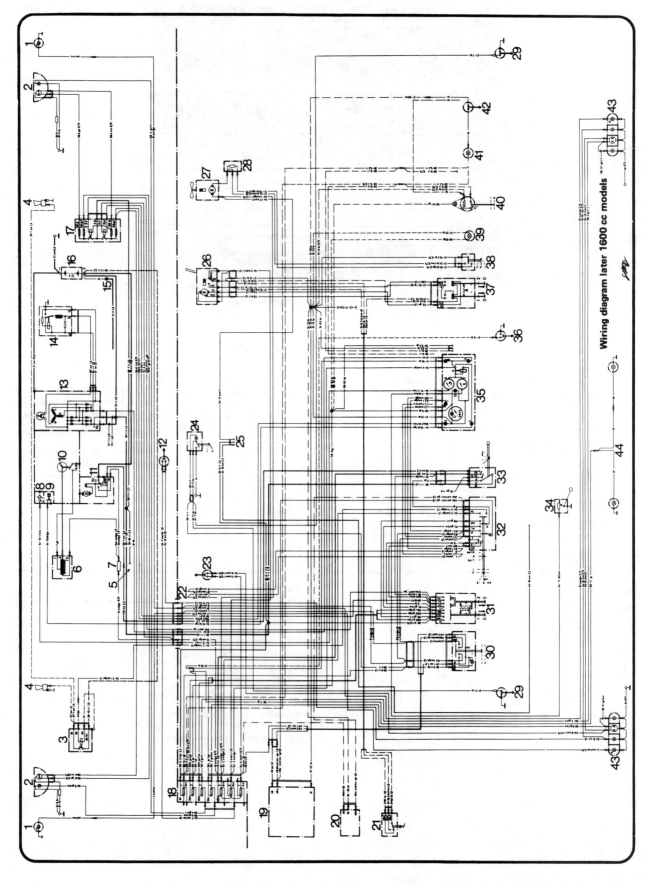

Wiring diagram later 1600 cc models

Key to Wiring Diagram later 1600 cc models

1	Front indicator		27	Heater motor
2	Head lamp		28	Series resistance, heater motor
3	Relay horn		29	Courtesy light switch
4	Horn		30	Hazard flasher switch
5	Relay - automatic transmission		31	Light switch
6	Ignition coil		32	Indicator switch
7	Series resistance - ignition coil		33	Steering lock ignition switch
8	Temperature gauge sender unit		34	Fuel gauge sender unit
9	Oil pressure switch		35	Instrument cluster
10	Distributor			1 Flasher warning light (red)
11	Starter motor			2 Main beam warning light (blue)
12	Back-up lamp switch			3 Ignition warning light (green)
13	Alternator			4 Oil pressure warning light (red)
14	Regulator			6 Temperature gauge
15	Fuse wire - alternator (Ford UK)			7 Fuel gauge
16	Battery			8 Handbrake warning light
17	Headlamp relay			9 Voltage regulator
18	Fuse block			12 Instrument lighting
19	Flasher unit		36	Handbrake warning light switch
20	Flasher unit (Ford UK)		37	Wiper motor switch
21	Wiper motor - foot switch		38	Heater blower switch
22	Vehicles without hazard flasher system		39	Lighting, heater blower switch
23	Stop light switch		40	Cigarette lighter
24	Interior light		41	Glove box lamp
25	Heated rear window		42	Glove box lamp switch
26	Wiper motor		43	Rear lamp assembly
			44	Number plate lamps

Wiring Loom on standard instrument panel has no connections for any auxiliary instrumentation

Fuses (fuse block)

1	Interior lights, hazard flasher system, cigarette lighter, electric clock, glove box lamp		4	Side light LH, rear lamp LH
2	Instrument lighting, number plate lamps		5	Heater blower motor, horn, heated rear window
3	Side light RH, rear lamp RH		6	Wiper motor, back-up lamps, instrument cluster
			7	Indicator lamp, brake light

Unmarked fuses are 8 amps

Colour codes - Key

sw	black		rs	pink		ge	yellow	
ws	white		gn	green		bl	blue	
rt	red							
						gr	grey	
						br	brown	
						vi	violet	

Applications

_____ Standard, L and XL

— · · — · — · — · · — · — · · — Standard only

— — — — — — — — — — — — — XL

— · — · — · — · — · — · — · L and XL

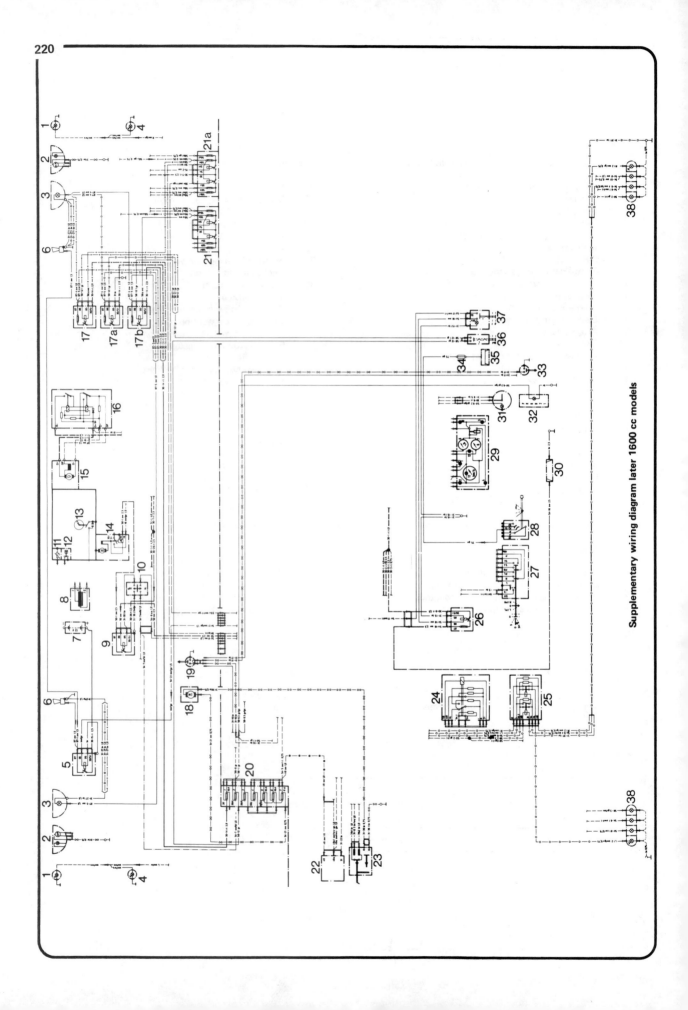

Supplementary wiring diagram later 1600 cc models

Key to supplementary Wiring Diagram later 1600 cc models

1	Front indicator	20	Fuse block
2	Headlamp	21	Headlamp relay
3	Fog lamp	21a	Headlamp relay (Italy and France)
4	Front side repeater lamp	22	Flasher unit
5	Horn relay	23	Wiper foot switch
6	Horn	24	Operational relays for double lighting intensity
7	Battery	25	(Ford UK)
8	Ignition coil	26	Heater rear window relay
9	Relay - automatic transmission	27	Indicator switch
10	Inhibitor switch - automatic transmission	28	Steering lock/ignition switch
11	Temperature gauge sender unit	29	Instrument cluster
12	Oil pressure sender unit	30	Heater rear window
13	Distributor	31	Clock
14	Starter motor	32	Quadrant lamp
15	Alternator	33	Handbrake warning light switch
16	Regulator	34	Fuse - radio (medium delay action)
17	Relay - fog-lamp (France)	35	Radio
17a	Relay - fog-lamp (Ford UK)	36	Fog lamp switch
17b	Relay - fog-lamp (special equipment)	37	Heater rear window switch
18	Washer motor	38	Rear lamp assembly switch
19	Dual braking system warning light switch		

Fuses (Fuse block)

1	Interior lights, hazard flasher system, cigarette lighter, clock, glove box lamp	4	Side light - LH, rear lamp - LH
2	Instrument lighting, number plate lamps, quadrant lamp	5	Heater blower motor, horn, heated rear window
3	Side light - RH, rear lamp - RH	6	Wiper motor, back-up lamps, instrument cluster
		7	Indicator lamp, brake light

All unmarked fuses are 8 amps

Colour codes - Key

sw	black	rs	pink	ge	yellow	gr	grey
ws	white	gn	green	bl	blue	br	brown
rt	red					vi	violet

Applications

————————————————— Wire for special equipment

— — — — — — — — — Standard wire (as shown in wiring diagram for standard models)

— o — o — o — o — o — o — o — o Ford UK

— · — · — · — · — · — · — · — · Italy, Portugal and France

— ·· — ·· — ·· — ·· — ·· — ·· — Italy

— o o — o o — o o — o o — o o — o o — Sweden

—+—+—+—+—+—+—+—+—+—+— France

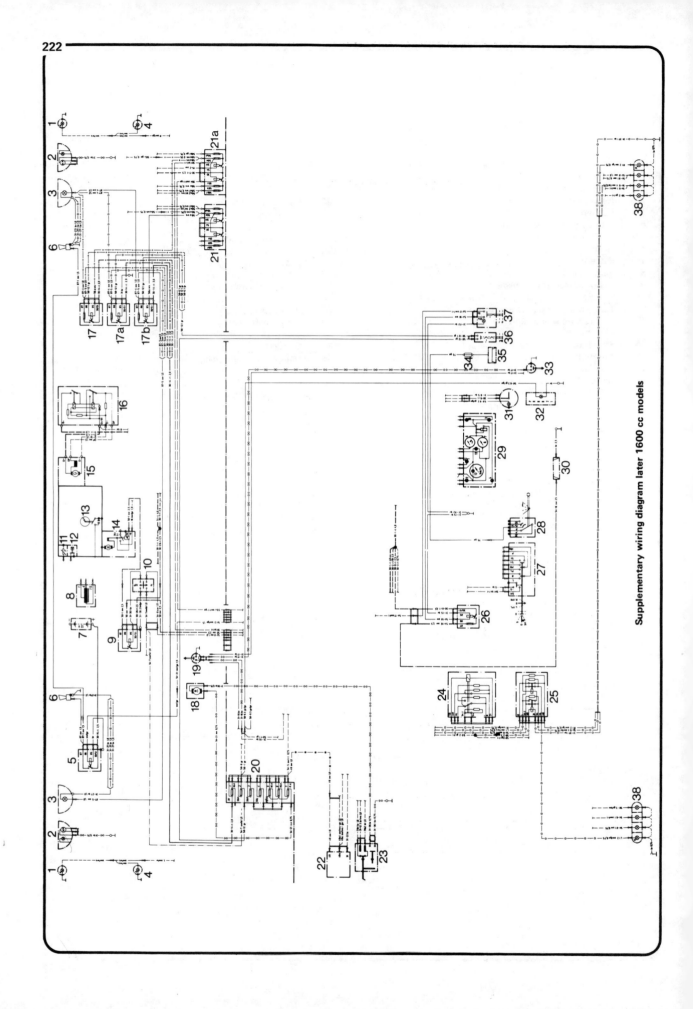

Supplementary wiring diagram later 1600 cc models

Key to Wiring Diagram later 1600 cc GT models

1	Front indicator	29	Heated rear window
2	Headlamp	30	Direction indicator lamp switch
3	Fog lamp	31	Steering lock ignition switch
4	Horn	32	Instrument cluster
5	Two-tone horn relay	1	Indicator warning light (red)
6	Dual braking system warning light switch	2	Main beam warning light (blue)
7	Battery	3	Ignition warning light (green)
8	Ignition coil	5	Oil pressure gauge
9	Series resistance - ignition coil	6	Temperature gauge
10	Temperature gauge sender unit	7	Fuel gauge
11	Distributor	8	Brake warning light (red)
12	Starter motor	9	Voltage regulator
13	Alternator	10	Ammeter
14	Relay automatic transmission	11	Tachometer
15	Regulator	12	Instrument lights
16	Relay fog lamp	33	Fuel gauge sender unit
17	Headlamp relay	34	Wiper motor switch
18	Fuse block	35	Clock
19	Flasher unit	36	Handbrake warning light switch
20	Wiper foot switch	37	Fog lamp switch
21	Brake light switch	38	Heater motor switch
22	Interior light	39	Lighting, heater motor switch
23	Wiper motor	40	Cigarette lighter
24	Heater blower motor	41	Map reading light
25	Series resistance, heater blower motor	42	Glove compartment lamp
26	Courtesy light switch	43	Glove compartment lamp switch
27	Hazard light switch	44	Rear lamp assembly
28	Light switch	45	Number plate lamps

Fuses (Fuse block)

1	Interior lights, hazard flasher system, cigarette lighter, clock, glove box lamp	4	Side light - LH, rear lamp - LH
2	Instrument lighting, number plate lamps	5	Heater blower motor, horn, heated rear window
3	Side light - RH, rear lamp - RH	6	Wiper motor, back-up lamps, instrument cluster
		7	Indicator lamp, brake light

All unmarked fuses are 8 amps

Colour codes - Key

sw	black	rs	pink	ge	yellow	gr	grey
ws	white	gn	green	bl	blue	br	brown
rt	red					vi	violet

Applications

———————————————————— Model GT and GTR

— — — — — — — — — — — — — GTR only

224

Supplementary wiring diagram later 1600 cc GT models

Key to supplementary Wiring Diagram later 1600 cc GT models

1	Headlamp	19	Fuse block
2	Fog lamp	20	Flasher unit
3	Horn	21	Wiper motor foot switch
4	Front side repeater lamp	22	Optional relays for double luminous intensity
5	Washer motor	23	(Ford UK)
6	Dual braking system warning light switch	24	Light switch
7	Battery	25	Relay - heated rear window
8	Inhibitor switch (automatic transmission)	26	Direction indicator switch
9	Temperature gauge sender unit	27	Steering lock/ignition switch
10	Oil pressure switch	28	Heated rear window
11	Distributor	29	Fuse - radio (2 amps medium relay)
12	Starter motor	30	Radio
13	Alternator	31	Quadrant lamp
14	Regulator	32	Handbrake warning light switch
15	Relay - automatic transmission	33	Fog lamp switch
16	Relay - fog lamp (Ford UK)	34	Heated rear window switch
17	Relay - fog lamp (France	35	Rear lamp assembly
18	Headlamp relay		

Fuses (Fuse block)

1 Interior lights, hazard flasher system, cigarette lighter, clock, glove box lamp
2 Instrument lighting, number plate lamps, quadrant lamp
3 Side light - RH, rear lamp - RH
4 Side light - LH, rear lamp - LH
5 Heater blower motor, horn, heated rear window
6 Wiper motor, back-up lamps, instrument cluster
7 Indicator lamp, brake light

All unmarked fuses are 8 amps

Colour codes - Key

sw	black	rs	pink	ge	yellow	gr	grey
ws	white	gn	green	bl	blue	br	brown
rt	red					vi	violet

Applications

Wire for special equipment

Standard wire (as shown in wiring diagram for model GT)

Ford of Britain

Italy, Portugal, France and Ford of Britain

Italy and France

Italy

Sweden

France

Safety first!

Professional motor mechanics are trained in safe working procedures. However enthusiastic you may be about getting on with the job in hand, do take the time to ensure that your safety is not put at risk. A moment's lack of attention can result in an accident, as can failure to observe certain elementary precautions.

There will always be new ways of having accidents, and the following points do not pretend to be a comprehensive list of all dangers; they are intended rather to make you aware of the risks and to encourage a safety-conscious approach to all work you carry out on your vehicle.

Essential DOs and DON'Ts

DON'T rely on a single jack when working underneath the vehicle. Always use reliable additional means of support, such as axle stands, securely placed under a part of the vehicle that you know will not give way.

DON'T attempt to loosen or tighten high-torque nuts (e.g. wheel hub nuts) while the vehicle is on a jack; it may be pulled off.

DON'T start the engine without first ascertaining that the transmission is in neutral (or 'Park' where applicable) and the parking brake applied.

DON'T suddenly remove the filler cap from a hot cooling system – cover it with a cloth and release the pressure gradually first, or you may get scalded by escaping coolant.

DON'T attempt to drain oil until you are sure it has cooled sufficiently to avoid scalding you.

DON'T grasp any part of the engine, exhaust or catalytic converter without first ascertaining that it is sufficiently cool to avoid burning you.

DON'T allow brake fluid or antifreeze to contact vehicle paintwork.

DON'T syphon toxic liquids such as fuel, brake fluid or antifreeze by mouth, or allow them to remain on your skin.

DON'T inhale dust – it may be injurious to health (see *Asbestos* below).

DON'T allow any spilt oil or grease to remain on the floor – wipe it up straight away, before someone slips on it.

DON'T use ill-fitting spanners or other tools which may slip and cause injury.

DON'T attempt to lift a heavy component which may be beyond your capability – get assistance.

DON'T rush to finish a job, or take unverified short cuts.

DON'T allow children or animals in or around an unattended vehicle.

DO wear eye protection when using power tools such as drill, sander, bench grinder etc, and when working under the vehicle.

DO use a barrier cream on your hands prior to undertaking dirty jobs – it will protect your skin from infection as well as making the dirt easier to remove afterwards; but make sure your hands aren't left slippery.

DO keep loose clothing (cuffs, tie etc) and long hair well out of the way of moving mechanical parts.

DO remove rings, wristwatch etc, before working on the vehicle – especially the electrical system.

DO ensure that any lifting tackle used has a safe working load rating adequate for the job.

DO keep your work area tidy – it is only too easy to fall over articles left lying around.

DO get someone to check periodically that all is well, when working alone on the vehicle.

DO carry out work in a logical sequence and check that everything is correctly assembled and tightened afterwards.

DO remember that your vehicle's safety affects that of yourself and others. If in doubt on any point, get specialist advice.

IF, in spite of following these precautions, you are unfortunate enough to injure yourself, seek medical attention as soon as possible.

Asbestos

Certain friction, insulating, sealing, and other products – such as brake linings, brake bands, clutch linings, torque converters, gaskets, etc – contain asbestos. *Extreme care must be taken to avoid inhalation of dust from such products since it is hazardous to health.* If in doubt, assume that they *do* contain asbestos.

Fire

Remember at all times that petrol (gasoline) is highly flammable. Never smoke, or have any kind of naked flame around, when working on the vehicle. But the risk does not end there – a spark caused by an electrical short-circuit, by two metal surfaces contacting each other, by careless use of tools, or even by static electricity built up in your body under certain conditions, can ignite petrol vapour, which in a confined space is highly explosive.

Always disconnect the battery earth (ground) terminal before working on any part of the fuel or electrical system, and never risk spilling fuel on to a hot engine or exhaust.

It is recommended that a fire extinguisher of a type suitable for fuel and electrical fires is kept handy in the garage or workplace at all times. Never try to extinguish a fuel or electrical fire with water.

Fumes

Certain fumes are highly toxic and can quickly cause unconsciousness and even death if inhaled to any extent. Petrol (gasoline) vapour comes into this category, as do the vapours from certain solvents such as trichloroethylene. Any draining or pouring of such volatile fluids should be done in a well ventilated area.

When using cleaning fluids and solvents, read the instructions carefully. Never use materials from unmarked containers – they may give off poisonous vapours.

Never run the engine of a motor vehicle in an enclosed space such as a garage. Exhaust fumes contain carbon monoxide which is extremely poisonous; if you need to run the engine, always do so in the open air or at least have the rear of the vehicle outside the workplace.

If you are fortunate enough to have the use of an inspection pit, never drain or pour petrol, and never run the engine, while the vehicle is standing over it; the fumes, being heavier than air, will concentrate in the pit with possibly lethal results.

The battery

Never cause a spark, or allow a naked light, near the vehicle's battery. It will normally be giving off a certain amount of hydrogen gas, which is highly explosive.

Always disconnect the battery earth (ground) terminal before working on the fuel or electrical systems.

If possible, loosen the filler plugs or cover when charging the battery from an external source. Do not charge at an excessive rate or the battery may burst.

Take care when topping up and when carrying the battery. The acid electrolyte, even when diluted, is very corrosive and should not be allowed to contact the eyes or skin.

If you ever need to prepare electrolyte yourself, always add the acid slowly to the water, and never the other way round. Protect against splashes by wearing rubber gloves and goggles.

When jump starting a car using a booster battery, for negative earth (ground) vehicles, connect the jump leads in the following sequence: First connect one jump lead between the positive (+) terminals of the two batteries. Then connect the other jump lead first to the negative (–) terminal of the booster battery, and then to a good earthing (ground) point on the vehicle to be started, at least 18 in (45 cm) from the battery if possible. Ensure that hands and jump leads are clear of any moving parts, and that the two vehicles do not touch. Disconnect the leads in the reverse order.

Mains electricity

When using an electric power tool, inspection light etc, which works from the mains, always ensure that the appliance is correctly connected to its plug and that, where necessary, it is properly earthed (grounded). Do not use such appliances in damp conditions and, again, beware of creating a spark or applying excessive heat in the vicinity of fuel or fuel vapour.

Ignition HT voltage

A severe electric shock can result from touching certain parts of the ignition system, such as the HT leads, when the engine is running or being cranked, particularly if components are damp or the insulation is defective. Where an electronic ignition system is fitted, the HT voltage is much higher and could prove fatal.

General repair procedures

Whenever servicing, repair or overhaul work is carried out on the car or its components, it is necessary to observe the following procedures and instructions. This will assist in carrying out the operation efficiently and to a professional standard of workmanship.

Joint mating faces and gaskets

Where a gasket is used between the mating faces of two components, ensure that it is renewed on reassembly, and fit it dry unless otherwise stated in the repair procedure. Make sure that the mating faces are clean and dry with all traces of old gasket removed. When cleaning a joint face, use a tool which is not likely to score or damage the face, and remove any burrs or nicks with an oilstone or fine file.

Make sure that tapped holes are cleaned with a pipe cleaner, and keep them free of jointing compound if this is being used unless specifically instructed otherwise.

Ensure that all orifices, channels or pipes are clear and blow through them, preferably using compressed air.

Oil seals

Whenever an oil seal is removed from its working location, either individually or as part of an assembly, it should be renewed.

The very fine sealing lip of the seal is easily damaged and will not seal if the surface it contacts is not completely clean and free from scratches, nicks or grooves. If the original sealing surface of the component cannot be restored, the component should be renewed.

Protect the lips of the seal from any surface which may damage them in the course of fitting. Use tape or a conical sleeve where possible. Lubricate the seal lips with oil before fitting and, on dual lipped seals, fill the space between the lips with grease.

Unless otherwise stated, oil seals must be fitted with their sealing lips toward the lubricant to be sealed.

Use a tubular drift or block of wood of the appropriate size to install the seal and, if the seal housing is shouldered, drive the seal down to the shoulder. If the seal housing is unshouldered, the seal should be fitted with its face flush with the housing top face.

Screw threads and fastenings

Always ensure that a blind tapped hole is completely free from oil, grease, water or other fluid before installing the bolt or stud. Failure to do this could cause the housing to crack due to the hydraulic action of the bolt or stud as it is screwed in.

When tightening a castellated nut to accept a split pin, tighten the nut to the specified torque, where applicable, and then tighten further to the next split pin hole. Never slacken the nut to align a split pin hole unless stated in the repair procedure.

When checking or retightening a nut or bolt to a specified torque setting, slacken the nut or bolt by a quarter of a turn, and then retighten to the specified setting.

Locknuts, locktabs and washers

Any fastening which will rotate against a component or housing in the course of tightening should always have a washer between it and the relevant component or housing.

Spring or split washers should always be renewed when they are used to lock a critical component such as a big-end bearing retaining nut or bolt.

Locktabs which are folded over to retain a nut or bolt should always be renewed.

Self-locking nuts can be reused in non-critical areas, providing resistance can be felt when the locking portion passes over the bolt or stud thread.

Split pins must always be replaced with new ones of the correct size for the hole.

Special tools

Some repair procedures in this manual entail the use of special tools such as a press, two or three-legged pullers, spring compressors etc. Wherever possible, suitable readily available alternatives to the manufacturer's special tools are described, and are shown in use. In some instances, where no alternative is possible, it has been necessary to resort to the use of a manufacturer's tool and this has been done for reasons of safety as well as the efficient completion of the repair operation. Unless you are highly skilled and have a thorough understanding of the procedure described, never attempt to bypass the use of any special tool when the procedure described specifies its use. Not only is there a very great risk of personal injury, but expensive damage could be caused to the components involved.

Conversion factors

Length (distance)
Inches (in)	X 25.4	= Millimetres (mm)	X 0.0394	= Inches (in)
Feet (ft)	X 0.305	= Metres (m)	X 3.281	= Feet (ft)
Miles	X 1.609	= Kilometres (km)	X 0.621	= Miles

Volume (capacity)
Cubic inches (cu in; in³)	X 16.387	= Cubic centimetres (cc; cm³)	X 0.061	= Cubic inches (cu in; in³)
Imperial pints (Imp pt)	X 0.568	= Litres (l)	X 1.76	= Imperial pints (Imp pt)
Imperial quarts (Imp qt)	X 1.137	= Litres (l)	X 0.88	= Imperial quarts (Imp qt)
Imperial quarts (Imp qt)	X 1.201	= US quarts (US qt)	X 0.833	= Imperial quarts (Imp qt)
US quarts (US qt)	X 0.946	= Litres (l)	X 1.057	= US quarts (US qt)
Imperial gallons (Imp gal)	X 4.546	= Litres (l)	X 0.22	= Imperial gallons (Imp gal)
Imperial gallons (Imp gal)	X 1.201	= US gallons (US gal)	X 0.833	= Imperial gallons (Imp gal)
US gallons (US gal)	X 3.785	= Litres (l)	X 0.264	= US gallons (US gal)

Mass (weight)
Ounces (oz)	X 28.35	= Grams (g)	X 0.035	= Ounces (oz)
Pounds (lb)	X 0.454	= Kilograms (kg)	X 2.205	= Pounds (lb)

Force
Ounces-force (ozf; oz)	X 0.278	= Newtons (N)	X 3.6	= Ounces-force (ozf; oz)
Pounds-force (lbf; lb)	X 4.448	= Newtons (N)	X 0.225	= Pounds-force (lbf; lb)
Newtons (N)	X 0.1	= Kilograms-force (kgf; kg)	X 9.81	= Newtons (N)

Pressure
Pounds-force per square inch (psi; lbf/in²; lb/in²)	X 0.070	= Kilograms-force per square centimetre (kgf/cm²; kg/cm²)	X 14.223	= Pounds-force per square inch (psi; lbf/in²; lb/in²)
Pounds-force per square inch (psi; lbf/in²; lb/in²)	X 0.068	= Atmospheres (atm)	X 14.696	= Pounds-force per square inch (psi; lbf/in²; lb/in²)
Pounds-force per square inch (psi; lbf/in²; lb/in²)	X 0.069	= Bars	X 14.5	= Pounds-force per square inch (psi; lbf/in²; lb/in²)
Pounds-force per square inch (psi; lbf/in²; lb/in²)	X 6.895	= Kilopascals (kPa)	X 0.145	= Pounds-force per square inch (psi; lbf/in²; lb/in²)
Kilopascals (kPa)	X 0.01	= Kilograms-force per square centimetre (kgf/cm²; kg/cm²)	X 98.1	= Kilopascals (kPa)

Torque (moment of force)
Pounds-force inches (lbf in; lb in)	X 1.152	= Kilograms-force centimetre (kgf cm; kg cm)	X 0.868	= Pounds-force inches (lbf in; lb in)
Pounds-force inches (lbf in; lb in)	X 0.113	= Newton metres (Nm)	X 8.85	= Pounds-force inches (lbf in; lb in)
Pounds-force inches (lbf in; lb in)	X 0.083	= Pounds-force feet (lbf ft; lb ft)	X 12	= Pounds-force inches (lbf in; lb in)
Pounds-force feet (lbf ft; lb ft)	X 0.138	= Kilograms-force metres (kgf m; kg m)	X 7.233	= Pounds-force feet (lbf ft; lb ft)
Pounds-force feet (lbf ft; lb ft)	X 1.356	= Newton metres (Nm)	X 0.738	= Pounds-force feet (lbf ft; lb ft)
Newton metres (Nm)	X 0.102	= Kilograms-force metres (kgf m; kg m)	X 9.804	= Newton metres (Nm)

Power
Horsepower (hp)	X 745.7	= Watts (W)	X 0.0013	= Horsepower (hp)

Velocity (speed)
Miles per hour (miles/hr; mph)	X 1.609	= Kilometres per hour (km/hr; kph)	X 0.621	= Miles per hour (miles/hr; mph)

Fuel consumption*
Miles per gallon, Imperial (mpg)	X 0.354	= Kilometres per litre (km/l)	X 2.825	= Miles per gallon, Imperial (mpg)
Miles per gallon, US (mpg)	X 0.425	= Kilometres per litre (km/l)	X 2.352	= Miles per gallon, US (mpg)

Temperature
Degrees Fahrenheit = (°C x 1.8) + 32   Degrees Celsius (Degrees Centigrade; °C) = (°F - 32) x 0.56

*It is common practice to convert from miles per gallon (mpg) to litres/100 kilometres (l/100km),
where mpg (Imperial) x l/100 km = 282 and mpg (US) x l/100 km = 235

Index

Printed by
J H Haynes & Co Ltd
Sparkford Nr Yeovil
Somerset BA22 7JJ England